Death & Co

Death & Co

MODERN CLASSIC COCKTAILS

....

DAVID KAPLAN | NICK FAUCHALD | ALEX DAY

PHOTOGRAPHS BY WILLIAM HEREFORD

ILLUSTRATIONS BY TIM TOMKINSON

TEN SPEED PRESS

BERKELEY

CONTENTS

FOREWORD

TOBY CECCHINI

The following is an excerpt from an email that Mr. Cecchini, a noted New York City bartender and cocktail writer who was largely responsible for the Cosmopolitan craze of the 1990s—and who authored a memoir by the same name, Cosmopolitan—*sent to a friend after his short stint as a guest bartender at Death & Co in 2009.*

My Reidy, here is a very long response to your note:

Holy Christ, was it ever bittersweet to hear from you last night when I stepped in at two in the morning from doing my third guest bartender training shift at this freakish cocktail geek stronghold here called Death & Co. My hands are all cut to pieces and my lower back is stabbing me in perma-rictus, but the larger damage has been done to my psyche.

Some background: There is this fairly tight coterie of extreme cocktail fanatics that stretches from London to San Francisco and Seattle, with outposts in Tokyo and Portland and certain bars in Boston and Philadelphia. However, New York and London are, I would say, the central hubs. I'm acquainted with most of the big players and everyone kind of knows who I am, but I've always been fairly peripheral to it all.

This is a very young, earnest, geeky set—all of them madly debating so-and-so's take on the real recipe for Abbott's bitters or crème de violette (both products that disappeared decades ago) or issuing raging diatribes on ice (the shapes; the purification processes; whether to chip block ice, like the Ginza school in Japan; whether it's okay to use a Scotsman machine to make crushed ice or must one hammer it in a canvas Lewis bag to get the perfect consistency). Meanwhile, they're busy crafting every conceivable tincture and infusion and finding thousands of liqueurs, pimento drams, amari, you fucking name it. It is, in short, a subworld, like many others: in cooking, in music, in writing, you will always have these überfanatics who just like to push it to the outer limit of exclusivity.

Some of this is kind of great, but a lot of it I've always found fairly exhausting. Overall, the movement (and it is a movement at this point, really) reinforces my belief that drinks should be made with care and knowledge and employ the best and freshest ingredients. On the other hand, a waxed mustachio or gold-plated Hawthorne strainer does not a good drink make. And so I was quite interested to see if style would supersede substance among this new crop of bartenders.

There is one place I have found where this slavish allegiance to the craft of fine cocktail making is all for the good—where the drinks are just so skillfully and artfully constructed that even an old cynic like me has to sit back and take note. This is Death & Co, a quite well-known, very small and intense cocktail bar in the East Village. A few weeks ago, Brian Miller—a very nice chap and the place's head bartender—called me and asked if I would be amenable to stepping behind the bar to fill in some shifts while the staff was at a cocktail convention in New Orleans. They're all super nice cats and ferociously fast, adept bartenders. Very admirable.

I like Death & Co, and I've always found that, unlike most of these geeky cocktail joints, the guys are superspiff bartenders and spot-on in their knowledge and execution. When I walk in and ask for a Scotch on the rocks, they don't try to talk me into a cumin-lavender-habanero Rob Roy instead. I must admit that they all know who I am too, and so are very respectful, and that has always buttered me up and brought me back there. Once when I took some friends there, the place was closing up and turning people away, but they spotted me, called us back, and bade us come in and drink with them while they closed up. Quite nice.

So it was that when Brian called and said he didn't mean to insult me, but that they would consider it an honor if I would deign to step behind their bar and help them out when everyone was gone, and possibly as a backup after that, I thought, *You know, of all the serious bars I'm familiar with, that may be the only one I would, in fact, step behind.*

I laughed at the offer and assured Brian I was flattered to be asked. I told him I thought maybe it would be good for me to get off my ass from staring at a computer screen all day working on this diabolical book proposal, and get back behind the stick. He was very excited and grateful and said all the guys were vying to work with me, to see what Toby Cecchini would teach them about this and that. I warned him that knocking a year's rust off would be an endeavor in itself, and that I always tread very lightly in someone else's sandbox, so it would be quite enough for me to trail for a bit to get the hang of how they did things there.

I did three trail shifts this week, which is what a new recruit does in a bar or restaurant, trailing about after the workers. All I can say at the end of three shifts is this: If the devil is in the details, then this bar is truly diabolical. Everything they do, from start to finish, is completely ass-backward from the way I've always done it. That doesn't mean they're wrong at all—nor that I am—it just means our base assumptions are not the same.

It starts with their entire philosophy of how a drink should be made. The new current thinking is that you want to chill the drink as quickly as possible with the least possible dilution. I've always felt and preached that dilution is one of the most essential aspects of making cocktails, and I geared my building and shaking directly on that, so my building starts with taking a large tin and filling it with ice, where theirs begins with taking a small tin and starting "dry," meaning without ice. They build from the smallest ingredient to the largest, which is smart, so that if you mess up, you're typically throwing out two shakes of bitters and an ounce of lemon juice rather than two ounces of expensive gin. But I always build from the base spirit down, and that's how I cue my memory. Their setup is huge and impressive, much like a *mise en place* in a professional kitchen, with dozens of juices, infused liquors, homemade tinctures and bitters, fresh fruits, herbs, spices, and vegetables for muddling,

and so on. It's all quite impressive, but I just keep thinking, *Why do these guys want to make all of this so hard on themselves?*

Nowhere does that question come more into play, however, than with the drink list, which has been winnowed down to a mere fifty-seven selections from the seventy-three it had been, apparently, the week before last. It has separate sections for swizzles, cobblers, slings, and all the old categories of classics, and they tell me I'm lucky to have come after they cut out the flips section, which are made with port and separated egg whites and yolks, but all of these, mind you, are house concoctions, and so don't even take in the vast array of common or actual classic cocktails. This guarantees that even the most seasoned bartender, and I include myself in that category, can find no bearings whatever in navigating the drinks menu, being that they are all unknowns.

Most drinks have well over six ingredients, some as many as twelve, and they are made with several different kinds of ice, many to be shaken in one kind and strained into another, with very specific shaking vessels, glassware, garnishes, and flourishes like floats, rinses, specific twists, and so on for each.

It is, in a word—and in a way I cannot stress enough—utter madness. There are two duty stations behind the bar: the "service," where you stand taking orders out of an electronic ticket dispenser and making drinks for the tables, and the "point," where you stand serving the twelve seats at the bar. I have no possibility, because of the confounding breadth of the drinks list, of working either one after my three days of trailing. I have, in point of fact, been turned into a virtual deer in the headlights on my last two nights, flailing about, Lucille Ball-like, as tickets spat from the feeder and I just looked at them in uncomprehending horror, going back and forth in comic futility to this extensive recipe cheat sheet to begin building these monstrosities one at a time. I never thought anything could make me feel like such an utter novice behind a bar, like a terrified child, really, but it has turned me into a blithering idiot. I'm truly just in these guys' way. It literally felt like I was in a nightmare, and not surprisingly my sleep on each subsequent night was frenetically peopled with muddling strawberries with mint and cucumber and trying to reach the currant-infused Old Overholt rye. Ach!

The bartenders at Death & Co are as sharp as daggers. There are only four of them in total. They invented and honed their list, and they know it back and forth. They have this list memorized to the point where they shout the recipes back and forth to one another in digital code ("The Miss Behavin' is a quarter, quarter, half, one and a half, and two?").

I have, I very much fear, bitten off more than I can chew.

Jim Meehan, a very competitive friend of mine who runs another serious bar, called PDT (for Please Don't Tell), is taking bets that there's no way I can handle the speed and volume. Perhaps Jim is right, and I can't hack it with the fast kids anymore. Yes, I have developed ways to juke the twenty-year-olds on the basketball and tennis courts, even if I'm no longer as fast as they, but maybe on the killing floor my moves aren't good enough anymore. It makes me angry—and makes me want to dig in my heels until I get it right and am not freaked by it anymore. Part of me thinks that would be some kind of huge, Pyrrhic victory, while a perhaps more experienced part of me understands it would be a huge, narcissistic waste of my time. I am certainly learning some expansive new stuff that is completely different from the ways I did things, but that I would now incorporate if I opened another bar of my own, which certainly has an intrinsic worth. If you're not curious, you can't learn, and that goes especially for those, like me, who think they know everything.

And it's amazing how the guys there, witnessing how flustered I am, are being so extraordinarily kind and encouraging about it, stressing how hard the list is. They keep saying how they discussed among them who they thought might be able to hack it back there, and they unanimously decided on me. Whether any of this is true, it is certainly extremely kind and makes me feel all the worse that I am absolutely miserable over this whole thing. Even as I'm writing this, I just got a text from Alex Day, who worked with me during last night's bloodbath and wrote, "Hey man, ya did great last night and it's an honor to have shared time behind the stick—hope you're gonna stay on with us a bit." I don't know right now. Kill vs. make stronger? My back is stabbing me and I'm leaning on furniture as I walk around, but at least for now, the plan is to go back for another shift.

Much, T.

INTRODUCTION

DAVID KAPLAN

I'd been playing bar owner for a long time. I opened my first short-lived pop-up when I was eighteen years old. It was a tiki-themed joint that my friend Bryce and I built in his dirt-floor garage, with umbrellas hanging from the ceiling and a four-page laminated cocktail "menu" full of sweet, Technicolor drinks. At the end of the summer we threw an elaborate party with a faux waterfall, Astroturf on the floor, paper umbrellas, the works.

When I left for college, I packed my surplus of booze in a trunk and moved it to upstate New York, where I was starting art school as a photography major. I lived in a dorm and turned my room into a makeshift bar, more interested in playing host and making cocktails for my friends than actually drinking them. The dorm scene quickly got old, and in an effort to escape my particularly bad building, I pledged a fraternity. I quickly realized that my frat brothers were a bunch of idiots, but I was impressed by their efficient, hyperorganized parties.

Before my junior year, I bought a cheap Victorian house near downtown. In the parlor I built a fifteen-foot corner bar, complete with upholstered panels and a mosaic top. I retrofitted a chest freezer into a two-tap beer fridge. I fitted it with speed rails and filled them with cheap booze recommended by the old *Mr. Boston Official Bartender's Guide*, which, as far as I was aware, was the only drinks tome available. The bar worked on an honor system: all of my friends had a tab and would (ostensibly) mark down how many drinks they'd consumed. My roommates were stoners and couldn't care less about the bar, but my friend Karen and I would hang out and dream up cocktails like the Green Dragon: marijuana-infused vodka blended with honey and cranberry juice, topped with Sprite. I thought I was brilliant (and to be fair, that drink *was* tasty).

Questionable cocktail creations aside, I did see a future for myself in nightlife hospitality, so after college I moved to Las Vegas and landed a job as a VIP host at Rain, a nightclub in the Palms Casino. I worked from 8 p.m. to 4 a.m., wore a billowing "fitted" suit and earpiece, and had a microphone sticking out of my sleeve. It was a painfully boring job, so I treated it like a study in sociology. During my shift I filled notebooks with observations on how people interact at bars and lists of what did and did not work at this massive club. On my four-day weekends I sought out the anti-Vegas experience, so I often flew to New York to soak up art and culture. At the time, the city's cocktail renaissance was starting to take shape. Bars like Milk & Honey, Angel's Share, Little Branch, Pegu Club, and the Flatiron Lounge were teaching the city's nightlife crowd to trade their blue martinis and whiskey gingers for Moscow Mules and Sazeracs. Under their influence, I started dreaming up a bar of my own.

I lasted nine months in Vegas before I moved to New York in 2006, when I was twenty-three years old. I moved into an apartment on Seventh Street and Avenue A in the East Village and took at job at *Vice* magazine's retail store. In my free time I visited other bars, devoured business books, design books, and bar manuals, and began looking for a space to create my kind of nightlife experience: a friendly, accessible bar where I'd go for one cocktail and end up staying all night. Below my apartment was the Bourgeois Pig, a sexy, closet-size beer-and-wine drinking den owned by Ravi DeRossi. Ravi and I became friends and started talking about opening a bar together.

A few weeks later, we found a space one block away in a defunct Indian fusion restaurant named Raga. We negotiated, I convinced my father to back a line of credit, the owners carried a note on the business, Ravi and I pooled some money, and we closed on the space in July.

With no interior design background, I sketched a simple layout and wrote a one-page walk-through at the behest of my contractors. We began the build-out without a general contractor or an architect (or any usable architectural plans), so I spent my days making design decisions on the fly, relying on the builders to tell me which elements were feasible and which were not (apparently, countertops need "support"). I wanted an interior that felt enveloping, a safe haven in which you could forget the outside world. We added a marble bar top and antique mirrors behind the bar to give the space a feeling of permanence, like it had been there for years. I wanted deep-brown suede booths and chandeliers hanging from gold-leaf insets. I hired my tattoo artist, Scott Campbell, to design laser etchings for the black granite tables. The ceiling was very important: I'd long been in love with the layered wood ceiling at the Rendezvous Bistro in my hometown of Jackson Hole, Wyoming, so we mimicked its design. To balance all of the shiny, polished surfaces and make the space feel less fussy, I gave the long wall opposite the bar a gritty, multi-layered finish with various washes of color.

Outside, I wanted a sculpted brass door and a symmetrical, cedar-panel façade outlined in burnished brass. An artist from Connecticut crafted a massive brass door handle that depicted an angel in repose. I planned to have the name of the bar inlaid in stone just in front of the door—again, a way to that sense of permanence in the details. It would tell our customers, "This bar has been, and will be, here forever." The only problem was, "this bar" didn't have a name.

My girlfriend at the time had given me a decoupage plate covered with some pre-Prohibition propaganda. Below an illustration of drinking and corruption labeled "Devil's Toboggan Slide" were the words "Death & Co, Proprietors." I researched this and learned that it was often used as an encrypted map to underground speakeasies. Then I looked into the phrase "Death & Company" and ran across a short story of the same name by Dashiell Hammett, the author of my favorite detective series and the epic cocktail tribute movie *The Thin Man*. I took it as a sign. I sheepishly floated the name past Ravi and he loved it. Before we could change our minds, I had the name cut out of steel and inset in the doorway.

At home, I had begun experimenting with cocktails more deliberately. I was visiting every serious cocktail bar in the city regularly, though it was easier back then (there were only five or so). I read every cocktail book I could find and replicated the recipes. I played around with infusions and used fresh citrus juice for the first time. I wanted to learn everything I could before we opened, so I signed up for the inaugural Beverage Alcohol Resource (BAR) program, an immersive, five-day course in spirits and cocktails created by six of the industry's godfathers: Dale DeGroff, Doug Frost, Steven Olson, F. Paul Pacult, Andy Seymour, and David Wondrich.

At BAR, I was a babe in the woods; most of my fellow students were already top bartenders or spirits professionals. Our instructors dumped volumes of information on us about the history and production of spirits as we blind tasted dozens and dozens of products. Then we had a crash course on cocktail history and hands-on seminars in bartending skills. The final day of the course was full of tests: a written exam, a cocktail-making practical, blind spirits and cocktail exams, and a very blunt critique of the cocktail menus we'd each been asked to develop. I passed the course, but the results did not come out until after Death & Co opened, and to this day, I think that had something to do with my passing grade.

When the time came to staff the bar, I knew I wanted bartenders with some experience, but who would also understand my vision for the drinks program: inventive cocktails with a wink and nod to the classics. I posted an ad on Craigslist and my inbox filled with applications—including two pictures of topless women, ten of shirtless dudes, and at least one hundred half-assed resumes—but few, if any, seemed like a good fit. They were either too inexperienced or too entitled to do the work necessary to open a new bar.

Then I opened an email from Phil Ward. It was a short, one-line response: "I've been head bartender at two top cocktail bars in New York." I asked Phil to come to an open call we were having at the bar that weekend, and he showed up—a lanky, moppy-headed fellow from Pittsburgh with a bone-dry sense of humor. He looked dubious, at best. He entertained my interview long enough to fill out a questionnaire I'd written up for candidates. The last question was "Name as many bitters as you can." In 2006, most bartenders only knew Angostura (if that). Phil listed sixteen types of bitters. Then Phil interviewed me—several times, in fact. "What kind of ice machine will you use? What kind of glassware will you buy? Will we have to serve Red Bull? Will we be open on Sunday?" I offered him a job as head bartender.

Around Thanksgiving, our staff began to take shape. The news that Phil Ward was on board at a new bar created ripples in the incestuous local cocktail community and brought us a wave of more talent who wanted to work with him. He convinced his friend and fellow Pegu Club alum Brian Miller to work for us while waiting for his next job, at a fancy downtown nightclub, to begin; Brian ended up staying at Death & Co for three years. Joaquín Simó, a charming, enthusiastic, fresh-faced bartender, who was working the brunch shift at the Stanton Social, joined the team and quickly settled into the role of good cop to his more cantankerous coworkers. I hired a few cocktail waitresses, including Jessica Gonzalez (along with Joaquín and Phil, she was one of our three Craigslist hires), who would soon become our first female bartender. We made sure our waitresses could understand and explain the drinks as well as the bartenders so our guests would have an enlightening experience no matter where they sat. Because I had lucked out online a few times with finding staff, I posted again for a door host and got Frankie Rodriguez. I called him moments after our interview and offered him the job. Now he's the bar's general manager and longest-standing employee.

As I hired the bartenders, I told each the same thing: "You're probably not going to make more money here than you could at some other bars, but I'll get out of your way and give you whatever you need to make the best drinks possible. You will stand behind your cocktails and take the credit they earn. This is not my bar; this is *our* bar."

As we hustled to finish construction before Christmas, Phil put together a cocktail program. He'd been working at top cocktail bars for four years but had only seen a few of his original drinks make their way onto a menu. Here, he was free to showcase his own style of cocktails. Our first menu contained seven drinks, most of them containing four or five ingredients. If Phil were a writer or an artist, he'd be Raymond Carver or Richard Serra: his cocktails were minimalist and grounded in the classics, yet each took an innovative leap forward. One let the Moscow Mule

run free by pairing raspberries and rye (see Monongahela Mule, page 201). In another he took the classic Widow's Kiss and split its base spirit—calvados—into equal parts rye and apple brandy (see Wicked Kiss, page 209). Phil has a special affection for agave-based spirits, one that was as intense as his hatred—no, *phobia*—for vodka, developed by years of slinging vodka and tonics for screaming bar patrons. Tequila and pear eloped in a classic sour template (see St. Matilda, page 188). And mezcal—still a mysterious, smoky elixir in the cocktail world—was thrust into the spotlight in Phil's Oaxaca Old-Fashioned (page 273), a drink that would become Death & Co's totem.

We quietly opened for business just after Christmas 2007. Would people show up? Would they order from the menu or ask for appletinis? We didn't know what to expect, and had hedged our bets by adding sixty-some bottles of wine to the menu, along with a dozen beers and even a few sakes. Not knowing what we would one day become, I included bottles of Southern Comfort and Jägermeister in our initial liquor orders. Of course, it pains me now to admit it (and my staff never lets me forget). I made Phil promise that no matter what guests ordered, he'd smile and make them the best drink they ever tasted. We also hired a chef and developed a food menu that included hot crab dip, duck quesadillas, and mango and scallop ceviche.

Our first few nights were quiet, as expected, and relatively easy. Our industry friends showed up and ordered cocktails, the reception was warm, and everyone was happy. Well, almost: I'd had the crazy idea to eschew the standard computerized point-of-sale system that virtually all bars and restaurants use in lieu of an antique cash register. Our checks were all recorded in old-fashioned triplicate books, which kept us at the bar every night until 6 a.m. counting cash and checking it against receipts. This endured only a few weeks before we wised up and bought a point-of-sale system.

We threw our opening party on New Year's Eve, with just friends and family. We blocked out the madness that is New York on December 31 and enjoyed each other's company, taking pause to celebrate our opening before actual paying customers started showing up. Everyone stumbled out, toasted and happy, in the wee hours of January 1, 2007. It's an annual tradition that continues today.

A few days later I opened the Sunday *New York Times* to see Death & Co splashed across the front page of the "Sunday Styles" section. So much for a soft opening. On

Monday, a crowd of people were waiting outside the door when we opened for business. We were bombarded with more press, and the average wait to get in the bar increased to one or two hours, and sometimes as much as three. I quickly initiated a door policy that remains in place to this day, and that I've now repeated thousands of times: "We operate on a first-come, first-served basis, and if there is a wait at the time of your arrival, our door host will take your name and number and call you as soon as we have availability." We had agreed that the bar would be seating only. Our drinks were labor-intensive from day one and we wanted to ensure the highest level of service even on a Friday night, but the driving motivator was and continues to be ensuring a friendly, relaxed atmosphere and letting our guests escape the noise and bustle of everyday city life, so we had to give everyone a comfortable, uncrowded place to enjoy their drink. Not having a scrum of customers at the bar also engendered a higher level of expectation from the guest; we couldn't hide behind the chaos.

I never wanted the door to be a barrier; the exterior of the bar is foreboding enough. It has always been a challenge to sweetly tell someone, "No, the bar's full right now." Our door host has to be welcoming and warm, even when breaking the news that there's a two-hour wait, even for a stool at the bar. Convincing people that the bar doesn't allow standing, that our host truly will call you back, or that the pretty or famous people aren't being let in preferentially is still a nightly battle.

The first couple of months are still a blur. I'd stay at Death & Co until finishing the night's accounting, then walk outside to see the sunrise and go home to sleep for a few hours before returning to prepare for the next night. I had my first night away from the bar about two months after we opened. I went to a local dive bar and overheard someone mentioning Death & Co. The bartenders stopped what they were doing and peppered the guest with questions: "What was it like?" "What did you drink?" I'd had my head down in the details for so long that, despite the press, I didn't know whether our bar had a real life outside its doors. For the first time I was able to relax a little and feel proud of what we'd built. We hadn't planned on opening one of the best cocktail bars in New York, but that's what people were already calling it. And thanks to our staff, I knew we were capable of living up to the hype.

Death & Co brought me many firsts: my first plumbing problems, my first staffing issues, my first police visits—though none of them would be my last. I was particularly ill-prepared for one event more than any other, but in hindsight, it's clearly just part of the bar owner package.

One of our upstairs neighbors wasn't happy that a bar had opened below his apartment, and he found some folks in the neighborhood to join his cause. Soon we were visited several times a week by the police, who were receiving complaints of excess noise and other imagined misbehavior. One night I found myself nose-to-nose with a Ninth Precinct detective who issued thinly veiled threats to "make life very difficult" or simply shut us down completely. Our license was up for renewal (in NYC this happens every two years), and, thanks to our upstairs neighbor, we were facing renewal with a rich complaint history and had to appear before the local community board. We were blindsided by 45 minutes of complaints by a neighbor whom I'd never met, our less-than-friendly upstairs nuisance, and a congregate of the synagogue up the street. The member from the synagogue said our name frightened people in the community, that the black flag (that used to hang above our door) represented devil Nazism, and our façade resembled an Auschwitz rail car. When I was finally allowed to speak in our defense, I stood up and said, "My name is David Jacob Kaplan, and if that leaves any doubt, I am in fact Jewish," and sat down, less than happy that I had to stand up for myself in the face of these ridiculous claims.

The State Liquor Authority launched an investigation that lasted more than a year, and ultimately resulted in their fining us, closing us for one week, and then revoking our liquor license after the forced closure—ostensibly because of some minor mistakes in our application. Knowing that this wasn't within their legal right, I hired a lawyer and sued the SLA for denying a license without claim. I told our staff not to worry, that the good guys always win, and to ignore the hailstorm around them and focus on making drinks. The threat of permanent closure seemed imminent. This was a crucial, gut-check moment for everyone at Death & Co: We were either going to give up the fight and find other jobs, or we were going to double-down on our bar and treat every shift like our last.

Nobody quit. Instead, the staff banded together, dug in deeper, and only worked harder. Everyone who worked at the bar had found a place in their careers that they could call home, and coworkers they considered family. How do you make a Plan B for that? Death & Co became the most important thing in our lives, and we managed to turn all of the negativity and uncertainty into better drinks, better service, a tighter team, a better bar. The back bar filled up with exciting new products, each inspiring new drinks. Every bartender brought his skills and interests into the mix. Brian was obsessed with tiki drinks, so he started blending other spirits the way tiki uses rums in harmony. Joaquín raided the kitchen and brought new flavors and novel combinations to cocktails and infusions. We ignored the rules and conventions of classic cocktails and pushed each other to keep innovating.

We added more talent behind the bar: Alex Day came on in 2008 and turned us on to the potential of sherry and a host of other techniques and ingredients. Later that year, Thomas Waugh left his post as one of San Francisco's best bartenders to join the team and eventually become head bartender. Jillian Vose took the reins after him as our first female head bartender, and we've enjoyed several new talents under her leadership.

At one point in our early days, another bartender friend of ours, Jim Meehan, referred to our staff as the Yankees. This was a testament to our depth of talent, but I always liked to think of our staff as the Beatles: every member had a different style, philosophy, and skill set, but we were always best as a unit, always learning from and pushing each other to be better.

In those first years, however, the identity and emotional state of the bar was bipolar. As we became more and more recognized for our work, our legal troubles and fate of the bar became more precarious. But no matter how bad it got, it never crossed my mind to walk away. My whole life was wrapped up in that bar; it felt like being hopelessly in love with someone you couldn't walk away from, no matter how bad it gets. Our staff believed in the bar and themselves so completely that we only fought harder to make our team stronger, to do more and push harder.

That was how, at the tender age of twenty-five, I found myself walking up the steps of the New York Supreme Court, more than mildly terrified. At this point we had been under investigation by the State Liquor Authority for three years—during which time we'd been operating with a conditional license, abbreviated hours, and unapologetic NYPD harassment and hazing. But finally, after filing countless actions and reconsiderations, the fates smiled upon us: the courts issued us a liquor license with our name on it.

That same year we won Best Cocktail Bar in America and World's Best Cocktail Menu at Tales of the Cocktail, the world's premier cocktail festival. Our cocktail recipes had spread to menus around the globe, and we'd received more press and awards than we could keep track of. Our bartenders were considered among the most elite and were invited to represent us at numerous conferences and events around the world. We'd been so focused on our work that we were shocked and humbled—and, of course, elated—by what the bar had become.

Opening Death & Co taught me countless lessons: how to (and how not to) build a bar, the ins and outs of the legal system, how pennies become dollars, how to hire and fire, and where perception and reality differ. It also taught me how to deal with other people, the community, an unruly customer, or an ego—be it a bartender's, a business partner's, or one's own. But most of all, Death & Co has been a lesson in passion. If you love and believe in something, it's never a hard sell. Every night we try to make our passion transparent and contagious from the moment guests walk through our door. We hope this book will bring our passion for cocktails to your own bar or home for many years to come.

HOW TO
READ & ENJOY THIS BOOK

DAVE, NICK & ALEX

There are plenty of great cocktail books out there—old and new—filled with pages of recipes and carefully researched historical references. But when we set out to write our own, we realized that very few bar books actually teach readers how to make and create a tasty, well-balanced cocktail and explain why certain tools, ingredients, and techniques are best for any given drink.

These two questions—*how?* and *why?*—are the secrets to Death & Co's success, and our bartenders ask them constantly: How can we make drinks more efficiently and consistently? Why should we use this kind of ice over that one? How can we make a better Manhattan? Why are four rums better than one? When we opened the bar, we scrutinized every norm, convention, and lesson we'd been taught and threw out anything that didn't hold up. And as soon as we figured out a better way to make a drink—or found a better bottle of gin—we put it to the test. Before any drink earns a place on our menu, it's subjected to numerous rounds of tasting, tweaking, substitution, collaboration, and improvement. This book contains the collective knowledge of the Death & Co staff, amassed over seven years and tens of thousands of hours of practice and introspection, and we're excited as hell to share it with you.

This book is intended for anyone with a passion or curiosity for cocktails, from seasoned professionals to novice home bartenders. We want to share our enthusiasm for our craft and the ingredients, tools, techniques, and creativity essential to it. Each chapter builds upon the previous chapter's lessons. In chapter 1, "A Night at Death & Co," we show you what goes into creating and running a world-class bar. In chapter 2, "Building a Bar," we'll introduce you to many of the key ingredients we use at our bar. Chapter 3, "Building a Drink," covers the tools and techniques that help us do our job consistently and efficiently, night after night. Chapter 4, "Creating New Classics," demystifies the process of inventing new cocktails. Then, once you've learned how to work and think like a Death & Co bartender, we give you hundreds of original recipes in chapter 5, "The Specs," along with recipes for our favorite classic cocktails. Throughout the book, you'll be introduced to a handful of our favorite regular customers and hear their stories from the other side of the bar.

We can't guarantee that you'll love every Death & Co cocktail you try; after all, not every drink fits every person or every mood. But we do believe there's a perfect cocktail (or many) for everyone. Also, don't feel as though you need to follow every recipe to the letter. Personal preferences and the ingredients available vary from person to person and place to place. If you improvise on—and perhaps improve upon—our recipes, we'll be even happier.

Most of all, we hope this books inspires you to seek out better cocktails, to create your own concoctions, and to start asking your own hows and whys. And if you have any unanswered questions after you finish this book, we welcome you to stop by the bar, pull up a stool, and ask away while we mix you a drink.

Chapter One

A NIGHT
AT DEATH & CO

OAXACA OLD-FASHIONED

PHIL WARD

We didn't know it when Phil added this drink to Death & Co's first menu in 2007, but the Oaxaca Old-Fashioned would go on to symbolize our approach to cocktails: a simple recipe grounded in the classics, but with a level of innovation that comes from a deep understanding of the ingredients at play. The drink also represents an important breakthrough for us. Phil had started with a tequila-based old-fashioned he'd previously created and added an aggressively flavored spirit—mezcal—as a modifier. At the time, bartenders were struggling to make mezcal—a relatively recent addition to the craft cocktail scene—work in mixed drinks. Nobody had thought to cast it in a supporting role until Phil—and this opened the gates to countless exciting, more evenly balanced mezcal recipes. Today the Oaxaca Old-Fashioned is the most-requested drink we've ever produced, and the most replicated. We've found it on cocktail menus all over the world.

1½ OUNCES EL TESORO
REPOSADO TEQUILA

½ OUNCE DEL MAGUEY SAN LUIS
DEL RIO MEZCAL

1 TEASPOON AGAVE NECTAR

2 DASHES ANGOSTURA BITTERS

GARNISH: 1 ORANGE TWIST

Stir all the ingredients over ice, then strain into a double rocks glass over 1 large ice cube.
To garnish, flame the orange twist over the drink, then drop it in.

There's no such thing as a "typical" night at Death & Co: every shift spent and every drink ordered presents its own set of challenges, chances, and small victories. But if you picked a night at random from the 2,500-some we've had since opening the place, it might look something like this.

FRIDAY, 8:00 A.M.

Frankie Rodriguez, our general manager, arrives and opens up the front gate. He's here early to meet an electrician—who doesn't show up.

9:00 A.M.

Frankie starts his daily office duties: reviewing the previous night's sales, processing invoices, running payroll, organizing private parties, and calling repairmen (something is always leaking).

11:30 A.M.

Head bartender Jillian Vose arrives to place liquor orders and receive the first of the day's deliveries.

12:00 P.M.

The prep cook arrives and begins preparing the night's fresh juices (a process that takes about three hours) and ingredients for the kitchen.

1:00 P.M.

A repairman comes to service the dishwasher. Jillian runs inventory and makes a list of what the bar needs for the week: liquor, wine, beer, glassware, produce, and so on.

2:30 P.M.

Afternoon liquor shipments arrive. Someone wanders in the front door. Jillian says, "Sorry, we open at six!" (This will happen six more times before 6 p.m.)

3:00 P.M.

A liquor distributor comes by to taste samples with Jillian. During their tasting, another liquor rep makes an unscheduled visit to show Jillian a new "erotic ginseng liqueur." With as much politeness as she can muster, Jillian tells him she's not interested. The chef arrives and sets up the kitchen for service. The barback arrives and pulls trays of block ice from the standing freezer to let them

defrost. Then he sets up the bar: unrolling mats, arranging garnish boxes, restocking glassware, and organizing and restocking the service station.

4:00 P.M.

The other bartender, Scott Teague, arrives and begins making infusions and syrups in the basement. The barback fills fresh juice bottles and backup juice containers while Jillian pulls the seventy-some cheater bottles from the refrigerator and replenishes those that need filling.

4:30 P.M.

The barback arranges the cheater bottles across the bar and tops them with speed pourers. Then he replenishes the liquor in the speed rack and jots down a restocking list for beer, wine, liquor, soda, and other ingredients.

5:00 P.M.

A server, Brittany Chadbourne, arrives and starts on opening duties: filling water bottles, cleaning and refilling candles, restocking bathrooms, cleaning mirrors, loading change drawers, wiping down tables and bar stools, and counting menus (at least a couple are stolen each night).

5:15 P.M.

The barback fills ice wells with Kold-Draft cubes and crushed ice. Garnish trays are filled with crushed ice. Jillian and Scott set up their stations; Jillian is working the point, and Scott is on service.

5:30 P.M.

Jack, the door host, arrives and sweeps. The chef places food for the staff on the bar. Everyone's too busy to eat. The barback stocks the ice well with block ice and ice spheres. Jillian and Scott change into service clothes: a black dress for her, and shirt, tie, and pants with suspenders for him.

5:45 P.M.

Brittany lights candles and lines up bar stools and tables.

5:50 P.M.

Brittany turns down the lights, and Jillian switches the music to the house playlist. Jack assumes his post outside, where a line of guests has formed.

5:55 P.M.

GDT (gangster daiquiri time): Scott makes a round of mini daiquiris and the staff toasts to the night ahead. Everyone finishes in one gulp.

6:00 P.M.

Jack escorts the first guests inside. To prevent a logjam of drink orders, he seats them in the order in which they lined up. Brittany greets guests at their tables, fills their water glasses, and passes out menus.

6:05 P.M.

Guests place their first drink orders.

6:15 P.M.

The bar is filling up quickly. Conversations are punctuated by the sound of shaking.

6:30 P.M.

The first food orders are placed. Jillian greets a couple of regulars who grab a seat at the bar.

7:00 P.M.

The bar is at capacity, so Jack takes names and numbers in his notebook and directs guests to nearby bars to have a drink while they wait.

8:00 P.M.

The barback replenishes fresh juices and ice. Scott is making between four and six drinks at a time at the service station.

9:00 P.M.

Jillian makes a drink in progress for Scott. "That doesn't suck," he says. The wait for a seat is forty-five minutes. Jack's notebook is filled with names and phone numbers.

9:30 P.M.

The barback begins his closing duties checklist: refilling ice trays, restocking citrus for tomorrow's juice, organizing the liquor room, and breaking down boxes.

10:00 P.M.

Jillian makes her one hundredth cocktail of the night.

11:30 P.M.

Staff shot, aka "time to feed the kids." A round of glasses are filled with rum, clinked, and quickly consumed.

SATURDAY, 12:00 A.M.

The doorman has worked his way through the list of guests waiting for a spot inside.

1:30 A.M.

Last call. Frankie finishes his office work and goes home.

1:45 A.M.

Cooks and waitstaff from neighborhood restaurants stop by for a quick after-work drink. (These late arrivals are known as scumbagging.) Jillian and Scott serve them beers, shots of whiskey, and unfinished bottles of wine.

2:00 A.M.

The last customers shuffle out of the bar. Brittany turns up the lights. Scott switches the music over to something more raucous.

2:30 A.M.

Scott and Jillian disassemble their stations. Any remaining ice is "burned" in the sinks with hot water. The barback works through his closing checklist. Brittany tallies sales, prints reports, and fills out time sheets.

2:45 A.M.

Brittany sorts and counts receipts and cash in the basement, then refills money drawers with cash. Scott and the barback finish cleaning the bar. Jillian makes a prep list for the next day (well, later that same day).

3:00 A.M.

Tips are tallied and divided among the staff. Jillian passes out a round of beers and the staff sits (for the first time in many hours) to chat about the night's happenings.

3:30 A.M.

Night porters arrive to finish cleaning the bar. The music is turned off, the front doors are locked, and the staff heads out for a Guinness and shot of whiskey at a nearby pub before heading home.

THE DEATH & CO LEXICON

A glossary of relevant and irreverent cocktail colloquialisms, bartender lingo, and juvenile slang.

ANGO Short for Angostura, as in Angostura bitters, the most widely used bitters in the world—and at Death & Co. For example, "Does our mai tai get one dash *Ango* or two?" (See *DAB*.)

BACK BAR A collection of about two hundred bottles of liquor, loosely organized by category and arranged on cascading tiers. Bottles used occasionally or rarely reside on the back bar; those used more frequently are found in the *speed rack*.

BASE The ingredient that anchors a cocktail, usually (though not always) a high-proof spirit.

BATCH To blend all or a portion of a drink ahead of time (see page 129) to save time when making complex drinks. Batches are usually stored in *cheater* bottles. Batching is also used to make large volumes of drinks for off-site catering events. (See *bullshit*.)

BEHIND THE STICK Used to describe a bartender at work. For example, "Frank was *behind the stick* that night." The phrase derives from the taps used to dispense beer (though it must be noted that Death & Co does not have a beer tap).

BOOMERANG A shot of liquor covered in cellophane and delivered by hand to another establishment, usually as a way of saying hello to industry friends.

BROWN An adjective used—usually by Phil Ward—to describe a drink whose flavor is complicated yet indiscriminant, usually as a result of one or more unnecessary ingredients in the recipe. For example, "This cocktails tastes *brown*. Take an ingredient or two out?" Also known as "muddy."

BULLSHIT Slang for a *batch*. For example, "We're using the Red Ant *bullshit* for the Pisco Inferno now." Also known as "biz."

CHEATERS A motley array of small bottles atop the bar that contain syrups, *batches*, spirits from ludicrously shaped bottles, and other ingredients used frequently but in small amounts on the current cocktail menu.

CONCEPT DRINK A cocktail developed around a specific theme or name. Popularized by Brad Farran, whose *concept drinks* include Botany of Desire (page 162), Good Humor (page 157), and Cynaro de Bergerac (page 229). (See "Death & Co's Worst Drink Names" on page 125.)

DAB Acronym for "dash of Angostura bitters."

DILUTION The sweet spot attained when just the right ratio of water has been introduced into a drink through stirring or shaking. For example, "This drink is a bit *hot*; I don't think it reached full *dilution*."

DOESN'T SUCK An ambiguous form of praise offered by certain Death & Co bartenders. *Doesn't suck* can range in meaning from "This is awesome" to "This isn't awesome, but it's not terrible, either."

DOUBLE STRAIN To strain a shaken drink through both a Hawthorne strainer (see page 73) and a fine-mesh cone strainer (page 73) to eliminate any fruit, vegetable, or herb particles. For example, "This cocktail has bits of mint in it. Do you want to try it again and *double strain* it?" Also known as "fine strain."

FAMILY MEAL A staff-wide shot taken nightly around 11:30 p.m., typically in the form of Siembra Azul tequila, Appleton rum, Rittenhouse rye, or Buffalo Trace bourbon (though we've never discriminated). Also known as "time to feed the kids."

FAT A sweetener (syrup) used to add viscosity to a *thin* drink. For example, "That swizzle tastes great but needs a little *fat*. Add some *simple* or agave?"

GDT Gangster daiquiri time, between 5:50 and 6:00 p.m., when a round of daiquiris is assembled and distributed among the staff to toast the start of a shift.

GET SKINNY A more polite way to say "get the fuck out of the way" when another bartender blocks you.

HOME A tool's or bottle's designated place behind the bar, which is essential to efficiency and organization. A less affected way of referring to *mise en place*.

HOT Used to describe a drink that tastes too alcoholic. For example, "This Sazerac is *hot*. Needs more *dilution*."

IRKSOME A small measure of booze left in a bottle that is easier to drink than to decant into a new bottle. Also used to refer to a very small amount of an ingredient in a cocktail *spec*.

KD Shorthand for Kold-Draft, this refers to the 1¼-inch ice cubes used to shake and stir drinks at Death & Co, produced by a large, expensive, and temperamental machine made by the Kold-Draft company.

KETCHUP Nickname given to St-Germain, an elderflower-flavored liqueur that was especially popular at the bar in 2007 and 2008. Its ability to enhance a seemingly endless variety of cocktail styles (and subsequent overuse) earned it various other monikers in the cocktail community, including "bartender's butter" and "bartender's duct tape."

MISE Pronounced MEEZ and short for *mise en place*, a French cooking term referring to the preparation and organization of one's equipment and ingredients. At the bar it refers to the arrangement of tools, garnishes, *cheaters*, and other ingredients at the *service* and *point* stations.

MR. POTATO HEAD A technique for creating a new drink by substituting one or more ingredients into an established (usually classic) cocktail recipe. For example, "The Final

Ward is a *Mr. Potato Head* riff on the Last Word, with rye and lemon in place of gin and lime."

NEEDS A BUMP Used to describe a drink that tastes good but needs a little something extra.

NG Short for "no garnish," to indicate a drink that is served unadorned.

POINT The bar station nearest the door, where the bartender prepares drinks for (and entertains) customers seated around the bar. (See *service*.) Also known as the "personality station."

PRO Short for "professional," when referring to admirable behavior, technique, or decorum exhibited by staff members. Often used in conjunction with "job." For example, "Thanks for setting set up the bar on your day off; that was a real *pro* job." Also used sarcastically to comment on blunders; breaking an expensive mixing glass is "very *pro*."

SCUMBAG Used as either a noun or a verb when referring to a drinks industry person who shows up and orders a drink as we're attempting to close the bar, then hangs on for a few shots and barely tips. For example, "So-and-so *scumbagged* me last night. It was annoying." Also applied to instances when our drinks show up on other bars' menus without credit.

SERVICE The bar station nearest the kitchen, where the bartender receives orders via printed ticket for customers seated at the tables (aka the floor).

SHAKING ICE Large, 2-inch cubes of ice used to shake drinks, and a cause

of many shoulder injuries at the bar. Also known as "block ice."

SIMPLE Short for "simple syrup," a solution of equal parts sugar and water. (See *fat*.) Also abbreviated as SS.

SPEC A cocktail recipe written or verbally described in cryptic shorthand. For example, "Is your *spec* for a daiquiri two, one, three-quarter, or two, three-quarter, three-quarter?"

SPEED RACK The two rows of troughs that run the length of the bar and contain the vast majority of the ingredients (other than the *cheaters*), used to make the current menu of cocktails. Also known as "the rack."

SPLIT Using two or more different base spirits to anchor a cocktail. For example, "I *Mr. Potato Headed* this old-fashioned by swapping out the bourbon and *splitting* the base between tequila and mezcal."

THIN The opposite of *fat*.

TIN ON TIN Our preferred shaker setup. For example, "At my last job everyone used Boston shakers, but switching to *tin on tin* has saved my shoulder."

WASH LINE The level to which a cocktail fills its serving glass. In most cases, an ideal wash line reaches the very top of a glass. A low wash line indicates an underdiluted drink. For example, "The *wash line* on your daiquiri looks low. Did you shake it long enough?"

WAYNE GRETZKY Slang for a snobby mixologist—or someone who sports the mini mullet popular among hockey players.

THE REGULARS
FATHER BILL DAILEY

Father Bill Dailey is one of our favorite customers. He's also a Roman Catholic priest and a lawyer.

Death & Co is an 85-minute walk from the Holy Trinity Parish on Eighty-Second and Broadway. When I first moved to New York, I'd leave the church on Sunday night (which is a priest's Friday night) and walk downtown to the bar. If there was a wait to be seated, I'd read my book or chat with Frankie, the doorman, about his screenplay in progress. He was always politely amused that I would sit under the awning and wait. Later I found time to come down on Tuesdays and Thursdays as well. Then Death & Co became my home away from home.

I like to begin the evening with a Ti Punch. Each bartender makes it differently and swears his or her variation is the best. Joaquín's is essentially a rum snow cone, and Thomas's doesn't have a hint of ice. After the Ti Punch, I'll have a one-to-one martini, then a Rob Roy (page 150). I can't be in bar where I don't feel comfortable ordering a martini.

Though you usually go to a bar to turn off your brain, sometimes you want to turn it on. In the latter case, the Death & Co bar staff are always willing to teach their craft, and their depth of experience means that you're always in excellent hands, no matter who's behind the bar. Being a bartender there is a hard job. Those folks could be making more money slinging rum and Cokes anywhere else. Every night they have to explain to someone why the bar doesn't serve vodka, and they're constantly asked, "What's your favorite drink?"

I regard the work of the priesthood largely as encountering people who feel lost. Everyone eventually wonders about his or her place in the world, and that tends to be when they go to church. I think my task is to show them that we're all at home in this universe and that it's a good place that's warm and inviting. That's hospitality—creating a sense of home for people. It's not a stretch to say a bartender performs a similar service.

TI PUNCH

½ LIME

1 TEASPOON CANE SUGAR SYRUP (PAGE 276)

2 OUNCES LA FAVORITE RHUM AGRICOLE BLANC

In a double rocks glass, muddle the lime and cane syrup until the lime is well juiced. Add the rum and cracked ice and stir until cold. No garnish.

Chapter Two

BUILDING A BAR

APERITIVO JULEP

ALEX DAY

Here's an example of what great a cocktail should be: a whole that's much better than the sum of its parts. Anytime a bottle of something new or foreign shows up at Death & Co, we taste it and keep it in mind for creating new drinks. The afternoon the deliciously bittersweet Amaro CioCiaro showed up, Alex had a sip that lingered in his head through that night's service. At some point he was mixing a drink made with Massenez Crème de Pêche, and a whiff of that heady peach liqueur synced up with the amaro and Dolin dry vermouth, another new favorite at the bar. Bartenders often scoff at low-alcohol drinks, so he thought it would be fun to serve this drink in a vessel that usually indicates a boozy concoction—the julep tin—and give it an oxymoronic name.

2 OUNCES DOLIN DRY
VERMOUTH

¾ OUNCE AMARO CIOCIARO

1 TEASPOON MASSENEZ CRÈME
DE PÊCHE PEACH LIQUEUR

GARNISH: 1 MINT BOUQUET

Put all the ingredients in a julep tin. Fill the tin halfway with crushed ice. Stir with a bar spoon, churning the ice as you go, for about 10 seconds, holding the drink by the rim so the entire tin can eventually frost up. Add more crushed ice to fill the tin two-thirds full and stir until the tin is completely frosted. Add more ice to form a cone above the rim. Garnish with the mint bouquet in the center of the ice and serve with a straw.

This chapter conveniently skips over the chemistry and minutiae of how spirits and other alcoholic ingredients are produced. Instead, we'll concentrate on the spirits, liqueurs, and other modifiers we use most frequently at Death & Co and explain why they're our favorite ingredients to use. This chapter isn't intended to be a comprehensive list of every tasty spirit under the sun; rather, it's a curated list of ingredients that shine in cocktails. We don't expect you to replicate our collection at home or in your establishment. Instead, we want to give you the tools to taste and evaluate spirits to start building your own bar.

We start this chapter with the primary base spirits: gin, rum, tequila and mezcal, whiskey (and whisky), and brandy. (You may wonder why we omit vodka. Honestly, we almost never use it at Death & Co; when the bar opened, in the early days of the current cocktail movement, our goal was to introduce people to *new* spirits—specifically those with flavor and depth. These days our hard stance against vodka has mellowed some, and we'll happily make a vodka cocktail if you request one. But out of tradition, and a near-endless array of more interesting options, we still don't feature it on our menu and most likely never will.)

After base spirits, we cover a couple of more unusual spirits (absinthe, aquavit) that may serve as bases but more often play a supporting role as modifiers. Next up are more dedicated modifiers, such as liqueurs, amari, vermouths, sherries, aperitif wines, and bitters. Finally, we round out the chapter with discussions of sweeteners, infusions, juices, garnishes, and ice.

To be a creative cocktail maker is to be a student of your ingredients. Compared to chefs and sommeliers, bartenders are incredibly lucky to work with ingredients that are usually consistent (booze). That said, these products sometimes do change and, over the years, we've experienced a number of our favorite spirits going downhill. In one case, a favorite tequila brand was purchased by an international conglomerate, and our hearts broke as we watched it torturously decline in quality. In another,

a popular rye whiskey began to taste weaker and less like itself in what we suspect was an attempt by the producer to fill demand by bottling younger whiskey. It just goes to show that even products that seem to be consistent year after year will sometimes change. Our job is to constantly test and taste products to see whether they're as we expect them to be and, if not, strategize what we need to do to adjust our specs so our cocktails stay up to snuff.

Additionally, new and game-changing products are introduced all the time, more so now than ever before. One of the greatest joys of working at Death & Co is our access to new products. When something new comes on the market, we're lucky to be some of the first to taste it. If it passes muster, it enters the active ranks at the bar. For a time, it will enjoy the limelight in a privileged position just in front of the wall of spirits on our back bar, placed strategically between both bartenders. It sits there during a shift, usually accompanied by a tasting glass, and when time allows, the bartenders have a taste. Then they go about serving our guests while mulling over this new product and its potential. Some bartenders find inspiration simply by tasting alone, while others dig deep into the product's history, searching for intellectual connections that inspire a new drink. At some point, a light bulb goes off and an idea begins to take shape. Between orders, the back bar begins filling up with cocktails in progress, sometimes lined up ten drinks long. Other bartenders offer suggestions in these early stages, tweaks are made, the floor staff gets into the game, and when something concrete begins to take shape, trusty regulars are brought in for some honest feedback. And voilà, that new product just became indispensable—and we just created a whole new headache for ourselves in trying to find a place for it on our already-crowded shelves.

By the time this book is in print, we will certainly have new favorite ingredients that we're regularly using in our drinks, and we encourage you to bring a similar spirit of adventure to your cocktail making. Keep an eye out for new products: the ever-growing arsenal of spirits and other ingredients we get to play with ensures that no one will ever get bored and there will always be new cocktails to create!

TASTING & EVALUATING SPIRITS

Almost every day, one or more importers or producers stops by to share a new product with us. Death & Co has been lucky to play test bed for many important new releases in their infancy, often as early prototypes, as well as in their final tweaking stages. This is probably because importers and producers see the bar as a safe place to get an honest assessment of their product. Our bartenders don't hold back on their opinions. If they love what they taste, they'll say so; if they hate it, they'll be equally unabashed.

When tasting a new product, we follow a methodology taught by the gents at Beverage Alcohol Resource (see Resources, page 288), which we think is the best way to evaluate its merits. Here are the general rules.

ALWAYS TASTE WITH SOMEONE ELSE.
It doesn't matter whether others are inexperienced tasters or their preferences are wildly different than your own. Tasting and evaluating spirits by yourself is a bad idea because a monologue is never as productive as a dialogue. When tasting, we like to gather bartenders and other staff as well.

SET UP SOME BASELINE COMPARISONS.
A tasting is only valuable if it's done comparatively. We don't pit products against one another in the spirit of one-upmanship, but rather to start a conversation and, often, a debate. Having something to relate the product to is vital in establishing a baseline. We usually do this in a blind tasting of several spirits in the same category, such as an array of mezcals, rye whiskeys, or gins. We often include our favorite bottles in this tasting—again, served blind—as a point of comparison.

ESTABLISH A PURPOSE FOR THE TASTING.
Sometimes we're tasting a spirit to determine its quality. In those instances, we always taste the unadulterated spirit first: just the product in a glass. But more often than not, we're tasting to determine the best application for a spirit: how we can best use this product in a cocktail and whether it's better than what we already use. To determine this, after first tasting individual spirits, we do another round of tasting using the spirits in simple, well-known cocktails. Rums are tested in a daiquiri, whiskeys in a Manhattan or an old-fashioned, gins in a martini, and so on.

TASTE THE SPIRIT.
After assembling your spirits—not only the new product that's to be analyzed but also a couple of comparative examples—start tasting. Keep a glass of water handy for cleansing your palate and, if needed, diluting any high-proof samples so they can reveal all of their potential. Begin by nosing the spirit. Spirits have a lot higher alcohol content than beer and wine, and if you were to smell them as you would a wine, you'd quickly burn your nose and ruin the whole exercise. For this reason, you should bring the glass up close to your nose, open your mouth, and breathe in. This simple action allows you to bypass the strong alcohol and get to the spirit's underlying aroma. After a few smells, discuss what you notice with your cohorts. Use the first sip to rinse any lingering flavors in your mouth, left over from your last cup of coffee, meal, cigarette, or what have you. Then take two more sips, swirling the spirit in your mouth and pausing between sips to chat about what you're tasting. Add a small amount of water as necessary if the alcohol is getting in the way of the spirit's aromas and flavors.

FIND USEFUL, MEANINGFUL WORDS TO DESCRIBE EACH SPIRIT.
We work hard to avoid esoteric descriptors—words like "supple" or vague phrases like "a hint of stone fruit." Instead, we try to offer feedback that's relaxed and conversational. Tasting spirits is about a connection to a personal experience, a way of articulating a memory or an association with what you smell or taste. A peaty Scotch might remind you of a campfire near the ocean, for example, or a sherry rich with dried fruit and baking spice might evoke Christmas in a glass.

You don't need extensive experience in tasting spirits to be good at it; you just have to be open to whatever is personally relevant, not be shy with what senses and memories come to mind, and, ultimately, be comfortable speaking about it. The deepest and most honest comments come this way, and they enliven what might otherwise be a dour mood among a bunch of polite people sitting around a table nosing and tasting quietly. Boring. We want emotion, excitement, and active engagement.

GIN

We use gin as a base spirit more often than any other at Death & Co. Why? Because it gets along with pretty much everything. Gin offers a strong foundation for a drink while allowing other ingredients to build upon its flavor profile. All of its delicious botanicals (juniper, cardamom, coriander, citrus, and so on) act as little fingers, grasping onto other flavors and enhancing every element of a cocktail. It's both sturdy enough to stand out in boozy stirred drinks and delicate enough for refreshing, citrusy cocktails. Gin is our prom king *and* Miss Congeniality.

RAW MATERIALS

Gin is made by redistilling a high-proof neutral spirit with botanicals, which always includes juniper, but may also include orange peel, lemon peel, angelica root, anise, caraway, cassia, coriander, cocoa, bitter almonds, orris root, and many others, depending on the brand. After redistillation, the spirit is cut to proof with water.

GEOGRAPHY

Originally from Holland, where it was called *genever*, gin is now made all over the world. However, the majority of popular gin brands are distilled in the United Kingdom.

CATEGORIES

London dry: A big, high-proof (usually at least 45% ABV), aggressive, crisp style of gin with prominent flavors of juniper and citrus. The London dry style is widely considered the benchmark for all other gin. While it is associated with the city, it does not need to be made in London; in fact, only a couple of London dry gins are actually made in London proper. London dry is an invaluable tool in the bartender's arsenal, being indispensable for citrusy and boozy cocktails alike. A gimlet is a thing of beauty with a sharp gin like Beefeater, just as the strong personality of a Tanqueray is perfect in a Negroni.

Plymouth: A gentle, citrus-forward style of gin similar to traditional London dry but with a lower ABV of 41.2%. Plymouth gin is distilled at a specific distillery in Plymouth, England. Also available in the higher-proof (at least 57% ABV) navy strength—the perfect platform for a stiff martini.

Old Tom: London dry's historical cousin, boasting a similar juniper-forward flavor profile but with a richer body and sweeter flavor. Traditionally, Old Tom gin was sweetened with sugar and had added botanicals. Although this stemmed from the need to cover up poorly made distillates, it also provided an opportunity to increase the amount of botanicals in the gin. After largely disappearing from cocktaildom in the latter half of the twentieth century, Old Tom has made a recent comeback and has evolved into a distinct category, unique in its vibrancy and punch. Most old cocktail recipes that call for gin are actually referring to the Old Tom style, and a Tom Collins made with a quality Old Tom is a revelation.

Genever: The granddaddy of all gin, genever was created by the Dutch as a delivery system for juniper, which was thought to offer protection from the plague. Genever is distilled from a malted wine base and then redistilled with botanicals. Its flavor profile is sweeter and richer than that of any other style of gin, almost like an unaged whiskey with a hint of botanicals.

New style: Also called "New Western" or "American" to indicate that this is the Wild West of gin. The category encompasses basically any style of botanical distillate that doesn't fall directly under one of the categories above. Most take flavor or style cues from the classic gin styles, then add or subtract botanicals and experiment with different raw materials for the base spirit. As with all gins, juniper is a constant, though in varying degrees of intensity.

AGING

Though not traditionally aged, some gins spend time in oak. Genever has a long tradition of aging, and in recent years, certain London dry labels (Beefeater Burrough's Reserve is an example) and traditional Old Tom gins have gotten into the game (Ransom Old Tom is a favorite). More often than not, these are mildly aged—nowhere near as extensive as with whiskey or brandy.

RECOMMENDED BOTTLES

··· *London Dry* ···

Beefeater London Dry Gin: Death & Co opened with two gins in its speed rack: Beefeater and Plymouth. Beefeater is a benchmark London dry gin that says hello with juniper on your first whiff, then opens up with orange, peppery, and spicy notes. It's versatile enough to attach itself well to a variety of ingredients, and it can be part of a rowdier party in bracing cocktails like the Last Word (page 144).

Plymouth Gin: Both a brand and a style in itself, Plymouth is a softer and more elegant gin best utilized in drinks with delicate modifiers and citrus or floral flavors, including classics like the Aviation (page 139) and French 75 (page 143). Plymouth is also a great gateway gin: if customers swear they don't like gin, we make them a South Side (page 151) with Plymouth and watch them become converts.

Tanqueray London Dry Gin: Like Beefeater, Tanqueray is another quintessential London dry gin, and once we realized how well it stands up to—and collaborates with—other strong flavors, we added it to our repertoire. You can throw pretty much anything at Tanqueray and its assertive piney aroma will come through, especially when bridging the distinctive flavors found in amari and herbaceous liqueurs such as Chartreuse. Its high proof (47.3% ABV) gives body to drinks that don't have added sugar. Our house Negroni (page 147) is made with Tanqueray, which is our highest form of praise.

··· *Old Tom* ···

Hayman's Old Tom Gin: Hayman's relaunched their version of this formerly forgotten style around the time we opened the bar, and although we rarely use it as the sole foundation for a drink, its delicate, approachable flavor makes for a versatile split base.

Ransom Old Tom Gin: Our pal and cocktail historian David Wondrich helped Oregon's Ransom distillery re-create what they say is a more classic Old Tom, which they assert was not sweetened and was aged in barrels. Thus is the history of booze: rife with strong assertions but sometimes short on hard facts because everyone was drunk. Ransom is drier and has a more subtle maltiness than Hayman's version, and the two play nice as a split base in our house Martinez (page 145). Ransom stands alone admirably in drinks like the Tom Bomb (page 161).

··· *Genever* ···

Bols Genever: Unlike more modern styles of gin, this progenitor has a malt-forward flavor with subtle juniper and citrus notes. Bols reintroduced the style to the United States not long after Death & Co opened, and we quickly adopted it in drinks in which we wanted a malty, grainy base without reaching for whiskey, such as the Racketeer Julep (page 244). Not long after, Bols released a barrel-aged genever that adds a touch of spice and mint. We use it often in concert with other gins in split bases.

··· *Other* ···

Anchor Distilling Company Junipero Gin: Sometimes you need gin to be a president, other times you need it to be a tyrant. This aggressive gin is the latter, with the proof (49.3% ABV) and focused botanicals that can carry classic, "ginny gin" drinks like a dry martini or Last Word (page 144).

Perry's Tot Navy-Strength Gin: One of our early and most loyal regulars, Allen Katz, crafted this navy-strength (57% ABV) gin with cocktails in mind. Bold, spicy, and sweetened with wildflower honey, it can carry its complexity through drinks like the Commandant (page 155) and is our favorite gin in a classic Gimlet (page 143).

THE REGULARS
DON LEE

Don Lee left a career in IT to work behind the bar (including exactly one shift at Death & Co).
He's also the beverage director of the New York bar Golden Cadillac.

My friend John Deragon had heard a rumor that Death & Co was having its soft opening on New Year's Eve, so we showed up. My first impression was it didn't look like other cocktail bars. It was darker, more romantic—and a little more goth, I guess—than the other cocktail bars in the city.

I'd known Phil and Brian from their time at Pegu Club and tasting some of their creations there, but the menu at Death & Co was completely different than anything I'd seen before. It was like finally listening to an entire album after just hearing a few singles.

I started going to the bar at least three times a week. I was part of the early crowd: we'd get in at 6 p.m., hang out for a couple of hours, then get out before it got too busy. The evening was a great time to chat with the bartenders and try new things. Whereas most New York cocktail bars were very focused on classics, sours, and other shaken drinks, Death & Co was pushing the boundaries of boozy, stirred drinks and using a lot of nonstandard cocktail ingredients: amaro, mezcal, punches, loads of bitters, everything infused with everything. All these things became the foundation for what we now call the "New York style" of cocktails.

A few months after the bar opened, Phil asked me if I wanted to take a shift here or there. He said something like, "Hey assholes, we want to take a vacation, but don't have enough staff to cover. At this point you know our drinks well enough to fill in." So I trailed a couple of shifts to learn the basics.

One Sunday Phil had tickets for a concert, so I took his shift. In those days Sundays were quiet enough that there was only one bartender and one barback. The beginning of the shift was easy enough. I set up the bar, cut some garnishes. Then two older guys came in and ordered a Fish House Punch. I had the recipe, so I made one for them while I went into a little speech on the history of punch. I overheard their conversation as they drank their punch and realized I'd just served Dave Wondrich and Jared Brown, two of the most important and knowledgeable cocktail historians of our time. (Dave later told me that my punch was okay.)

By 10 p.m. the bar had filled up and I was slammed. I couldn't keep up with the drink orders, and I could feel the whole situation going down in flames. Then Phil showed up, wasted from his concert, and jumps behind the bar. He looked at the drink tickets and banged out thirty drinks in a row, then said "See ya" and disappeared. That was my first and last shift at Death & Co.

FISH HOUSE PUNCH

4 SUGAR CUBES

2 OUNCES CLUB SODA

1 OUNCE LEMON JUICE

1 OUNCE HINE H COGNAC

1 OUNCE APPLETON V/X RUM

½ OUNCE MASSENEZ CRÈME DE PÊCHE PEACH LIQUEUR

GARNISH: PEACH SLICES

In a mixing glass, muddle the sugar cubes with 1 ounce of the club soda until the sugar is fully broken up. Add the remaining ingredients (except the remaining club soda) and stir over ice until cold, then strain into a brandy snifter over 1 large ice cube. Top with the remaining 1 ounce club soda. Garnish with peach slices.

RUM

Whereas gins and whiskeys can be somewhat interchangeable in cocktails, the rums we stock at the bar have such distinct personalities that swapping out one for another is likely to dramatically change the flavor profile of a drink. This is largely due to the fact that rum is the world's most varied spirit. It's made in dozens of countries, many with their own long-standing styles of production. We tend to go down two avenues with rum in drinks: daiquiris and other refreshing shaken drinks, and stirred, boozy drinks in which rum (or in the case of tiki-style drinks, multiple rums) offers the same depth and complexity as other barrel-aged spirits.

RAW MATERIALS

Rum is made by fermenting fresh-pressed sugarcane juice, cane sugar, or cane sugar by-products (most commonly molasses), then distilling, and, in many cases, aging the resulting spirit in oak casks.

GEOGRAPHY

Rum hails predominately from the Caribbean, though great rums are made all over, including in Australia, the United Kingdom, Asia, and the United States.

CATEGORIES

Spanish: A lighter style typically distilled from molasses.

English: A richer style, this is often distilled from demerara sugar.

Jamaican: Also known as "navy rum," Jamaican-style rum has a uniquely funky complexity.

French: This distinct, grassy, earthy style is distilled from freshly pressed sugarcane juice. It's largely produced in the French West Indies, where it's designated as rhum agricole.

AGING

The majority of rum produced is bottled with no discernable color and is neither matured nor stored in oak barrels. However, most of the rum we use at Death & Co has spent some time in oak.

RECOMMENDED BOTTLES

··· *Spanish-Style Rums* ···

Caña Brava (Panama): Our good friends Simón Ford and Dushan Zaric worked tirelessly to bring an authentic Cuban-style rum to the United States. For now, Caña Brava is as close as we can get to Havana Club (thanks to our ongoing embargo with Cuba), and some of us insist it's even better. There are few things as beautiful as a daiquiri with Caña Brava—a litmus test we take very seriously.

Flor de Caña Extra-Dry White Rum (Nicaragua): A great entry into Spanish-style rums. In cocktails, it brings just enough to the party without offending any of the other guests, thanks to time spent in oak, which also adds spice and vanilla flavors that play well with citrus and other tropical fruit.

Ron del Barrilito 3-Star Rum (Puerto Rico): Intensely fruity for an aged rum, it's often used to add brightness to tiki-style drinks that include several varieties of rum.

Santa Teresa 1796 Ron Antiguo de Solera Rum (Venezuela): A unique bottling made by progressive aging of rum using the Spanish solera method: after some rum from the oldest cask is bottled, rum from the next-youngest cask is transferred in, and so on down the line, thereby ensuring that every cask is filled and every bottle contains a mixture of a variety of vintages. The result is a very dry, flexible rum that tastes mature but can be integrated into both stirred and shaken drinks.

··· *English-Style Rums* ···

El Dorado 12-Year Rum (Guyana): Made from a combination of stills (including an old wooden still once used by the British Royal Navy), this rum has deep caramel flavors that work well in concert with other rums in tiki-style drinks.

Gosling's Black Seal Rum (Bermuda): This dark, syrupy rum is most famous for its role in the Dark and Stormy (page 142), but it's surprisingly handy when you want to add a rich, molasses-y flavor to either stirred or shaken drinks.

Lemon Hart 151 Rum (Guyana): Yes, you can light the bar on fire with this rum, but that would be a waste. Until it returned to the U.S. market, this overproof rum was the missing ingredient in zombies and other classic tiki drinks we wanted to re-create at the bar.

Scarlet Ibis Rum (Trinidad): Originally developed as our own private-label rum, Scarlet Ibis is made from a blend of pot-distilled rums aged three to five years. Full-bodied (thanks to its 49% ABV) and boldly flavored, it mixes well with lighter-style rums and boosts the spice notes when paired with aged rums from other islands. One of our favorite bottles for Manhattan-style rum drinks.

··· *Jamaican-Style Rums* ···

Appleton Estate V/X Rum (Jamaica): This is our favorite bottle when we want to add the telltale fruity funk of Jamaican rum to a cocktail. We use it in varying amounts in everything from fizzes to tiki drinks and punches. Appleton V/X paired with a light rhum agricole is a match made in heaven.

Smith & Cross Rum (Jamaica): Its navy-strength proof (57% ABV) and intense levels of *hogo* (a term used to describe the funky, almost gamy flavor associated with molasses-based spirits) make this rum a hard beast to tame, though it's worth the fight.

··· *Rhum Agricole* ···

Barbancourt White Rhum (Haiti): A rum for when you want the sharpness and tanginess of agricole without as many vegetal notes. A great base for the classic daiquiri and its many interpretations.

La Favorite Rhum Agricole Ambre (Martinique): Less vegetal than its unaged brother, it's perfectly balanced with spicy and buttery notes from barrel aging. A perfect example of a spirit that's just as much at home in a cocktail as it is served neat.

La Favorite Rhum Agricole Blanc (Martinique): The funky and petrol-like flavors (a good thing, we maintain) may put some novice rum drinkers off, so we're wary of serving it to the uninitiated. But it's what we reach for most when we want fresh, grassy sugarcane flavors to be noticeable in a drink.

Rebel Rebel, page 193

TEQUILA AND MEZCAL

Tequila and mezcal are the wines of the distillate world. More than any other spirit, their flavor and quality depend so much on how their base ingredient—agave—is handled: the soil and location in which it's planted, when it's harvested (typically maturing for ten to twelve years before harvest), how it's processed, and which yeasts control the fermentation all affect the final result. A great agave-based spirit is the product of hard work and dedication; a bad one is the victim of cutting corners.

TEQUILA

Most of the tequila we use in our cocktails is of the unaged, or blanco, style. Aged tequilas (see "Aging," page 28) are delicious on their own (and in a few specific drinks), but we lean heavily on the blanco style for its honest expression of the agave plant. When you leave tequila in wood for a long time, it loses some of that agave magic and inches closer in flavor to other oak-aged spirits, especially whiskey. We also tend to favor blanco tequila because it's a touch less expensive, but there are certainly times when a delicious reposado or añejo is the right call.

RAW MATERIALS

Tequila is made from the succulent agave and, in the case of some lesser styles, additional sugar. Tequila can only be made from the blue agave (*Agave tequilana* Weber var. *azul*). The agave plants must be harvested at a precise moment after spending more than a decade in the ground. That moment is decided by the *jimador*, a farmer who has spent years cultivating agave and has developed an innate sense of when it is ready to be pulled from the ground. The plants are then cooked and shredded before the juice can be extracted for fermentation. They are cooked either by steaming in stainless steel pressure cookers or by baking in neutral clay ovens.

GEOGRAPHY

Tequila is produced exclusively in the Mexican states of Jalisco, Nayarit, Michoacán, Guanajuato, and Tamaulipas in governmentally designated zones covering more than twenty-six million acres. Most of the agave is grown in the highland and the lowland areas of Jalisco, though it thrives at elevations more than five thousand feet above sea level. Tequila that comes from highland agave has a sharp, fresh, grassy note that we usually prefer in cocktails, whereas lowland agave tequilas have broader, fattier flavor profiles.

CATEGORIES

100 percent agave: These higher-quality tequilas are distilled twice using only blue agave (*Agave tequilana* Weber var. *azul*) and without adding sugars of any kind.

Mixto: Made from at least 51 percent agave, mixtos may contain up to 49 percent other sugars. Mixtos are considered the lesser of the two categories and are often lower-quality spirits. At Death & Co we use only 100 percent agave tequila and leave mixto tequila (the artificially colored crap) to the college kids.

AGING

Blanco, plata, platinum, or white: No aging, though sometimes these tequilas are rested in neutral holding tanks for up to two months.

Reposado: Matured in oak barrels for at least two months and up to one year.

Añejo: Matured in oak barrels with a capacity no larger than 600 liters for at least one year and up to three years.

Extra añejo: Matured in small oak barrels for at least three years.

RECOMMENDED BOTTLES

Siembra Azul Blanco Tequila: By far our favorite blanco for cocktails, this tequila is clean, dry, and well balanced and has an honest, pure agave flavor. It's an especially great base spirit for chile pepper infusions.

Siete Leguas Blanco Tequila: Crafted in one of Mexico's oldest distilleries (the same one from which the ubiquitous Patron brand sprung), Siete Leguas is made from agave roasted in a stone oven. It bursts with sharp fruit, spice, and floral notes that stand out even when part of a split base.

El Tesoro Platinum Tequila: The gold standard of highlands blanco tequila, El Tesoro platinum is a benchmark by which we judge all new blanco tequilas professing quality. A bright grassiness meets fresh citrus and a deeply lingering fresh fruit character.

El Tesoro Reposado Tequila: When we want both the body and the bright agave notes of blanco tequila and the spicy, sweet flavors that come from barrel aging, we reach for this reposado. Yet it's also full-bodied and bold enough to hold its own against an aggressive mezcal, as is the case in our Oaxaca Old-Fashioned (page 273).

Siete Leguas Reposado Tequila: Just because a distillery does a blanco right, that doesn't mean it'll be successful with aging—not an issue for Siete Leguas. They apply just the right amount of time in oak to their reposado, maintaining all the brightness and youth of the blanco while softening some of its aggressive edges.

El Tesoro Añejo Tequila: Two years of oak aging smoothes out this intensely aromatic tequila and adds spice and vanilla notes you won't find in younger styles. We use it as the base spirit in both stirred drinks (Coralillo, page 190, and Te Amo, page 195) and shaken drinks (Dolores Park Swizzle, page 249).

MEZCAL

The usual wisdom is that mezcal is the overarching category for all spirits made from agave, with tequila being a type of mezcal made specifically in the areas surrounding the city of Tequila. While this is a convenient way of categorizing agave spirits, mezcal and tequila are stylistically distinct. Whereas tequila is all about the vegetal brightness drawn from the agave, mezcal highlights the unique flavors of different varietals of agave and employs a special technique wherein the agave is cooked underground for many hours. The resulting spirit has a smoky, telltale personality. Yes, there is lots of cheap, terrible mezcal to be had in Mexico, but the bottles we use at Death & Co are truly artisanal, made in small batches in Oaxaca's mountain villages using ancient methods and materials. Mezcal's penetrating smoky and briny flavors are sometimes too powerful for a base spirit in a cocktail, so we often split it with tequila or apply it in tiny amounts as a modifier, similar to how we often use peaty Islay Scotch. Mezcal is often distilled to proof, which varies depending on the distiller's process; they usually range from just over 40% to almost 50% ABV.

RAW MATERIALS

Mezcal is made from either wild or cultivated agave. Unlike tequila, which is made from one type of agave, mezcal can be made from a number of varieties, with a type often referred to as *espadin* being the most common. As with tequila, the agave must be cooked and shredded before the juice can be extracted in preparation for fermentation; with mezcal this cooking process happens in pits filled with hot rocks, where the agave is cooked for several days and up to several weeks at a time, giving mezcal its smoky character.

GEOGRAPHY

Mezcal is traditionally made in five Mexican states: Oaxaca, Durango, San Luis Potosí, Guerrero, and Zacatecas.

CATEGORIES

The style of mezcal is tied to the type of agave used for its production. Notable examples include, but certainly aren't limited to, *espadin*, *tobala*, *barril*, and *cupreata*.

AGING

Blanco or joven: No aging, though sometimes these mezcals are rested in neutral tanks for up to two months. Most mezcals on the market are blancos, and these have become our go-to style.

Reposado or madurado: Matured in oak barrels for at least two months and up to one year.

Añejo or añejado: Matured in oak barrels with a capacity no larger than 200 liters for at least one year.

RECOMMENDED BOTTLES

Del Maguey Chichicapa Mezcal: Once we caught the mezcal bug, we started playing with the portfolio of single-village mezcals imported by Ron Cooper, one of the first and most notable importers of artisanal mezcal. This one has become a favorite for its rich, chewy texture and distinct chocolate and vegetal notes. Though often doled out by the teaspoonful in drinks, it's the star player in a beguiling drink called Terrible Love (page 195).

Del Maguey Crema de Mezcal: Sweetened with unfermented syrup from roasted agave, this lower-proof (40% ABV) mezcal adds a fruit basket to the usual briny, smoky, and vegetal flavors.

Del Maguey Vida Mezcal: Most artisanal mezcals run $50 and up per bottle, so this affordable blend of single-village mezcals has been a real game changer. It is briny, moderately smoky, and highly mixable and works equally well as a base spirit, a split base, or a modifier.

Los Amantes Joven Mezcal: Stars aligned when Death & Co opened around the same time that this accessible, high-quality mezcal hit the New York market. This bottle's intense agave flavor and considerable (though not overwhelming) smokiness inspired a bunch of drinks.

WHISKEY AND WHISKY

Whiskey is the George Clooney of the cocktail world: It's typically found in the lead role, with a supporting cast that amplifies its best qualities; it can shine across many genres of drinks; and it was prominently featured in *O Brother, Where Art Thou?* But seriously, with its long history in both America and Europe, whiskey (generally spelled without an "e" in Scotland and Canada, and with an "e" in Ireland and the United States) is the foundation for many classic cocktails. Some of our favorite whiskeys are high proof (over 45% ABV), providing a strong foundation for complex drinks and great infusions.

While some people might take issue with using a fine single-malt Scotch or rare bourbon in a cocktail, we've always considered every spirit fair game if handled correctly. This is particularly true of whiskey, where so many unique bottlings can be found. Purists might scoff at the use of an Islay Scotch in a swizzle-style drink, but when Phil came up with the Myra Breckinridge (page 250), the combination of peat and lime flavors was a revelation. When Brian toasted pecans and infused them into one of our favorite bourbons (Buffalo Trace), a new Death & Co classic was born in the Buffalo Soldier (page 204).

AMERICAN WHISKEY

RAW MATERIALS

All whiskey is essentially a hopless beer that has been distilled and aged in oak barrels. As with beer, it can be made from various grains, including corn, rye, wheat, and malted barley, and the specific grains or blend of grains imparts a great deal of the whiskey's flavor. The flexible approach to grain selection originated to make use of the grains local to any given area. When European settlers arrived in what would eventually become the United States, they found an abundance of rye, and thus rye whiskey was born. When distillers moved over the Appalachian Mountains and settled in what is present-day Kentucky, they found that corn grew abundantly, giving rise to America's national treasure: bourbon.

GEOGRAPHY

While the majority of American whiskey is made in the southern United States, especially Kentucky, many small distilleries are cropping up around the country, including in Death & Co's hometown, New York City.

CATEGORIES

Bourbon: The term *bourbon* applies to any whiskey made from at least 51 percent corn. Note that bourbon whiskey doesn't *have* to come from Bourbon County, Kentucky (although it does *have* to come from the United States). Rather, bourbon is defined by a high corn content, its aging process (it must be aged in charred new-oak barrels for at least two years to be labeled "straight" bourbon), and a strict prohibition against any additives except water. Bourbon typically has a rich, sweet taste and full mouthfeel. Almost all bourbon is blended from many casks, though there are a few examples of single-barrel and small-batch blends, and its age designation refers to the youngest bourbon in the blend.

Rye: Made from at least 51 percent rye grain, it typically has a crisper, spicier taste and sharper mouthfeel than bourbon. As with bourbon, rye must be aged in charred new-oak barrels for at least two years to be labeled "straight" rye, and the only additive allowed is water.

Tennessee sour mash whiskey: Made using between 51 and 79 percent corn, this spirit must be filtered through maple charcoal chunks before aging, a step known as the Lincoln County process.

Bottled in bond: The Bottled-in-Bond Act of 1897 was passed to ensure the authenticity of the whiskey inside a bottle and prevent unscrupulous bottlers from diluting good whiskey into swill. The act dictates that the whiskey be aged a minimum of four years, be bottled at a minimum of 100 proof, and be the product of one distillery and one distiller, and from one season. For us, bonded whiskey status indicates not only that it's good booze but also that its proof is high enough to make it suitable in a spirituous cocktail like a proper Manhattan.

RECOMMENDED BOTTLES

Buffalo Trace Kentucky Straight Bourbon: Many of our favorite sipping bourbons are too pricey to mix into drinks; we'd rather not charge $18 for an old-fashioned. Buffalo Trace is an exemplary bourbon for its affordable price tag, with a buttery, corny flavor profile and a distinct nuttiness that's amplified even more when infused with pecans (page 282).

Elijah Craig 12-Year Kentucky Straight Bourbon: Thanks to this bourbon's copious caramel and honey flavors and assertiveness, it works great in sour-style cocktails, but we've also been known to throw it into a Manhattan or an old-fashioned.

Old Grand-Dad 114 Kentucky Straight Bourbon: Its spicy kick makes Old Grand Dad a rye-lover's bourbon, and at 57% ABV, it gives juleps, old-fashioneds, and other whiskey drinks served on ice the benefit of extra body without the unpleasant hammer that overproof booze often hits you with. For such a high proof, Old Grand-Dad 114 is surprisingly drinkable.

Old Overholt Kentucky Straight Rye: Like Rittenhouse, Old Overholt is a rye, but the two couldn't be more different. Overholt is soft and creamy, with a stony, almost dusty nose that seems to last forever. It loves being matched with fruit, especially grapefruit and raspberries, and lends itself particularly well to infusions, including our workhorse chamomile-infused rye (page 281). We use this rye so much at Death & Co that it's earned the nickname Old Overpour.

Rittenhouse Bonded 100-Proof Kentucky Straight Rye Whiskey: When we opened, rye was having its moment in craft cocktails, and Rittenhouse, because of its high proof (50% ABV) and low price tag, was many a bartender's favorite bottle. At one point Rittenhouse was so popular that we'd stockpile twelve cases at a time, fearing a shortage (which is exactly what happened). With an in-your-face spiciness that plays well with a variety of ingredients, Rittenhouse always asserts itself in just the right amount, letting you know that you're drinking a rye-based cocktail. We use it in everything from citrusy cocktails (Double Fill-Up, page 199) to stirred, boozy drinks (Manhattan Transfer, page 206).

SCOTCH WHISKY & IRISH WHISKEY

RAW MATERIALS

Scotch and Irish whiskey are made primarily from malted barley, along with other grains, such as corn and wheat.

GEOGRAPHY

Just to state the obvious, Scotch whisky hails from Scotland, and Irish whiskey is produced in Ireland.

CATEGORIES

··· *Scotland* ···

Single-malt whisky: The holy grail of Scotch whisky for discerning aficionados, single-malt must be made from 100 percent malted barley in small pot stills in at least two distillation runs, produced by a single distillery, and aged for a minimum of three years in oak casks. The pot still, or alembic still, is an ancient distilling tool, one that has remained nearly unchanged for millennia. It produces a rich and complex spirit, a defining characteristic of single-malts. While some people tend to categorize single-malts by their

region of origin (Islay, Speyside, Lowlands, and so on), we've taken a cue from our mentor Paul Pacult and instead think of single-malts (and Scotches in general) as being either maritime or inland. Maritime Scotch absorbs the smell of the sea and has the brininess that comes with aging whisky so close to the ocean (Islay and Orkney Scotches are examples). Inland Scotch is typically more floral and reminiscent of Scotland's vast plains.

Blended malt whisky: This term refers to a blend of 100 percent malted barley whiskies from two or more distilleries.

Blended whisky: Blended whiskies are made by combining single-malts with whiskies made from other grains such as corn or wheat.

Single-grain whisky: Used mostly for blending, these 100 percent corn or wheat whiskies are produced in a column still, creating spirits with a lighter body than those made in small pot stills.

··· *Ireland* ···

Single-malt whiskey: As in Scotland, Ireland's single-malts are 100 percent malted barley and made in a pot still by a single distillery.

Grain whiskey: Typically lighter than single-malts, Irish grain whiskeys are made in a column still using wheat or corn.

Blended whiskey: This is a combination of single-malt and grain whiskeys.

Single pot still whiskey: Unique to Ireland, this style is made with 100 percent barley, both malted and unmalted, in a pot still.

AGING

Because bourbon producers are required to use brand-new barrels for aging, used bourbon barrels are abundant and have historically been the most common aging vessel for Irish whiskey and Scotch whisky. Sherry, port, madeira, and other wine barrels have also had a strong tradition with Scotch, but their scarcity—and the popularity of Scotch—has meant that whiskey aged in wine barrels has become increasingly rare. Both types of whiskey must be aged for at least three years.

NOTABLE INFORMATION

• Pot stills used to make Irish whiskey are much larger than those used to make Scotch whisky and yield a slightly milder flavor.

• The smoky flavor of some Scotch whisky is a result of the process by which the barley is prepared for distillation: after the barley is soaked to release crucial enzymes, the grains are dried over burning peat (an accumulation of partially decayed vegetation), imparting flavors into the grains that are retained even after distillation. This peaty flavor, often the hallmark of Scotch whiskies, is particularly prevalent in those produced on the island of Islay, in western Scotland.

RECOMMENDED BOTTLES

Compass Box Asyla Blended Scotch: This blended whisky has a broad "Scotchiness" to it, with a distinct heather note that lends itself well to classics like the Rob Roy (page 150) or Sazerac-style drinks.

Famous Grouse Blended Scotch: This blended Scotch is a great foundation for infusions, especially fruit infusions, and we often pair it with apples. It has just enough smokiness for classic Scotch drinks like the Bobby Burns (page 140).

Knappogue Castle 12-Year Irish Whiskey: We reach for this clean, elegant bottling when we want a less-assertive whiskey that will pair well with floral ingredients like honey, lavender, and rosebuds. It's lovely in concert with our Chamomile-Infused Old Overholt Rye (page 281) in drinks like the Trembling Bell (page 209).

Laphroaig 10-Year Islay Single-Malt Scotch: A couple of drops of this pungent Scotch goes a long way, which is why we often use it as a modifier or to rinse a glass to give it an ethereal wisp of peatiness. Other times it's fun to use as a base spirit for extra-smoky drinks like the Myra Breckinridge (page 250).

Redbreast 12-Year Irish Whiskey: This one-of-a-kind Irish whiskey is made in a pot still from both malted and unmalted barley, then aged in oloroso sherry casks, giving it a big, unctuous texture, lots of cereal flavors, and a distinct, apple-y finish. It's a key component in some of our most successful simple drinks, like the Cooper Union (page 255).

BRANDY

The term *brandy* refers to any spirit distilled from fermented fruit juice. This vague definition results in a wide array of beverages from all corners of the globe, from France's famous grape brandies to the apple brandy made by America's first licensed distillery (Laird & Company) to the intensely aromatic eaux-de-vie produced from peak-season fruit.

· ·

GRAPE BRANDIES

RAW MATERIALS

Grape brandies are made from wine grapes. Specific varietals are listed in the spirit categories below.

GEOGRAPHY

The great grape brandies of the world come mainly from France, Italy, and the Americas.

CATEGORIES

Armagnac: Spicier and lighter bodied than cognac, Armagnac is distilled mostly from Ugni Blanc grapes, with small amounts of the other cognac varietals, using a combination of column and pot stills and then aged in oak. It is produced exclusively in the Armagnac region of France.

Cognac: Cognac is double distilled in pot stills using Ugni Blanc, Folle Blanche, and Colombard grapes and aged in French Limousin oak, which imparts subtle, spicy notes (whereas American oak typically offers rich vanilla flavors). Cognac is exclusively produced in the Cognac region of France.

Grappa: This Italian spirit is a "pomace brandy"—meaning it's pot distilled from the skins, seeds, and stems of grapes, traditionally those left over from making wine. Although grappa originated in Italy, there are some beautiful grappas coming from North America these days.

Marc: Another pomace brandy, marc is a French product that's also made from grape skins, seeds, and stems and pot distilled.

Pisco: Often unaged, this grape-based brandy is distilled from any number of varietals (Torontel, Moscatel, Quebranta, Italia, Albillo, Uvina, and Negra Corriente in Peru; Muscat, Pedro Ximénez, and Torontel in Chile). Peruvian pisco tends to favor pot stills, while Chilean favors column still. Pisco usually isn't aged (though there are some very cool, sipping-worthy aged ones from Chile); instead, it's rested in neutral vessels for a minimum of three months.

AGING

··· *Armagnac & Cognac* ···

VS (Very Special/Superior) or Three Star: At least two years in oak casks.

VSOP (Very Special/Superior Old Pale), Réserve, or Five Star: At least four years in oak casks for cognac or five years for Armagnac.

XO (Extra Old), Napoleon, Extra, or Hors d'Age: At least six years in oak casks.

Hors d'Age: Refers to Armagnac aged at least ten years in oak casks.

··· *Grappa & Marc* ···

Mostly unaged, though some fine grappas are matured in oak barrels.

··· *Pisco* ···

Peru: Aged at least three months in copper, glass, clay, or stainless steel. No wood-aging permitted.

Chile: Aging in wooden barrels is permitted but used sparingly.

RECOMMENDED BOTTLES

Campo de Encanto Acholado Pisco: Fellow bartender Duggan McDonnell helped craft this blended style of Peruvian pisco with cocktails in mind. The combination of distillate from Quebranta, Torontel, and Italia grapes makes for a balanced pisco with floral, citrus, and spice notes. Because pisco is unaged, it has a great deal of texture and a gritty, floral flavor and aroma. In cocktails, this works amazingly well in citrusy drinks like the P-Five Punch (page 238) or a classic Pisco Sour (page 149), but recently pisco has been showing up increasingly in boozy drinks, like the Sweet Hereafter (page 219).

Hine H VSOP Cognac: If there is such a thing as a work-horse cognac, dry, full-bodied Hine H is it. As a base spirit, it cooperates with a spectrum of ingredients, yet it isn't a neutral player; rather, it adds its rich, fruity flavor profile to both stirred and shaken drinks.

Pierre Ferrand 1840 Cognac: Cognac isn't as deeply rooted in classic cocktail culture as gin or whiskey. The Sidecar (page 151) is probably its best-known vehicle. The Sazerac (page 151) was originally made with cognac, until the European phylloxera epidemic in the late 1800s wiped out grape production and bartenders switched to rye. At 90 proof, Pierre Ferrand's 1840 bottling is perfect for these classic cognac-based drinks and is assuredly destined to appear in a host of new concoctions.

Pierre Ferrand Ambre Cognac: This amber-colored cognac can add a basket of fall-fruit flavors (pear, apple, apricot) sans sweetness, which comes in handy for making stirred drinks like the Ingénue (Brian Miller's tiki-scented Manhattan variation, page 267) and the Vieux Carré (page 153). We often pull for the Ambre bottling when a softer, more elegant spirit is needed, compared to the spiciness of the 1840.

APPLE BRANDY

RAW MATERIALS

The apples used to make brandy aren't the kind you get at your local grocery store. Apple brandy is most often made from cider apples, which are small and intensely flavored. The apples are pressed and made into cider, which is then distilled into brandy.

GEOGRAPHY

Apple brandy typically hails from France and North America. The idea of terroir, which is integral to winemaking, is particularly relevant when tasting apple brandies. Apples grown alongside rolling pastures in Normandy taste very different from apples that grow in the crisp, clean air of the Pacific Northwest, and those distinctions are reflected in the resulting brandies.

CATEGORIES

Calvados: This French apple brandy, produced in the Calvados region, is defined by production and aging regulations similar to those for cognac and Armagnac. It tends to have crisp apple flavor with loads of barnyard funk.

Straight apple brandy: This term refers to American apple brandy. Laird's bonded apple brandy adheres to the same set of standards required for bonded whiskey, yielding a rich, deeply aged, spicy spirit.

Applejack: Though traditionally produced by freeze distillation (a process known as jacking), modern applejack is typically a combination of apple brandy and a neutral grain spirit (30 and 70 percent, respectively).

AGING

Fine, Three Star, Original: At least two years in oak.

Vieux or Réserve: At least three years in oak.

Vieille Réserve, VO, VSOP: At least four years in oak.

Hors d'Age, Extra, Age Inconnu: At least six years in oak.

··· *Bonded Apple Brandy* ···

Same rules as bonded whiskey (see page 31).

RECOMMENDED BOTTLES

Laird's Bottled-in-Bond Straight Apple Brandy: By far our most-used brandy, Laird's has kept its spot in our speed rack since the day Death & Co opened. Its elemental apple flavor has a natural affinity for rye (evident in one of our original drinks, the Wicked Kiss, page 209), and thanks to its fiery proof (50% ABV), it works well as a base spirit in a host of boozy stirred drinks.

Busnel Calvados Pays d'Auge VSOP: This French apple brandy is all finesse, which comes in handy whether its used as a modifier or in concert with Laird's (as in our house Jack Rose recipe, page 144), to round out its rowdy American cousin.

EAU-DE-VIE OR FRUIT BRANDY

The main difference between eau-de-vie and other types of brandy is that eau-de-vie is meant to be the purest possible expression of the fruit from which it is distilled. It can be very helpful in adding a boost of flavor to fresh ingredients; for example, 1 teaspoon of pear eau-de-vie can do wonders in a cocktail featuring fresh pear. Because the flavors in fruit brandies are extremely concentrated, they can easily dominate other flavors, so it's best to exercise restraint while mixing with them. Although their fresh fruit aromas trick your mind into thinking you're drinking something sweeter, eaux-de-vie are actually quite dry, so we either augment eau-de-vie with a sweetener or reach for a fruit-flavored liqueur.

RAW MATERIALS

Eaux-de vie can be made from any fermentable fruit, but they usually employ full-flavored, hearty fruits such as pear (poire, poire Guillame), cherry (kirschwasser), apple (pomme), and raspberry (framboise).

GEOGRAPHY

Eaux-de-vie may be produced anywhere in the world, but the best-known varieties largely hail from France, Eastern Europe, and the Pacific Northwest.

AGING

Fruit brandies typically aren't aged, though some are rested in neutral holding tanks.

RECOMMENDED BOTTLES

Clear Creek Pear Brandy: Made in Oregon using local Williams or Bartlett pears, this intense eau-de-vie delivers big fruit flavors, which is why we use it in small doses as a modifier or an accent in a drink. The exception to this rule is Brian Miller's Miss Behavin' (page 226), in which it is used to great effect as a base spirit.

G. E. Massenez Kirsch Vieux Cherry Brandy: An intense cherry bomb of flavor, this spirit is usually used in small doses in stirred drinks, such as Thomas Waugh's extra-complex Manhattan-style cocktail the Red Ant (page 269).

G.E. Massenez Crème de Pêche Peach Liqueur: When it's perfectly ripe, there are few fruits that can compare to a peach. This liqueur captures that distinctive flavor in drinks like the Moon Cocktail (page 167) and Stick the Landing (page 215).

36 | DEATH & CO

OTHER SPIRITS

The spirits that follow don't all fit into one tidy package, but they play an important role in our repertoire. Most are used as modifiers rather than base spirits, though we do like to challenge ourselves to create cocktails around them from time to time.

AQUAVIT

Aquavit, produced primarily in Scandinavia, is made from neutral grain or potato spirits and flavored with spices, herbs, and other botanicals. It's predominantly flavored with licorice-like caraway and often contains dill, anise, cardamom, fennel, and citrus peel. Like gin, aquavit can be made with a wide variety of ingredients, giving distillers the freedom to create signature flavor profiles. We love the complex spice flavors aquavit can add, whether as a base spirit or as a modifier. As a result, we probably use more aquavit than most cocktail bars.

RECOMMENDED BOTTLES

Linie Aquavit: This Norwegian spirit is loaded into sherry casks and carried in ships that cross the equator twice before bottling, based on the belief that the movement of the seas and changes in temperature and humidity improve its flavor. The reward from this long maritime journey is a spirit driven by caraway and other baking spices and a lovely, nutty note that works well in both stirred and shaken drinks.

Krogstad Aquavit: Not bound by European Union regulations, which call for aquavit to be caraway- or dill-dominant, Oregon's Christian Krogstad makes his eponymous aquavit with a heavy star anise note that's great in refreshing shaken drinks.

ABSINTHE

Absinthe is an overproof spirit whose main flavor is anise. For absinthe to be acknowledged as legitimate, it must contain the leaves and flowers of grande wormwood (*Artemisia absinthium*), a plant in the same family as tarragon, anise seed, fennel, melissa (aka lemon balm), and hyssop, another shrub with a long medicinal history. There are many misconceptions about absinthe, mostly centering around the idea that it causes people to go crazy or hallucinate. It's true that the wormwood in absinthe contains thujone, a substance once thought to be a powerful hallucinogen. However, true absinthe contains only trace amounts of thujone, as this compound barely survives distillation. And thanks to advances in modern science, thujone levels in absinthe can now be tested, so this spirit is no longer banned in the United States.

RECOMMENDED BOTTLE

Emile Pernot Vieux Pontarlier Absinthe: A classic French absinthe with prominent wormwood and anise flavors. We load the stuff into dasher bottles and use it frequently but sparingly, in a similar manner to bitters. It's also our go-to rinsing absinthe for Sazerac-style cocktails.

VAN OOSTEN BATAVIA ARRACK

Distilled from sugarcane and red rice, Batavia arrack is believed to be the historical precursor to rum and the ingredient first used in punch, which was invented by British soldiers stationed in India. It's funky and pungent—and a required ingredient for many classic punches. It has become a rite of passage for Death & Co bartenders, many of whom have had at least a passing obsession with it at some point in their career.

MODIFIERS

The ingredients highlighted here are the supporting cast of cocktails, supplementing base spirits and adding extra layers of complexity. By our definition, any alcoholic ingredient that isn't the base of a cocktail can be a modifier. This broad category includes liqueurs and amari as well as vermouth, sherry, and other fortified wines.

LIQUEURS

Generally speaking, liqueurs are spirits combined with flavorings and sweeteners. The category as a whole is large and diverse, with liqueurs clocking in with wildly varying alcohol and sweetness levels. Most liqueurs have a neutral base spirit (essentially a high-proof vodka), flavored with various ingredients, including fruit, herbs, bark, roots, nuts, seeds, and spices. Some, such as fruit-based liqueurs, add the simple, pure essence of the primary flavoring ingredient, while more complex herbal liqueurs (like Chartreuse, made from an ultrasecret recipe with 130 botanicals known only to two monks) add a chorus of flavors.

RECOMMENDED BOTTLES

Bénédictine: This brandy-based liqueur contains twenty-seven herbs and spices, with heavy notes of angelica and hyssop and a deep, dark honey flavor that pairs well in drinks with aged brown spirits and apple brandies.

Chartreuse: Carthusian monks have produced this liqueur since the early eighteenth century using a highly guarded secret blend of herbs, flowers, and plants. We're especially blessed in that it comes in two varieties: green, which is high proof (55% ABV) and extremely herbal, and yellow, which is lower in proof (40% ABV) and less herbaceous in flavor, with more sweet, honeyed notes. We add them to cocktails to bringing extra complexity to the party, and also use them to balance out strong bitter

and sour flavors; a good example of this is the Naked and Famous (page 185), in which yellow Chartreuse bridges smoky mezcal and bittersweet Aperol.

Cointreau: Triple sec is a category of orange liqueur, and Cointreau, with its perfect balance of sweetness, body, and clean orange flavors, is far and away our favorite triple sec. It adds an incredible brightness to drinks, especially in classic cocktails that depend on triple sec, like the Margarita (page 145) or Sidecar (page 151). Try either cocktail with a cheap orange liqueur and you'll see the difference.

Galliano l'Autentico: Commercial interests sometimes get the better of spirits and liqueurs, and there are numerous cases over the last century when a historical spirit has been dumbed down for less adventurous palates. For much of the past fifty years, Galliano l'Autentico was a shell of its former, intense self. But a few years back, the makers of this golden nectar smartly reverted back to their original recipe, upping the proof (to 42.3% ABV), cutting back on the sweetness, and better balancing the vanilla and anise flavors with the other botanicals in the formula.

Grand Marnier: A blend of cognac and triple sec, Grand Marnier is sweeter than Cointreau and has a rounder, richer profile and an earthier flavor.

Kalani Ron de Coco Coconut Liqueur: The most natural-tasting coconut liqueur we've come across comes from Mexico's Yucatán Peninsula, where it's made from locally grown coconuts and sugarcane.

Luxardo Maraschino Liqueur: At some point every bartender develops a crush on this cherry-flavored liqueur because of the funky flavor profile that comes from using the whole marasca cherry—pits and all—in the distillation process. Just a splash can add an insane amount of complexity to an otherwise simple drink (try making an Aviation, page 139, without it to see what we mean).

Marie Brizard White Crème de Cacao: This classic chocolate liqueur is distilled from cocoa beans and flavored with vanilla. It has an unctuous texture and pure, natural flavors that set it apart from most other chocolate liqueurs. Marie Brizard also makes a brown variation of this liqueur.

Rothman & Winter Orchard Apricot Liqueur: A combination of Klosterneuburger apricot juice and an eau-de-vie distilled from the same fruit, this spirit is a great way to introduce fresh apricot flavors into a drink. It has a delicate sweetness that leaves room for other sweet ingredients.

Strega: An Italian digestif similar in color and complexity to yellow Chartreuse, but with more anise and vanilla flavors. It's best used in tiny amounts; any more and it turns into the playground bully.

St. Elizabeth Allspice Dram: A rum-based liqueur with concentrated flavors of the allspice berry, a spice that earned its name because of its inherent flavors of cinnamon, cloves, and nutmeg. Often called pimento dram in older cocktail recipes, this spirit is especially useful in punches and tiki-style drinks.

St-Germain: This lovely elderflower liqueur has been a victim of its own success. When it was first released, around the same time we opened Death & Co, bartenders found that its potent lychee aroma and citrus flavors harmonized surprisingly well with almost any ingredient, earning it the nickname "bartender's ketchup." After getting distracted by other new modifiers for a few years, we've come back around to this old fling, as it's still our favorite slave to citrus.

Suze Saveur d'Autrefois Liqueur: Sometimes described in similar terms to Campari, Suze is a bracingly flavored French aperitif. Pale yellow in color, Suze has a strong aroma of earth, roots, gentian, and lemon.

John D. Taylor Velvet Falernum: A longtime staple of Carribean cocktails, Falernum is a clove- and lime zest-flavored cordial from Barbados. We often use it in tiki-style drinks, such as the Coffey Park Swizzle (page 249) to add body and a subtle, astringent spiciness.

AMARI, APERITIFS, AND DIGESTIFS

An amaro is a bittersweet Italian liqueur traditionally consumed after a meal as a digestif. In cocktails, a small amount can add many times its weight in depth and complexity. Since Death & Co opened, a number of new amari have become available in the United States. Each release is like a new toy: all of us play around with it for a few days, then it either finds its way onto the cocktail menu or languishes forgotten on the back bar until a new kid comes along to show it some love. Every bartender has one or two favorites that see repeated use.

While all amari (the plural of amaro) share the quality of being both bitter and sweet, in different proportions depending on the brand, each boasts a unique flavor profile imparted by a proprietary blend of some combination of roots, herbs, flowers, barks, and citrus peels. Amaro is made by macerating this special blend in either a neutral grain spirit or wine, then adding sugar to the filtrate and allowing the mixture to age. Their alcohol content can range between 16% and 40% ABV.

RECOMMENDED BOTTLES

Amaro Averna: The best way we've been able to describe this amaro is that it tastes like flat Coca-Cola, with flavors of chocolate, vanilla, and citrus.

Amaro CioCiaro: CioCiaro's profile has pronounced bitter orange and earthy flavors. In cocktails, it makes a fine substitute for drinks that call for Amer Picon, a French aperitif used in some classic recipes that's now difficult to obtain in the United States.

Amaro Meletti: Meletti has a distinctive violet nose and flavors of saffron and anise.

Amaro Nardini: Nardini has a menthol character similar to that found in Fernet-Branca, minus Fernet's overarching bitterness.

Amaro Nonino Quintessentia: Relatively subtle compared to others in the category, this grappa-based amaro is flavored with alpine herbs and can be used in larger quantities without squashing other ingredients.

Aperol: Aperol is less bitter and more sweet than Campari and has a more pronounced orange flavor that adds lightness and brightness to cocktails.

Campari: Campari is one of those special ingredients that can be either refreshing or settling, depending on what quantity you use and what you pair it with. Every bartender becomes obsessed with its bittersweet grapefruit and orange profile at some point. There is no Negroni without Campari, and without Negronis the world is a far less beautiful place.

Cynar: Though the bottle depicts an artichoke and the name comes from the vegetable's Latin name (*Cynara cardunculus*), Cynar doesn't really taste like artichokes—though artichoke is one ingredient in the overall recipe. Its flavor profile transitions from sweet to sharp and citrusy with some vegetal notes. In a drink, it adds a quick spike of flavor that mellows after a few seconds.

Fernet-Branca: This is amaro on crack, with an aggressive medicinal, mentholated flavor profile derived from forty-plus herbs and spices, including myrrh, chamomile, and cardamom. In addition to being a popular shot among the beverage industry as a way to say "Hello," "Good-bye," "How are you?" or any other number of things, we use it in small quantities as a modifier.

Ramazzotti: This popular amaro is sweeter than most, with vanilla and root beer flavors and a big orange character that loves to be mixed with whiskey.

....

VERMOUTH

In its most simplistic definition, vermouth is fortified wine flavored with herbs, barks, and spices. In modern terms, a relatively neutral white wine stands as the base for most vermouths (generally made from Clairette Blanche, Piquepoul, Catarratto, or Trebbiano grapes), and a small amount of neutral spirit is added. This practice, common throughout the wine-producing world (for example, in sherry, port, and Lillet), is an old technique to help preserve wine, as the higher alcohol content helps ward off microbial spoilage. The flavorings used in vermouth are proprietary to each manufacturer, but common ingredients include clove, cinnamon, quinine, citrus peel, cardamom, marjoram, chamomile, coriander, juniper, hyssop, and ginger.

There are three main types of vermouth. Dry vermouth is pale in color, slightly bitter, and dry, as the name implies. Sweet vermouth is red and sweeter, and white, or blanc, vermouth is transparent and stylistically falls somewhere between dry and sweet vermouths. It's tricky to generalize about using vermouths in cocktails, but we've found that, as a rule, dry vermouth does best with lighter spirits, like gin, and sweet vermouth has an affinity for aged spirits. Blanc vermouth is a switch hitter, able to get along with both lighter and aged spirits.

The word *vermouth* comes from the German word *wermut*, meaning "wormwood," and vermouth did indeed originally contain wormwood (and sometimes still does). Vermouth has a long and storied history and was made in different ways in different regions until the two main centers of vermouth production were established: Italy and France. The Italians are credited with producing a rich, bitter style of sweet vermouth today referred to as vermouth di Torino; prime examples are Carpano Antica Formula vermouth and Cocchi vermouth di Torino. Not long after, the French got into the game and created a drier, light style. Spurred by a resurging interest in vermouths, many American producers have taken to making unique vermouths from local ingredients, and some of these have found their way into Death & Co's arsenal.

Most vermouths in use today are European and governed by the regulations of the European Council. Those rules specify that vermouth must be based on wine made according to EU wine legislation, and that wine must constitute no less than 75 percent of the finished product. Further, it must be fortified by the addition of distilled alcohol to between 14.5% and 22% ABV; flavored with natural flavorings, aromatic herbs, and/or spices; and sweetened with caramelized sugar, sucrose, and/or grape must.

RECOMMENDED BOTTLES

Carpano Antica Formula Vermouth: This sweet vermouth is equally delicious on its own as it is mixed into a cocktail. Its bitter, full-bodied flavor profile includes cocoa, orange, caramel, and figs, along with a big vanilla note. In cocktails it's a versatile modifier that can both complement and contrast with other flavors, though it can sometimes be a bully in the glass compared to other vermouths. There was a time when we were putting Carpano in everything, especially any variation on the Manhattan. Those were the days when Death & Co was defining "stirred and bitter" as a category. Since then we've mellowed a bit to include other vermouths.

Cocchi Vermouth di Torino: Like Carpano Antica (to which it is stylistically similar), this sweet vermouth has a strong vanilla note and a rich, compelling body, but unlike Carpano it lets other ingredients shine through in cocktails.

Dolin Blanc Vermouth: With its full body and sweetness, Dolin blanc works like a red vermouth and pairs well with base spirits that would overpower a dry vermouth, especially blanco tequila. We reach for this when introducing guests to stirred, boozy drinks, as it lightens the intensity of the drink without masking other flavors.

Dolin Dry Vermouth: This beautiful, soft, dry vermouth has gentle herbaceous flavors and a touch of sweetness. It pairs nicely with subtly flavored base spirits by stretching out their flavors and is the base ingredient in Alex's Aperitivo Julep (page 242).

Dolin Rouge Vermouth: Made from wine and botanicals from Chambéry, France, Dolin rouge is drier and lighter bodied than Carpano Antica or Cocchi Torino, which makes it too wimpy to stand up to bigger brown spirits (unless we're making a Manhattan with a wheat-heavy bourbon; then it's just right). To remedy this, we mix equal parts Dolin rouge and Punt e Mes to make our House Sweet Vermouth (page 284).

Punt e Mes: This very poignant sweet vermouth is almost amaro-like in its sharp bitterness and has a balsamic vinegar quality to its flavor profile. We discovered that it loves grapefruit, and our Grapefruit-Infused Punt e Mes (page 281) has become a staple ingredient in many drinks. The heavy bitterness of Punt e Mes has led many to question whether it is truly a vermouth or whether it would be better categorized as an amaro.

SHERRY

Sherry gets a bad rap. It's a sad fact that most people consider it to be simply a sweet wine that's best consumed by doting grandmothers and snooty intellectuals. But sherry is amazing in its variety, running the spectrum from the driest wines in the world to the richest.

Sherry is a fortified wine produced in the "sherry triangle" region of Andalusia, on the southern coast of Spain. The primary grapes used in its production are Palomino, Moscatel, and Pedro Ximénez. There are many different categories of sherry, ranging from bone dry (manzanilla, fino), to just a hint of sweetness (amontillado), to very sweet (Pedro Ximénez, Moscatel, cream). The sweetest types of sherry (Pedro Ximénez and Moscatel) start with grapes that have been dried and concentrated under the sun until they're almost raisin-like; the resulting intensely sweet wine is, in our view, nature's finest sweetener.

The process for aging sherry is one of the most unique and complicated in the wine world. Generally speaking, sherries are aged in one of three ways:

- **Biological aging:** The wine is fortified to about 15% ABV and then develops a layer of indigenous yeast on the surface, known as flor, which protects the wine from contact with air and oxidation while still allowing it to mingle with the cask. This is the process used for the driest categories, such as fino and manzanilla.

- **Oxidative aging:** The wine is fortified beyond 17% ABV and is in constant contact with the air in the cask—the same type of aging used for most wines and spirits. This process introduces another level of flavors, concentrating the richness and introducing spice notes. Oloroso sherry is aged in this way and therefore concentrates into a relatively sweet-tasting wine as it ages.

- **Mixed aging:** In the case of amontillado, the sherry starts as a fino (aged under flor), then the proof is raised, killing the flor. Next, it undergoes oxidative aging, creating a sherry that's rich on the nose and generally very light on the palate.

Aging takes place using the solera system, which is designed to produce a fairly consistent product from year to year. A solera is comprised of a number of different barrels, or *criaderas*. Each layer of barrels represents a different year; the first layer contains the youngest wine, the second layer the second-youngest wine, and so forth. Several times a year, some of the wine from barrels in the oldest layer is bottled, and the barrels are then topped off with wine from the next-oldest layer, which is then replenished from the next-oldest layer, and so forth, until new

wine is added to the youngest layer. This ensures that each bottling has some sherry from each layer, which in turn means that each bottle contains a variety of vintages.

Before 2008, sherry was rarely used in cocktails. Then our friends Steve Olson and Andy Seymour, who were doing work for the Sherry Council of America, stopped in to throw us a comprehensive sherry tasting. We started experimenting with the bottles they left behind, and our minds were quickly opened to sherry's versatility in cocktails. In addition to its compelling, oxidized-wine character, sherry can add loads of sweet flavors—particularly dried fruit, honey, and nuts—to the glass without making a drink cloying. The drier styles of sherry, such as amontillado and oloroso, work especially well as base spirits, as in the Coffey Park Swizzle (page 249), its variation, the Dolores Park Swizzle (page 249), and La Viña (page 206).

RECOMMENDED BOTTLES

Alvear Festival Pale Cream Montilla-Moriles: Produced just outside the designated sherry region, the fortified wines of Alvear might as well be sherry; they're made in the same method and styles as their cousins, with the exception that all of them are made from Pedro Ximénez grapes. They impart strong savory and fruity flavors and are dry enough to use as either a base or a modifier. The pale cream version is light and sweet, with flavors of melons, apricots, and pears.

La Gitana Manzanilla Sherry: A bone-dry sherry with a salty, savory, herbal flavor. Because it's not as intense as sweeter sherries, we can get away with using it in larger quantities in cocktails.

Lustau East India Solera Sherry: This has the same intense aroma and sweetness as an oloroso sherry but

opens up into orange and spice notes that reach out and grab other flavors in the cocktail.

Lustau Los Arcos Amontillado Sherry: Though it smells like raisins and figs, this sherry is dry on the palate, with a nutty, oxidized character to boot. Of all sherries, it's the one we use most as a base ingredient.

Williams & Humbert Dry Sack Medium Sherry: A blended style of sherry that's stylistically close to an amontillado. It's on the dry side but has a richness and spice flavors that marry well with rum.

PORT

Best known as an after-dinner dessert wine, port has a long history as a cocktail ingredient. Over the years we've used port extensively; it adds a rich texture, body, depth, and structure to drinks.

Port is made exclusively in the Duoro River Valley of Portugal. By law, winemakers can use over a hundred different variatals of grapes in making the wine; in reality, though, there are five main varietals: Tinta Barroca, Tinta Cão, Tinta Roriz, Touriga Francessa, and Touriga Nacional. Port's typical sweetness comes from the special way in which it is made: grapes are pressed, allowed to ferment, and then fortified with a base spirit. This raises the overall alcohol content and kills off the yeast before they have the chance to consume the sugars within the wine, and thus results in a "sweet" but stable wine.

There are two main styles of port we use: tawny and ruby. Tawny port is made by blending several vintages of oak-aged wine. The time in oak barrels produces nutty flavors, a quality that comes with oxidative aging. Tawny often improves with age in the bottle. Ruby port, by contrast, is stored in neutral tanks then bottled and sold.

RECOMMENDED BOTTLES

Graham's "Six Grapes" Reserve Ruby Port: Full-bodied and rich, with ripe plum and dark chocolate flavors.

Warre's Otima Ten-Year Tawny Port: A dry-ish tawny with ripe fruit and honey richness on the nose and a deep, dried-apricot flavor.

APERITIF WINES

A decade ago, we were lucky if we could find a handful of quality vermouths on the market, let alone any other fortified wines to play with aside from Lillet blanc. Today, with vermouth's rising popularity, other fortified wines are constantly coming into the spotlight in every style from light to sweet. Traditional aperitif wines have been popular throughout Europe for centuries. Most are fortified to preserve them from degrading and flavored with ingredients local to the area where they're produced. In this way, aperitif wines offer an exciting journey through different regions and drinking traditions.

RECOMMENDED BOTTLES

Bonal Gentiane-Quina: Produced by Alpenz, the same company that makes our beloved Dolin vermouths, Bonal Gentiane-Quina is partially fermented grape juice infused with cinchona bark and gentian (both bittering agents) and is characterized by dark fruit and herb flavors.

Cocchi Americano: This Italian aperitif dates back to the nineteenth century but was only recently released in the United States. Flavored with orange and spices, it gets its sharp bitterness from cinchona bark. Many compare it to the original formula for Kina Lillet, which was replaced in the 1980s with Lillet blanc, a milder version of its venerated forebear.

Lillet Blanc: Lillet blanc is a blend of Semillon, Sauvignon Blanc, and Muscadelle wine fortified with citrus liqueur. It's less bitter than Cocchi Americano, with a floral nose and bright orange flavor, and is used much like a blanc vermouth in cocktails.

Lillet Rouge: Made from a Merlot-based red wine blended with the addition of cinchona bark, it's lightly tannic and mildly bitter, like a dainty sweet vermouth.

Lillet Rosé: As with rosé wine, this relatively new product splits the difference between Lillet blanc and rouge. It's less potent than a sweet vermouth but not as rich as a blanc vermouth, with floral aromas and a big strawberry flavor.

CHEATER BOTTLES

When making drinks during service, any time bartenders have to spin around or leave their post to retrieve a bottle, they lose precious time (and, ultimately, money). But at Death & Co we use literally hundreds of ingredients to create our drinks, so it's impossible to keep everything needed close at hand. Not long after we opened the bar, Phil decided to decant some of the most commonly used combinations of essential ingredients—typically added in small amounts—into small bottles topped with speed pourers. This shortcut seems like a no-brainer now, but at the time we hadn't seen anyone do this.

Over the years, our assortment of cheater bottles has multiplied like bunnies, and now we have a mass of seventy-some vessels of various shapes and sizes—repurposed soda bottles, antique glassware, whatever we can scrounge up at flea markets—containing a wide array of ingredients, from syrups to assorted modifiers and batches (see page 284).

Not one shift goes by without a guest asking, "Do you really know what's in all of those little bottles?" Our response: "Of course; it's our job!"

A large (and painful) part of our daily preservice prep involves cleaning, filling, and organizing our cheaters. When we create a new menu, it's a puzzle to figure out the most convenient and efficient organization for the bottles, with the most-used cheaters in the easiest-to-reach spots. We train our bartenders to have a purpose for every movement and to never be empty-handed. When new bartenders start working at Death & Co, we cut them a break and add labels to the cheaters for their first few shifts. But soon enough we remove the labels and expect them to memorize the layout—until we completely change it when we introduce the next menu. Then everyone has to learn it all over again.

BITTERS

Bitters are a bar's spice rack. In addition to contributing their own flavors, they draw out and bind unexpected flavors from other ingredients in a drink. When they are used correctly, you probably won't be able to identify which bitters are present; they should do their work in the background. Bitters are often the answer to the question "What else does this drink need?" In addition to pulling out flavors that might otherwise be buried, bitters can affect the texture of a drink, sometimes tricking your mind into thinking the drink is creamier, more tannic, or richer than it is. At Death & Co, we occasionally use bitters to boost the aromatics of a drink by dashing them on top of a finished cocktail (see Pisco Sour, page 149) or directly onto a citrus or mint garnish.

When creating new cocktails, we often try several different bitters near the end of the development process, after the rest of the spec has been locked in. It's astonishing how a dash of certain ingredients can completely transform a cocktail, even at this late stage in its development.

Each year since we opened Death & Co, the number of bitters at our disposal has increased exponentially. As with other booze, we taste every product that comes across the bar, and only a few earn a permanent spot in our rotation. We've also extended our "more is more" philosophy to bitters. Our House Orange Bitters (page 284) is actually an equal-parts blend of three brands: Fee Brothers West Indian orange bitters has a pure, sweet flavor; Regans' orange bitters adds a distinct cardamom note and some bitterness; and Angostura orange bitters adds cinnamon and clove flavors. Likewise, our House Peychaud's Bitters (page 284) combines two parts of the classic brand with one part Bitter Truth creole bitters, which boosts the bitterness and spice flavors.

We break bitters down into two categories: lifting bitters and binding bitters.

LIFTING BITTERS

These bitters heighten and brighten other similar flavors in a drink. They usually have a simple flavor profile created around one or two main ingredients. Here are some examples:

- Bittercube cherry bark and vanilla bitters
- Bitter Truth celery bitters
- Bittermens 'Elemakule Tiki bitters
- Bittermens hopped grapefruit bitters
- Bittermens Hellfire habanero shrub
- House Orange Bitters (page 284)

BINDING BITTERS

These are more complex in formula and act like a zipper to connect disparate ingredients. Just one dash can rescue an otherwise muddy flavor profile, as in the Conference cocktail (page 270). Here are some examples:

- Angostura bitters
- Bittermens Xocolatl mole bitters
- Bitter Truth aromatic bitters
- Bitter Truth Jerry Thomas' bitters
- Fee Brothers whiskey barrel–aged bitters
- House Orange Bitters (page 284)
- House Peychaud's Bitters (page 284)

INFUSIONS

We never planned on infusions being a big part of Death & Co's bar program, but in the early days Phil fell in love with a chamomile-flavored grappa he'd tasted and wanted to make something similar with rye. A few experiments later, the Chamomile Julep (page 242) debuted on our menu, and our minds and palates were opened to the potential of Chamomile-Infused Old Overholt Rye (page 281), which has become one of our most-used spirits over the years and served as the springboard for a family of tea-based infusions. Before long, we started infusing blanco tequila with jalapeño peppers, a concoction we use both as a foundation for myriad spicy drinks and in lesser quantities as modifiers, to bring a little heat to the party.

There are many high-tech tools and methods you can use to make infusions: whip cream chargers, immersion circulators, cryovacs, fat washing, and so on. However, we prefer simple, room-temperature macerations using everyday ingredients. After all, alcohol is a wonderful solvent. It can pull both flavor and aroma from the ingredients it touches without any effect on its own color, clarity, texture, or proof. Using infused spirits in cocktails leaves room for more ingredients, and it also speeds up the drink-making process by adding a level of consistency and allowing the introduction of various flavors that are otherwise impossible to add at the last minute. Recipes for many of the custom infusions we use at Death & Co appear in appendix 1, starting on page 276.

SWEETENERS

The function of sweeteners in a cocktail is twofold: they tame the burn of alcohol and round off a drink's rough edges, and they add body and texture to the drink. Anyone in the "I don't like sweet cocktails" camp should omit the simple syrup in their next daiquiri and reconsider their stance. Cloying cocktails are awful (and awfully prevalent), but sweetness is a stanchion, an essential component to a properly balanced drink.

If a cocktail doesn't get its necessary sweetness from an alcoholic ingredient (usually a liqueur), it must come from a syrup of some sort, most commonly simple syrup (one part sugar to one part water, see page 277), which is the most neutral-tasting sweetener possible. We use other sugars, such as demerara or cane, when we want to enhance the complexity of a drink. Simple syrup acts as a neutral platform on which the other ingredients stand, but demerara and cane sugars bring their own unique flavor to cocktails. Both Demerara Syrup (page 277) and Cane Sugar Syrup (page 276) use two parts sugar to one part water, so they're are also denser and sweeter. Therefore, we most often use them in spirituous stirred drinks in which we want as little dilution as possible.

Both of these syrups also do a wonderful job of amplifying the sweeter flavors of aged spirits, so we usually pair them with rum and whiskey. Likewise, we typically pair the natural sweetness of agave nectar with agave-based spirits. We use Grade B maple syrup (which is more robust than the quotidian Grade A) in small amounts to echo similar characteristics in whiskey and rum. And honey syrup adds a floral note that's best buddies with gin and rum; for our version (page 276) we use acacia honey thinned with water, which makes it easier to measure and pour. Recipes for all of the sweeteners we use at Death & Co appear in appendix 1, starting on page 276.

FRESH JUICE

We prepare fresh juice each day before service and make more as needed to replenish our supply during the evening. Once juice is made, oxidation and enzymatic reactions kick in, causing the flavor to deteriorate over time. At home, you'll probably want to squeeze citrus right before you start making drinks, since any leftover juice only retains good flavor for a day at best. This is particularly true of lemon and lime, which lose their freshness within a few precious hours. Grapefruit and orange can be more forgiving; depending on the type fruit used, the juice can keep up to two days.

We juice most of our citrus using a Sunkist commercial juicer, then double strain them to remove pulp. For home use, we recommend a handheld citrus press or a countertop swing-arm citrus press. To make juices from other fruits and vegetables, we use a juice extractor. If you don't own an extractor, you can puree the fruit in a blender and strain the pulp through cheesecloth. We keep all of our juices in sealed containers, either in glass bottles placed in ice during service or in plastic containers under refrigeration.

Always use the freshest, best-quality fruit you can find, organic whenever possible. Wash the fruit well before juicing to remove any wax or pesticide residues. Here are some pointers on the juices we use most often:

Apple juice: We extract most of our apple juice from Fuji or Granny Smith apples. One medium apple yields about 2 ounces of juice. When we make large batches, we add 1 teaspoon of ascorbic acid per quart of juice (or 3 grams per liter, if you have a scale) to prevent browning.

Lemon juice: Lemon deteriorates slightly less quickly than lime but should still be juiced as close to service as possible. One lemon yields 1 to 1½ ounces of juice.

Lime juice: Limes oxidize more quickly than other citrus and should be juiced as close to service as possible. One lime yields about 1 ounce of juice.

Grapefruit juice: Ruby Red grapefruits are our preferred variety for juicing and garnishes. White grapefruits aren't as sweet, so if you use them, you might need to adjust the drink with additional sweetener. One medium grapefruit yields about 8 ounces of juice.

FRESH INGREDIENTS FOR MUDDLING

When muddling fresh fruit, vegetables, or herbs into a drink, consider the ingredient being used before deciding how long and hard to muddle it. Herbs and delicate fruits (such as raspberries) only need a brief, gentle muddling to release their oils and juices; sturdy fruit and vegetables (apples, pears, citrus, celery, etc.) will need more intense muddling to extract their flavors. Fruit and vegetables should be cut into pieces (1 inch or smaller) to make the task easier. Fruit doesn't need to be seeded before muddling, but take care not to crush the seeds, as they can impart a bitter flavor.

Some fresh ingredients you'll find muddled into our drinks:

Apples	Cilantro	Nectarines
Basil	Citrus	Peaches
Blackberries	Cucumbers	Pears
Celery	Grapes	Raspberries
Cherries	Kaffir lime	Sage
Cherry	leaves	Strawberries
tomatoes	Mint	Tangerines

Orange juice: Fresh orange juice isn't used in many cocktails, so we prepare it in smaller batches using oranges left over from garnish preparation. One medium orange yields 3 to 4 ounces of juice.

Pineapple juice: Pineapples are skinned and passed through a juice extractor, then double strained to remove pulp. One pineapple yields roughly 16 ounces of juice.

In lesser quantities, we use a few other fresh juices at the bar:

- Blood orange
- Cantaloupe
- Carrot
- Celery
- Red bell pepper
- Watermelon

OTHER INGREDIENTS

These unique ingredients don't fit neatly into any specific category, but they occassionally show up in Death & Co creations.

ACID PHOSPHATE

Once a staple of soda fountains, this bygone ingredient has found a new home at the bar. We use it to add acidity and sourness to a drink without the added sweetness and flavor that comes from citrus juice.

COCO LOPEZ

This cane sugar–sweetened coconut cream hails from Puerto Rico and is a key ingredient in the Piña Colada (page 148) and many tiki-style drinks.

POMEGRANATE MOLASSES

This sweet-tart syrup is a staple in Middle Eastern and Mediterranean cooking and also makes an excellent cocktail ingredient. It's one of Phil Ward's favorite secret weapons, and he prefers the Al-Wadi brand. "I can mix 1 teaspoon of pomegranate molasses with 2 ounces of panther piss and it will probably be palatable," he says. (We do not suggest trying this at home.)

ROSE WATER

A by-product of rose petal distillation, a process used to make rose oil for perfumes, rose water is common in Indian and Middle Eastern cooking. Just a couple of drops of this fragrant liquid will add big floral aromas to a cocktail.

VERJUS

Verjus (vair-ZHOO) is fresh, nonalcoholic juice pressed from unripened grapes. In sweetness and acidity, it falls between wine and vinegar. It adds a fresh grape flavor and a bit of tartness to cocktails and can be used in place of other acidic ingredients, such as citrus juice. We primarily use Fusion verjus blanc, made from Napa Valley Chardonnay grapes, in our drinks.

Garnishes

Garnishes are pretty, but first and foremost they should be functional. We definitely don't believe in sticking a citrus wedge on the lip of every glass. We find that a de facto garnish sometimes allows people to revert to the bad habit of squeezing in the citrus before tasting the drink. This type of garnish is much like salt and pepper in food: it's there for adjusting the flavor to personal preference.

With our cocktails, we want people to first taste the intended balance of flavors. Then we closely monitor their reaction and, if need be, lead them to a different cocktail on their next round should they prefer something different, perhaps sweeter or more tart.

If a garnish won't enhance the drinking experience, we don't use one. A dramatic, ornate garnish can distract from—and sometimes decimate—an otherwise fine drink. More than half of our drinks have no ornamentation at all, and citrus twists are often discarded after their oil is expressed over a drink. When we drop a twist into a drink, it's for a deliberate purpose: we want it to continue flavoring the cocktail. Other garnishes, such as fresh fruit, vegetables, and herbs, are used to visually or aromatically echo ingredients within a drink.

Garnishes should be prepared at the last moment, right before you shake a cocktail or, with a stirred drink, immediately before you pour it into the glass. We cut citrus wedges and wheels before service to save time, but twists are always cut right before we serve the drink, as citrus peel dries out quickly.

CITRUS GARNISHES

Select fruit that is firm and unblemished. Shininess is usually a plus and means the peel has good oil content. Buy organic and unwaxed if available. Always wash citrus first, and remove any wax with a vegetable brush.

CITRUS WEDGES

Some bars like to lop off the ends of citrus fruits, but we try to remove as little as possible and only trim the small nubs on either end. Wedges are simple to make, but if you need any pointers, here's how we prepare ours:

1. Cut the fruit in half lengthwise, then make a crosswise notch across the center of each half from pith to pith to create a split for fitting the fruit on the rim of a glass later.

2. Quarter each half lengthwise to make 4 wedges.

3. Slice any membrane from the straight edge of each wedge and pluck out any seeds with the tip of a knife.

CITRUS WHEELS, CRESCENTS, AND FANS

Citrus wheels are an aromatic garnish that we either skewer on a cocktail pick or float on top of a drink. Larger citrus fruits, like oranges and grapefruit, are usually cut into crescents rather than wheels. Here are tips on making wheels, crescents, and fans:

1. To make wheels, working from the less-tapered end, cut the fruit into ¼-inch crosswise slices.

2. To make crescents, cut the wheels in half, trimming any membrane from the straight edge and removing any seeds with the tip of a knife.

3. Citrus fans are a wheel or crescent skewered on a cocktail pick.

CITRUS FLAGS

Citrus wheels and crescents are often wrapped around cherries or other fruit and skewered on a cocktail pick to make a flag.

CITRUS TWISTS

Our twists are always long pieces of citrus peel removed with a sturdy, sharp Y-shaped vegetable peeler. We never use a channel knife, which cuts away too much of the pith. To create a twist, place the peeler near the top of the fruit and move the fruit against the peeler at an angle to shave off a twist about 1 inch wide and 3 to 4 inches long. Be sure to remove as little of the white pith as possible. If you'll be leaving the twist in the drink, clean up the edges by using a sharp knife to trim the long edges, then trim the top and bottom at an angle to make a long parallelogram. Here are some pointers on garnishing with twists:

1. Grab the peel between your thumbs and index and middle fingers with the pith side facing you.

2. Hold the twist an inch or so above the cocktail and squeeze it to release its oils over the glass; this is called expressing the twist. You should see a fine mist of citrus oil hit the surface of the drink.

3. If you want to add more citrus flavor, lightly rub the twist once around the rim of the glass.

4. Either discard the twist or drop it into the drink, pith side down. It will release more of its flavor as it sits in the cocktail.

FLAMED TWISTS

Flaming twists is an impressive pyrotechnic trick, but it's also abused. Too many cocktails have been ruined by a slick of burnt, sulfury oil floating on top of the drink. We flame twists for only a handful of drinks, though we get plenty of practice at it because our most popular drink, the Oaxaca Old-Fashioned (page 273), calls for a flamed orange twist. Here's the procedure:

1. Using a sharp knife, cut a quarter-size round of peel with enough pith attached to it to keep it from splitting when you squeeze it.

2. Light a match (never a lighter) and let the sulfur burn off, then, with your other hand, grab the twist between your thumb and first two fingers.

3. Hold the twist a few inches above the match to let the citrus oils warm up, then squeeze the twist at a 45-degree angle over the match and toward the drink, about 4 inches from the top of the glass. The extracted orange oils will ignite over the flame and land on top of the drink, giving it a lightly caramelized flavor.

4. Drop the twist in the drink, if desired. We don't rub flamed twists around the rim, as it imparts too much flavor.

5. For a fancier garnish, twist the peel into a coil and balance one end on the rim (if using a coupe) or drop it into the glass (if using a champagne flute).

OTHER FRUIT & VEGETABLE GARNISHES

A garnish should always be functional and easy to understand. As such, we like to stick to the standards. Exotic garnishes—and those that require lots of meticulous preparation—only slow down the bartender and distract from the magic that happens *inside* the cocktail glass.

APPLES

We use apple slices to garnish both shaken and stirred drinks and prefer Fuji apples for their pure, sweet-tart apple flavor and firm texture. Granny Smiths are also great, though slightly more tart. Here are instructions for apple slices and apple fans:

1. For slices, cut the apple into quarters, then cut away enough of the straight edge to remove the core. Slice the apples lengthwise into ⅛-inch crescents and rub them with a lemon to prevent browning.

2. To make an apple fan, stack four or five thin apple slices and skewer them through one end with a cocktail pick.

CHERRIES

Luxardo Marasche brandied cherries are the gold standard. Though we've tried other brands and have even tried making our own, we keep coming back to these.

CUCUMBER

We like your standard garden cucumber to make both wheels and ribbons. Because the peel is used, opt for organic cucumbers if possible. Always wash and scrub the cucumbers well to remove any waxy coating, then trim away the ends. Prepare cucumbers just before you use them, as they dry out quickly. We use cucumbers as wheels, ribbons, and spears.

1. To make wheels, slice the cucumber crosswise into ¼-inch rounds. Cut a notch halfway through the wheel if placing the cucumber on the rim of a glass.

2. To make a cucumber ribbon, use a Y-shaped vegetable peeler to remove a long piece of peel (discard this), then use it again to remove a long strip of cucumber. Snake the ribbon back and forth and skewer it onto a cocktail pick.

3. Cucumber spears should be about 6 inches long and 1 inch wide.

MINT

Mint is a very aromatic garnish. We use it in amounts ranging from a single leaf to a lavish bouquet, depending on the style of drink and how much aroma we want the drinker to detect. Single leaves are floated on top of shaken drinks served up, while sprigs and bouquets are almost always used in conjunction with crushed ice. We prefer spearmint's sharp, refreshing aroma over peppermint's mentholated bite. Here are a couple of tips on mint garnishes:

1. To garnish with a single mint leaf, place it in the palm of your hand and give it a good spank, then place it on top of the drink.

2. Prepare a mint sprig by removing any leaves below the sprig's top plumage. Store the sprigs in water until ready to use. To garnish, shake off any excess water, then smack the sprig against your palm to release its oils. Insert the stem into the crushed ice until the bottom leaves are almost in contact with the surface of the drink.

3. A mint bouquet is several sprigs gathered into a bunch.

OTHER FRESH HERBS

We also use cilantro, basil, and Thai basil sprigs and leaves for garnish. Follow the same method as preparing mint.

CURRY AND KAFFIR LIME LEAVES

Fresh curry and Kaffir lime leaves are both highly aromatic garnishes that can be found in Asian markets and specialty food stores. Only one leaf is necessary, floated on top of the drink in the same manner as mint leaves.

PEARS

We use both Bartlett and Anjou pear slices as garnishes. Follow the same method as apple slices to prepare pears.

PINEAPPLE

Wedges of pineapple, a highly aromatic fruit, are a common garnish for tiki-style drinks. To make pineapple wedges, cut an unpeeled pineapple crosswise into ¼-inch rounds. Leaving the core intact, cut the rounds into wedges about 2 inches wide at their widest point. Cut a notch in the core if placing the pineapple on the rim of the glass. Occasionally we use a single pineapple leaf for garnish.

RASPBERRIES AND BLACKBERRIES

We'll sometimes use a single raspberry or blackberry to add a simple yet dramatic garnish to a shaken drink. Use the freshest, plumpest berries you can find.

STRAWBERRIES

Strawberries are used halved or whole, with a notch sliced in the bottom for fitting on the rim of the glass. Never hull strawberries, as the leaves add a nice bit of color.

OTHER GARNISHES

BITTERS

In addition to using bitters as an ingredient, we often finish cocktails with a few drops to add intense aromatics on top. In some swizzles, such as the Hyde Park Swizzle (page 250) and Coffey Park Swizzle (page 249), we add a considerable amount to the top of the drink and swizzle it to create a dramatic layer that rests atop the other ingredients, slowly seeping into the liquid as the guest drinks it. Bitters can also be dashed on top of mint sprigs, citrus wheels, or other garnishes to further add to its bouquet, or on top of an egg-white sour or fizz to diffuse the pungency of egg and add an aromatic contrast (see Grouse Rampant, page 200).

CHOCOLATE

Once in a while we'll coarsely grate chocolate over a drink, as in the Mudslide Flip (page 147). Choose a high-quality dark chocolate and use a coarse Microplane grater (or, in a pinch, a vegetable peeler) to shave some small, fine ribbons over the drink.

CINNAMON

While we use flavorful Ceylon cinnamon in syrups and infusions, we use the more common (and cheaper) cassia cinnamon sticks whole or grated directly over a drink. If using whole cinnamon sticks as garnish, lightly grate one side of the stick away from the drink (to release its flavors without introducing any cinnamon shavings into the drink) before dropping it in.

NUTMEG

Occasionally we grate fresh nutmeg over a drink. Use this aromatic spice sparingly; a couple of grates go a long way.

DEATH & CO COLLABORATIONS

Over the years we've worked with several of our favorite spirits brands to produce special bottlings specifically for our bar. This has been a highly enlightening experience. In addition to helping us fine-tune our palates and preferences, it's taught us so much about how one distillate can vary based on how, where, and how long it was aged. It's also given us a deeper connection to the spirits we showcase at the bar and an additional layer of control we can exercise over our cocktails. Here are a few of our favorite collaborations:

Scarlet Ibis Rum

A few years ago, there weren't any high-proof, molasses-based rums on the market that worked well in boozy stirred cocktails. There were overproof rums, like El Dorado 151, but most available on the market were firewater in a bottle—not good for mixing in a Manhattan-style drink. So we teamed up with Eric Seed, an importer who's brought many game-changing new products to the American market, to create a custom rum for Death & Co. He brought us a bunch of barrel-strength samples sourced from around the Caribbean and not previously imported into the United States. We tasted through them, test-drove them in cocktails, and landed on our favorite: an aged, dry rum from Trinidad, laden with bergamot and dried fruit, that worked equally well in both shaken and stirred drinks. Then we cut the rum down into various proofs using a store-bought hygrometer and New York tap water to settle on 49% ABV. Scarlet Ibis, which we named after Trinidad's national bird, is now available in many markets across the United States and on back bars across the country.

Pierre Ferrand Cognac & Plantation Rum

For our five-year anniversary, we wanted to create something special for the bar. We approached Alexandre Gabriel, owner of the cognac brand Pierre Ferrand, and coaxed him into producing a custom bottling of their excellent cognac. He obliged, and surprised us with an extra gift: a funky five-year Barbados rum.

Willett Rye

A couple years back, three neighborhood bars—Death & Co, PDT, and the Beagle—combined forces to purchase one barrel of Willett rye as a way to celebrate the East Village as a cocktail destination. To select it, we tasted many samples at our respective bars, and we all unanimously landed on the same barrel— surprising for a group of picky palates. For such a high-proof whiskey (58.6% ABV), it's incredible drunk neat and makes one of the best Manhattans we've ever tasted.

Wild Turkey Single-Barrel Bourbon

In 2010, the folks at Wild Turkey let Death & Co and a few other New York cocktail bars each pick out a specific barrel to be bottled and delivered to the bar. We tried some twenty samples before landing on our choice, which was a beautiful marriage of the roundness of good bourbon and a spike of spice. It's equally at home neat or in a big, boozy cocktail. The day our last bottle dries up is going to be a sad one.

ICE

It's easy to forget that cocktails—like human bodies—are mostly water. Most drinks contain between 20 and 25 percent water from melted ice. This doesn't take into account the water inherent in other ingredients, such as spirits, modifiers, fresh juice, and sweeteners.

With very few exceptions, water is added to a drink in its solid state: ice. Both a tool and an ingredient, ice performs two key functions in cocktails: dilution and temperature change. In shaken cocktails, ice also agitates the drink.

One of the biggest advancements in modern cocktail making is the ready availability of good ice. We define good ice as being cold, dry, and neutral in flavor. We don't make a big fuss over clarity. Cloudy ice works just as well in a cocktail as crystal clear cubes, though a large, glimmering block of perfectly transparent ice always makes for a sexier drink. Cloudiness is simply caused by dissolved gases, which get pushed toward the center as the ice freezes from all directions, and won't diminish the quality of a cocktail.

At Death & Co we use a few styles of ice, choosing among them depending on the type of drink we're making: Kold-Draft ice, block ice, crushed or pellet ice, and punch ice.

KOLD-DRAFT

The Kold-Draft machine is probably the biggest technical innovation in bartending since the invention of the freezer. It creates dense, 1¼-inch cubes of crystalline ice by spraying water upward into a metal mold. The ice freezes slowly from the top down, so it has fewer impurities.

We use Kold-Draft (aka KD) ice for all of our stirred cocktails. We usually crack the ice cubes before dropping them into the mixing glass. This increases the surface area of the ice, limits the amount of melting that occurs when sitting in the ice bin, and lets it chill and dilute the drink more quickly, which is helpful during a busy service. At home, you don't need to crack ice for stirred drinks, though you will have to stir a bit longer (more on this in chapter 3).

We also use KD ice when shaking a drink that will be served over ice cubes or crushed or pellet ice. The smaller cubes quickly chill the drink and blend the ingredients before they're strained. At home, you can make ice somewhat similar to KD ice using 1-inch silicone ice molds.

BLOCK ICE

We use the term *block ice* to refer to large, 2-inch ice cubes. We freeze them in silicone molds in a dedicated freezer so that no funky flavors will make their way into the ice. Block ice is our preferred shaking ice for drinks served up, and we use two cubes for most drinks. This allows for shaking a drink longer before it reaches proper dilution, resulting in a cold, well-aerated cocktail. It also allows a larger margin of error; it's harder to overshake (that is, overdilute) a drink when using 2-inch cubes. We also use block ice for any drinks served over a single large cube.

CRUSHED OR PELLET ICE

A Scotsman machine in Death & Co's basement spits out gallons of round ice pellets every hour. We use these crunchy nuggets to fill glasses destined for juleps, swizzles, tiki-style drinks, or anything else served over crushed ice. We often use this ice to whip (see page 95) ingredients that will be served over such drinks; a few small pieces will quickly blend ingredients while slightly chilling them, which slows down the rate of dilution once the drink is poured into the ice-filled glass, julep tin, or tiki mug.

At home, you can make your own crushed ice by placing ice cubes in a clean towel or Lewis bag (see page 78) and whacking it with a mallet, muddler, or small saucepan.

PUNCH ICE

Our communal punches are served with one large puck of ice frozen in a round plastic pint container (the same type you often get when you order take-out). At home, any small, clean bowl or plastic food storage container will do the trick. For certain punches, we throw fresh fruit into the container and freeze it in the ice. This is a beautiful addition to any punch, especially if you use raspberries.

MAKING ICE AT HOME

Producing ice can be as simple as filling your desired ice tray with tap water and sticking it in the freezer. If your tap water isn't good, use bottled or purified water. Over time, the ice in your freezer will absorb flavors from any other food nearby, so cover your ice trays with plastic wrap or dedicate your freezer to only making ice. (It's all about priorities.)

However, homemade freezer ice will probably be cloudy due to dissolved gases in the water. If you want to make clearer ice, boil the water first to release any dissolved gases. Place boiled water into ice molds inside the freezer while still hot. Aside from cosmetics, clear ice is denser and more structurally sound, so it will break apart less quickly than cloudy ice when shaken.

MAKING ICE FROM BIG BLOCKS

If you're lucky enough to procure a large block of ice (from a frozen lake, perhaps, or a commercial ice company), you can cut it down into any desired shape and size. Or you can make your own block of ice by filling a small cooler with hot water and placing it in the freezer, uncovered. The insulated sides will force the ice to slowly freeze from the surface downward. After a couple of days, you'll have a large block of crystal clear ice with a cloudy layer of trapped gases on the bottom, which can be chipped off.

To break down a large block of ice, use a serrated knife that you don't care too much about (chipping ice will quickly dull the teeth). Let the ice sit at room temperature for a few minutes. (If you start hacking it up right away, the ice will shatter into shards.) Score one side of the block until you have a ⅛-inch-deep crease down one side. We usually begin by scoring 2 inches from one side, to create a 2-inch slab. Turn the block over and saw another line the same distance from the edge, and repeat until you've scored four sides. Next, use the knife to tap around the perimeter, following the lines you've scored. The knife's teeth will work like tiny ice picks, and eventually a slab of ice will break off from the block. You can then shape this into smaller cubes using the same method.

WORKING WITH SHITTY ICE

We often find ourselves someplace—be it a hotel, a friend's house, or an unfamiliar bar—where the only ice on hand is small, barely frozen chips or those cloudy half-moons that home freezers spit out of their doors. Fret not: you can still make excellent drinks when faced with these subpar hailstones. If you're making a shaken drink, pack the shaker full of ice and shake hard but briefly—about five seconds. This will quickly chill the drink without overdiluting it. If stirring a cocktail, fill the mixing vessel with ice and strain out any water before adding the cocktail ingredients. Be aware that the ice will melt rather quickly, so stir briskly but for less time than usual.

THE REGULARS

TOM CHADWICK

Tom Chadwick is a bartender and co-owner of Brooklyn's Dram bar.

I was a cocktail nerd before I could afford to be one. I worked at a dive bar and used to read about Death & Co, and when I could eventually afford a $13 drink, that's where I went.

I remember walking in and getting hit first by the smell of mint and citrus oils. My friend ordered me a Pink Lady, which was the most delicious thing I'd ever tasted. I asked Phil how he made it, and he explained his recipe for grenadine. Then someone else ordered a swizzle, which I'd never seen before. That huge glass of crushed ice with its plumage of mint blew me away. After that I started coming in every week.

A lot of cocktail joints are full of prima donna bartenders. Death & Co always felt, first and foremost, like a bar. The bartenders can discuss sports or literature as easily as they can the history of Chartreuse—and they're more than happy to serve me a beer. Late at night we do shots together, just like at any other bar. And these folks can *drink*.

After I opened Dram, Phil came in and picked up some shifts behind the bar. He taught me so much about simplicity and modesty when creating cocktails. He can make magic happen with just three or four ingredients.

In the years since Death & Co opened, cocktail culture has exploded—not just in New York, but everywhere. There's a generation of bartenders coming up who didn't have to swim upstream and figure everything out for the first time. Bartenders no longer have to justify to the owner why they need a Kold-Draft machine or four kinds of pisco. They don't have to explain to customers why their drinks take five minutes to make, why they don't serve vodka tonics, or why a $12 cocktail isn't the most ridiculous thing ever.

In five or ten years, cocktail culture will have come full circle. We'll have better drinks everywhere, and your average dive bar will make a decent old-fashioned. We'll keep the good stuff and shake off most of the preciousness and pretension. Then we'll be able to focus on the fact that great cocktails are just one part of a larger drinking experience. And when that day comes, I'm sure Death & Co will have aged gracefully into an institution.

PINK LADY

1½ OUNCES PLYMOUTH GIN

½ OUNCE LAIRD'S BONDED APPLE BRANDY

¾ OUNCE LEMON JUICE

¾ OUNCE SIMPLE SYRUP (PAGE 277)

¼ OUNCE GRENADINE (PAGE 284)

1 EGG WHITE

GARNISH: 3 BRANDIED CHERRIES ON A COCKTAIL PICK

Dry shake all the ingredients, then shake again with ice. Double strain into a rocks glass over 1 large ice cube. Garnish with the cherries.

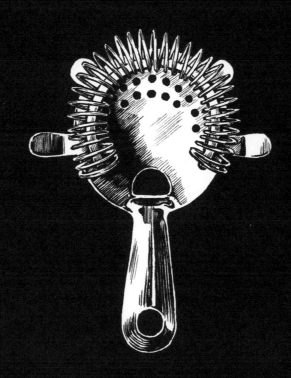

Chapter Three

BUILDING A DRINK

STRANGE BREW

THOMAS WAUGH

This refreshing cocktail pairs two of Thomas's favorite things: juniper-forward gin and hoppy beer. What's especially interesting about this drink is how it uses beer like a modifier: to add a spicy, aromatic flavor, enhancing the base spirit rather than overwhelming it. Thomas also did an ingenious thing with pineapple juice here. Cocktails made with pineapple juice are often flabby or overtly tiki-esque, whereas here he uses it as the focus of the drink. The resulting composition surrounds the tropical richness of pineapple with the spice of gin and hoppy IPA.

2 OUNCES TANQUERAY
NO. TEN GIN

¾ OUNCE VELVET FALERNUM

1 OUNCE PINEAPPLE JUICE

½ OUNCE LEMON JUICE

GREEN FLASH IPA BEER

GARNISH: 1 MINT SPRIG

Short shake all the ingredients (except the IPA) with 3 ice cubes, then strain into a pilsner glass filled with crushed ice. Top with IPA. Garnish with the mint and serve with a straw.

TOOLS

As bartenders hone their craft, they naturally begin gravitating toward tools that allow them to do their jobs best. Much like a cook who fanatically protects a coveted knife, we view our jiggers, mixing glasses, and strainers as vital to our technique. As we increasingly focus on making drinks better and faster, we've developed deep appreciation for certain tools.

THE BARTENDER'S TOOL KIT

Before the early 2000s, even the most serious bartenders used the cheap, disposable bar tools found at restaurant supply stores. Our profession had been underequipped for decades because the once-thriving barware industry (not to mention the craft of making cocktails) largely disappeared during Prohibition and has since struggled to rebuild itself. However, even though our trade toiled in the cocktail Dark Ages throughout the second half of the twentieth century, American cocktail culture (and its tools) did find its way to other parts of the world, most notably Japan, where it flourished, evolved, and begat its own arsenal of neoclassical gear. These amazing Japanese bar tools, made specifically for cocktails (as opposed to kitchen tools repurposed for cocktail use), spawned an industry-wide fascination with Japanese technique that's still going strong.

At Death & Co, we take the same approach to tools as we do technique: everyone figures out what works best for them and which tools allow them to make the best drinks they can as consistently as possible. We all have our favorite spoons, sentimental shakers, quirky gadgets, and random liquor-industry swag. Most of us ferry our personal bar kits to and from the bar. Others (well, just Phil) leave their tools in not-so-secret hiding places around the bar. All of that said, most of us do end up using similar stuff.

For the purposes of this book, we're well aware that home bartenders have a different set of priorities than the pros. You don't need to turn out hundreds of drinks each night, and you want tools that are economical, easy to clean, and easy on the eyes. Our advice for home bartenders is the same as for our own staff: start simple, with gear that feels good, then build up your tool kit as you gain proficiency and hone your own style of making drinks.

STIRRERS

BARSPOONS { *for stirring mixed drinks*}
We've all mixed drinks with a chopstick, butter knife, or index finger in a pinch, but a long, slender barspoon allows you to stir quickly and fluidly, thus chilling and diluting

the drink smoothly without adding texture (read, air bubbles) to the drink. This method accomplishes the goal in a properly stirred cocktail: silky mouthfeel.

There are myriad styles and lengths of barspoons out there, but almost everyone at Death & Co uses the long-handled, Japanese-style spoons illustrated here. (They can be purchased online or at any specialty barware store; see appendix 3, page 288.) They're made from a single piece of metal twisted into a tight coil, allowing the spoon to be kept in a consistent place in the hand while stirring. On the business end of the long, twisted handle is the bowl, which is used to move liquid around the mixing glass.

Although it's often assumed that a barspoon measures out 1 teaspoon (5 ml) of liquid, their capacity can

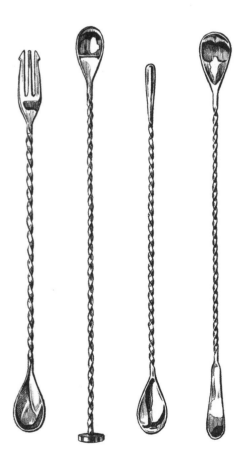

vary dramatically from model to model, ranging from ½ teaspoon up to 2 teaspoons, which is rather annoying and can result in inaccurately measured cocktails. As such, at Death & Co we only use culinary measuring spoons for quantities smaller than ¼ ounce or measures that don't easily translate into ounces, such as 2 teaspoons (⅓ ounce). If you decide to use a barspoon to measure, it's best to figure out the exact volume of your spoon and calibrate your drinks accordingly. Our mantra: accuracy is important, but consistency is vital.

The opposite end of a barspoon can vary in both form and function. Some feature a slender, curved tongue that can be used to ease large cubes or spheres of ice into a cocktail glass, preventing splashing. Others have a bad-ass trident on the end for spearing garnishes. "Serpent-tongued" spoons serve the same function. Both are also great at impaling the arms and faces of busy bartenders, so be careful where you keep them. But perhaps the most multipurpose version, made by the UK-based company Bonzer, has a flat disk on the end for crushing sugar cubes, building layered drinks (such as pousse-cafés), and, in a pinch, light muddling duties.

One of our favorite models has a teardrop-shaped weight on the end that doesn't serve a secondary purpose, but it looks elegant and offers great counterbalance for a smooth stirring rhythm. Stay away from any barspoon with a red plastic nub—or no weight at all—on the end; this is a sign of a flimsy, poorly balanced implement made from cheap metal that will bend and be tossed into the garbage.

Whatever style you choose, there are a few things to look for when purchasing a barspoon:

- **Material:** The spoon should be forged from a single piece of stainless steel. Two-piece spoons with welded bowls will eventually break if you use them to crack ice. Expect to pay $20 or more for a quality spoon. On the fancier side, you can buy one coated with copper, silver, or, if you really want it to get stolen, gold. Japanese-made spoons, which are fetishized in the bartending community for their craftsmanship, can cost $80 or more.

- **Length and balance:** Most barspoons range from 8 to 20 inches in length. The length you choose comes down to your personal stirring style and preference. Likewise, choose a spoon that's weighted and balanced to your liking. Most bartenders opt for one with a heavier weight opposite the bowl, which allows for faster stirring.

- **Spiral shaft:** Look for a slender, tightly twisted shaft. A tighter spiral creates less resistance in the glass, which results in quicker stirring without introducing too much air into the drink. If you're a beginning bartender or amateur enthusiast, we recommend that you start with a spoon that has a smooth, threadless (untwisted) shaft. This will help you learn to stir without twisting the spoon in your hand, but rather allowing the outside of the spoon to travel smoothly along the inside of the glass.

- **Comfort:** When you pick up a spoon, you shouldn't feel any sharp edges along the handle, as they can quickly lead to a painful blister. You'll eventually develop a callus on your finger from any barspoon if you mix enough drinks, and this is one of the badges of honor earned while tending bar. But we've notices that the tighter the thread, the more gentle the spoon is on the hand.

SWIZZLE STICKS
{ for mixing crushed ice-based cocktails}

Until recently, bartenders had trouble getting their hands on the spindly wooden sticks known as *bois lélé*—the original swizzle sticks. Supply lines were limited to "a guy who knows a guy" and usually involved a trip to Martinique and some clever luggage packing. These sticks are harvested in the Lesser Antilles from *Quararibea turbinate* (aka swizzlestick tree), a native shrub that grows in protected forests. (The shrub itself, however, is not protected.) The branches of the shrub are clipped to leave a circle of small prongs (twigs) at the end, which aid in blending.

In the Caribbean they're used to whip cream, but at Death & Co we use them to make juleps, swizzles, and other drinks mixed in crushed ice, as well as Ti Punch (page 152), a rum-based drink popular in the French-speaking Caribbean. The prongs on the stick act like a manual immersion blender, diving deep into the drink and swirling the crushed ice around. The increased surface contact of the drink with the crushed ice causes it to get cold very quickly—a vital consideration for crushed ice  drinks, as longer stirring would result in too much dilution.

Swizzle sticks usually come with a longer handle and more spindles than necessary; you're supposed to trim both to length. We cut ours so the spindles will span the diameter of a pilsner glass (in which we build our swizzles), and we trim the shaft so it's long enough to accommodate two hands performing the swizzle technique, which involves spinning the stick between your hands—not unlike the drum technique featured in *The Karate Kid, Part II.*

MIXING VESSELS

MIXING GLASSES *{ for making stirred drinks}*

There isn't one perfect vessel for making a stirred drink; each has its benefits and drawbacks. The cheapest and most readily available mixing glass is the standard pint glass. It's important to use one made from durable tempered glass, which can handle the rapid temperature changes it will face, say, when going from the dishwasher into the freezer. The pint glass's tapered shape also makes stirring a bit easier, as it allows you to use move the spoon around the perimeter of the glass with the forgiveness of a gentle angle. If the glass were perfectly vertical and as narrow as a pint glass, your stirring position would have to be very tightly controlled.

A shaking tin also makes a passable stirring vessel, but has two major drawbacks. First, metal is a poor insulator, as it has a higher thermal conductivity than glass. This makes it harder to chill the drink before it exceeds its ideal dilution (see "The Science of Stirring," on page 93). Geekery aside, metal also doesn't let you see what's happening to the drink as you stir, which prevents you from gauging dilution by sight and most importantly, metal cheats your guests out of the theater of watching their drink being crafted.

Japanese-style mixing glasses have a lot of good things going for them. These straight-sided vessels have a handy spout, which makes pouring drinks easier than from a pint glass. Also, they're made from extra-thick glass, which will help you achieve a colder drink. Glass, a fairly efficient insulator, holds on to its cold temperature well when chilled before making a cocktail. When liquid and ice are placed inside the chilled mixing glass, the temperature will leach out into the cocktail rather than bleeding off into the air, and it will equalize with those ingredients at a lower temperature than would be possible with a room-temperature glass. For this reason, we always chill our mixing glasses. No lukewarm martinis are allowed at Death & Co!

Two of our favorite mixing glasses are the Yarai and paddle glasses sold by Cocktail Kingdom and others (see appendix 3). Another Japanese style resembles a large wine glass with a squat stem; it's equally gorgeous and is big enough for stirring multiple drinks. The drawback to all three is that they are fragile and expensive ($40 and up), making them a somewhat risky investment for a commercial bar, especially when the glass is being moved into and out of the freezer during service. A good alternative to these, especially for home use, are the straight-sided glass vessels used in French press coffeemakers, which are cheaper than Japanese-style glasses, though they are a bit more fragile.

Clockwise, from top left: pint glass, stemmed glass, paddle glass, Yarai glass

SHAKERS { *for shaking drinks* }

Cocktail shakers vary more in material, shape, and functionality than any other bar tool. You can shake a drink in pretty much any vessel that can hold ice and liquid and seals tightly. Heck, even a screw-top water bottle will work in a MacGyver-esque pinch. But some shakers make the task easier than others.

Boston shakers: Until fairly recently, the standard setup was the Boston shaker, which consists of a pint glass and a large metal shaking tin. Back when most bartenders free poured their spirits instead of measuring them with a jigger, the pint glass allowed them to eyeball how much booze was going into the glass. Now that jiggering is more the rule than the exception, using glass to shake drinks isn't as necessary. That's a good thing, because the Boston setup has numerous drawbacks: the difference in weight between the pint glass (heavy) and the tin (light) makes for an awkwardly balanced shake; a room-temperature pint glass won't get the drink as cold as a room-temperature metal tin (a fine point of thermodynamics we'll explain later in this chapter), and Boston shakers generally terrify us, as pint glasses tend to crack and shatter without warning or come unsealed from the tin and turn into a deadly projectile while spraying the drink all over the bar. Every bartender who has used a Boston shaker has war stories.

Cobbler shakers: Thankfully, the modern cocktail movement has brought us an improved arsenal of shakers and has also repopularized some classic models. The cobbler shaker is a three-piece outfit that dates back to the late nineteenth century. It features a large metal tin, a tapered top with a built-in strainer, and a cap, which makes for a nice all-in-one cocktail device. Many top bartenders favor the cobbler, especially those who have built their shaking technique specifically around this design. However, the cobbler has its faults: when a cocktail is shaken in any vessel, the volume contracts as the ice turns into water, creating a vacuum in the container, and this vacuum makes it a real pain in the ass to remove the tiny cap atop a cobbler shaker. Furthermore, the cobbler's built-in strainer doesn't have a control mechanism like the Hawthorn strainer, which has an adjustable tab; therefore, you can't change the size of the strainer's holes to moderate the texture. As a result, your drinks may end up including tiny ice chips, citrus pulp, and other solids that you could block with a better strainer.

From left: Boston shaker, 18-28 set, cobbler shaker, Parisian shaker

Parisian shakers: Parisian shakers are gorgeous vessels comprised of two stainless steel tins that join with the appearance of an almost seamless seal. Some bartenders like this because it results in fewer rough edges inside the shaker (unlike in a Boston shaker), which tend to chip little pieces off the ice as it bounces around. But Parisian shakers aren't ideal for busy bar service, as that attractive seal isn't secure, so they require two hands to operate—unless you have enormous hands. This means you can only shake one cocktail at a time. Fun fact: In Paris, they call these "continental shakers."

18-28 set: Our favorite workhorse shaker is something we call the 18-28 set, which is a pair of weighted stainless steel tins, one small and one large (18 and 28 ounces, respectively, though some folks prefer a 30-ounce tin for the larger one). In cocktail lingo we call this tin on tin. It essentially combines the best of the Boston shaker setup (an airtight seal) with the best of a cobbler or Parisian setup (all-metal surfaces, and therefore better thermal conductivity), and it's lightweight enough for any bartender to double shake, which is crucial when cranking out drinks during service. The tin-on-tin method didn't gain traction in NYC until the early 2000s, after Toby Maloney introduced it at the groundbreaking neo-speakeasy Milk & Honey. The two tins easily form a tight seal when pressed together, but the metal is pliable enough for them to separate with relative ease when you're ready to pour the drink. Anyone who has a drink at Death & Co quickly notices the *sssssNACK* sound punctuating the bar's din; this is the sound of the two shaking tins being pulled apart. We also love tin on tin

because these setups are pretty cheap and very durable. If you choose to go this route, make sure you buy tins that are weighted at the bottom. Koriko and Vollrath are two brands that make this weighted style. You'll probably come across 16- and 24-ounce shaking tins in kitchen supply stores, but these don't fit together well and tend to come apart at the most inconvenient times. Plus, they're made from cheap metal that warps into sharp, finger-slicing edges.

STRAINERS

JULEP STRAINERS { *for straining stirred drinks* }

The julep strainer, originally crafted in the mid-1800s, has a shallow, bowl-like shape designed to strategically fit inside a julep cup, remaining there while imbibers drank the eponymous cocktail. (Dentistry not being what it is today, the julep strainer was necessary to keep the drinks' crushed ice away from your teeth.) At Death & Co we use julep strainers for all manner of stirred drinks. It fits neatly inside a mixing glass, holding the ice back as its tiny holes allow liquid to pass through quickly and evenly, which helps the cocktail maintain its silky texture. (Again, air bubbles are a stirred drink's enemy.) Another plus is that, should any unwanted ice fall into the cocktail glass, the julep's perforated bowl does double duty and can scoop them from the glass.

Good julep strainers are made from a single piece of stainless steel, but you can get away with a cheaper model as long as you find one that fits snugly inside your favorite mixing glass, without any big gaps that would let ice slip through. Some julep strainers have perfectly round bowls and fit pint glasses well; others have an oval shape and are better for larger Japanese-style mixing glasses.

HAWTHORNE STRAINERS
{ *for straining shaken drinks* }

The Hawthorne strainer dates back to 1892, when a patent was issued to its inventor, William Wright, and Dennis P. Sullivan, who owned Boston's Hawthorne Café (and, conveniently, a bar-products manufacturing company, D. P. Sullivan and Co.). The specs featured a flat, circular disk of perforated metal with a self-adjusting spring coil that fits snugly inside the rim of a shaker or mixing glass, thereby holding the implement in place as you strain a cocktail.

A Hawthorne strainer can be used to strain stirred cocktails, and many bartenders use only Hawthorne strainers for both shaken and stirred drinks. In our opinion, it's the only strainer you should use for shaken cocktails. Why? Two words: *gate control* (see page 99).

Wright's original design has been tweaked and improved upon in countless iterations throughout the last century. Most are still referred to as Hawthorne strainers, although models that are more true to the original design will bear the word *Hawthorne*, spelled out in the holes of the plate. The most common improvements are a tab that lets you adjust the flow, two or more small thumbs that hold the strainer in place against the rim of a shaker, and a pair of slots that direct the flow of the drink into two streams, thereby allowing two drinks to be poured at once. Whatever style of Hawthorne strainer you choose to use, here are some qualities you want to look for:

- **Tightness of the spring:** You want a sturdy spring that will hold the strainer in place. More importantly, a tighter spring will do a better job of holding back ice

and other fine particles as you strain the drink. Here's an easy hack for a cheap spring: remove the spring from another Hawthorne strainer and thread it onto the same base to create a tighter spring.

- **Gauge of steel:** A heavier strainer will provide better balance and control, and the strainer will be more durable—a useful quality, as bartenders tend to toss these tools around quite a bit.

- **Size and symmetry of the circle:** The circular edge should span across the diameter of your tin or mixing glass to prevent any liquid or ice from splashing out around the sides of the strainer.

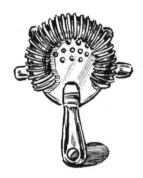

CONE STRAINERS { *for double straining drinks* }

Some cocktails require a two-stage straining process to ensure that the finished drink is free of ice chips and tiny particles, usually muddled fruit or herbs. For these you need a fine-mesh cone strainer, which is basically a small sieve. An inexpensive kitchen sieve will do the trick, but at Death & Co we use strainers created specifically with cocktails in mind. They have a deep cone that will hold an entire drink's worth of liquid, and their V shape directs the liquid into the glass, instead of spraying it all over the place.

MEASURING AND POURING DEVICES

JIGGERS

{ *for precisely measuring spirits, fresh juices, and syrups* }

Using jiggers is not an indication of a new or inexperienced bartender; rather, it shows that the bartender has a vested interest in the quality of his or her drinks. It ensures that cocktails are consistent, while also showing guests that every drop of liquid in a drink is intended to be there. In a commercial bar, using jiggers can also save a great deal of money. Later in this chapter, we'll make our case for always measuring ingredients, versus free pouring. So for now, let's just assume you want to make consistently delicious cocktails. For that, you'll need jiggers.

Jiggers come in many shapes and sizes, but most bartenders use the double-sided, hourglass-shaped jiggers that accurately measure two volumes of liquid. We use multiple configurations of jiggers at Death & Co, such as a combined 2-ounce and 1-ounce jigger, and a combined ½-ounce and ¾-ounce setup. The most useful of these also have etchings inside the vessel for smaller measurements (1½ ounces, ¼ ounce, and so on).

There are two subsets of this style of jigger: the shorter, angular variety, and the taller, rounded Japanese-style jigger. There are pros and cons to each, with the former being very precise and the latter being a bit faster. And as gorgeous as the taller models are, they do tend to tip over and roll around the bar. We're particularly fond of Oxo's stainless steel 1½-ounce/1-ounce jigger for home use, which also has interior markings for ¼, ½, ⅓ and ¾ ounces, making it as close to an all-in-one jigger as we've seen.

Whatever style you choose, look for jiggers with enough heft to give you lots of control while measuring and pouring; lighter-weight models are harder to hold steady. Also, be aware that jiggers can be maddeningly inaccurate. A "1-ounce" jigger can measure up to ¼ ounce more or less, even when perfectly filled. Therefore, we recommend measuring the exact capacity of your jiggers. You can do this using accurate measuring spoons (1 ounce of water equals 2 tablespoons) or with a gram scale (1 ounce of water weighs 29.57 grams). Once you know the accuracy—or inaccuracy—of your jiggers, you can adjust accordingly. Remember: Consistent inaccuracy is better than inconsistent accuracy! We've noticed that it helps to stick with one brand of jigger, as jiggers made by the same company tend to be off somewhat consistently across the brand.

MEASURING SPOONS

{ *for precisely measuring small amounts of ingredients* }

As discussed above, a barspoon shouldn't be used to measure ingredients except in a pinch or if you know the exact capacity of the bowl. Jiggers can accurately measure down to ¼ ounce; for measurements smaller than that, we use standard sets of kitchen measuring spoons. Some of our bartenders like the adjustable models made by KitchenArt, which allow them to make multiple precise measurements without having to switch spoons.

DASHER BOTTLES

{ *for precisely measuring bitters, tinctures, and other small-volume ingredients* }

All of the myriad bitters we use at Death & Co are poured from Japanese-made dasher bottles. These pretty, teardrop-shaped glass bottles have a screw-on metal dasher spout that can pour smaller and more precise quantities than the plastic tops on off-the-shelf bitters bottles—especially given that the size of the plastic aperture can vary from one bitters company to the next, so dash size can be remarkably different from brand to brand. As a general rule of thumb, one dash from a plastic-topped bottle equals three dashes from a Japanese dasher bottle. In the recipes in this book, when we call for a dash of bitters, that's a dash as measured from a dasher bottle; if you're using a Japanese dasher bottle, you should triple the number of dashes.

If you make your own bitters or tinctures at home, we highly recommend investing in Japanese dasher bottles. And even if you use store-bought bitters, you may want to transfer them into Japanese dasher bottles so you can pour uniform dashes of any bitters. Additionally they look rather sexy, like tiny crystal decanters for your bitters.

SPEED POURERS
{ for ensuring flow of liquid is consistent from every bottle}

The name *speed pourer* is somewhat counterintuitive, as it's much faster (albeit messier) to pour liquor straight from the bottle. However, speed pourers give you a slower, more consistent stream of liquid with less waste once you learn how to use them properly. They aren't totally necessary for the home bartender unless you make a lot of drinks or want to practice your flair—both of which we highly endorse! However, speed pourers are vital in a busy bar. At Death & Co, the bottles on the back bar get to keep their pretty caps on, but in our speed rack and on cheater bottles on the bar top, where about 90 percent of the booze used in the current cocktail menu lives, every bottle is capped with a speed pourer.

A good speed pourer will have a long, slightly angled metal spout with a plastic collar that fits tightly inside the neck of the bottle to prevent leaks. Avoid models with short, plastic spouts, and also steer clear of those with hinged lids at the top, as they inevitably stick before shooting a jet of booze everywhere but inside the jigger. You also want an air hole, or carb, at the base of the spout, which allows you to slow the speed of the pour by putting your finger over the carb.

ICE-SHAPING TOOLS

ICE PICKS
{ for breaking and shaping larger pieces of ice}

At Death & Co we use picks only occasionally, to shape or break apart a piece of 2-inch block ice. But an ice pick will come in handy if you want to shape your own ice at home. We generally find that cheap ice picks with long, straight spikes are more dangerous than useful. If you're going to carve lots of ice, opt instead for a wooden-handled Japanese-style ice pick, which has a shorter spike and an anvil-shaped end for delicate carving duties.

SERRATED KNIVES
{ for breaking down large blocks of ice}

When we need to break down a giant block of ice into cubes, we use a long, serrated kitchen knife to do the work; its teeth act like many tiny ice picks. Look for one with a curved cutting edge and deep teeth; it will be much easier to use for sawing and chipping away at the block than a straight-edged bread knife. And don't spend much money on it. An inexpensive restaurant supply model is preferable, as cutting and chipping ice will wear the teeth down very quickly.

WOOD CHISELS
{ for breaking down large blocks of ice}

Another great tool for carving large blocks of ice can be found in your toolbox. We usually use a 1- or 2-inch-wide wood chisel, along with a rubber mallet, to break ice blocks down into large cubes. Bonus: Once you get the hang of it, you can make an ice luge!

LEWIS BAGS { *for making crushed ice* }

At Death & Co we use a commercial Scotsman machine to keep us supplied with pellet ice by the bucketful. For making crushed ice at home, though, we find a canvas Lewis bag ideal. It's much better for the task than hand-cranked ice crushers. It's a pretty simple—and rewarding—process: fill the bag with ice, then whack it with a wooden mallet, muddler, or small saucepan until the ice is crushed to your liking. The canvas will soak up any water that melts during the process.

TAP-ICERS { *for cracking ice* }

Named for the manufacturer that popularized this simple tool in the mid-twentieth century, the Tap-Icer is a long, flexible plastic wand with a smooth steel disk at the end used for cracking ice cubes. Some bartenders use the back of a heavier barspoon for this task, but a good Tap-Icer can shatter a big block of ice with a gentle snap of the wrist, saving the bartender a lot of energy over the course of a shift. The original Tap-Icer has been out of production for years, but they're easy to find on eBay and the design has been adopted and updated by modern manufacturers. We've also played around with some antique ice crackers, which usually feature a metal wand with a spring in the middle and a small metal ball at the ice-cracking end. However, we quickly realized that this design is hard to control, resulting in as many cracked hands as ice cubes. Ouch!

OTHER TOOLS AND GADGETS

MUDDLERS
{ *for muddling herbs, fruit, and sugar cubes* }

Muddlers can be gorgeous objects—elegant pieces of exotic wood shaped on a lathe by the sturdy, careful hands of an earnest artisan, then varnished and buffed to a lustrous patina. Unfortunately, these muddlers are better left on your mantle and out of your cocktail shaker.

For starters, most wooden muddlers are too short to do the job: once you have them in a mixing glass or shaking tin, there's not enough handle sticking out to hold. The coating on a varnished muddler will eventually chip or peel, and varnish isn't an ingredient we like to put in our drinks. Unvarnished wooden muddlers also have their shortcomings. The wood can also chip off during use. Plus, untreated wood likes to soak up whatever it touches and takes its time to dry, thereby creating a petri dish type of environment for fun bacterial experiments.

That's not to say you should run the other way when you encounter a wooden muddler. We have a couple of them in our arsenal at Death & Co, but we're careful to regularly clean and oil them.

Another popular style of muddler features a steel handle and a plastic bottom dotted with small spikes. These are practically useless, as the nubs tend to shred herbs, and ingredients often get caught up in them—and if you're muddling four raspberries, you don't want two sticking to the muddler.

Our favorite muddlers at Death & Co are as inelegant as they come: heavy black PVC cylinders that look like short nightsticks or menacing S&M props. They're heavy enough to do most of the work for you, which is much appreciated after an eight-hour shift. Also, they have a flat bottom with sharp edges, allowing you to dig into the corner of the tin, unlike muddlers with rounded bottom edges. In addition, they're cheap, infinitely durable, and easy to wash.

CITRUS JUICERS { *for juicing . . . what else?* }

If you work in a bar, you'll probably use an electric juicer for most of your citrus juice. Sunkist makes the most popular commercial juicers, and ours can crank out about ten gallons of juice per hour. But a handheld citrus press or a countertop swing-arm citrus press is the most sensible option for making drinks at home. You can find either in most kitchen supply stores, but pass on anything coated in enamel, as the paint tends to chip away with use.

GRATERS { *for grating ingredients over a drink* }

There is no comparison between freshly grated cinnamon and nutmeg and their preground counterparts. We use a standard handheld kitchen grater (the kind you'd use to finely grate hard cheese) for these ingredients as well as citrus, and a coarse Microplane grater for grating dark chocolate.

VEGETABLE PEELERS { *for preparing citrus peels* }

The strategy for creating a citrus garnish is usually to carve away a wide swath of peel while leaving behind the bitter white pith. Some bartenders prefer to carve each twist or piece of citrus peel with a sharp paring knife, but we (and many others) have found that a vegetable peeler produces a more consistent and less pithy peel. Look for a heavy-duty, Y-shaped peeler with a sharp, nonserrated blade that will easily shave off pieces of peel, leaving the bitter pith behind. Oxo makes a great version with a nonslip rubber handle. Plastic peelers are too wimpy for the task, and their blades tend to pop away when you least expect it.

THE REGULARS

SHERI HARRISON

Sheri Harrison is a technology manager at a nonprofit.

I moved into a place around the corner from Death & Co in 2009. I'd come from San Francisco, where I was a whiskey drinker. After my first visit to Death & Co, I was quickly converted into a cocktail geek. I'd sit at the bar and ask a lot of questions, and the bartenders were always generous with their knowledge. I'm not shy about asking for recipes, and they've never turned me down. I love just staring at the hundreds of bottles on the back bar; it's like a huge chemistry set.

I'm a two- or three-ingredient drink person. I think it's because of my personality: I'm picky and I don't like a lot of fuss. You can wrap your brain around a simple cocktail and really think about the chemistry in the glass. I will drink a Manhattan (page 145) any day. I remember one blustery winter night when I came in and dusted off the snow, and Thomas made the most unforgettable Boulevardier (page 140, also at right). Phil turned me to Beefeater martinis and White Negronis (page 259). Alex introduced me to my all-time favorite drink, the Tailspin (page 152), a simple recipe that tastes so much more complex than it really is. And Jessica was my Martinez (page 145) muse.

Being a regular is such a personal thing. There's a level of comfort to it that's hard to describe. If I have a shitty day, I come in knowing that I'll be served with graciousness. I can talk about cocktail geekery, or I can enjoy my drink in peace and just feel comforted.

I always sit at the bar. Sitting at a table is like being at the kids' table at Thanksgiving; there's no action. It's fun to sit next to cocktail tourists, who are either literally tourists or locals who have never been to Death & Co before. They often arrive very wide-eyed and sometimes intimidated, but they usually throw themselves at the mercy of a bartender and leave happy.

If I'm describing Death & Co to people, I tell them it's the best of both worlds. It's a world-class cocktail bar, but it's also a down-to-earth neighborhood bar where you'll always be cared for. Not everyone sees it this way—it's New York, after all, and this place can seem exclusive—but having gotten to know the staff, I see it as my friendly local watering hole.

BOULEVARDIER

1½ OUNCES ELIJAH CRAIG 12-YEAR BOURBON

¾ OUNCE HOUSE SWEET VERMOUTH (PAGE 284)

¾ OUNCE CAMPARI

GARNISH: 1 LEMON TWIST

Stir all the ingredients over ice, then strain into a coupe. Garnish with the lemon twist.

GLASSWARE

We pair a cocktail with a particular serving piece for a variety of reasons. The shape of a glass can affect how quickly and intensely a drink's aroma hits your nose. Higher-volume drinks—those served over ice, topped with bubbles, or both—require a larger glass, of course. Tradition also comes into play: serving martinis and fizzes in anything but their eponymous glassware would just be plain wrong.

The temperature of a glass is vitally important. Whenever possible, store glassware in a freezer until just before you pour and serve the cocktail. In addition to keeping the drink cold longer than a room-temperature vessel, the tactile sensation of a cold stem between your fingers, the frosty patina that envelopes the glass, and the bracing jolt from its rim against your lip triggers an emotional reaction to the drink.

UP DRINKS

Coupe (all-purpose, 5 ounces; and large, 6 ounces): Our favorite glass for both stirred and shaken cocktails served up, and the occasional champagne cocktail, is the coupe. We usually use all-purpose 5-ounce coupes, but also have deeper, 6-ounce coupes for more voluminous drinks and drinks that are rinsed with a spirit before other ingredients are added.

V martini glass (4½ ounces): Used most often for Manhattans and their variations, this glass also makes an elegant serving piece for intensely boozy drinks such as Thomas Waugh's Red Ant (page 269).

Nick & Nora glass (5 ounces): This pretty tulip-shaped glass can be used in place of a coupe for stirred drinks, especially those that have an elegant garnish on top, such as the apple fan in Brad Farran's Botany of Desire (page 162).

Port glass (7 ounces): We use port glasses for both stirred and shaken drinks that need their aromatics amplified; the port glass's depth and sloped sides helps direct the aromas up and into your nose.

Fancy fizz glass (6 ounces): In addition to serving as our "classy" house shot glasses, these small, tapered vessels are great for flips and other shaken drinks that are served up and meant to be consumed quickly.

Fizz glass (10 ounces): This slender, U-shaped glass is used for fizzes and not much else. The strong vertical sides are important for a fizz involving egg white; when soda is added, this shape allows the foam to rise above the glass.

Champagne flute (7 ounces): If a drink includes sparkling wine (and isn't a punch), it goes in a flute. We like flutes that are large enough that there's an inch or so of room above the wash line, which leaves room for a garnish.

ICED DRINKS

Single rocks glass (9 ounces): The single rocks glass is also known as a Sazerac glass, and for good reason. We serve all iterations of Sazeracs in this glass.

Double rocks glass (13 ounces): Also known as an old-fashioned glass, the double rocks glass is used most often for drinks served over one large ice cube (aka block ice). A good double rocks glass has a heavy bottom that will keep the drink cold if the glass is chilled beforehand.

Snifter (22 ounces): Snifters make terrible spirit-sipping glasses because they overly concentrate the alcohol content on the nose, making nuanced tasting almost impossible, but they're excellent for cocktails. The sloped sides of this bulbous stemmed glass direct a drink's

Coupe

V martini

Nick & Nora

Port

Fancy fizz

Fizz

Champagne flute

Single rocks

Double rocks

Snifter

Julep tin

Tiki mug

Ceramic coconut

Pilsner

Highball

Punch bowl

aromas up and into the nose of the drinker. Because they're too large to be used for up drinks, we usually use them for shaken cocktails served over a large ice cube.

Julep tin (13 ounces): The best julep tins are silver-plated and highly burnished, allowing them to show off the icy sheath created by a properly built drink.

Tiki mug (22 ounces): Popularized by tiki forefather Donn Beach, our jet-black porcelain gods are about as low-kitsch as they come; the drinks we serve in them can speak for themselves. Ooga mooga! (Available at barproducts.com.)

Ceramic coconut (20 ounces): A slightly more kitschy version of the tiki mug, these faux palm fruit are mounded full of crushed ice for many tiki drinks that contain coconut.

Pilsner glass (16 ounces): We borrow these tall, gently sloping glasses from the beer shelf and fill them with all manner of swizzles and other tall drinks served over crushed ice.

Highball glass (11 ounces): Slings, smashes, and other verb-based rocks drinks are served in these no-nonsense vessels, also known as collins glasses.

Punch bowl and cups: Any glass bowl can be used to serve punch, but a beautiful antique vessel will definitely add to the allure of a communal drink. We use an assortment of antique punch sets made from opaque milk glass.

THE REGULARS

GLEN T. WU

Glen T. Wu is a real estate agent and New York City native.

I lived on First Avenue and Tenth Street when Death & Co first opened. I came in on a Sunday. I work in real estate, so Sunday is my Friday. Because I talk all the time when I work, I just wanted to be quiet for a bit and enjoy my drink. The first cocktail I ordered was a Sazerac. I consider that my gold standard, and I order one everywhere I go. I still haven't been served one anywhere else that's quite as good. I'm not sure what their secret is.

A lot of people find cocktail bars intimidating. They've been to too many cold, inaccessible bars where you have to prove yourself worthy of a bartender's attention. But good bars make you feel comfortable no matter who you are and what you know. The vibe at Death & Co on a Sunday night is great. A lot of hospitality industry people come by, and it feels like a big reunion.

I'm not the kind of person who says, "Make me whatever." You don't walk into a four-star restaurant and say, "Cook me something good." You have to at least give the bartender someplace to start. They must hate it when customers ask for "whatever *you* want to drink," but I hear it all the time.

Even after I moved to Jackson Heights, in Queens, Death & Co remained my home base. I'm here pretty much every Sunday. I always start my evening with a Sazerac, then I move on to something else that's stirred and boozy, maybe a Vanderbilt (page 259), Toronto (page 152), or Oaxaca Old-Fashioned (page 273). I feel like I'm drinking with friends, even when I'm here by myself.

SAZERAC

VIEUX PONTARLIER ABSINTHE

1½ OUNCES RITTENHOUSE 100 RYE

½ OUNCE PIERRE FERRAND 1840 COGNAC

1 TEASPOON DEMERARA SYRUP (PAGE 277)

4 DASHES PEYCHAUD'S BITTERS

1 DASH ANGOSTURA BITTERS

1 LEMON TWIST

Rinse a rocks glass with absinthe and dump. Stir the remaining ingredients (except the lemon twist) over ice, then strain into the glass. Squeeze the lemon twist over the drink and discard. No garnish.

Technique

Technique is the refinement of many little tasks that—when learned, combined, and eventually perfected—form a personal bartending style. At Death & Co, our collective style has evolved from watching each other at work, adopting and adapting the small tricks our coworkers have pick up over the years, endless experimentation, and a measure of innovation, always with the goal of making great drinks more quickly, efficiently, and, most importantly, consistently. The goal of anyone who makes drinks, whether at home or in a bar, should be to master the basics and improve technique. That way, you can more easily and reliably mix drinks, which will free you to innovate more confidently.

MEASURING & POURING INGREDIENTS

Measuring every last ingredient that goes into a cocktail is vital to making consistently balanced drinks. Many of our cocktails teeter on a balance of incredibly nuanced ingredients, leaving little leeway for over- or underpouring ingredients. At Death & Co we use two jiggers to make most of our drinks. The larger jigger measures 1 and 2 ounces; the smaller ½ and ¾ ounce. Many of our recipes also call for ¼-ounce and teaspoon measures as well; for these we use jiggers with ¼-ounce interior markings or measuring spoons. Generally speaking, ingredients called for in the smallest amounts are the most potent and flavorful in a drink, making it all the more important to measure exactly: inaccuracies of just a few drops can quickly throw off the balance of a drink.

HOW TO JIGGER

The best way to learn how to measure ingredients with a jigger is to fill a liquor bottle with water and practice over and over again until you feel comfortable with the motions. The goal is to pour your ingredients quickly, smoothly, and without spilling anything on the bar (which is sloppy and a waste of precious ingredients) or, worse yet, onto your guest. Once you get the hang of it, test yourself by placing a mixing glass on a white sheet of paper; you should be able to build a drink without any liquid hitting the paper (a trick we learned from Milk & Honey's Sasha Petraske). Then repeat the entire process with your opposite hand until it feels just as natural. Ambidexterity in all techniques allows bartenders to make drinks much more quickly and efficiently without having to twist or turn their back to their guests.

Our bartenders vary in where they hold jiggers as they measure and pour. You'll see some hold the jigger at six o'clock to the glass and others at nine or twelve o'clock. What follows is what we've found to be the most natural and efficient way to jigger. These instructions are written for right-handed people; lefties need to reverse the hand placement. Or better yet, follow the advice above and master the art of jiggering with both hands.

1. Place a mixing glass in front of you and the bottle of whatever you intend to pour, opened, to the right of the glass.

2. Pick up a jigger with your left hand, holding it at its narrowest point between your thumb an d index finger and using your middle finger to steady the jigger. You can also hold the jigger between the first and second knuckles of your index and middle fingers with your hand flat, palm down and parallel to the bar. This style is more graceful, but it can also be slower and less steady until you take the time to master it.

3. Hold the top of the jigger just above the rim of the glass somewhere between nine and ten o'clock. Aligning the top of the jigger with the top of the glass will make it easier to see if you're holding the jigger level.

4. Pick up the bottle with your right hand. If you're using a speed pourer, grab the bottle by the neck to allow you to pivot quickly and cut off the pour in a precise way; otherwise, hold the bottle near the middle.

5. Pour the liquid into the jigger, keeping the tip of the speed pourer or mouth of the bottle as close to the lip of the jigger as possible. If you're using a speed pourer, the liquid will pour faster as you lift the bottom of the bottle higher. We prefer starting our pours at a high angle and tapering down as we finish the measure. Start with a slow stream and pour with a fluid motion, focusing on precision and control. Slow and precise trumps fast and inaccurate every time. If need be, you can place your finger over the air-intake hole, aka carb, of the speed pourer to slow the stream even more.

6. Fill the jigger completely full. This is the most important part of jiggering, and the most difficult to master. If you under- or overfill the jigger even slightly, you could throw off the flavor of the drink considerably. To assess the fullness of the jigger, look at the meniscus—the surface of the liquid. It should be as flat as possible. If you overfill, the meniscus will be convex, bulging up above the rim of the jigger; if you underfill, it will be concave. The density and surface tension of cocktail ingredients vary dramatically, and in some cases it's possible to add as much as ¼ ounce of extra liquid to a jigger before the meniscus breaks and the liquid spills out.

7. If using a speed pourer, turn your wrist toward your body to cut off the stream.

8. Tilt the jigger to pour the liquid into the glass, pulling the jigger across the top of the glass toward your body. Pouring toward your body ensures that any overzealous or misguided pours will end up on your side of the mixing glass, not your guest's.

STIRRING VS. SHAKING

Our general rule of thumb: If a cocktail contains any opaque or cloudy ingredients, such as fruit juices (citrus or otherwise), egg, or cream, it should be shaken—vigorously. It takes a good deal of effort to integrate these kinds of ingredients into the drink. Conversely, if a cocktail consists entirely of transparent ingredients—spirits, vermouth, sweeteners, bitters, and so on—it should be stirred.

Why? It all comes down to texture. With a shaken drink, you're looking to liven up the ingredients and add texture to the drink via air bubbles and emulsification. Or to paraphrase Harry Craddock, who wrote *The Savoy Cocktail Book*, you are trying to wake the cocktail up, not send it to sleep. Agitating a citrusy cocktail creates a frothy texture on top and a refreshing aroma and lightly effervescent first sip.

Stirring a cocktail, on the other hand, is intended to chill and dilute a drink without adding any air bubbles. The finished drink should have the mouthfeel of extremely cold silk, smooth over the tongue and down the throat.

STIRRING COCKTAILS

In *The Karate Kid*, Mr. Miyagi begins his martial arts tutelage by first having Daniel do monotonous, arm-numbing chores around his house. After days of waxing cars, sanding floors, and painting fences, an embittered Daniel-san realizes he's mastered the essential movements of karate, all while giving Miyagi's bachelor pad a free facelift.

We approach instruction in stirring in much the same way, with a sequence of many small, seemingly inconsequential tasks eventually becoming effortless and natural. The first step is to master control of the tool in its environment: the push and pull of a barspoon inside an empty mixing glass. Next is changing the perception of what stirring a cocktail is; it's not stirring, after all, but allowing the outside of the spoon to travel along the inside bevel of the glass. Only then do we introduce ice and liquid to the practice. The goal is to stir as quietly as possible, never agitating the liquid beyond a gentle rattle of ice.

HOW TO STIR

The best way to build good stirring technique is to take an empty mixing glass and spoon and sit or, better yet, stand in front of the television. Stir as you watch; this will help you get comfortable with the motion, build muscle memory, and teach you how to multitask when you make drinks—a vital skill for every bartender.

The process that follows will sound finicky, but being precise and paying attention to detail here will inform the rest of your stirring technique and make the difference between accuracy and sloppiness. When training new bartenders, we can usually tell how well they will work by how seriously they take this part of the process ("Either you karate do yes, or karate do no . . .").

1. Hold a mixing spoon bowl end down between the middle and ring finger of your dominant hand. The neck should rest between the first and second knuckles.

2. Rotate the spoon so the inside of the bowl faces your body. Let the spoon slip through your fingers so your knuckles are toward the top of the spoon. Relax your hand so the spoon can rotate between your fingers.

3. Insert the bowl of the spoon into an empty mixing glass with the back of the spoon facing twelve o'clock and pressed against the mixing glass. Imagine a line that connects the middle of the glass and the ceiling; the top of the spoon should stay connected to this line. Keep your elbow raised so your forearm is parallel with the bar.

4. To practice using only your middle and ring fingers to move the spoon (still in a mixing glass without liquid or ice), pull the spoon from twelve o'clock to six o'clock with your middle finger, then push it in the opposite direction with your ring finger. The top of the spoon should stay in place (still connected in that imaginary line to the ceiling), and the face of the spoon shouldn't rotate. Following a steady cadence, tap one side of the glass then the other, like a metronome.

5. Practice actually revolving the spoon around the mixing glass. Start with half circles, beginning at twelve o'clock and pulling the spoon clockwise around the glass (if you're right-handed; counterclockwise if you're a lefty) with your middle finger, stopping at six o'clock. The curved side of the bowl should always be touching the side of the glass. Then, with your ring finger, push the spoon back the way you came, to twelve o'clock. Repeat in a steady rhythm, pausing each time exactly at the top and bottom of the glass (push, pull . . . push, pull . . .).

6. Practice making a full rotation. Fill the mixing glass with ice. Starting with the bowl of the spoon at twelve o'clock, draw it clockwise around the glass for one full revolution (or counterclockwise if you're a lefty). After pushing with your middle finger to the six o'clock position, complete the rotation by pulling with your ring finger. Stop precisely at twelve o'clock each time around; this will help you learn control.

7. After you're comfortable with one revolution, do two revolutions, stopping at twelve o'clock after every two turns. Work your way up to a dozen or more revolutions until you're make one continuous, smooth motion around the glass.

8. Once you're comfortable with the stirring motion, repeat the entire process with your nondominant hand. This will be frustrating at first. To get the hang of it, routinely go back to your dominant hand to remind yourself how the motion should feel.

BUILDING A STIRRED COCKTAIL

When making stirred cocktails, always start with a cold mixing glass or pint glass (see "Mixing Glass," page 93). Keep your mixing glass in the freezer between uses, or fill it with ice water for a few minutes and then dump it out.

1. Add the ingredients, starting with the cheapest and/or smallest volume ingredients first. This way, if you mess up you can start over without wasting large quantities of ingredients or more expensive spirits and modifiers.

2. Give the mixture a couple of quick stirs.

3. Add enough ice cubes to fill the glass about three-quarters full (use Kold-Draft ice or 1-inch ice cubes; see "Ice," page 60), layering the ice as tightly as possible. If you're using a pint glass or large chunks of ice, you may need to crack the ice so it fits more tightly into the glass; otherwise, you'll end up with a stack of cubes, and it will take forever to chill and dilute the drink.

4. Hold the mixing glass steady near its base with two or three fingers; any more or higher, and the heat from your hand will warm the glass.

5. Stir the drink in a steady rhythm, stopping after about 15 seconds.

6. Taste the drink. Trap a bit using a cocktail straw and your finger, or spoon a small amount onto the back of your hand; don't slurp from the spoon you're using to stir the drink. Is it cold and diluted to your liking? If the answer is no, stir for a few more seconds and taste again.

7. Strain the drink into a chilled cocktail glass and take a look: Are there bubbles in the drink? If so, you stirred or poured too aggressively. Give it a taste: Does the drink taste balanced and glide down your throat like a ribbon of cold silk? Good job!

If you make stirred cocktails under similar conditions each time (same tools, similar ice, and so on), you'll soon get a feel for when they're close to proper temperature and dilution, so you won't have to taste as often (bummer). You can also watch for visual cues. In particular, the ice will shrink as it melts into the drink, and the wash line (the amount of liquid in the glass) will rise accordingly.

There are a couple of other factors to consider as you decide how long to stir. First is whether the drink will be served up or over ice. Most stirred drinks are served up, but with cocktails served over ice, like the old-fashioned and Vieux Carré, we stop short of mixing the drink all the way to dilution, knowing that ice will continue to melt into the drink as it's consumed. Second, small cubes melt faster than large, block ice, so you should definitely stir less if using smaller cubes or cracked ice in the finished drink.

HOW TO DOUBLE (AND QUADRUPLE!) STIR

Once you've mastered the stirring motion independently with both hands, you're ready to double stir. This involves exactly the same movements, but in duplicate: place two cocktail glasses in front of you and repeat the same steps listed above, with your right-hand spoon moving clockwise and your left hand moving counterclockwise. Moving the spoons in opposite directions makes it easier to stir both drinks at the same speed, thereby achieving equal dilution. Master this technique and you can move on to the crane kick of cocktails: the quadruple stir, which involves using two spoons in each hand to simultaneously mix four cocktails. Few of us have mastered this technique (it helps to have enormous hands).

THE SCIENCE OF STIRRING

The goal of making a stirred drink is twofold: chilling and dilution. You want to mix the ingredients until they're very cold. The ideal temperature is between 18°F and 23°F. You also want the drink to reach its ideal dilution. Water is the most underrated ingredient in a drink. Too little and the drink will taste too hot, or alcoholic; too much and it will taste too weak.

A number of factors can affect how quickly or slowly these aims are achieved: the temperature and size of the mixing glass, the size and quantity of ice cubes, the ingredients themselves, and the speed and duration of stirring. We addressed speed and duration of stirring above. Here's how the other three factors will affect the drink, along with what we've found to work best for us at Death & Co.

MIXING GLASS

We'll spare you the refresher course on thermodynamics, but know this: The temperature of a mixing glass has a considerable impact on the interaction between the ice and liquid it contains. Your goal should be to slow the dilution process enough that the cocktail is very cold by the time it reaches proper dilution. A room-temperature mixing glass will transfer its heat to the cooler liquid within, speeding up the dilution process. On the other hand, a cold mixing glass will chill the liquid within (at least until the two reach equilibrium), thereby diluting the cocktail more slowly, which means you can chill the drink more thoroughly without diluting it too much.

This is why we keep our mixing glasses in the freezer whenever possible. During a busy shift this isn't practical, but in that case we're using the glasses frequently enough that they stay cold. At home, we recommend keeping your mixing glasses in the freezer. We also prefer a Japanese-style mixing glass, as its width allows more ice to interact with the liquid than in a narrow-bottomed pint glass, helping the drink reach its target temperature and dilution simultaneously.

ICE

It all comes down to size. You can make a proper stirred drink with anything from tiny ice pellets up to one giant chunk of ice, and you can certainly use ice made in a home freezer, which isn't as bad as people like to say. With different sizes of ice, what changes is how long you have to stir to achieve proper dilution. In a working bar, the trick is to find the right balance of speed, efficiency, and control. We can chill and dilute a drink very quickly with crushed ice or tiny pellets, which puts more surface area of ice in contact with the drink, but this also makes it dangerously easy to overdilute the drink. Conversely, we can stir a cocktail over a single ice cube, which has less surface area and therefore provides a larger margin of error, meaning the drink will chill and dilute more slowly; but in this case we'd end up stirring ourselves dizzy while our customers find someplace else to drink.

The happy medium is Kold-Draft ice, which we use to make most of our stirred drinks. Our machine produces pristine 1¼-inch cubes that stack in neat layers inside our mixing glasses. They're large enough to dilute a drink slowly but offer enough surface area to keep stirring time fairly short. For making drinks at home, approximately 1-inch ice cubes will perform similarly.

INGREDIENTS

How much dilution a drink needs varies from cocktail to cocktail. A drink made mostly from high-proof spirits (such as a Sazerac or dry martini) needs more water and will take longer to reach dilution. A less boozy drink (such as a Manhattan or classic, fifty-fifty martini) will reach dilution more quickly.

....

SHAKING COCKTAILS

While *The Karate Kid* is the best metaphor we could come up with for stirring (sorry!), Major League Baseball is the most apt we've come up with for shaking. In baseball, you see dramatic differences in throwing motion among pitchers, even in the most elite ranks of hurlers. Most pitchers throw overhand, a smaller subset throws sidearm, and a handful of freaks throw underhand (called a submarine pitch, if you care to know). But beyond these basic categories lie a panoply of variations and quirks that give each pitcher's motion its signature. Some of these pitchers are poetry in motion, while others look like they're trying to detach a snapping turtle from their hand. But all have one thing in common: they can put the ball over the plate.

Among Death & Co bartenders you'll notice a similarly varied array of shaking styles. A bartender's shake is his or her unique signature, a combination of nature and nurture, and often the purest expression of personality behind the bar, developed and tweaked through thousands of hours spent working behind the rail. As such, we don't try to foist an ideal shaking technique on our bartenders. The fact that they're working at Death & Co signifies that they've figured out how to make consistently excellent drinks, so whether they shake over their shoulder, in front of their body, or between their legs matters not—as long as they can deliver.

Phil Ward's giant hands and wristy, over-the-shoulder motion evokes a heavy metal drummer banging on cymbals. Thomas Waugh's shake is elegant, deliberate, and adaptable: he switches between several distinctive motions depending on the drink. Joaquín Simó holds his shaker near his waist and delivers a cadence that starts slow and builds into a full-body convulsion.

Many of us have completely overhauled our shaking motion over the years, whether due to experimentation, emulation, or injury. As in baseball, throwing out a shoulder is probably the bartender's most common—and career-threatening—impairment, and it often requires adopting a new technique in order to stay in the game. Before he threw out his shoulder, Brian Miller would begin his angry-gorilla shake by cocking his arm back like a quarterback, then unleashing a violent convulsion that stopped conversations and turned heads around the bar. When Alex Day hurt his shoulder, he moved his motion from next to his head to down in front of his body.

Despite our many different styles, there are some commonalities to an efficient and effective shake. Once you understand the principles behind a good shake, you can adapt them to develop your own personal technique.

HOW TO SHAKE

Shaking a cocktail is like walking or sex: everyone has a rhythm and motion that works best for them. The motion we describe below isn't necessarily the *best* shake in the world, but it's one we've found to be both efficient and ergonomic—that is, it inflicts the least amount of wear and tear on your body. After you're comfortable with it, experiment with different motions and grips to find your own style.

At Death & Co we shake the vast majority of our drinks using a combination of small and large weighted shaking tins, typically 18 and 28 ounces in volume, and that's the setup we reference in the following instructions. As discussed earlier in this chapter, we're not fans of the traditional Boston shaker setup; however, this technique can easily be adapted for any shaker type:

1. Set the small tin on the bar, then measure the ingredients into it, without ice. Fill the large tin about half full of ice.

2. Coming in at an angle, place the large tin over the small tin so one side of the shakers forms a straight line. Seal the shaker by hitting the top of the large tin with the palm of your hand. The shaker is sealed when you can grab it by the top tin and lift it off the bar without the bottom half separating.

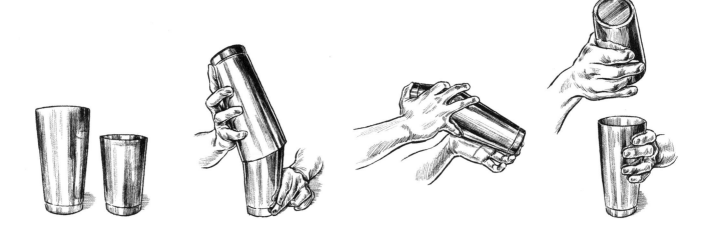

3. Pick the shaker up with the top of the small tin facing your body. This way, if it leaks or opens while shaking, the drink will spill on you and not your guest. Place one hand on either end, finding a comfortable position for your hands. Most Death & Co bartenders grasp the shaker like a football with their dominant hand—with a thumb near the seam and two fingers on either tin—and cradle the bottom of the large tin with their nondominant hand. The key is to find a secure grip that uses as little body contact as possible. Having your palms all over the shaker will add body heat to the cocktail and result in a drink that's warmer when it reaches proper dilution.

4. Give the shaker a couple of turns to temper the ice, making it less likely to shatter as you shake.

5. Keeping the shaker in front of your body, push it away from your body, then pull it back in. There should be a slight arc to your motion, rather than a back-and-forth piston action. The goal is to make the ice move in a circular pattern, which will round off the edges instead of busting the ice into pieces. It's important to shake hard but comfortably. If it hurts to shake, you're doing it wrong.

6. Set the shaker down with the larger tin on the bottom. Squeeze the sides of the larger tin as you push the smaller tin away to unlock and separate the two halves. Strain the drink as soon as possible. (We'll cover straining in the next section.)

OTHER STYLES OF SHAKING

The technique described above is what we use for most of our shaken drinks. However, there are a few other specialty shakes we employ for specific styles of drinks.

DRY SHAKING

When making cocktails that contain eggs—whether whites, yolks, or both—we start by dry shaking the drink, meaning without ice. Egg whites are jumbles of tightly packed protein, and when they're agitated without ice, those proteins unfold and bond around air molecules more easily, resulting in better emulsification and more prominent foam atop the drink. To dry shake, build the drink, close the tins, and shake until the ingredients are emulsified, which takes about as long as shaking a drink with ice. You'll be able to hear the ingredients inside the shaker transitioning from a sloshy-sounding mixture into something thicker and more homogenous. Separate the tins as above, so the ingredients remain in the large tin. Fill the small tin with ice, quickly reseal, then proceed with a normal shake.

DOUBLE SHAKING

When you master shaking one drink at a time, you're ready to move on to the double shake, which is just what it sounds like: shaking two cocktails at once. Make sure you have a secure grip on both shakers, then bring them up next to your head and shake back and forth, with the shakers moving in opposite directions. You can try shaking with both hands in sync, but you'll quickly find that the motion is as unbalanced and awkward-looking as it is painful.

SHORT SHAKING

When a cocktail is served over ice or topped with an effervescent ingredient (club soda, ginger beer, and so on), you don't need to shake it as vigorously or for as long, as it will be diluted in the glass by the ice or additional ingredients. We use the short shake when making collins-style drinks as well as some tiki drinks. The goal is to shake the ingredient just long enough to mix them well and chill them slightly, the latter being helpful for preventing the drink from diluting too quickly when you pour it over ice.

WHIPPING

We use this technique for cocktails served over a lot of crushed ice, such as swizzles and mai tais. Shake the drink using only one cube or a few nuggets of ice (we use pellets made by a Scotsman machine), just long enough to melt the ice completely and incorporate the ingredients. The mixture won't be very cold or diluted, but chilling and dilution will be taken care of in the glass.

THE SCIENCE
(OR LACK THEREOF)
OF SHAKING

The purpose of stirring a drink is to chill and dilute it. Shaking adds a third element: modifying the texture of the drink by adding air bubbles and emulsifying the ingredients. Cocktails that contain solids (such as fruit or herbs) or cloudy ingredients (citrus juice, dairy, and so on) are usually shaken. This much we can agree on.

Yet shaking remains one of the most mysterious and hotly contended techniques in the cocktail world. We (and many others) have experimented with different vessels, motions, durations, and types of ice over the years and have been left with more questions than answers. That said, it helps to understand all the variables that contribute to the a good-quality shake: ice, motion, and duration.

ICE

You can make a proper shaken drink with any kind of ice, even the stuff that comes out of a home ice maker. The trick is adjusting the amount of ice and the duration and intensity of shaking. Smaller ice will expose more surface area to the liquid and dilute the drink more quickly, so you'll need a shorter shake. Larger pieces of ice will dilute the drink more slowly, which means you'll have to shake longer. And if you shake aggressively with small ice, it will shatter into smaller pieces, further increasing the surface area and diluting the drink even more quickly.

The other thing ice contributes to a shaken drink is aeration, which is created as the ice moves through the liquid, creating tiny bubbles. The larger the ice, the harder you'll have to shake to get the aeration you want.

At Death & Co we use two large, 2-inch block ice cubes for drinks that will be served neat. The large size ensures the drink will be as cold as possible when it reaches its target dilution. (Our target temperature for a shaken drink is between 32°F and 41°F). For drinks served over ice, we short shake the drink using three Kold-Draft ice cubes. This chills the drink more quickly, which is fine, as dilution will continue in the glass.

MOTION

The best shaking motion is one that works for you. But there are two things to consider here. First, does your motion cause the ice to bounce around the shaker? Ideally it will move the ice around in a circular pattern, rounding off the edges of the ice cubes. A good way to know if you've done this is to look at the ice after shaking to see if it's round. A straight, back-and-forth motion will cause the ice to piston between the two ends, which tends to shatter the ice, creating more surface area and diluting the drink too quickly. You'll see some great bartenders using this style, but they've figured out how to adjust other variables to achieve the right results.

Second, does the motion allow you to shake hard and long (for hours on end, if you work in a bar) without hurting yourself? We like the "push-pull" technique described in "How to Shake," page 94, because it puts less stress on the shoulders. Some bartenders move the shaker up and down as they shake, which helps create a steady, consistent rhythm and encourages the ice to move in a circular pattern.

DURATION

It's hard to give precise guidelines on how long to shake. So many variables affect how much time is required to reach proper dilution, chief among them the size and amount of ice used (big? small? wet? dry?) and the intensity and speed of shaking (hard and fast? slow and wimpy?). Just as important is the style of drink you're preparing. For cocktails served up, you should shake all the way to dilution. Drinks served on the rocks are shaken about three-quarters of the way to dilution, with the exact amount depending on the size and amount of ice they will be served over and whether they will be further diluted with soda, champagne, or other such ingredients.

It takes a bit of experience and intuition to know when a drink has been shaken to its ideal temperature, dilution, and aeration. The good news is that it's easier to underdilute than overdilute a drink, so when it doubt, stop shaking, taste the drink, and shake a bit more if it's not there yet. As you gain more experience, you'll develop an awareness, sort of a sixth sense, about this based on how the cocktail *feels* inside the shaker when it's been shaken enough. This only comes with shaking hundreds of drinks.

That said, here are a few general guidelines: An up cocktail shaken with two large (2-inch) ice cubes (our preferred ice setup) should take between ten and fifteen seconds of hard, fast shaking to reach proper dilution (that's longer than it sounds). Short shaking with three Kold-Draft ice cubes (or their equivalent) should take eight to ten seconds.

As to how to develop that "sixth sense" for shaking, use your other senses. Although it's impossible to see all of what's going on inside the shaker, you can listen as the ice melts and the volume of liquid increases, resulting in a more sloshy sound. If you hear the ice cubes breaking apart, it's a good sign that the drink is close to dilution. Over time, you'll learn to detect the sound of a properly shaken drink. Your sense of touch is equally important. By the time the drink is properly shaken, the tin will be very cold and your hands will start to stick to it.

BUILDING A ROUND

If we made each of our drinks one at a time during service, we'd have some mighty sober guests. To speed things up, bartenders often make two or more drinks at once; this is called building a round.

Every round is its own little puzzle. You have to figure out the fastest and most efficient order in which to build the cocktails, then stir or shake them, so that they all reach the guests at the same time.

As with building any drink, start by adding the cheapest ingredients and smallest amounts to the shaker or mixing glass first. The order is typically bitters, then sweeteners, citrus, modifiers, and finally base spirits. (By the way, this is opposite the order in which ingredients are listed in the recipes in this book, or by a bartender if you ask him or her for a recipe; this means our staff literally knows our drinks forward *and* backward.) In addition to saving money if you screw up, you can also work from one set of ingredients to the next while preparing multiple cocktails. Group mixing glasses and shakers together and work from right to left (or left to right, as long as you're consistent), repeating any ingredients that appear in multiple drinks before putting them away. For example, if three drinks contain Angostura bitters, you can add it to all three before moving on to the next ingredient. Rinse jiggers before moving to the next ingredient if using ingredients that are noticeably flavorful. And for very pungent ingredients, like ginger syrup or mezcal, we give jiggers an extra rinse, since their flavors tend to stick around. On the other hand, rinsing isn't necessary in many situations. For example, if you're using simple syrup, you don't need to rinse the jigger before moving on to citrus. Likewise, jiggers need not be rinsed between some citrus juices (lemon, lime), but should be between others (orange, grapefruit).

Most rounds contain a combination of shaken and stirred drinks. In this case, build the stirred drinks first, then fill their mixing glasses with ice and give them a couple of stirs to start the cooling process. Next, build the shaken drinks in small tins. Prep any garnishes needed for the round, then finish stirring the up drinks. Grab chilled glasses from the freezer and place them on the bar. Strain any stirred drinks into the glasses, then add ice to the shakers and shake them to completion. Strain the shaken drinks into the glasses and garnish the entire round. If you're serving the cocktails yourself, always serve the shaken drinks first, followed by the stirred.

To speed things up even more, you can learn to shake one drink and stir another simultaneously— and ambidextrously. This is tricky at first, not unlike patting your head while rubbing your belly, but it's an important skill to learn if you work at a busy bar.

STRAINING

Most of the hard work of building a cocktail happens in the mixing glass or shaker; straining is the easy part.

STRAINING STIRRED DRINKS

If you're using a julep strainer, position the handle of the strainer between your index and middle fingers, with the base of the handle (where it connects to the bowl of the julep strainer) pressed against the rim of the mixing glass, on the side opposite the glass's pouring spout. Hold the strainer in place by grabbing the rim of the mixing glass with your thumb, ring, and pinky fingers. Using the edge of the glass as a fulcrum, flex your middle and index fingers to press the bowl of the julep strainer inside the glass and over the ice so that it rests tightly against the front of the glass below the spout. Slowly pour the drink so that the spout side is perpendicular to the guest (never pour toward people lest you splash them), being careful not to create air bubbles or splash the drink out of the glass.

If you're using a Hawthorne strainer, set the strainer over the glass with the handle opposite the glass's pouring spout. Grab the glass beneath the handle of the strainer and place your index finger against the tab (if there is one). Push the strainter toward the front of the glass and slowly pour the drink sideways or at an angle toward your body, giving it a gentle shake at the end to knock any liquid sticking to the ice into the drink.

STRAINING SHAKEN DRINKS

The main concern when straining a drink is to get it all into the glass as quickly as possible so as not to lose the aeration you worked so hard to create, and to do so without leaving any liquid behind in the shaker and without any of the cocktail hitting the bar or, worse, your guest. Assuming you're using a Hawthorne strainer (which you should always use for shaken drinks), follow the same method described above but take into consideration what we call gate control: how tightly you push the front of the strainer against the edge of the mixing tin. How tightly you close the gate depends on whether you want any small ice chips to fall into the drink. This is a matter of personal preference, but it can be an important consideration depending on what happens to ice during shaking. If it breaks up at all, we close the gate tight to avoid ice chips on top of the drink.

DOUBLE STRAINING

For most shaken cocktails served up, we don't want any ice chips or small pieces of muddled fruit or herbs in the drink, so we use a Hawthorne strainer (gate closed) plus a fine-mesh cone strainer to double strain the drink. This is especially important with drinks that contain egg white, as any tiny ice chips can ruin the foamy head that rests on top of the drink. In addition, we find that the mesh strainer aerates the head even more than when the cocktail is poured

From left: straining a stirred drink, straining a shaken drink, double straining a shaken drink

only through a Hawthorne strainer. To double strain, use the Hawthorne strainer as describe above and hold the mesh strainer over the serving glass. Pour, then knock the side of the cone strainer with the bottom of the shaker to speed up the flow of liquid.

MUDDLING

It's painfully common to watch a bartender throw some mint into a shaker and jackhammer it into a sludgy mess with their muddler. (If you've ever ordered a mojito, you've probably witnessed this process.) This is wrong on so many levels. First, crushing mint, or any other herb, releases bitter, stemmy flavors you don't want in the drink. It also breaks the cells and releases chlorophyll, along with its green color, into the drink.

All of the essential oils you need can be coaxed out of herbs with minimal effort. To prove this point, place a mint leaf on your tongue, press it against the roof of your mouth, and gently rub it around. It should taste pleasantly minty. Now, chew the mint and taste the bitter, unpleasant flavor that ensues; this is what happens when you muddle too hard.

When muddling herbs, we often put some kind of sweetener in the shaker first, then add the herb. Then, all that's required is to gently press the muddler down and twist it a few times to release its oils.

When muddling citrus and other fruit you need to press and twist a bit harder to release the oils (in the case of citrus peels) or juice (when muddling citrus pieces or other types of fruit). It helps to look inside the shaker as you do this so you can target the fruit to extract as much oil or juice as possible.

For drinks that require muddling both fruit and herbs, such as a smash, put the sweetener and herb in the shaker first, then add the fruit. The fruit will act as a cushion and keep the herb from tearing during muddling.

RIMMING

To rim a glass with salt, sugar or other ingredients before straining the cocktail into it, wet the outside of the rim with water or a piece of citrus fruit (preferably the same citrus used in the cocktail), then dip the glass into the rimming mixture. Roll the glass on the outside only to keep particles from falling into the finished drink. For some drinks, such as a margarita, we apply a thick swath of salt to half the glass, allowing the guest to choose if they want salt or not. After applied, while the glass is upside down over a trash bin, lightly tap the base of the glass, shedding excess granules.

RINSING

Many cocktails are rinsed with an aggressively flavored spirit (most often absinthe, mezcal, or a peaty Scotch) before adding the drink. To rinse a glass, pour a small amount (about ¼ ounce) of the spirit into the glass. Slowly rotate the glass so the rinse coats the entire interior. Discard the rinse—down the drain (if you're wasteful), back into the bottle (if you're miserly) or discreetly into a shot glass for later consumption (if you're anything like us).

THE REGULARS
GARO YELLIN

Garo Yellin is a professional cellist whose work encompasses multiple genres of music, including classical, jazz, and rock. He was a member of the experimental rock group the Ordinaires and has toured with Pere Ubu.

I almost never drink cocktails—I should get that out there right away. I like to be the easiest customer in the room. When bartenders are busy, they have a lot of pressure on them, so I tell them to pour me an ounce of anything brown, no ice. A glass of whiskey doesn't suck after ten minutes like a martini does. Martinis are an amateur drinker's drink. You have to consume a martini quickly, then order another and drink that one quickly. Before you know it you're done for the night. It's like a fight scene in a movie: you watch someone getting punched in the face thirty-seven times and they're still standing up, and you know that in real life you can only take one or two punches before you hit the floor.

Certain bars have a glorious half-life when they're perfect every night of the week. You can go by yourself and have a 95 percent chance of having a great time. It feels like a nineteenth-century French or Viennese café, where you show up and are expected to hold your own with smart, interesting strangers. You talk to beautiful women without feeling awkward. Then the clientele changes, or the staff turns over, or the assholes show up and chase away the interesting strangers and the beautiful women, and the bar's moment has passed, never to return.

Death & Co has been consistently perfect since my first visit. I never don't want to go there. I often drive down Sixth Street on my way home from a gig, and if there's a parking spot I stop in no matter how I feel. It's also a versatile bar. If a friend's parents are visiting from out of town and want a touch of NYC hipness, I send them to Death & Co. If I'm on a date and don't know where to go, the bar has never failed me. I can take anyone there, and if they don't like the place, I know it's their fault, not mine.

The key to great cocktail bars in general, and Death & Co in particular, isn't the decor, the lighting, the music, or the quality of the cocktails. It comes down to the staff—always the staff. At Death & Co that starts before you even step inside. The door hosts have the impossible job of making people feel okay about not getting into the bar right away. They're honest and straightforward about it, and they take your number and actually call you back when a seat opens up. And they're genuinely happy when you come back.

Inside, it's one of the fanciest bars in the world, yet I've never felt weird about not being a cocktail guy. A bar is defined by the ineffable quality of its vibe. Death & Co has an atmosphere I want to breathe. There have been times when I've been away on tour for months and returned to find new faces at the door or at the bar, but I always feel right at home. A good bar staff doesn't try hard to make you feel like a regular; they make everyone feel like a regular from their first drink. For me, it comes down to this: what kind of bar do I want to walk into?

WHISKY NEAT

2 OUNCES JAPANESE WHISKY

Pour into a rocks glass. No garnish.

Chapter Four

CREATING NEW CLASSICS

FLOR DE JEREZ

JOAQUÍN SIMÓ

Oh, sherry. Sometime around 2009 every one of our bartenders fell hard for this fortified wine because of how its flavors and acidity mingle so well with other cocktail ingredients. (We also loved that it's a cheap-as-hell base ingredient—you can buy a great bottle for under $12.) Joaquín was particularly smitten with the amontillado style of sherry, which is dry but smells sweet, leaving room for the bartender to add other sweeteners to a drink. In his Flor de Jerez, Joaquín uses rum to bring out the sherry's darker, raisiny flavors, and apricot liqueur to bring out its fruity notes.

½ OUNCE APPLETON ESTATE
RESERVE RUM

1½ OUNCES LUSTAU
AMONTILLADO SHERRY

¼ OUNCE ROTHMAN & WINTER
APRICOT LIQUEUR

¾ OUNCE LEMON JUICE

½ OUNCE CANE SUGAR SYRUP
(PAGE 276)

1 DASH ANGOSTURA BITTERS

Shake all the ingredients with ice, then strain into a coupe. No garnish.

THE TASTING

On a Monday morning in early spring, Dave and a group of bartenders—a ragged, sleep-deprived bunch, several of whom have just left the bar a few hours ago—shuffle into Death & Co. Sausage-and-egg sandwiches, black coffee, and bottles of water are distributed. A few tattered, recipe-filled notebooks are scattered across the bar. As is custom, the bar's newest staff member, Tyson Buhler, is selected to go first. He steps behind the bar and mixes a drink, then passes it around for his peers to taste.

TYSON The idea was to combine bourbon, port, and aquavit—three ingredients I love. I also added lemon juice and cane syrup.

PHIL When you said you were combining bourbon and aquavit, I thought, *What a fucking moron*. But you have some affinity here. I think it can work, but it needs a little tweaking. What's your spec?

TYSON One and a half Eagle Rare, three-quarters tawny port, half Krogstad aquavit, three-quarters lemon, half cane, egg white.

JOAQUÍN Have you tried Linie? Its aged flavors might play better with Eagle Rare.

Tyson repeats the drink with Linie aquavit.

JILLIAN Now it tastes like a fruit and nut chocolate bar. I think it's well balanced and tastes good, but it needs one more thing to stand out. Nutmeg?

Tyson grates some nutmeg over the drink.

BRAD I liked the first one better. It was flowery. But the cane syrup was overwhelming. Try it with simple?

JOAQUÍN It's also got a bit of a chalky texture. A weird thing can happen with egg white drinks. If it feels chalky you actually need to add more whites to make it less so.

Tyson repeats the first version of the drink, this time with simple syrup and more egg white.

DAVE It's an interesting idea, but there are still some kinks to work out. Let's try it again at the next tasting.

To the uninitiated, this shorthand exchange of cocktail lingo may be indecipherable. At Death & Co we call it "the tasting," and it's our core creative process. Every few months we overhaul our cocktail menu, which consists of some sixty drinks. The tasting takes place over two daylong sessions, and in the process a new menu is crafted by committee, one drink at a time. Each bartender presents a series of original drinks while the rest of the staff—a mix of current and past employees—provides unfiltered feedback. Few if any cocktails are perfect on the first try. Most go through several iterations before a consensus is reached, with the head bartender getting the final say on what makes the menu. Drinks that still don't work after a few tries are shelved for more tinkering or scrapped altogether.

We don't take this ritual lightly. Over six years and dozens of tastings, there have been hurt feelings, broken egos, and even the occasional scuffle, but after each tasting the staff emerges united and more excited about its craft.

After forty minutes and four drinks, Tyson's turn is up. One cocktail makes the cut, and the rest go back into development. Brad Farran is up next.

BRAD I'm calling this drink Tommy and the Ron-Dels. I wanted to do a Ron del Barrilito rum drink based on the Tommy's margarita spec, but that was boring, so I goosed it with Galliano and tiki bitters. I used a scant half of Galliano; otherwise, that's all you taste.

Brad shakes the drink, then strains it into a rocks glass and passes it around.

THOMAS Did you use a full half of agave? It looked like a quarter.

JOAQUÍN It looked short to me. If it's going to get served on the rocks, it needs sugar or it will taste thin.

THOMAS You used two rums?

BRAD One and a half rum, half crema de mezcal.

JOAQUÍN You forgot to say that. I was wondering why it's so smoky.

THOMAS You think the rum is too strong?

JOAQUÍN It's a fruit bomb. I like rum and Galliano together, but not with crema. Maybe another rum in place of Ron del?

THOMAS What about a smokier tequila?

BRAD I like the softness and roundness of crema.

THOMAS It does need more sugar.

BRAD I'll make another with more agave.

THOMAS And El Tesoro repo instead of crema. Sound good?

JOAQUÍN Blanco would be too green, añejo too soft. It wouldn't stand up at all.

BRAD I'll make another with more agave and repo.

Brad moves on to his next drink.

BRAD I call this one Cynaro de Bergerac.

PHIL What?

BRAD It's a concept drink.

PHIL What the fuck is a concept drink?

BRAD It's when I come up with the name first. In this case we have a great wine from Bergerac, so I wanted to come up with something made with that. Then I saw Cynar and "Cynaro de Bergerac" jumped into my head. Boom.

PHIL Let's taste it before you induct yourself into the hall of fame.

JILLIAN It just looks like a glass of cold red wine.

PHIL It's a concept drink, Jillian.

To everyone's surprise, Brad's concept drink eventually meets universal approval, while the rest are left to him for tinkering before he presents them again the following day. The next bartender, Eryn Reece, replaces Brad behind the bar and mixes her first drink.

ERYN I wanted to try a stirred Hemingway with grapefruit-infused Punt e Mes, tequila, and an absinthe rinse.

BRAD Why did you rinse with absinthe? I'd put a couple dashes in.

JOAQUÍN With the wash line on this drink, the rinse is pointless.

THOMAS I like to do both.

BRAD I'm not wild about this drink. It's confusing me.

JOAQUÍN It's brown, muddy. Nothing's distinctive here.

THOMAS What could you take out of it?

JOAQUÍN Maybe a little less Punt e Mes and cut the absinthe?

BRAD How dedicated are you to tequila? What if you used whiskey?

ERYN I'm not dedicated to tequila.

JOAQUÍN What about Ibis? It's a really dry rum.

BRAD Or split Ibis and Flor de Caña 7. Flor is so subtle that it will let the Ibis speak but not dominate.

Eryn mixes a second version with rum in place of tequila.

THOMAS I think it would be tasty with whiskey.

ERYN Scotch or Japanese?

THOMAS Bourbon.

Eryn makes a third drink, this time with bourbon.

DAVE It's still dry and too tannic. I think we have to go back to the drawing board.

THOMAS The infusion gives it a pithy bitterness. And now it's too sweet. Take the simple out and use a teaspoon of maraschino liqueur.

BRAD What if you kill the infusion and just twist the grapefruit in before you stir?

Eryn makes a fourth iteration.

DAVE This works.

THOMAS Agreed.

BRAD The finish is interesting. I can get down with that. Can you pass it back to me so I can get down with it?

After Eryn finishes her drinks, the current head bartender, Jillian Vose, takes her turn behind the bar.

JILLIAN I made this at the end of my shift last night, so it needs some work. I did an old-fashioned variation with Willett, IPA syrup, sherry, Jerry Thomas, and orange bitters. It's inspired by a beer and a shot.

THOMAS This smells like a boilermaker. Two, half, quarter?

JILLIAN Two, quarter, quarter.

DAVE It's superdry, but the flavor profile is great.

BRAD Hot, too.

JOAQUÍN Painfully hot—needs more water. Can you try stirring longer to dilute more?

BRAD What if you split the rye with something lower proof?

JILLIAN Like Overholt?

BRAD Like Russell's. Then it will be sweet but not hot.

JOAQUÍN What kind of sugar did you use for the beer syrup?

JILLIAN Superfine.

JOAQUÍN I'd try cane instead, and a little more.

Jillian makes another version with two whiskeys and cane syrup.

DAVE Now it's too sweet.

THOMAS I told you fuckers it wasn't dry. A half ounce of sweet in a stirred drink is too much. Let's take it back down.

Alex Day, a former Death & Co bartender and now co-owner of the bar, lives in Los Angeles, has stopped in for the tasting and is put on the spot to make a drink. He makes a drink and passes it around.

ALEX There might be sherry in my cocktail. Hold your surprise.

JILLIAN This is the first time Alex has used sherry in a drink. Be nice.

ALEX So this is grapefruit, lemon, dry sack, Perry's Tot, simple.

JILLIAN It will be nice to mix it up by putting some lower-alcohol sherry cocktails on the menu. Most of our drinks kick your ass hard.

PHIL I feel like it's a little abrasive. The sherry up front is nice, but the second wave ends bitter. Gin and sherry are banging heads. Let one dominate the other.

BRAD I don't think the Tot and sherry are playing well together. What about Old Tom? Something sweeter, rounder, not as forceful.

Alex tries another version with a new gin.

PHIL It's nice but needs a bump. A dash or two of Ango?

JILLIAN Ango is too clove-y. Needs something more interesting than that.

Alex adds tiki bitters to his next version.

PHIL Something went really wrong there. It's amazing what a dash of bitters can do to a drink.

ALEX Ango makes everything better. I'll use that.

TASTING AND EVALUATING COCKTAILS

It's very easy to pour a few ounces of booze into a mixing glass or shaking tin and call it a cocktail. Sometimes that cocktail will even be delicious, but more often it will taste like what it is: a random assortment of liquids that's more or less palatable.

The drinks that enjoy a long, sometimes immortal lifetime among the world's canon of classic cocktails—and those that make their way onto the menu at Death & Co—are born from a combination of careful thought, applied knowledge, tireless trial and error, and, sometimes, informed dumb luck.

Within the genesis of every new drink lies an important question: are you trying to present a new idea in cocktail form, or are you creating just for the sake of creation? If the latter, it's probably not going to be very good. It will lack the soul that all of the best drinks possess. A successful drink needs a focus, be it an inspiring ingredient, a new flavor combination, or a thematic idea, and sometimes employs a combination of these.

At Death & Co, our bartenders arrive at new cocktails using various strategies and tricks (more on these in a bit), but before any bartender—professional or otherwise—begins working on new drinks, he or she must first have a thorough understanding of some core principles. Chief among them is balance.

Cocktails are, above anything else, about balancing aggressive flavors and ingredients. The combination of sour, sweet, and strong is the three-legged stool of any drink. If one leg is too long or short, the drink will topple and be ill suited to its purpose. The margin of error between bad, good, and great is maddeningly fickle and sometimes amazingly thin, but a well-balanced cocktail will at least ensure a drink that's pleasant to consume.

When considering balance, we break drinks down, rather loosely, into three families: sours, old-fashioned-style cocktails, and Manhattan- or martini-style cocktails.

SOURS

With three basic elements—strong (liquor), sour (citrus), and sweet (sugar of some sort)—the basic sour formula of two parts strong to one part each sour and sweet is the foundation for almost every cocktail involving citrus, and it's a platform on which we create countless drinks. The magic comes in the nuance, increasing one element or another by a small amount. We enjoy our sours with slightly less sweetener and a touch more sourness than some, though never to the point of being too tart. To get an idea of how these three basic elements influence a sour, let's do an experiment.

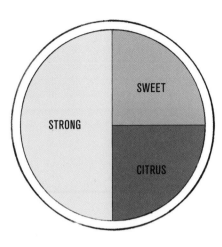

··· The Goldilocks Experiment 1 ···
The Daiquiri, Three Ways

The best litmus test for a bartender's craft is a daiquiri. A simple drink (rum, fresh lime juice, and sugar), the daiquiri is the perfect vehicle for testing the ability to make a properly balanced drink, as it's very obvious when one is made incorrectly. But reading about balance is rather dry and in no way delicious. It's more fun to *experience* balance by having a drink (or three) to taste the difference between what we deem too sweet, too tart, and just right. So we recommend that you make three daiquiris using the following recipes. Be careful with your measurements, as the variations in measurements between the three versions is small, and the flavor of each drink will be significantly altered if you're off by even the smallest amount. If after tasting all three drinks you think we're crazy and prefer one of the other daiquiris, that's just fine: everyone has a different palate. That's part of what makes cocktails fun. Of course, you'll want to use the same type of rum for all three versions. We recommend Caña Brava or Flor de Caña extra-dry white rum.

DAIQUIRI 1: TOO SWEET

2 OUNCES HIGH-QUALITY WHITE RUM
¾ OUNCE FRESH LIME JUICE
1 OUNCE SIMPLE SYRUP (PAGE 277)
GARNISH: 1 LIME WEDGE

Shake all the ingredients with ice, then strain into a coupe. Garnish with the lime wedge.

DAIQUIRI 2: TOO TART

2 OUNCES HIGH-QUALITY WHITE RUM
1 OUNCE FRESH LIME JUICE
½ OUNCE SIMPLE SYRUP (PAGE 277)
GARNISH: 1 LIME WEDGE

Shake all the ingredients with ice, then strain into a coupe. Garnish with the lime wedge.

DAIQUIRI 3: JUST RIGHT

2 OUNCES HIGH-QUALITY WHITE RUM
1 OUNCE FRESH LIME JUICE
¾ OUNCE SIMPLE SYRUP (PAGE 277)
GARNISH: 1 LIME WEDGE

Shake all the ingredients with ice, then strain into a coupe. Garnish with the lime wedge.

OLD-FASHIONED-STYLE COCKTAILS

Styles of cocktail that don't contain a sour element can still suffer from imbalance. An old-fashioned is another simple recipe on the surface: booze of any kind (rye whiskey in this case), a small proportion of sugar, bitters, and citrus twists. (For our old-fashioned recipe, see page 147.)

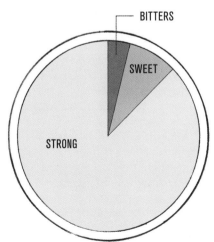

In an old-fashioned, balance manifests in a different way than in a sour. It's all about enhancing the flavor of the base spirit in a pronounced and focused way while rounding off the edges, making it easier to consume than straight booze. Add just a bit too much sweetener and the drink tastes bland. Skip the bitters and it's just sweet. And an old-fashioned without a twist of citrus (we prefer ours with both lemon and orange twists) lacks the bright aroma that will lighten the drink's booziness. As for forgoing the whiskey, we can't help you there. Have a beer or something.

MANHATTAN- AND MARTINI-STYLE COCKTAILS

Manhattans and martinis are somewhat similar to old-fashioneds, but fortified wine (usually vermouth) replaces the sweetener, typically in larger proportions. The same principles apply (enhancing the base spirit while rounding its edges), but the bitters or bittering ingredients serve a more important function in bridging the other flavors.

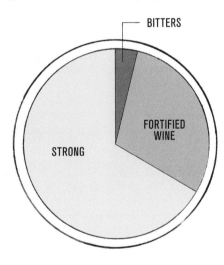

··· The Goldilocks Experiment 2 ···
The Manhattan, Three Ways

Let's get back to drinking. Achieving perfect balance in a well-made Manhattan is one of the greatest cocktail accomplishments. Beyond accurate measurement, it requires a thoughtful consideration of every single ingredient in the drink and how they fit together. At Death & Co, our standard Manhattan recipe contains Rittenhouse 100 rye matched with our House Sweet Vermouth (page 284) and a couple of dashes of Angostura bitters. There's nothing revolutionary here, but we love the balance between those three ingredients: the rye takes center stage, but the vermouth shares the spotlight, offering a round texture and extra depth of flavor. The bitters connect them harmoniously and add just a hint of spicy bite. Although it's unquestionably a stiff drink, it's a balanced recipe. If you were to make it any boozier, it would taste like diluted whiskey. And without bitters, it just wouldn't make sense.

MANHATTAN 1: TOO BOOZY

2½ OUNCES RITTENHOUSE 100 RYE

½ OUNCE HOUSE SWEET VERMOUTH (PAGE 284)

2 DASHES ANGOSTURA BITTERS

GARNISH: 1 BRANDIED CHERRY

Stir all the ingredients over ice, then strain into a coupe. Garnish with the cherry.

MANHATTAN 2: NO CONNECTION

2½ OUNCES RITTENHOUSE 100 RYE

¾ OUNCE HOUSE SWEET VERMOUTH (PAGE 284)

GARNISH: 1 BRANDIED CHERRY

Stir all the ingredients over ice, then strain into a coupe. Garnish with the cherry.

MANHATTAN 3: JUST RIGHT

2½ OUNCES RITTENHOUSE 100 RYE

¾ OUNCE HOUSE SWEET VERMOUTH (PAGE 284)

2 DASHES ANGOSTURA BITTERS

GARNISH: 1 BRANDIED CHERRY

Stir all the ingredients over ice, then strain into a coupe. Garnish with the cherry.

GARNISHES

Balance extends into garnishes. Placing a wedge of citrus on the rim of a glass offers the drinker an opportunity to adjust the cocktail to his or her liking: with a quick squeeze, tartness levels can be increased as desired. But a garnish also imparts aroma, a valuable but often overlooked component of balance. A lime wedge, for example, has an intense fragrance, creating a greater impression of freshness and acidity, and as the first sip is taken, its aroma will mingle with the liquid and impact the overall composition of the drink. In boozy cocktails, a strategic garnish can have an even greater impact. Citrus twists have the advantage of offering the suggestion of acidity in a drink without contributing excessive flavor. A martini garnished with a lemon twist isn't lemony, but its flavors are certainly brightened.

Throughout the more than four hundred recipes that begin on page 138, you'll probably notice that the basic formulas outlined above reveal themselves time and time again. When making a fizz-style drink, for example, we start with a sour template but decrease the citrus a bit, serve it in a fizz glass, and top it with club soda. For a collins, a fizz is poured over ice in a taller glass. Swizzles and tiki-style drinks are centered around aggressive ingredients, but they too are fundamentally sours. And although many of our old-fashioned variations may seem very much unlike an old-fashioned, if you parse the ingredients, you'll spot the classic formula. And almost any of our cocktails combining a strong spirit with fortified wine and bitters can be traced back to the Manhattan or martini.

BEYOND BALANCE

Once you can identify a balanced drink—and adjust one that isn't—creating new cocktails gets a hell of a lot easier. But before you begin throwing a half dozen (or more) ingredients into the mixing glass, consider this: in cocktails, simplicity will always reign supreme (though you won't always get that impression when looking at our recipes). There will never be a drink that can match the elegance of a well-made gin martini (page 145). A daiquiri (page 141) will refresh your mind and senses better than a

day at the spa. And nothing is better before a meal than a Negroni (page 147). These are just facts, people.

Knowing this—that all of the finest drinks are profoundly delicious because of their simplicity—we approach the creation of new cocktails first as an exercise in moderation. After defining for ourselves what the focus of the cocktail will be, we begin to carefully—and intellectually—assemble its elements. We ask ourselves what will go best with a key ingredient, and more importantly, we strive to understand why certain ingredients pair well. A lot of liquor can be wasted when developing cocktails, so we try to have a solid estimation of how it will all come together before we start actually fiddling around with the ingredients.

This process is informed by a fanatical interest in ingredients and an ever-evolving awareness of how they play with one another. From this foundation, we begin trying out ideas. There are times when simplicity gets trumped by an exciting combination of many ingredients, often used in very small quantities. But there is a fine line between complexity and extravagance. As more ingredients get added to a drink, we always ask ourselves if they belong: Are they adding something to the drink, or just resulting in a complicated soup? More often than not, less is more: it's easy to make a ten-ingredient drink taste like nothing (or worse) and incredibly difficult to turn that same number of ingredients into something greater than the sum of its parts. When you see recipes in this book with long lists of ingredients, it's hopefully because we accomplished just that.

It's much easier to describe and discuss the various components of a drink—which range from texture and temperature to the specific aromas and flavors present—when you have a common language to work from. Use the wheel at right to enhance your cocktail vocabulary—or simply to help you decide what you're in the mood to drink.

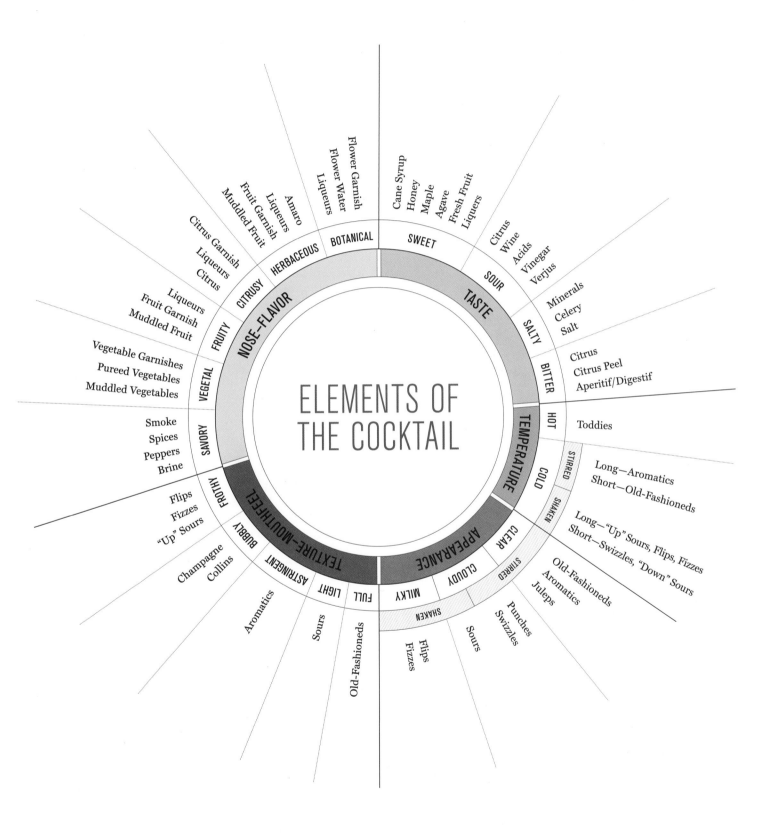

ELEMENTS OF THE COCKTAIL

Flower Garnish
Flower Water
Liqueurs

BOTANICAL

SWEET

Cane Syrup
Honey
Maple
Agave
Fresh Fruit
Liquers

Amaro
Liqueurs
Fruit Garnish
Muddled Fruit

HERBACEOUS

Citrus
Wine
Acids
Vinegar
Verjus

SOUR

Citrus Garnish
Liqueurs
Citrus

CITRUSY

TASTE

Minerals
Celery
Salt

SALTY

Liqueurs
Fruit Garnish
Muddled Fruit

FRUITY

NOSE-FLAVOR

Citrus
Citrus Peel
Aperitif/Digestif

BITTER

Vegetable Garnishes
Pureed Vegetables
Muddled Vegetables

VEGETAL

HOT

Toddies

TEMPERATURE

Smoke
Spices
Peppers
Brine

SAVORY

COLD

STIRRED

Long—Aromatics
Short—Old-Fashioneds

Flips
Fizzes
"Up" Sours

FROTHY

SHAKEN

Long—"Up" Sours, Flips, Fizzes
Short—Swizzles, "Down" Sours

Champagne
Collins

BUBBLY

TEXTURE-MOUTHFEEL

CLEAR

STIRRED

Old-Fashioneds
Aromatics
Juleps

Aromatics

ASTRINGENT

CLOUDY

Punches
Swizzles

Sours

LIGHT

APPEARANCE

SHAKEN

Sours

Old-Fashioneds

FULL

MILKY

Flips
Fizzes

FOUR STRATEGIES FOR
CREATING DRINKS

The creative origins of many of the drinks we've created at Death & Co can be traced back to a few simple strategies.

....

MR. POTATO HEAD: PLUG AND PLAY

Phil Ward coined the term *Mr. Potato Head* around the time he was developing Death & Co's inaugural menu. Phil's head

is filled with hundreds, if not thousands, of specs: ratios of ingredients that are the basis of countless classic cocktails. By substituting one or more elements from an existing template with a different ingredient, like changing Mr. Potato Head's nose—or even swapping out an eye for his nose—you can create a variation that tastes drastically different. In Phil's words, "Every great drink is the blueprint for many other drinks." An early example of this technique can be found in his Scotch Lady (page 202), in which he swaps the gin in the classic Pink Lady recipe (page 148) for blended Scotch. He used a similar substitution in his Pete's Word (page 202), a variation on the Last Word (page 144), a not-quite-classic drink that dates back to the 1950s.

The easiest way to get accustomed to the Mr. Potato Head technique is to start with a simple, spirituous cocktail and play around with different base spirits. Beginning on page 255, you'll find variations on the classic Sazerac (page 151) made with cognac, rum, gin, numerous styles of whiskey, and even aquavit. The Negroni (page 147) is another favorite template for Mr. Potato Head variations: Like apple brandy? Try the Vanderbilt (page 259). More a fan of tequila? Make yourself a Range Life (page 259).

Keep in mind that not every substitution should be one for one. Some spirits are more alcoholic or assertive than others, and amounts of these, or the other ingredients in the cocktail, will need to be increased or decreased accordingly to restore balance.

After you're comfortable with swapping base spirits, try substituting modifiers, then fresh juices, sweeteners, and bitters. You'll find that certain ingredients and flavors across these categories work better together; for example, tequila loves lime, while whiskey prefers lemon. To help you get started, we created a chart of some of our favorite flavor pairings; see page 123.

DRESSING UP NAKED DRINKS: A LITTLE SOMETHING EXTRA

Another easy way to create new drinks is to transform a simple, standard (aka naked) cocktail by adding an extra layer of complexity. One of our favorite ways to do this is by infusing additional flavors into base spirits or modifiers. With this approach, you can transform the flavor profile of the drink without altering the other ingredients. A great example of this is the Chamomile Julep (page 242), in which rye infused with chamomile tea turns the boozy Derby-day favorite into something more elegant. And we love jalapeño-infused blanco tequila (page 279) and use it often to add an invigorating kick to popular tequila drinks, as in the Spicy Paloma (page 188).

Flavored syrups, which are basically sweet infusions, are also fair game for enhancing naked drinks. In his Boukman Daiquiri (page 261), Alex Day swaps Cinnamon Bark Syrup for simple syrup in a daiquiri variation, making a traditionally warm-weather cocktail ready for wintertime drinking.

We also add small amounts of intensely flavored modifiers to increase the depth and complexity of otherwise simple classics. Phil's Bitter French (page 220) turns the classic French 75 into an aperitif with the addition of a small amount of Campari. The daiquiri is particularly well suited to this technique, as seen in the Jovencourt Daiquiri (page 262), in which just ¼ ounce of mezcal turns an otherwise standard daiquiri into something smoky and beguiling. Another good example is the D.W.B. (page 261), a daiquiri made extra-funky with the addition of intense Batavia arrack.

To take this idea a step further, we often combine an infusion with an extra modifier, as in the Short Rib (page 187), a margarita (page 145) made with jalapeño-infused tequila and a small splash of syrupy pomegranate

molasses, or Thomas Waugh's Coffee and Cigarettes (page 205), a variation on the Rob Roy (page 150) made with coffee liqueur.

SPLITTING HAIRS: TWO IS BETTER THAN ONE

Using a combination of base spirits in a cocktail seems like an obvious springboard for creativity now, but when we opened Death & Co, few bartenders were doing this. Phil was the first at our bar to experiment with split bases. His Martica (page 218) was his initial foray into this technique; it includes 1 ounce each of cognac and Jamaican rum as the base for a variation on the Martinez (page 145; but as you'll see, our house Martinez uses both a split base and a split modifier). Another early example is the Wicked Kiss (page 209), in which the base for the Widow's Kiss—a nineteenth-century drink made with calvados—is split into equal parts of rye and apple brandy.

Although very few classic cocktails feature split bases (the cognac- and rum-based Between the Sheets is one exception), the practice has a long history in tiki cocktails, in which two or more rums are often blended to achieve a more complex (and extra-boozy) foundation. One night, our in-house tiki expert, Brian Miller, decided to use the same tactic on a whiskey-based drink he was asked to make on the fly. His Conference (page 270)—an old-fashioned variation made with equal parts rye, bourbon, calvados, and cognac—was a revelation to us all, and soon split bases were showing up in many of our new drinks.

When implemented poorly, multiple base spirits can turn a drink into a muddy mess, as in Long Island Iced

Tea, so this method requires more attention than just simple division. Even if two spirits taste fine together, they will often clash when combined with other ingredients in a cocktail. Sometimes you need to use more of one spirit and less of the other, or one brand of a spirit will work well while another falls completely flat. Patient experimentation is key. And be prepared to be more surprised by what does work than what doesn't. On paper, aquavit and tequila sound like bitter rivals, but after trying several brands and amounts, Jillian Vose was able to make them best friends in her Enemy Lines (page 256), a variation on the Sazerac (page 151).

After you grow comfortable with splitting base spirits, try playing around with split modifiers and sweeteners. Eventually you'll be able to adapt drink recipes extensively, splitting multiple components and watching the ingredient count add up, as in the Shattered Glasser (page 194), which contains two base spirits and four modifiers.

CONCEPT DRINKS: THE ZIGGY STARDUST OF COCKTAILS

Sometimes a new drink will be born out of a simple stroke of inspiration, be it an ingredient, a flavor combination, a song, a movie, a mood, or just about anything else. Such cocktails, created to express a unified idea, are what we call concept drinks.

Whereas Mr. Potato Head, dressing up naked drinks, and splitting base spirits and modifiers are all ways to remodel existing cocktails, concept drinks are created from the ground up. As a result, they require a lot of patience and tinkering to get right. To best illustrate the process of developing a concept drink, we asked Brad Farran, our resident conceptual cocktail artist, to explain the process behind a few of his concept drinks:

JULIUS ORANGE {*page 172*}

"I loved Orange Julius as a kid and wanted to re-create that flavor in a sophisticated cocktail. For a base spirit I started with dry curaçao, which has an orangey flavor, obviously, but also a strong vanilla note, as does an Orange Julius. Then I started playing around with rums as a modifier, particularly rums that could enhance that vanilla flavor. It's fun to use a modifier as a base spirit and vice versa. After that it was a matter of adding other elements to balance it out: lemon juice for acidity, a little bit of cream for richness, and a teaspoon of Vanilla Syrup (page 277) to really pump up that flavor. Originally I didn't include orange bitters in the drink, but when I added them it made it taste a lot more like a cocktail and less like something you might buy at the mall."

CRANE KICK {*page 198*}

"I love the original *Karate Kid* movie and decided to create a drink based on Daniel's signature move. I asked myself, What does the name imply? The answer: Japanese whiskey. I like pairing whiskey with tropical flavors, so I went in a tiki direction. I tried to find a modifier that would showcase the Yamazaki whiskey's flavor profile, and found it, of all places, in coconut liqueur. Sweetness came from orgeat, another tiki staple, and acidity from a combination of orange juice and lemon juice. At that point the drink tasted fine, but it wasn't very complex. A teaspoon of peaty Scotch fixed that, resulting in a drink that was graceful yet deadly."

GOOD HUMOR {*page 157*}

"I woke up one day wanting one of those strawberry short-cake ice cream bars I'd bought as a kid from the Good Humor truck. I couldn't find one, so I decided to turn my craving into a cocktail. I knew the hardest part would be getting the malty flavor of the coating into the drink, so I reached for an unaged genever as a base spirit, but it was too malty on its own. So I split the base three ways with bourbon, unaged genever, and barrel-aged genever, which did the trick. Heavy cream and orgeat provided the richness, and Vanilla Syrup (page 277) added the ice cream flavor. All that was left was the strawberry. It took only a half teaspoon of strawberry liqueur to get all of the flavor I needed."

Pit Stop Flip, page 246

FLAVOR BUDDIES

We're constantly discovering new and surprising flavor combinations at the bar. Below you'll find some of our all-time favorite affinities between various base spirits, modifiers, and fresh ingredients.

BASE SPIRITS

GIN Everything (almost), herbs, citrus, aperitif wine, dry vermouth, blanc vermouth, Chartreuse, honey, calvados, bitters, champagne, ginger

VODKA Anything with flavor

AQUAVIT Gin, pepper, pineapple, celery, lemon, blanc vermouth, rye, sweet vermouth, dry vermouth, amari, chamomile, ginger

BOURBON Crème de cacao, honey, grapefruit, figs, apple, cognac, chamomile, rye

CALVADOS Chamomile, clove

APPLEJACK Smoky Scotch, lager

RUM Other rums, maple syrup, coffee, citrus (lime especially), herbs (mint, basil), ginger, curry leaf

TEQUILA Grapefruit, black pepper, yellow Chartreuse, salt, jalapeño, Thai basil, kumquats

MEZCAL Tequila (reposado), bell pepper, strawberry, Suze

SCOTCH (SMOKY) Pineapple, mint, lime

SCOTCH Apples and pears, cinnamon

JAPANESE WHISKEY pineapple, coconut

MODIFIERS

SHERRY Everything (almost)

DRY SHERRY Gin, cocchi Americano

AMONTILLADO SHERRY American whiskey, citrus, gin, cognac

OLOROSO SHERRY Blended Scotch

DRY VERMOUTH Peach, apricot

CARPANO ANTICA FORMULA Coffee

SWEET VERMOUTH Chai tea

BLANC VERMOUTH Chamomile, watermelon, sage

CAMPARI Chocolate, raspberries, sloe gin

APEROL Blanco tequila, Lustau East India solera sherry, mango, grapefruit

GREEN CHARTREUSE Coffee, chocolate

YELLOW CHARTREUSE Strawberry

AMARO Peach

CYNAR Crème de cacao, celery

ST-GERMAIN Everything

ANGOSTURA BITTERS Aged spirits

ORANGE BITTERS Citrus

OTHER INGREDIENTS

GRAPEFRUIT Cinnamon

CELERY Apple

VANILLA Passion fruit, pineapple

STRAWBERRIES Black pepper, cinnamon

CINNAMON Pineapple, pear, vanilla

CUCUMBER Mint, sage

PEACH Honey

PINAPPLE Sage

PEAR Orgeat

KAFFIR Cucumber

SNAP PEAS Gin

CHAMOMILE Yellow Chartreuse, peach

CHAMPAGNE COCKTAILS
{$16}

RADIO DAYS
Beefeater Gin, Sobea Genever,
Apricot, Acacia Honey Syrup, Fresh
Lemon Juice, Angostura Bitters,
Muddled Orange, Champagne

"Remember, gentlemen,
it's not just France
we're fighting for, it's
Champagne!"
...
— WINSTON CHURCHILL

PARLEY
WITH THE ENEMY
Coconut-Infused El Dorado 15
year Rum, Fresh Lime Juice, Fresh
Pineapple Juice, Cinnamon Syrup,
Champagne

THE BITTENBENDER
Russell's Reserve 10 year Bourbon,
Cognac-infused Campari,
Ginger Syrup, Fresh Lemon Juice,
Muddled Raspberries, Citrus Peel,
Champagne

PUNCH
{$60 SERVES 4-6}

CLASSICS
{$14}

DEATH: "There are better things in the world than
alcohol, Albert."
ALBERT: "Oh, yes, Sir. But alcohol sort of compensates
for not getting them."

NAMING DRINKS

We'd be thrilled if cocktails could somehow name themselves. While it might sound like a badge of honor to christen one's hard-earned original creation, coming up with a drink's name is usually the most frustrating part of the process. It's not as easy as, say, naming a baby or a car. You can't call a new cocktail Austin and move on. Nay, cocktail names need to be unique. For better or worse, there is only one Manhattan, and there will always be only one Slippery Nipple.

Most of our drinks are perfected long before they have a name, with the exception of a concept drink (explained on page 120). If bartenders fail to name their new creations (or give them names inappropriate for public consumption) before our next menu is finalized, the task falls to the head bartender, who often has to assign names to a queue of drinks, Ellis Island style, minutes before the menu is printed.

A very informal audit of our database of more than four hundred original Death & Co cocktails reveals a few commonly used drink-naming strategies.

THE MOVIE NOD Usually a reference to either lowbrow comedy or art-house cinema—rarely anything in between.

Examples: Crane Kick, Strange Brew, Sergio Leone, Blazing Saddles, Coffee and Cigarettes, Cider House Rules, Fair Lady, and Jack Sparrow Flip

THE NOSTALGIA TRIP Childhood favorites for grown-ups.

Examples: Good Humor, Pink Elephant, Camp Council, Little Engine, Dick and Jane, Koko B. Ware, and Rock, Paper, Scissors

THE SCHOLARLY REFERENCE Bartenders showing off how well read they are.

Examples: Dick Brautigan, Night Watch, Sling of Aphrodite, Hadley's Tears, Porfirian Punch, Myra Breckinridge, The Dangerous Summer, Botany of Desire

THE A SIDE A musical reference that most guests will recognize.

Examples: Cinnamon Girl, The Great Pretender, Rebel Rebel, Heart-Shaped Box, Lust for Life Punch, Dolly Dagger

THE B SIDE An obscure musical reference our guests would love to forget.

Examples: Eagle-Eye Cherry, Dr. Feelgood, Sade's Taboo, Hallyday, Nina's Moan

THE GENUS Various cocktails in the same category; often used for variations on classic drinks.

Examples: Cobra Verde, Coralillo, Vipera, Puerto Rican Racer (all variations on the Diamondback)

THE NAME DROP Shout-outs to our heroes, friends, and—perhaps too often—ourselves.

Examples: Gonzalez, Light and Day, Last Ward, Shattered Glasser, Ty Cobbler, the Bittenbender

THE INSIDE JOKE Probably best not to ask.

Examples: Slap 'n' Pickle, Stolen Huffy, Angie's Secret, 202 Steps, Sea B3, B.A.F.

--- *Death & Co's Worst Drink Names, Selected by the Staff* ---

DAI, DAI MY DARLING	MEXI-GIN MARTINI	SHORT RIB
DON'T SIT UNDER THE APPLE TREE	MIG ROYALE	SIPPING SEASONS
ENCHANTED ORCHARD	MRS. DOYLE	SLING OF APHRODITE
FAIR FAULT	PADDY MELT	SUNSET AT GOWANUS
GLANDULA DEL MONO	PELÉE'S BLOOD	VEJK SLING
LE BATELEUR	SADE'S TABOO	TUESDAYS WITH MOLE
LIGHT AND DAY	SENTIMENTAL JOURNEY	YEOMEN WARDER

THE REGULARS
AMADOR ACOSTA

Amador Acosta has cooked in some of New York City's finest restaurants, from Gilt with Paul Liebrandt to Tailor with Sam Mason, and is currently the kitchen operations manager and corporate chef at Michael White's Altamarea restaurant group.

Bartenders take a lot of cues and inspiration from chefs, but the bartenders at Death & Co teach me new ways to marry flavors in the kitchen. It's fun to sit at the bar and become part of the creative process. I'll throw out a couple of ingredients or flavors, and they'll create a new cocktail around them on the spot. They talk about balance, textures, and flavors the same way chefs do in the kitchen. Sometimes they engage me about a dish I'm working on and give me a new perspective on how to put it together.

In many ways Death & Co has become one of the city's centers of creativity. The bartenders love to experiment and are not afraid to fail. More importantly, they help each other work through ideas. This is how the best restaurant kitchens work, as well. At Death & Co, the customer becomes a key component of the process. The bartenders will share drinks they're working on and ask guests for feedback, then make it again. The more people you let into the process, the better the final product becomes. Nothing is proprietary, and there's no need to worry about your idea getting picked up and improved upon by the next guy.

The most important part of the creative process is having a firm understanding of the classics. Without this knowledge, creativity becomes novelty, not innovation. The reason the bartenders at Death & Co excel at innovation is because they have such a strong skill set and understanding of the classics.

I usually come to Death & Co after I'm done in the kitchen for the night, so I get there not long before last call. The old-fashioned is my default cocktail. It has a balance of bitter, sweet, and acidity that I appreciate. Tiki drinks have also taught me a lot about balance. With so many flavors and ingredients coming together in a glass, they are exceptionally hard to make right, yet a properly made tiki drink strikes a harmony you want to keep experiencing.

I tend to avoid clear, stirred drinks. They typically don't have enough going on for me. But one night Alex introduced me to the White Negroni. It had that balance of bitterness, booziness, and sweetness that I love. I'd already drunk so much that I couldn't finish my Negroni, so I dumped it into my coffee thermos and threw it in my backpack. The next night I pulled it out at a restaurant and poured it over ice. It was the ultimate roadie drink.

WHITE NEGRONI

1½ OUNCES FORDS GIN

¾ OUNCE DOLIN BLANC VERMOUTH

¾ OUNCE SUZE SAVEUR D'AUTREFOIS LIQUEUR

GARNISH: 1 LEMON TWIST

Stir all the ingredients over ice, then strain into a double rocks glass over 1 large ice cube. Garnish with the lemon twist.

PUNCH

In early 2007, we read a lengthy piece in the *New York Times* comparing the cocktail scenes in New York City and London. The article started with the proclamation—by an esteemed New York bartender, no less—that "London is the best cocktail city in the world right now." Phil and I (Dave) had never been to London, so a few months after Death & Co opened we planned a whirlwind tour of London bars to confirm or deny the claim.

The trip influenced more than one aspect of Death & Co. After three days of drinking our way around the city's best bars—we checked off some twenty-five establishments in all—we agreed with much of what the article said. The baseline for craft cocktails in London was indeed higher than NYC, in that there were more bars using fresh juice, good ice, and intriguing ingredients than our fair city. Still, these were familiar precepts—and ones we already adhered to at D&C. But London also brought us a couple of revelations.

First, we'd been told by New York's cocktail cognoscenti that a menu should contain no more than twelve drinks. Any more, they warned, and customers wouldn't be able to digest the content. Plus, the bar wouldn't be able to maintain a high level of quality and consistency. But in London, cocktail menus were crazy long. Many were exhaustive volumes filled with pages upon pages of drinks, mostly classic cocktails. We thought that if those London joints were able to manage their monumental menus, we could do the same but with our own original drinks. Upon our return, the menu at Death & Co swelled from ten drinks to sixty.

Our second revelation was punch service. At the Hawksmoor, a steakhouse with a bitchin' cocktail program, we watched as antique punch bowls were brought around to tables and guests were allowed to ladle themselves a drink. We loved the conviviality of punch service. There's something special about sharing the same drink with your friends and how punch passes the hospitality torch: order a bowl of punch for your table, and you become the host.

Punch predates the cocktail. British soldiers first created it in India in the sixteenth century and brought it back to the United Kingdom, where it became the preferred method of imbibing for some two centuries and spread famously throughout the world. However, nobody in the United States was making traditional punch at the time. What a shame.

Back at Death & Co, we started hunting for vintage bowls while Phil researched punch and began developing recipes. We added a few punches to our next menu, and guests began ordering it in waves. One bowl would go out, other tables would gawk, and the bar would soon be filled with the sound of clinking punch cups. We quickly received a lot of press for our punch program, and other bars took notice. Soon punch was popping up everywhere and being recognized for what it is: a communal drinking experience with deep roots in cocktail history—and fun.

Whenever we develop a new punch recipe, we follow a few guidelines:

- Classic punch contains five elements: spirits, sugar, citrus, water, and spice. The word *punch* is said to be derived from the Hindi word *panch*, which means "five," though recent scholarship calls this into question. (For a full history lesson on punch, read David Wondrich's thoroughly researched book on the topic; see page 287.) Tea was traditionally used as the spice component, so we often use a tea-infused spirit or vermouth, as in Mother's Ruin Punch (page 237).
- Sweetener can be added in solid form (granulated sugar or sugar cubes) or as a liquid, in the form of syrups. When creating Death & Co's first punch recipes, Phil came up with a method in which he muddled sugar cubes with club soda to make an instant simple syrup. He says using cubes makes measuring the sugar easier.
- Punch is always stirred. This breaks the rule of citrus = shaken, but we often finish punch with club soda or sparkling wine to add effervescence, so shaking isn't required. Instead, the punch is either stirred over ice in a pitcher or rolled (poured back and forth) between two pitchers with ice before straining it into the bowl.
- Punch is almost always served over one large block of ice. This slows down dilution while keeping the drink cold.
- Garnishes are floated in the punch bowl to be added to drinks as guests please.

Batching Cocktails

Making individual cocktails for people, one at a time, is an awful way to spend a dinner party. For entertaining large crowds, we fully support the practice of batching cocktails: premixing them to the extent possible a few hours ahead of time (or even the night before), then chilling the batch and making individual cocktails to order.

Most of batching involves simple math: Take a cocktail recipe, convert ounces to cups (or quarts or even gallons if serving a big crowd), mix, and chill. But there are a few rules of thumb to follow:

- **Proportions:** If you're preparing up to five drinks at a time, the balance won't change dramatically and you can get away with simply multiplying the recipe. But when batching more than five drinks at a time, a funny thing happens with citrus and other acidic ingredients, the sweeteners, and especially the bitters: their effect on the cocktail is enhanced. So you need to use less of these ingredients, by proportion, than in the base recipe. Start with about half the amount called for when you multiply the recipe, then add more to taste.

- **Dilution:** Don't forget that roughly 25 percent of a cocktail is water. If you're mixing ahead of time and refrigerating the batch, dilute it to taste with water just before serving, keeping in mind that any additional dilution that might occur if you're serving it over ice. A batch of stirred, boozy drinks can be diluted ahead of time and stored in the freezer; the alcohol will keep it from freezing. Shaken drinks should be batched without any added water and shaken with ice to order.

- **Bubbles:** Any cocktail that gets topped with champagne or another sparkling beverage is great for batching. Prepare the batch ahead of time without the bubbly ingredient, then add it just before you serve the cocktail to brighten it up.

BARTENDER'S CHOICE

Every night we're asked—dozens of times—to come up with a "bartender's choice" for a guest. If we took this request literally we'd rifle through our giant brain databases and offer the guest whatever cocktail we'd randomly fallen upon. Some bars do just this. But we take the responsibility of choosing a cocktail very seriously, and believe that there's a perfect drink out there for every guest. Finding it, however, requires a few questions and a lot of quick thinking on the part of our bartenders.

The chart below illustrates how Alex Day goes through the process. He generally starts with whatever menu we're serving at the time, then narrows down the choices from there. For brevity's sake, we've listed the specs of each drink in bartender's shorthand: each number represents the quantity (in ounces) of each ingredient, and DB stands for "dash of bitters."

WINTER 2014
DEATH & CO MENU

BELLA LUNA Gin, Shaken; page 154	**EAST INDIA TRADING** Rum, Stirred; page 176	**INGÉNUE** Manhattans; page 267	**PEARLS BEFORE SWINE** Flips & Fizzes; page 246	**SLAP 'N' PICKLE** Aquavit, Shaken; page 254
BLACK MAGIC Brandy, Stirred; page 216	**FIX ME UP** Whiskey, Shaken; page 200	**JIVE TURKEY** Manhattans; page 268	**PELÉE'S BLOOD** Rum, Shaken; page 173	**SOUTHERN EXPOSURE** Agave, Shaken; page 188
BLOODHOUND Punch; page 233	**FLOR DE JEREZ** Rum, Shaken; page 171	**KINGSTON NEGRONI** Negronis; page 259	**PENDENNIS CLUB** Classic; page 148	**STRANGE BREW** Gin, Shaken; page 160
BUMBOO Rum, Stirred; page 176	**GOLDEN BEAUTIFUL** Agave, Shaken; page 184	**KOKO B. WARE** Rum, Shaken; page 173	**PRESSURE DROP** Gin, Stirred; page 169	**STRAW DOG** Whiskey, Shaken; page 202
CHINGON Agave, Shaken; page 182	**GOLDEN GATE** Brandy, Shaken; page 211	**LAST TRAIN TO OAXACA** Agave, Stirred; page 192	**PRIMA CHINA** Agave, Stirred; page 193	**VALLEY OF KINGS** Punch; page 241
CORTADO Rum, Stirred; page 176	**GRAND STREET** Gin, Stirred; page 163	**LITTLE MISS ANNABELLE** Brandy, Shaken; page 213	**QUEEN PALM** Gin, Shaken; page 159	**YAMA BLANCA** Agave, Stirred; page 195
CURE FOR PAIN Whiskey, Stirred; page 205	**GREEN FLASH** Sparkling; page 223	**MORFEO** Sparkling; page 226	**RACKETEER** Juleps; page 244	**ZIHUATANEJO** Juleps; page 244
DICK AND JANE Sparkling; page 221	**HOI POLLOI** Brandy, Shaken; page 211	**NORTH GARDEN** Old-Fashioneds; page 273	**ROBERT JOHNSON SWIZZLE** Swizzles; page 251	
DOUBLE BARREL Juleps; page 242	**HONSHU** Gin, Shaken; page 200	**ONE, ONE, ONE** Aquavit; page 254	**ROB ROY** Classic; page 150	

BLACK MAGIC Brandy, Stirred; page 216 1, 1, ½, 1 tsp, 1 tsp, absinthe	**CURE FOR PAIN** Whiskey, Stirred; page 205 1½, ½, ½, ½, 1 tsp, 1 tsp	**GRAND STREET** Gin, Stirred; page 163 2, ¾, ¼, 1 tsp, GF twist	**KINGSTON NEGRONI** Negronis; page 259; 1, 1, 1	**ONE, ONE, ONE** Aquavit; page 254 1, 1, 1, DB	**RACKETEER** Juleps; page 244 2, ½, 1 tsp, 1 tsp, 1 DB
BUMBOO Rum, Stirred; page 176 2, 1 tsp, 1 tsp, 3 DB	**DOUBLE BARREL** Juleps; page 242 1½, ½, 1 tsp, 1 tsp, ¼, 4 DB	**INGÉNUE** Manhattans; page 267 2, 1, 1 tsp	**LAST TRAIN TO OAXACA** Agave, Stirred; page 192 1½, ¾, ½, 1 tsp	**PRESSURE DROP** Gin, Stirred; page 169 1½, 1, ½, 1 tsp, 1 DB	**YAMA BLANCA** Agave, Stirred; page 195 1½, ½, ¾, ¼
CORTADO Rum, Stirred; page 176 2, ½, ½, ¼, ½ tsp, 2 DB	**EAST INDIA TRADING** Rum, Stirred; page 176 2, ¾, ½, 2 DB	**JIVE TURKEY** Manhattans; page 268 1, ¾, ¾, ¾, ¼, 1 DB	**NORTH GARDEN** Old-Fashioneds; page 273 1½, ¾, ¼, 1 tsp, 1DB	**PRIMA CHINA** Agave, Stirred; page 193 2, ¾, ¼, 1 barspn, 1 DB	**ZIHUATANEJO** Juleps; page 244 2, 1 tsp, ½ float

GRAND STREET Gin, Stirred; page 163 2, ¾ , ¼, 1 tsp, muddled GF twist; coupe glass	**ONE, ONE, ONE** Aquavit; page 254 1, 1, 1, 1 DB; Nick & Nora glass	**PRESSURE DROP** Gin, Stirred; page 169 1½, 1, ½, 1 tsp, DB; coupe glass

GRAND STREET

ALEX DAY

1 GRAPEFRUIT TWIST

2 OUNCES BEEFEATER LONDON DRY GIN

¾ OUNCE PUNT E MES

¼ OUNCE CYNAR

1 TEASPOON LUXARDO MARASCHINO LIQUEUR

In a mixing glass, gently muddle the grapefruit twist. Add the remaining ingredients and
stir with ice, then strain into a coupe. No garnish.

THE REGULARS

ANTHONY SARNICOLA AND REGINA CONNORS

Anthony Sarnicola currently works as a technical project manager for an investment bank. Regina Connors is an independent consultant working with the financial industry.

ANTHONY My first experience here was not inside the bar. We lived in the neighborhood at the time, and I was out for a walk on a Saturday night. There was a huge line outside and a door guy. I thought that this was one of those places with an annoying door policy; for example, only the pretty people are allowed inside. But after stalking the door for a while, I realized that it was a completely egalitarian process. So I came back on a Wednesday as soon as they opened (6 p.m.), when there was no line. The first thing I noticed was that they had a bunch of ryes behind the bar. I asked the bartender, Joaquín, to make me a few different Manhattans, with a different rye in each. He obliged. My second trip there I ordered another Manhattan. Joaquín asked me if I'd ever had an Old Pal. That was the beginning of the end.

REGINA The first time I came in I'd just arrived home after a long flight. Anthony dragged me over and said, "You've got to taste these drinks."

ANTHONY I remember being served a Fog Cutter that night. I got about a quarter of the way through this tall, seemingly froufrou cocktail and said to Regina, "I must be a lightweight; I'm fucking buzzed already." Brian heard this and laughed, then said, "Dude, there's 6 ounces of rum in that drink."

REGINA Once the bartenders understand your palate, they like to broaden your horizons. I generally like my drinks not too boozy, whether they're shaken or stirred. While I like bitter drinks, Campari is not to my taste—ever. I loathe it. But I have to give the bartenders credit. They love to sneak Campari into drinks, and sometimes it helps me appreciate a new aspect of the spirit.

ANTHONY My usual now: brown, stirred, boozy—up or rocks; don't care.

REGINA I've lived and drunk in this city for decades and have had many fun experiences socializing with strangers. But Death & Co is unique in that the socializing has been around the drinks: the flavors, the shared sips, the shared stories that follow. On so many occasions the bonding led to friendships that lasted beyond the evening.

ANTHONY My favorite moments at Death & Co all revolve around the crowd and the random conversations you have with strangers. You meet people who have come to see what everyone's been talking about, who come to have some transcendent drinking experience. You meet people who are celebrating their twenty-first birthday and have decided that this is where they want to have their first proper cocktail.

REGINA After Death & Co's first anniversary they had some of the regulars' names engraved on silver plaques on the back of the bar stools. Dave grabbed us and went around the bar with a lighter to show us our names.

ANTHONY He held up a lighter under people's asses saying, "Excuse me, excuse me," until he found our stools.

OLD PAL

1½ OUNCES RITTENHOUSE 100 RYE

¾ OUNCE CAMPARI

¾ OUNCE DOLIN DRY VERMOUTH

GARNISH: 1 LEMON TWIST

Stir all the ingredients over ice, then strain into a Nick & Nora glass. Garnish with the lemon twist.

Chapter Five

THE SPECS

CONFERENCE

BRIAN MILLER

This is a tiki drink disguised as an old-fashioned, so it's no surprise that it comes from Brian Miller, Death & Co's resident scalawag and expert on all things Polynesian. One night a waitress asked Brian to make something stirred and boozy, so he took one of tiki's core principles—blending several base spirits to create a new flavor profile—and applied it to whiskey and brandy. It was another breakthrough moment for the bar, and these days it's not unusual to find two or more base spirits in our drinks.

½ OUNCE RITTENHOUSE 100 RYE

½ OUNCE BUFFALO TRACE BOURBON

½ OUNCE CALVADOS

½ OUNCE HINE H COGNAC

1 TEASPOON DEMERARA SYRUP (PAGE 277)

2 DASHES ANGOSTURA BITTERS

1 DASH BITTERMENS XOCOLATL MOLE BITTERS

GARNISH: 1 LEMON TWIST AND 1 ORANGE TWIST

Stir all the ingredients over ice, then strain into a double rocks glass over 1 large ice cube. Garnish with the lemon and orange twists.

The 450-plus recipes that follow represent most of the body of work we've produced at Death & Co in its first six years of business. If you follow a recipe to the letter, you should end up with a drink that equals one we'd serve at the bar. But if you like your cocktails a little sweeter or drier, can't find a particular bourbon, or are fresh out of Demerara Syrup, fret not: these specs are now yours to tweak, adapt, and overhaul as you please.

Because we view cocktails as formulas, we present ingredients added at the same time in a certain order. In almost all cases, they are arranged as follows:

- Rims, rinses, and other ingredients used in advance, such as muddled ingredients
- Base spirits
- Modifiers
- Fresh juices
- Sweeteners
- Oddball ingredients, such as egg, cream, or herbs
- Bitters
- Toppers, such as champagne or club soda
- Garnishes

CHAPTER CONTENTS

Generally speaking, we've organized these recipes by spirit, then by preparation method. In some instances we've grouped families of cocktails together into more specific categories (i.e., Old-Fashioned or Negroni variations). Here's an at-a-glance guide to the recipes that follow:

Classic and Vintage

The label "classic" gets attached to too many drinks—an old drink isn't necessarily a classic. We prefer to make a distinction between "classic" and "vintage" cocktails. In our view, to be deemed a classic a cocktail needs to have been both popular and pervasive since its invention. An esoteric recipe dug up from an old bar book isn't a classic; it's vintage. For example, the Last Word (page 144) had its moment, followed by a prolonged absence from cocktail culture, and has only recently become popular again. The Manhattan (page 145), on the other hand, was an immediate hit and has been ever since, so it's a classic. That said, the permanent "Classics" section on our cocktail menu contains our bartenders' interpretations and adaptations of both classics and vintage drinks.

In many cases, our recipes for classic and vintage cocktails that follow deviate from the original formulas. As palates evolve and new ingredients become available, we continuously update and tweak our specs. And although we're historically minded, we don't pretend to be historians. The origins of many classic cocktails are highly debatable at best, so we'll let these drinks speak for themselves.

20TH CENTURY

1½ OUNCES BEEFEATER LONDON DRY GIN

¾ OUNCE MARIE BRIZARD WHITE CRÈME DE CACAO

¾ OUNCE COCCHI AMERICANO

¾ OUNCE LEMON JUICE

Shake all the ingredients with ice, then double strain into a coupe. No garnish.

....

AIRMAIL

1 OUNCE RON DEL BARRILITO 3-STAR RUM

½ OUNCE LIME JUICE

½ OUNCE ACACIA HONEY SYRUP (PAGE 276)

DRY CHAMPAGNE

Shake all the ingredients (except the champagne) with ice, then strain into a flute. Top with champagne. No garnish.

....

AVIATION

2 OUNCES PLYMOUTH GIN

½ OUNCE LUXARDO MARASCHINO LIQUEUR

½ TEASPOON CRÈME YVETTE

¾ OUNCE LEMON JUICE

¼ OUNCE SIMPLE SYRUP (PAGE 277)

GARNISH: 1 BRANDIED CHERRY

Shake all the ingredients with ice, then strain into a coupe. Garnish with the cherry.

BAMBOO

1½ OUNCES DOLIN BLANC VERMOUTH

1½ OUNCES BARBADILLO PRINCIPE
    AMONTILLADO SHERRY

½ TEASPOON CANE SUGAR SYRUP (PAGE 276)

1 DASH HOUSE ORANGE BITTERS (PAGE 284)

1 DASH ANGOSTURA BITTERS

GARNISH: 1 LEMON TWIST

Stir all the ingredients over ice, then strain into a rocks glass. Garnish with the lemon twist.

. . . .

BEE'S KNEES

2 OUNCES TANQUERAY
    LONDON DRY GIN

¾ OUNCE LEMON JUICE

¾ OUNCE ACACIA HONEY
    SYRUP (PAGE 276)

3 DROPS SCRAPPY'S LAVENDER BITTERS

GARNISH: 1 BRANDIED CHERRY

Shake all the ingredients with ice, then strain into a coupe. Garnish with the cherry.

. . . .

BLOOD AND SAND

1 OUNCE SPRINGBANK 10-YEAR SCOTCH

½ OUNCE CHERRY HEERING

½ OUNCE HOUSE SWEET VERMOUTH (PAGE 284)

¾ OUNCE ORANGE JUICE

½ TEASPOON LEMON JUICE

GARNISH: 1 BRANDIED CHERRY

Shake all the ingredients with ice, then strain into a coupe. Garnish with the cherry.

BOBBY BURNS

2 OUNCES SPRINGBANK 10-YEAR SCOTCH

¾ OUNCE HOUSE SWEET VERMOUTH (PAGE 284)

¼ OUNCE DRAMBUIE

GARNISH: 1 LEMON TWIST

1 DASH ANGOSTURA BITTERS

Stir all the ingredients over ice, then strain into a martini glass. Garnish with the lemon twist.

. . . .

BOULEVARDIER

1½ OUNCES ELIJAH CRAIG 12-YEAR BOURBON

¾ OUNCE HOUSE SWEET VERMOUTH (PAGE 284)

¾ OUNCE CAMPARI

GARNISH: 1 LEMON TWIST

Stir all the ingredients over ice, then strain into a coupe. Garnish with the lemon twist.

. . . .

BROOKLYN

2 OUNCES RITTENHOUSE 100 RYE

¾ OUNCE DOLIN DRY VERMOUTH

¼ OUNCE AMARO CIOCIARO

1 TEASPOON LUXARDO MARASCHINO LIQUEUR

Stir all the ingredients over ice, then strain into a coupe. No garnish.

. . . .

BROWN DERBY

2 OUNCES ELIJAH CRAIG 12-YEAR BOURBON

1 OUNCE GRAPEFRUIT JUICE

1 TEASPOON LEMON JUICE

½ OUNCE ACACIA HONEY SYRUP (PAGE 276)

GARNISH: 1 GRAPEFRUIT TWIST

Shake all the ingredients with ice, then strain into a coupe. Garnish with the grapefruit twist.

....

CAIPIRINHA

6 LIME WEDGES

¾ OUNCE SIMPLE SYRUP (PAGE 277)

1 WHITE SUGAR CUBE

2 OUNCES AVUÁ AMBURANA CACHAÇA

In a shaker, muddle the lime with the simple syrup and sugar cube. Add the cachaça and shake with ice, then dump into a double rocks glass. No garnish.

....

CHAMPS-ÉLYSÉES

2 OUNCES PIERRE FERRAND AMBRE COGNAC

½ OUNCE GREEN CHARTREUSE

¾ OUNCE LEMON JUICE

½ OUNCE CANE SUGAR SYRUP (PAGE 276)

1 DASH ANGOSTURA BITTERS

GARNISH: 1 LEMON TWIST

Shake all the ingredients with ice, then strain into a coupe. Garnish with the lemon twist.

....

CHARLESTON COCKTAIL

½ OUNCE ANCHOR JUNIPERO GIN

½ OUNCE MASSENEZ KIRSCH VIEUX CHERRY
  BRANDY

½ OUNCE DOLIN DRY VERMOUTH

½ OUNCE PUNT E MES

½ OUNCE GABRIEL BOUDIER CURAÇAO

½ OUNCE MARASKA MARASCHINO LIQUEUR

Stir all the ingredients over ice, then strain into a coupe. No garnish.

COBRA'S FANG

1½ OUNCES APPLETON ESTATE RESERVE RUM

¾ OUNCE EL DORADO 151 RUM

1 TEASPOON MASSENEZ CRÈME DE PÊCHE
  PEACH LIQUEUR

2 DASHES VIEUX PONTARLIER ABSINTHE

¾ OUNCE LIME JUICE

½ OUNCE ORANGE JUICE

½ OUNCE PASSION FRUIT SYRUP (PAGE 277)

½ OUNCE CINNAMON BARK SYRUP (PAGE 276)

1 TEASPOON GINGER SYRUP (PAGE 277)

1 DASH ANGOSTURA BITTERS

GARNISH: 1 MINT SPRIG AND 1 LIME WHEEL

Short shake all the ingredients with 3 ice cubes, then strain into a tiki mug filled with crushed ice. Garnish with the mint sprig and lime wheel and serve with a straw.

....

CORPSE REVIVER #2

¾ OUNCE BEEFEATER LONDON DRY GIN

¾ OUNCE COINTREAU

¾ OUNCE LILLET BLANC

2 DASHES VIEUX PONTARLIER ABSINTHE

¾ OUNCE LEMON JUICE

Shake all the ingredients with ice, then strain into a coupe. No garnish.

....

DAIQUIRI

2 OUNCES FLOR DE CAÑA EXTRA-DRY WHITE RUM

1 OUNCE LIME JUICE

½ OUNCE CANE SUGAR SYRUP (PAGE 276)

GARNISH: 1 LIME WEDGE

Shake all the ingredients with ice, then strain into a coupe. Garnish with the lime wedge.

Cobra's Fang, page 141

DARK AND STORMY

2 OUNCES GOSLINGS BLACK SEAL RUM

¾ OUNCE LIME JUICE

1 OUNCE GINGER SYRUP (PAGE 277)

CLUB SODA

GARNISH: 1 LIME WHEEL AND CANDIED GINGER FLAG

In a shaker, combine all the ingredients (except the club soda) and whip (shake with a few pieces of crushed ice just until the ingredients are incorporated). Strain into a highball glass filled with ice cubes. Top with club soda. Garnish with the lime wheel and candied ginger flag and serve with a straw.

DIAMONDBACK

2 OUNCES RITTENHOUSE 100 RYE

½ OUNCE LAIRD'S BONDED APPLE BRANDY

½ OUNCE YELLOW CHARTREUSE

Stir all the ingredients over ice, then strain into a Nick & Nora glass.

....

FANCY-FREE

2 OUNCES RITTENHOUSE 100 RYE

½ OUNCE LUXARDO MARASCHINO LIQUEUR

1 DASH ANGOSTURA BITTERS

1 DASH HOUSE ORANGE BITTERS (PAGE 284)

GARNISH: 1 ORANGE TWIST

Stir all the ingredients over ice, then strain into double rocks glass over 1 large ice cube. Garnish with the orange twist.

....

FITZGERALD

2 OUNCES BEEFEATER LONDON DRY GIN

¾ OUNCE LEMON JUICE

1 OUNCE SIMPLE SYRUP (PAGE 277)

2 DASHES ANGOSTURA BITTERS

GARNISH: 1 LEMON WEDGE

Shake all the ingredients with ice, then strain into a double rocks glass. Garnish with the lemon wedge.

....

FLAMENCO

1½ OUNCES LUSTAU AMONTILLADO SHERRY

1 OUNCE BOLS GENEVER

½ OUNCE ORANGE JUICE

½ OUNCE LEMON JUICE

¾ OUNCE ORGEAT (PAGE 278)

2 DASHES ANGOSTURA BITTERS

Shake all the ingredients with ice, then strain into a coupe. No garnish.

....

FRENCH 75

1½ OUNCES PLYMOUTH GIN

¾ OUNCE LEMON JUICE

½ OUNCE CANE SUGAR SYRUP (PAGE 276)

DRY CHAMPAGNE

GARNISH: 1 LEMON TWIST

Shake all the ingredients (except the champagne) with ice, then double strain into a flute. Top with champagne and garnish with the lemon twist.

....

FRENCH 95

2 OUNCES BUFFALO TRACE BOURBON

¾ OUNCE LEMON JUICE

½ OUNCE CANE SUGAR SYRUP (PAGE 276)

DRY CHAMPAGNE

Short shake all the ingredients (except the champagne) with 3 ice cubes, then strain into a fizz glass over 2 ice cubes. Top with champagne. No garnish.

....

GIMLET

2 OUNCES PERRY'S TOT NAVY-STRENGTH GIN

1½ OUNCES TOBY'S LIME CORDIAL (PAGE 285)

GARNISH: 1 LIME WEDGE

Shake the gin and lime cordial with ice, then strain into a double rocks glass over cracked ice. Garnish with the lime wedge.

GIN FIZZ

2 OUNCES BEEFEATER LONDON DRY GIN

¾ OUNCE LEMON JUICE

¾ OUNCE SIMPLE SYRUP (PAGE 277)

1 EGG WHITE

CLUB SODA

Dry shake all the ingredients (except the club soda), then shake again with ice. Double strain into a fizz glass and top with club soda. No garnish.

....

GIN RICKEY

2 OUNCES BEEFEATER LONDON DRY GIN

1 OUNCE LIME JUICE

½ OUNCE SIMPLE SYRUP (PAGE 277)

CLUB SODA

GARNISH: 1 LIME WEDGE

Short shake all the ingredients (except the club soda) with 3 ice cubes, then strain into a highball glass filled with ice cubes. Top with club soda. Garnish with the lime wedge.

....

GRASSHOPPER

8 MINT LEAVES

1 OUNCE MARIE BRIZARD WHITE CRÈME DE MENTHE

1 OUNCE MARIE BRIZARD WHITE CRÈME DE CACAO

1 OUNCE HEAVY CREAM

GARNISH: 1 MINT LEAF

In a shaker, gently muddle the mint. Add the remaining ingredients and shake with ice, then double strain into a coupe. Garnish with the mint leaf.

HANKY-PANKY

2 OUNCES FORDS GIN
½ OUNCE CONTRATTO AMERICANO ROSSO VERMOUTH
½ OUNCE CARPANO ANTICA FORMULA VERMOUTH
¼ OUNCE FERNET-BRANCA
GARNISH: LEMON TWIST

Stir all the ingredients over ice, then strain into a Nick & Nora glass. Garnish with the lemon twist.

....

HONEYSUCKLE

2 OUNCES FLOR DE CAÑA EXTRA-DRY WHITE RUM
¾ OUNCE LIME JUICE
¾ OUNCE ACACIA HONEY SYRUP (PAGE 276)
GARNISH: 1 LIME WEDGE

Shake all the ingredients with ice, then strain into a coupe. Garnish with the lime wedge.

....

JACK ROSE

1 OUNCE LAIRD'S BONDED APPLE BRANDY
1 OUNCE BUSNEL VSOP CALVADOS
½ LEMON JUICE
½ OUNCE LIME JUICE
¾ OUNCE GRENADINE (PAGE 284)
GARNISH: 1 APPLE FAN

Shake all the ingredients with ice, then strain into a coupe. Garnish with the apple fan.

....

LA ROSITA

2 OUNCES EL TESORO REPOSADO TEQUILA
½ OUNCE CAMPARI

½ OUNCE COCCHI VERMOUTH DI TORINO
½ OUNCE DOLIN DRY VERMOUTH
1 DASH ANGOSTURA BITTERS
GARNISH: 1 ORANGE TWIST

Stir all the ingredients over ice, then strain into a Nick & Nora glass. Garnish with the orange twist.

....

LAST WORD

¾ OUNCE BEEFEATER LONDON DRY GIN
¾ OUNCE GREEN CHARTREUSE
¾ OUNCE LUXARDO MARASCHINO LIQUEUR
¾ OUNCE LIME JUICE

Shake all the ingredients with ice, then strain into a coupe. No garnish.

....

LUCIEN GAUDIN

1½ OUNCES TANQUERAY LONDON DRY GIN
½ OUNCE DOLIN DRY VERMOUTH
½ OUNCE CAMPARI
½ OUNCE COINTREAU
GARNISH: 1 LEMON TWIST

Stir all the ingredients over ice, then strain into a Nick & Nora glass. Garnish with the lemon twist.

....

MAI TAI

1 LIME WEDGE
1 OUNCE EL DORADO 15-YEAR RUM
1 OUNCE APPLETON ESTATE V/X RUM
¼ OUNCE LA FAVORITE RHUM AGRICOLE BLANC
½ OUNCE RHUM CLÉMENT CRÉOLE SHRUBB
1 OUNCE LIME JUICE

¾ OUNCE ORGEAT (PAGE 278)

1 DASH ANGOSTURA BITTERS

GARNISH: 1 MINT BOUQUET

Squeeze a lime wedge into a shaker and drop it in.
Add the remaining ingredients and short shake
with 3 ice cubes. Strain into a snifter filled with crushed
ice. Garnish with the mint bouquet and serve with a straw.

. . . .

MANHATTAN

2½ OUNCES RITTENHOUSE 100 RYE

¾ OUNCE HOUSE SWEET VERMOUTH (PAGE 284)

2 DASHES ANGOSTURA BITTERS

GARNISH: 1 BRANDIED CHERRY

Stir all the ingredients over ice, then strain into a coupe.
Garnish with the cherry.

. . . .

MARGARITA

KOSHER SALT

2 OUNCES SIEMBRA AZUL BLANCO TEQUILA

¾ OUNCE COINTREAU

1 OUNCE LIME JUICE

¼ OUNCE AGAVE NECTAR

GARNISH: 1 LIME WEDGE

Rim half of a double rocks glass with salt. Shake all the
ingredients with ice, then strain into the rimmed glass
over ice cubes. Garnish with the lime wedge.

. . . .

MARTINEZ

1½ OUNCES HAYMAN'S OLD TOM GIN

½ OUNCE RANSOM OLD TOM GIN

1 OUNCE HOUSE SWEET VERMOUTH (PAGE 284)

½ TEASPOON LUXARDO MARASCHINO LIQUEUR

½ TEASPOON MASSENEZ KIRSCH VIEUX CHERRY
   BRANDY

1 DASH HOUSE ORANGE BITTERS (PAGE 284)

GARNISH: 1 LEMON TWIST

Stir all the ingredients over ice, then strain into a Nick &
Nora glass. Garnish with the lemon twist.

. . . .

MARTINI

2½ OUNCES PLYMOUTH,
   BEEFEATER LONDON DRY, OR
   TANQUERAY LONDON DRY GIN

¾ OUNCE DOLIN DRY
   VERMOUTH

1 DASH HOUSE ORANGE BITTERS
   (PAGE 284)

GARNISH: 1 LEMON TWIST

Stir all the ingredients over ice,
then strain into a martini glass. Garnish
with the lemon twist.

. . . .

MEXICAN FIRING SQUAD

1½ OUNCES TAPATIO 110 BLANCO TEQUILA

¾ OUNCE LIME JUICE

½ OUNCE CANE SUGAR SYRUP (PAGE 276)

¼ OUNCE GRENADINE (PAGE 284)

2 DASHES BITTERMENS HELLFIRE HABANERO
   SHRUB

GARNISH: 1 LIME WHEEL AND CHERRY FLAG

Fill a highball glass with cracked ice. Short shake all
the ingredients with 3 ice cubes, then strain into the
glass. Garnish with the lime wheel and cherry flag
and serve with a straw.

Negroni

MINT JULEP

2 OUNCES BAKER'S BOURBON

¼ OUNCE SIMPLE SYRUP (PAGE 277)

GARNISH: 1 MINT BOUQUET

Put the bourbon and simple syrup in a julep tin. Fill the tin halfway with crushed ice. Stir with a teaspoon, churning the ice as you go, for about 10 seconds, holding the tin by the rim so the entire tin can eventually frost up. Add more crushed ice to fill the drink two-thirds full and stir until the tin is completely frosted. Add more ice to form a cone above the rim. Garnish with the mint bouquet in the center of the ice and serve with a straw.

....

MOJITO

6 MINT LEAVES

¾ OUNCE SIMPLE SYRUP (PAGE 277)

2 OUNCES CAÑA BRAVA RUM

1 OUNCE LIME JUICE

2 DROPS ANGOSTURA BITTERS

GARNISH: 1 MINT BOUQUET

In a shaker, gently muddle the mint and simple syrup. Add the remaining ingredients and whip (shake with a few pieces of crushed ice just until the ingredients are incorporated). Dump into a double rocks glass and fill the glass with crushed ice. Garnish with the mint bouquet in the center of the ice and serve with a straw.

....

MOSCOW MULE

2 OUNCES CHARBAY VODKA

½ OUNCE LIME JUICE

¾ OUNCE GINGER SYRUP (PAGE 277)

CLUB SODA

GARNISH: 1 LIME WHEEL AND CANDIED GINGER FLAG

Short shake all the ingredients (except the club soda) with 3 ice cubes, then strain into a highball glass filled with ice cubes. Top with club soda. Garnish with the lime wheel and candied ginger flag and serve with a straw.

....

MUDSLIDE FLIP

1½ OUNCES REDBREAST 12-YEAR IRISH WHISKEY

1 OUNCE COFFEE-INFUSED CARPANO ANTICA FORMULA VERMOUTH (PAGE 282)

¼ OUNCE DEMERARA SYRUP (PAGE 277)

1 EGG YOLK

½ OUNCE HEAVY CREAM

1 DASH ANGOSTURA BITTERS

GARNISH: DARK CHOCOLATE

Short shake all the ingredients with 3 ice cubes, then strain into a pilsner glass filled with crushed ice. Coarsely grate some dark chocolate over the drink and serve with a straw.

....

NEGRONI

1½ OUNCES TANQUERAY LONDON DRY GIN

1 OUNCE CAMPARI

1 OUNCE HOUSE SWEET VERMOUTH (PAGE 284)

GARNISH: 1 ORANGE TWIST

Stir all the ingredients over ice, then strain into a double rocks glass. Garnish with the orange twist.

....

OLD-FASHIONED

2 OUNCES EAGLE RARE 10-YEAR BOURBON

1 TEASPOON DEMERARA SYRUP (PAGE 277)

2 DASHES ANGOSTURA BITTERS

1 DASH BITTER TRUTH AROMATIC BITTERS

GARNISH: 1 ORANGE TWIST AND 1 LEMON TWIST

Stir all the ingredients over ice, then strain into a double rocks glass over 1 large ice cube. Garnish with the orange and lemon twists.

OLD PAL

1½ OUNCES RITTENHOUSE 100 RYE

¾ OUNCE CAMPARI

¾ OUNCE DOLIN DRY VERMOUTH

GARNISH: 1 LEMON TWIST

Stir all the ingredients over ice, then strain into a Nick & Nora glass. Garnish with the lemon twist.

....

PALOMA

KOSHER SALT

½ LIME

2 OUNCES EL TESORO PLATINUM TEQUILA

½ OUNCE GRAPEFRUIT JUICE

½ OUNCE SIMPLE SYRUP (PAGE 277)

SAN PELLEGRINO POMPELMO GRAPEFRUIT SODA

GARNISH: 1 LIME WHEEL

Rim a highball glass with kosher salt. Squeeze the lime into a shaker and drop it in. Add the tequila, grapefruit juice, and simple syrup and short shake with 3 ice cubes. Strain into a highball glass filled with ice cubes and top with grapefruit soda. Garnish with the lime wheel and serve with a straw.

....

PENDENNIS CLUB COCKTAIL

2 OUNCES PLYMOUTH GIN

¾ OUNCE PENDENNIS MIX (PAGE 284)

¾ OUNCE LIME JUICE

2 DASHES HOUSE PEYCHAUD'S BITTERS
    (PAGE 284)

GARNISH: 1 LIME WEDGE

Shake all the ingredients with ice, then strain into a coupe. Garnish with the lime wedge.

PIÑA COLADA

1 OUNCE SMITH & CROSS RUM

½ OUNCE EL DORADO 151 RUM

½ OUNCE EL DORADO 3-YEAR RUM

3 DASHES KALANI RON DE COCO COCONUT LIQUEUR

1 OUNCE PINEAPPLE JUICE

½ OUNCE LIME JUICE

¾ OUNCE COCO LOPEZ

2 DASHES ANGOSTURA BITTERS

GARNISH: 1 MINT BOUQUET

Short shake all the ingredients with 3 ice cubes, then strain into a coconut mug filled with crushed ice. Garnish with the mint bouquet and serve with a straw.

....

PING-PONG COCKTAIL

2 OUNCES PLYMOUTH SLOE GIN

½ OUNCE DOLIN DRY VERMOUTH

½ OUNCE PUNT E MES

2 DASHES HOUSE ORANGE BITTERS (PAGE 284)

GARNISH: 1 LEMON TWIST

Stir all the ingredients over ice, then strain into a coupe. Garnish with the lemon twist.

....

PINK LADY

1½ OUNCES PLYMOUTH GIN

½ OUNCE LAIRD'S BONDED APPLE BRANDY

¾ OUNCE LEMON JUICE

¾ OUNCE ACACIA HONEY SYRUP (PAGE 276)

¼ OUNCE GRENADINE (PAGE 284)

1 EGG WHITE

GARNISH: 3 BRANDIED CHERRIES ON A
    COCKTAIL PICK

Dry shake all the ingredients, then shake again with ice. Double strain into a rocks glass over 1 large ice cube. Garnish with the cherries.

Piña Colada

PISCO SOUR

2 OUNCES CAMPO DE ENCANTO ACHOLADO PISCO

½ OUNCE LEMON JUICE

½ OUNCE LIME JUICE

¾ OUNCE SIMPLE SYRUP (PAGE 277)

1 EGG WHITE

GARNISH: 3 DROPS ANGOSTURA BITTERS

Dry shake all the ingredients, then shake again with ice. Double strain into a coupe. Garnish with the bitters.

. . . .

PORT AU PRINCE

1 OUNCE BARBANCOURT 3-STAR RUM

1 OUNCE EL DORADO 3-YEAR RUM

¼ OUNCE LEMON HART 151 RUM

¾ OUNCE VELVET FALERNUM

¾ OUNCE LIME JUICE

½ OUNCE PINEAPPLE JUICE

¼ OUNCE GRENADINE (PAGE 284)

1 TEASPOON GINGER SYRUP (PAGE 277)

6 DROPS BITTERMENS 'ELEMAKULE TIKI BITTERS

GARNISH: 1 PINEAPPLE AND BRANDIED
    CHERRY FLAG

Short shake all the ingredients with 3 ice cubes, then strain into a pilsner glass filled with crushed ice. Garnish with the pineapple and cherry flag.

. . . .

PREAKNESS

1½ OUNCES OLD GRAND-DAD 114 BOURBON

¾ OUNCE CARPANO ANTICA FORMULA VERMOUTH

¼ OUNCE BÉNÉDICTINE

1 DASH BITTER TRUTH AROMATIC BITTERS

GARNISH: 1 ORANGE TWIST

Stir all the ingredients over ice, then strain into a coupe. Garnish with the orange twist.

QUEEN'S PARK SWIZZLE

10 MINT LEAVES

¾ OUNCE SIMPLE SYRUP (PAGE 277)

1 WHITE SUGAR CUBE

2 OUNCES CAÑA BRAVA RUM

1 OUNCE LIME JUICE

4 DASHES HOUSE PEYCHAUD'S BITTERS (PAGE 284)

4 DASHES ANGOSTURA BITTERS

GARNISH: 1 MINT SPRIG

In a shaker, gently muddle the mint with the simple syrup and sugar cube. Add the rum and lime juice and whip (shake with a few pieces of crushed ice just until the ingredients are incorporated). Dump into a pilsner glass filled with crushed ice. Swizzle until cold, then top with the bitters and swizzle them into the top of the drink. Garnish with the mint sprig and serve with a straw.

....

RAMOS GIN FIZZ

2 OUNCES PLYMOUTH GIN

½ OUNCE LEMON JUICE

½ OUNCE LIME JUICE

1 OUNCE SIMPLE SYRUP (PAGE 277)

1 OUNCE HEAVY CREAM

1 EGG WHITE

6 DROPS ORANGE FLOWER WATER

2 OUNCES CLUB SODA

Dry shake all the ingredients (except the club soda), then fill the shaker with ice cubes and shake until the tin is almost too cold to hold. Double strain into a highball glass and let rest for 30 seconds, then slowly top with club soda. Serve with a straw. No garnish.

REMEMBER THE MAINE

VIEUX PONTARLIER ABSINTHE

2 OUNCES RITTENHOUSE 100 RYE

¾ OUNCE COCCHI VERMOUTH DI TORINO

¼ OUNCE CHERRY HEERING

¼ OUNCE MASSENEZ KIRSCH VIEUX CHERRY BRANDY

2 DASHES VIEUX PONTARLIER ABSINTHE

GARNISH: 1 LEMON TWIST

Rinse a Nick & Nora glass with absinthe and dump. Stir the remaining ingredients over ice, then strain into the glass. Garnish with the lemon twist.

....

ROB ROY

2 OUNCES COMPASS BOX ASYLA SCOTCH

¾ OUNCE CARPANO ANTICA FORMULA VERMOUTH

2 DASHES ANGOSTURA BITTERS

GARNISH: 2 BRANDIED CHERRIES ON A COCKTAIL PICK

Stir all the ingredients over ice, then strain into a coupe. Garnish with the cherries.

....

RUM JULEP

¾ OUNCE LEMON HART 151 RUM

¾ OUNCE LEMON HART ORIGINAL RUM

½ OUNCE APPLETON ESTATE V/X RUM

¼ OUNCE VELVET FALERNUM

¼ OUNCE DONN'S SPICES #2 (PAGE 284)

½ OUNCE ORANGE JUICE

½ OUNCE LIME JUICE

½ OUNCE ACACIA HONEY SYRUP (PAGE 276)

GARNISH: 1 MINT BOUQUET

Short shake all the ingredients with 3 ice cubes, then strain into a julep tin filled with crushed ice. Garnish with the mint bouquet.

RUSTY NAIL

2 OUNCES SPRINGBANK 10-YEAR SCOTCH

¾ OUNCE DRAMBUIE

1 DASH BITTER TRUTH AROMATIC BITTERS

GARNISH: 1 LEMON TWIST

Stir all the ingredients over ice, then strain into a double rocks glass over 1 large ice cube. Garnish with the lemon twist.

....

SAZERAC

VIEUX PONTARLIER ABSINTHE

1½ OUNCES RITTENHOUSE 100 RYE

½ OUNCE PIERRE FERRAND 1840 COGNAC

1 TEASPOON DEMERARA SYRUP (PAGE 277)

4 DASHES PEYCHAUD'S BITTERS

1 DASH ANGOSTURA BITTERS

1 LEMON TWIST

Rinse a rocks glass with absinthe and dump. Stir the remaining ingredients (except the lemon twist) over ice, then strain into the glass. Squeeze the lemon twist over the drink and discard. No garnish.

....

SCOFFLAW

1½ OUNCES TEMPLETON RYE

½ OUNCE DOLIN BLANC VERMOUTH

½ OUNCE DOLIN DRY VERMOUTH

½ OUNCE LEMON JUICE

½ OUNCE GRENADINE (PAGE 284)

Shake all the ingredients with ice, then strain into a coupe. No garnish.

SIDECAR

2 OUNCES PIERRE FERRAND 1840 COGNAC

½ OUNCE COINTREAU

¾ OUNCE LEMON JUICE

¼ OUNCE CANE SUGAR SYRUP (PAGE 276)

GARNISH: 1 ORANGE TWIST

Shake all the ingredients with ice, then strain into a coupe. Garnish with the orange twist.

....

SINGAPORE SLING

1½ OUNCES BEEFEATER LONDON DRY GIN

½ OUNCE CHERRY HEERING

¼ OUNCE COINTREAU

¼ OUNCE BÉNÉDICTINE

2 OUNCES PINEAPPLE JUICE

½ OUNCE LIME JUICE

½ OUNCE GRENADINE (PAGE 284)

1 DASH ANGOSTURA BITTERS

GARNISH: 1 PINEAPPLE AND BRANDIED CHERRY FLAG

Short shake all the ingredients with 3 ice cubes, then strain into a highball glass filled with ice cubes. Garnish with the pineapple and cherry flag.

....

SOUTH SIDE

5 MINT LEAVES

2 OUNCES BEEFEATER LONDON DRY GIN

¾ OUNCE LIME JUICE

½ CANE SUGAR SYRUP (PAGE 276)

1 DASH ANGOSTURA BITTERS

GARNISH: 1 MINT LEAF

In a cocktail shaker, gently muddle the mint. Add the remaining ingredients, shake with ice, and strain into a coupe. Garnish with a mint leaf.

STINGER

2 OUNCES PIERRE FERRAND 1840 COGNAC

½ OUNCE MARIE BRIZARD WHITE CRÈME DE MENTHE

1 TEASPOON SIMPLE SYRUP (PAGE 277)

GARNISH: 1 MINT SPRIG

Short shake all the ingredients with 3 ice cubes, then strain into a double rocks glass filled with crushed ice. Garnish with the mint sprig and serve with a straw.

. . . .

TAILSPIN

CAMPARI

1½ OUNCES BEEFEATER LONDON DRY GIN

1 OUNCE CARPANO ANTICA FORMULA VERMOUTH

1 OUNCE GREEN CHARTREUSE

1 DASH HOUSE ORANGE BITTERS (PAGE 284)

GARNISH: 1 LEMON TWIST

Rinse a coupe with Campari and dump. Stir the remaining ingredients over ice, then strain into the coupe. Garnish with the lemon twist.

. . . .

TI PUNCH

½ OUNCE LIME JUICE

1 TEASPOON CANE SUGAR SYRUP (PAGE 276)

2 OUNCES LA FAVORITE RHUM AGRICOLE BLANC

In a double rocks glass, muddle the lime and cane syrup until the lime is well juiced. Add the rum and cracked ice and stir until cold. No garnish.

TOM COLLINS

2 OUNCES BEEFEATER LONDON DRY GIN

1 OUNCE LEMON JUICE

¾ OUNCE SIMPLE SYRUP (PAGE 277)

CLUB SODA

GARNISH: 1 ORANGE CRESCENT AND CHERRY FLAG

Short shake all the ingredients (except the club soda) with 3 ice cubes, then strain into a highball glass filled with ice cubes. Top with club soda. Garnish with the orange crescent and cherry flag and serve with a straw.

. . . .

TORONTO

2 OUNCES RITTENHOUSE 100 RYE

½ OUNCE FERNET-BRANCA

1 TEASPOON DEMERARA SYRUP (PAGE 277)

GARNISH: 1 LEMON TWIST

Stir all the ingredients over ice, then strain into a Nick & Nora glass. Garnish with the lemon twist.

. . . .

VESPER

1½ OUNCES PLYMOUTH GIN

¾ OUNCE CHARBAY VODKA

½ OUNCE COCCHI AMERICANO

GARNISH: 1 LEMON TWIST

Stir all the ingredients over ice, then strain into a Nick & Nora glass. Garnish with the lemon twist.

VIEUX CARRÉ

1 OUNCE RITTENHOUSE 100 RYE

1 OUNCE PIERRE FERRAND AMBRE COGNAC

1 OUNCE CARPANO ANTICA FORMULA VERMOUTH

1 TEASPOON BÉNÉDICTINE

1 DASH ANGOSTURA BITTERS

1 DASH HOUSE PEYCHAUD'S BITTERS (PAGE 284)

GARNISH: 1 LEMON TWIST

Stir all the ingredients over ice, then strain into a double rocks glass. Garnish with the lemon twist.

. . . .

WARD 8

2 OUNCES OLD OVERHOLT RYE

½ OUNCE LEMON JUICE

½ OUNCE ORANGE JUICE

½ OUNCE SIMPLE SYRUP (PAGE 277)

1 TEASPOON POMEGRANATE MOLASSES

Shake all the ingredients with ice, then strain into a coupe. No garnish.

. . . .

WHISKEY SOUR

2 OUNCES BUFFALO TRACE BOURBON

¾ OUNCE LEMON JUICE

¾ OUNCE SIMPLE SYRUP (PAGE 277)

1 EGG WHITE

GARNISH: 1 DASH ANGOSTURA BITTERS AND
1 ORANGE CRESCENT AND CHERRY FLAG

Dry shake all the ingredients, then shake again with ice. Double strain into a double rocks glass over 1 large ice cube. Add a dash of bitters on top and garnish with the orange and cherry flag.

ZOMBIE PUNCH

1½ OUNCES APPLETON ESTATE V/X RUM

1½ OUNCES RON DEL BARRILITO 3-STAR RUM

1 OUNCE LEMON HART 151 RUM

¾ OUNCE ZOMBIE MIX (PAGE 284)

½ OUNCE DONN'S SPICES #2 (PAGE 284)

¾ OUNCE LIME JUICE

1 DASH ANGOSTURA BITTERS

GARNISH: 1 MINT SPRIG

Shake all the ingredients with 2 ice cubes, then strain into a tiki mug filled with crushed ice. Garnish with the mint sprig.

GIN

ANJOU MAMA

JILLIAN VOSE, 2013

3 SMALL RIPE ANJOU PEAR SLICES

1 OUNCE PENNYROYAL-INFUSED HAYMAN'S
    OLD TOM GIN (PAGE 281)

1 OUNCE TANQUERAY NO. TEN GIN

¾ OUNCE LEMON JUICE

¼ OUNCE ORGEAT (PAGE 278)

¼ OUNCE CINNAMON BARK SYRUP (PAGE 276)

¼ OUNCE ACACIA HONEY SYRUP (PAGE 276)

GARNISH: 1 LEMON WHEEL

In a shaker, muddle the pear slices. Add the remaining
ingredients and shake with ice, then strain into a
Nick & Nora glass. Garnish with the lemon wheel.

. . . .

BELLA LUNA

BRIAN MILLER, 2009

2 OUNCES PLYMOUTH GIN

¾ OUNCE ST-GERMAIN

½ OUNCE CRÈME YVETTE

¾ OUNCE LEMON JUICE

1 TEASPOON SIMPLE SYRUP (PAGE 277)

Shake all the ingredients with ice, then strain into a port
glass. No garnish.

CÁDIZ COLLINS

ALEX DAY, 2008

*This is my way to get more people to drink sherry in
cocktails. The bitters and orange bring out the sherry's
spice flavors.—AD*

1 ORANGE WHEEL

3 DASHES FEE BROTHERS WHISKEY
    BARREL-AGED BITTERS

2 OUNCES PLYMOUTH GIN

¾ OUNCE LUSTAU AMONTILLADO SHERRY

½ OUNCE LEMON JUICE

½ OUNCE DEMERARA SYRUP (PAGE 277)

CLUB SODA

GARNISH: 1 ORANGE CRESCENT

In a shaker, muddle the orange wheel and bitters. Add
the remaining ingredients (except the club soda) and
shake with ice, then strain into a highball glass filled with
ice cubes. Top with club soda. Garnish with the orange
crescent and serve with a straw.

CITY OF GOLD SLING

JOAQUÍN SIMÓ, 2009

A handful of tiki-style drinks are gin based, most famously the Singapore Sling. This is a variation on that classic.—JS

1½ OUNCES HAYMAN'S OLD TOM GIN

½ OUNCE EL DORADO 12-YEAR RUM

¾ OUNCE DONN'S SPICES #2 (PAGE 284)

1 DASH VIEUX PONTARLIER ABSINTHE

1 OUNCE PINEAPPLE JUICE

½ OUNCE LIME JUICE

¼ OUNCE ORGEAT (PAGE 278)

1 DASH HOUSE PEYCHAUD'S BITTERS (PAGE 284)

GARNISH: 1 PINEAPPLE WEDGE

Shake all the ingredients with ice, then strain into a highball glass filled with ice cubes. Garnish with the pineapple wedge.

. . . .

THE COMMANDANT

TYSON BUHLER, 2013

Kaffir lime is a great way to add brightness to summer cocktails. The gin in this drink was named after Matthew Perry—not the actor, but the original commandant of the Brooklyn Navy Yard from 1841 to 1843.—TB

1½ OUNCES PERRY'S TOT NAVY-STRENGTH GIN

½ OUNCE KRONAN SWEDISH PUNSCH

¼ OUNCE VELVET FALERNUM

¾ OUNCE LIME JUICE

½ OUNCE COCO LOPEZ

1 SMALL FRESH KAFFIR LIME LEAF

GARNISH: 1 LIME WHEEL

Short shake all the ingredients with 3 ice cubes, then strain into a coconut mug filled with crushed ice. Garnish with the lime wheel and serve with a straw.

FRISCO CLUB

THOMAS WAUGH, 2008

This is a riff on the classic Pegu Club cocktail, with Fernet-Branca and grapefruit juice in place of the usual bitters and orange curaçao.—TW

2 OUNCES PLYMOUTH GIN

½ OUNCE SOLERNO BLOOD ORANGE LIQUEUR

¼ OUNCE FERNET-BRANCA

¾ OUNCE GRAPEFRUIT JUICE

¼ OUNCE LIME JUICE

½ OUNCE SIMPLE SYRUP (PAGE 277)

1 GRAPEFRUIT TWIST

Shake all the ingredients (except the grapefruit twist) with ice, then strain into a coupe. Squeeze the grapefruit twist over the drink and discard. No garnish.

. . . .

GIN HOUND

JOAQUÍN SIMÓ, 2009

Celery is a misunderstood ingredient. People think of it as bland and characterless, but it's actually quite intense. This gimlet-style drink is meant to showcase its big flavor.—JS

2 OUNCES TANQUERAY LONDON DRY GIN

½ OUNCE CELERY JUICE

½ OUNCE LIME JUICE

½ OUNCE ACACIA HONEY SYRUP (PAGE 276)

Shake all the ingredients with ice, then strain into a coupe. No garnish.

Muddled Mission, page 158

GOOD HUMOR

BRAD FARRAN, 2013

I wanted to mimic the flavors of a strawberry shortcake ice cream bar. The maltiness of the genever mimics the flavor of the cake, and the intensely flavored strawberry liqueur provides the fruit.—BF

1 STRAWBERRY

1 OUNCE BOLS GENEVER

½ OUNCE BOLS BARREL-AGED GENEVER

½ OUNCE ELIJAH CRAIG 12-YEAR BOURBON

½ TEASPOON MERLET CRÈME DE FRAISE DES BOIS STRAWBERRY LIQUEUR

½ OUNCE LEMON JUICE

½ OUNCE ORGEAT (PAGE 278)

¼ OUNCE VANILLA SYRUP (PAGE 277)

½ OUNCE HEAVY CREAM

GARNISH: 1 STRAWBERRY

In a shaker, gently muddle the strawberry. Add the remaining ingredients and shake with ice, then strain into a double rocks glass filled with crushed ice. Garnish with the strawberry and serve with a straw.

. . . .

GYPSY EYES

JESSICA GONZALEZ, 2009

GREEN CHARTREUSE

1½ OUNCES BEEFEATER LONDON DRY GIN

½ OUNCE APEROL

½ OUNCE LIME JUICE

½ OUNCE GRAPEFRUIT JUICE

¼ OUNCE SIMPLE SYRUP (PAGE 277)

Rinse a coupe with the Chartreuse and dump. Shake the remaining ingredients with ice, then strain into the coupe. No garnish.

GYPSY WEDDING

JILLIAN VOSE, 2012

TOASTED FENNEL SALT RIM (PAGE 283)

6 GREEN GRAPES

1½ OUNCES BOMBAY LONDON DRY GIN

½ OUNCE KROGSTAD AQUAVIT

¼ OUNCE VELVET FALERNUM

¾ OUNCE LIME JUICE

½ OUNCE GRAPEFRUIT JUICE

½ OUNCE ACACIA HONEY SYRUP (PAGE 276)

Rim half of a coupe with toasted fennel salt. In a shaker, muddle the grapes. Add the remaining ingredients and shake with ice, then double strain into the coupe. No garnish.

. . . .

KEW GARDENS COOLER

JOAQUÍN SIMÓ, 2009

2 THIN CUCUMBER WHEELS

2 OUNCES BEEFEATER 24 GIN

½ OUNCE APEROL

¾ OUNCE GRAPEFRUIT JUICE

½ OUNCE SCARLET GLOW SYRUP (PAGE 277)

GARNISH: 1 CUCUMBER RIBBON

In a shaker, muddle the cucumber wheels. Add the remaining ingredients and short shake with 3 ice cubes, then strain into a highball glass filled with crushed ice. Garnish with the cucumber ribbon skewered on a cocktail pick and serve with a straw.

MORTAL ENEMY

JILLIAN VOSE, 2013

The American Fruits Distillery in upstate New York makes a great line of cordials from peak-of-season fruit. It also happens to be located near the distillery where Allen Katz developed his Dorothy Parker gin, so I combined the two in this Last Word variation.—JV

¾ OUNCE DOROTHY PARKER GIN

¾ OUNCE MARIE BRIZARD WHITE CRÈME DE CACAO

¾ OUNCE AMERICAN FRUITS BLACK CURRANT CORDIAL

1 DASH VIEUX PONTARLIER ABSINTHE

¾ OUNCE LIME JUICE

¼ OUNCE SIMPLE SYRUP (PAGE 277)

Shake all the ingredients with ice, then strain into a Nick & Nora glass. No garnish.

MUDDLED MISSION

JOAQUÍN SIMÓ, 2008

1 STRAWBERRY

1½ OUNCES ANCHOR JUNIPERO GIN

1 OUNCE ST-GERMAIN

¼ OUNCE YELLOW CHARTREUSE

¾ OUNCE LEMON JUICE

GARNISH: 1 STRAWBERRY

In a shaker, gently muddle the strawberry. Add the remaining ingredients and shake with ice. Strain into a coupe. Garnish with the strawberry.

. . . .

OVERHEAD SMASH

JOAQUÍN SIMÓ, 2011

This is a reverse-engineered Pimm's Cup. The combination of Bonal (an amaro-like French aperitif), Carpano Antica, and gin creates a quaff similar to Pimm's, but with a more complex flavor profile.—JS

½ STRAWBERRY

2 CUCUMBER WHEELS

1½ OUNCES TANQUERAY LONDON DRY GIN

½ OUNCE BONAL GENTIANE-QUINA

½ OUNCE CARPANO ANTICA FORMULA VERMOUTH

¾ OUNCE LEMON JUICE

¼ OUNCE ORGEAT (PAGE 278)

¼ OUNCE GINGER SYRUP (PAGE 277)

1 DASH ANGOSTURA BITTERS

1 DASH HOUSE ORANGE BITTERS (PAGE 284)

CLUB SODA

GARNISH: 1 CUCUMBER RIBBON, 1 MINT SPRIG, AND 1 OR 2 DROPS ANGOSTURA BITTERS

In a shaker, muddle the strawberry and cucumber wheels. Add the remaining ingredients (except the club soda) and short shake with ice, then strain into a highball glass filled with ice cubes. Top with club soda. Garnish with the cucumber ribbon and mint spring, then dash the bitters on the mint. Serve with a straw.

PETTICOAT

JESSICA GONZALEZ, 2009

2 OUNCES SZECHUAN PEPPERCORN–INFUSED
   PLYMOUTH GIN (PAGE 283)
¼ OUNCE VELVET FALERNUM
¼ OUNCE MARIE BRIZARD APRICOT LIQUEUR
¾ OUNCE LIME JUICE
¼ OUNCE CANE SUGAR SYRUP (PAGE 276)

Shake all the ingredients with ice, then strain into a
coupe. No garnish.

....

PINK ELEPHANT

BRIAN MILLER, 2009

2 OUNCES TANQUERAY LONDON DRY GIN
1 TEASPOON LUXARDO MARASCHINO LIQUEUR
1 TEASPOON MASSENEZ CRÈME DE MÛRE
   BLACKBERRY LIQUEUR
¾ OUNCE GRAPEFRUIT JUICE
½ OUNCE LIME JUICE
1 TEASPOON SIMPLE SYRUP (PAGE 277)

Shake all the ingredients with ice, then strain into a
coupe. No garnish.

....

PINK FLAG

ERYN REECE, 2012

2 SAGE LEAVES
2 OUNCES TANQUERAY LONDON DRY GIN
¼ OUNCE CRÈME YVETTE
½ OUNCE LEMON JUICE
½ OUNCE PINEAPPLE JUICE
½ OUNCE ORGEAT (PAGE 278)

In a shaker, gently muddle the sage leaves. Add the
remaining ingredients and shake with ice, then double
strain into a coupe. No garnish.

PRETTY BIRD

THOMAS WAUGH, 2011

*Some drinks are so popular that we can't stand them
after a while. One of these drinks is Joaquín's Little Birdy
(page 213), which became a running joke that spawned
other ornithologically named drinks.—TW*

1½ OUNCES BOMBAY LONDON DRY GIN
½ OUNCE RHUM CLÉMENT CRÉOLE SHRUBB
¾ OUNCE GRAPEFRUIT JUICE
½ OUNCE LIME JUICE
¼ OUNCE GRENADINE (PAGE 284)
1 TEASPOON CINNAMON BARK SYRUP (PAGE 276)
GARNISH: 1 LIME WHEEL AND CHERRY FLAG

Shake all the ingredients, then strain into a double rocks
glass over 1 large ice cube. Garnish with the lime wheel
and cherry flag.

....

QUEEN PALM

THOMAS WAUGH, 2009

*I don't remember creating this drink. It was the Fourth
of July and we had our slowest night ever, so Brian and I
closed early, drank a few Zombie Punches, and went back
to his apartment, where we kept making drinks. I woke up
the next morning with this recipe scribbled on a piece of
paper in my pocket.—TW*

1½ OUNCES PLYMOUTH GIN
½ OUNCE DONN'S SPICES #2 (PAGE 284)
3 DASHES KALANI RON DE COCO COCONUT LIQUEUR
½ OUNCE GRAPEFRUIT JUICE
½ OUNCE LIME JUICE
½ OUNCE COCONUT WATER
1 TEASPOON CANE SUGAR SYRUP (PAGE 276)

Shake all the ingredients with ice, then strain into a
coupe. No garnish.

RAMBLE

PHIL WARD, 2008

2 OUNCES PLYMOUTH GIN

1 OUNCE LEMON JUICE

1¼ OUNCES SIMPLE SYRUP (PAGE 277)

3 RASPBERRIES

In a shaker, combine the gin, lemon juice, and ¾ ounce of the simple syrup. Short shake with 3 ice cubes, then strain into a highball glass filled with crushed ice. Empty the shaker, then add the raspberries and the remaining ½ ounce simple syrup. Gently muddle the raspberries, then pour over the top of the drink and serve with a straw.

....

RIGADOON

PHIL WARD, 2008

Kalamansi fruits look like tangerines but have a sour, acidic taste similar to that of limes. Though they're hard to come by, you can purchase frozen kalamansi puree from several online purveyors, including marquefoods.com.—PW

2 OUNCES TANQUERAY LONDON DRY GIN

¾ OUNCE BOIRON KALAMANSI PUREE

¼ OUNCE LEMON JUICE

¾ OUNCE SIMPLE SYRUP (PAGE 277)

4 THAI BASIL LEAVES

GARNISH: 1 THAI BASIL LEAF

Shake all the ingredients with ice, then double strain into a coupe. Garnish with the basil leaf.

....

THE RISK POOL

PHIL WARD, 2008

2 OUNCES HAYMAN'S OLD TOM GIN

¼ OUNCE ROTHMAN & WINTER CRÈME DE VIOLETTE

¾ OUNCE LIME JUICE

½ OUNCE GRAPEFRUIT JUICE

¾ OUNCE SIMPLE SYRUP (PAGE 277)

Shake all the ingredients with ice, then strain into a coupe. No garnish.

....

SHANTY TOWN

THOMAS WAUGH, 2012

This isn't technically a shaken cocktail—if anything it's a boilermaker—but it's a refreshing gin drink nonetheless.—TW

1 OUNCE PERRY'S TOT NAVY-STRENGTH GIN

DOC'S HARD APPLE CIDER

Fill a pilsner glass with ice cubes and add the gin. Top with cider and serve with a straw.

....

STRANGE BREW

THOMAS WAUGH, 2008

My friends and I used to go to Dolores Park in San Francisco and drink beer mixed with fresh fruit from the farmers' market, like the Germans do. My favorite combination was pineapple with IPA, which inspired this drink, named after the B side to EMF's hit song "Unbelievable."—TW

2 OUNCES TANQUERAY NO. TEN GIN

¾ OUNCE VELVET FALERNUM

1 OUNCE PINEAPPLE JUICE

½ OUNCE LEMON JUICE

GREEN FLASH IPA

GARNISH: 1 MINT SPRIG

Short shake all the ingredients (except the IPA) with 3 ice cubes, then strain into a pilsner glass filled with crushed ice. Top with IPA. Garnish with the mint sprig and serve with a straw.

SUNSET GUN

JOAQUÍN SIMÓ, 2011

2 FRESH KAFFIR LIME LEAVES

2 OUNCES DOROTHY PARKER GIN

¼ OUNCE VELVET FALERNUM

1 OUNCE LIME JUICE

½ OUNCE ORGEAT (PAGE 278)

GARNISH: 1 FRESH KAFFIR LIME LEAF

In a shaker, gently muddle the Kaffir lime leaves. Add the remaining ingredients and shake with ice. Double strain into a coupe and garnish with the Kaffir lime leaf.

....

TENEMENT YARD

JILLIAN VOSE, 2013

Génépy des Alpes is an herbal liqueur flavored with wormwood that tastes like a cross between Chartreuse and absinthe. I usually hate vegetables in cocktails, but peas have a fresh aroma and sweet flavor that plays well with the gin and Génépy.—JV

2 OUNCES SUGAR SNAP PEA–INFUSED PLYMOUTH
  GIN (PAGE 283)

½ OUNCE DOLIN GÉNÉPY DES ALPES LIQUEUR

¾ OUNCE LEMON JUICE

½ OUNCE ORGEAT (PAGE 278)

Shake all the ingredients with ice, then strain into a large coupe. No garnish.

TOM BOMB

JILLIAN VOSE, 2011

This was my first Death & Co drink. It uses the popular tiki flavor combination of pineapple, lemon, and spice, the latter in Donn's Spices #2.—JV

1½ OUNCES RANSOM OLD TOM GIN

¼ OUNCE DONN'S SPICES #2 (PAGE 284)

½ OUNCE LEMON JUICE

½ OUNCE PINEAPPLE JUICE

¼ OUNCE ORGEAT (PAGE 278)

¼ OUNCE ACACIA HONEY SYRUP (PAGE 276)

Shake all the ingredients with ice, then strain into a coupe. No garnish.

....

WATERLOO SUNSET

JOAQUÍN SIMÓ, 2011

7 MINT LEAVES

½ OUNCE CANE SUGAR SYRUP (PAGE 276)

1 OUNCE SZECHUAN PEPPERCORN–INFUSED
  PLYMOUTH GIN (PAGE 283)

1 OUNCE BEEFEATER LONDON DRY GIN

½ OUNCE DOLIN BLANC VERMOUTH

1½ OUNCES WATERMELON JUICE

¾ OUNCE LIME JUICE

GARNISH: 1 MINT SPRIG

In a shaker, gently muddle the mint leaves and syrup. Add the remaining ingredients and shake with ice, then double strain into a double rocks glass over 1 large ice cube. Garnish with the mint sprig.

GIN

STIRRED

BOTANY OF DESIRE

BRAD FARRAN, 2013

This drink was inspired by Botanist gin from Scotland, which is nuanced and difficult to mix with, so I paired it with other lighter flavors, including a verjus from Napa Valley, that wouldn't eclipse the gin.—BF

1½ OUNCES BRUICHLADDICH BOTANIST GIN

½ OUNCE BUSNEL VSOP CALVADOS

¼ OUNCE ÉLIXIR COMBIER

1½ OUNCES FUSION VERJUS BLANC

½ TEASPOON CANE SUGAR SYRUP (PAGE 276)

1 DASH HOUSE ORANGE BITTERS (PAGE 284)

GARNISH: 1 APPLE FAN

Stir all the ingredients over ice, then strain into a Nick & Nora glass. Garnish with the apple fan.

. . . .

CYNARTOWN

PHIL WARD, 2008

2 OUNCES BEEFEATER LONDON DRY GIN

¾ OUNCE CARPANO ANTICA FORMULA VERMOUTH

½ OUNCE CYNAR

GARNISH: 1 BRANDIED CHERRY

Stir all the ingredients over ice, then strain into a coupe. Garnish with the cherry.

DICK BRAUTIGAN

PHIL WARD, 2008

2 OUNCES BEEFEATER LONDON DRY GIN

¾ OUNCE GRAPEFRUIT-INFUSED PUNT E MES (PAGE 281)

½ OUNCE AMARO LUCANO

¼ OUNCE LUXARDO MARASCHINO LIQUEUR

Stir all the ingredients over ice, then strain into a coupe. No garnish.

. . . .

EUROPEAN UNION

ALEX DAY, 2008

The sweetness of the Old Tom gin is softened by calvados in this Martinez variation.—AD

1½ OUNCES HAYMAN'S OLD TOM GIN

1 OUNCE MARTINI SWEET VERMOUTH

½ OUNCE BUSNEL VSOP CALVADOS

1 TEASPOON STREGA

1 DASH BITTER TRUTH AROMATIC BITTERS

Stir all the ingredients over ice, then strain into a coupe. No garnish.

GONZALEZ

PHIL WARD, 2008

I named this after Jessica Gonzalez, who started at D&C as a cocktail waitress and became our first female bartender.—PW

2 OUNCES BEEFEATER LONDON DRY GIN

¾ OUNCE PUNT E MES

¼ OUNCE LUXARDO MARASCHINO LIQUEUR

2 DASHES BITTER TRUTH AROMATIC BITTERS

Stir all the ingredients over ice, then strain into a coupe. No garnish.

. . . .

GRAND STREET

ALEX DAY, 2009

Stirring citrus zest into a cocktail is one of our favorite tricks. It's like a quick infusion that adds a subtle depth of flavor.—AD

1 GRAPEFRUIT TWIST

2 OUNCES BEEFEATER LONDON DRY GIN

¾ OUNCE PUNT E MES

¼ OUNCE CYNAR

1 TEASPOON LUXARDO MARASCHINO LIQUEUR

In a mixing glass, gently muddle the grapefruit twist. Add the remaining ingredients and stir with ice, then strain into a coupe. No garnish.

. . . .

HOSTAGE SITUATION

JOAQUÍN SIMÓ, 2009

2 OUNCES RANSOM OLD TOM GIN

½ OUNCE COFFEE-INFUSED CARPANO ANTICA FORMULA VERMOUTH (PAGE 286)

½ OUNCE CARPANO ANTICA FORMULA VERMOUTH

¼ OUNCE RHUM CLÉMENT CRÉOLE SHRUBB

2 DASHES REGANS' ORANGE BITTERS

1 DASH ANGOSTURA BITTERS

GARNISH: 1 ORANGE TWIST

Stir all the ingredients over ice, then strain into a double rocks glass over 1 large ice cube. Garnish with the orange twist.

. . . .

HOWLIN' AT THE MOON

BRAD FARRAN, 2012

I wanted to create a genever-based old-fashioned and found that barrel-aged genever and chocolate played well together.—BF

1 LEMON TWIST

2 OUNCES BOLS BARREL-AGED GENEVER

2 TEASPOONS MARIE BRIZARD WHITE CRÈME DE CACAO

½ TEASPOON CANE SUGAR SYRUP (PAGE 276)

2 DASHES BITTERCUBE CHERRY BARK AND VANILLA BITTERS

GARNISH: 1 ORANGE TWIST

In a mixing glass, muddle the lemon twist. Add the remaining ingredients and stir over ice, then strain into a double rocks glass over 1 large ice cube. Garnish with the orange twist.

. . . .

IMPERIAL MARCH

JESSICA GONZALEZ, 2011

1½ OUNCES MARTIN MILLER'S WESTBOURNE-STRENGTH GIN

1 OUNCE ALVEAR FESTIVAL PALE CREAM SHERRY

¾ OUNCE COCCHI AMERICANO

1 TEASPOON LUXARDO MARASCHINO LIQUEUR

1 DASH HOUSE ORANGE BITTERS (PAGE 284)

GARNISH: 1 GRAPEFRUIT TWIST

Stir all the ingredients over ice, then strain into a fancy fizz glass. Garnish with the grapefruit twist.

The Joy Division

JESPER LIND

BRIAN MILLER, 2009

1½ OUNCES BEEFEATER LONDON DRY GIN

¾ OUNCE LUSTAU EAST INDIA SOLERA SHERRY

½ OUNCE LINIE AQUAVIT

1 TEASPOON VANILLA SYRUP (PAGE 277)

1 DASH HOUSE ORANGE BITTERS (PAGE 284)

Stir all the ingredients over ice, then strain into a coupe. No garnish.

. . . .

THE JOY DIVISION

PHIL WARD, 2008

2 OUNCES BEEFEATER LONDON DRY GIN

1 OUNCE DOLIN DRY VERMOUTH

½ OUNCE COINTREAU

3 DASHES VIEUX PONTARLIER ABSINTHE

GARNISH: 1 LEMON TWIST

Stir all the ingredients over ice, then strain into a coupe. Garnish with the lemon twist.

. . . .

KEY PARTY

JOAQUÍN SIMÓ, 2009

If you count all of the botanicals used to flavor the various spirits in this drink, you end up with more than two hundred ingredients in this cocktail. Not bad for something that only takes a minute to make.—JS

2 OUNCES PLYMOUTH GIN

½ OUNCE BONAL GENTIANE-QUINA

½ OUNCE AMARO NARDINI

¼ OUNCE GREEN CHARTREUSE

Stir all the ingredients over ice, then strain into a coupe. No garnish.

LE BATELEUR

ALEX DAY, 2008

2 OUNCES BEEFEATER LONDON DRY GIN

¾ OUNCE PUNT E MES

½ OUNCE STREGA

¼ OUNCE CYNAR

1 DASH ANGOSTURA BITTERS

GARNISH: 1 ORANGE TWIST

Stir all the ingredients over ice, then strain into a coupe. Garnish with the orange twist.

. . . .

LE SUBTIL

TOBY CECCHINI, 2009

2 OUNCES BOLS GENEVER

½ OUNCE CARDAMARO

½ OUNCE CARPANO ANTICA FORMULA VERMOUTH

2 DASHES BITTERMENS HOPPED GRAPEFRUIT BITTERS

GARNISH: 1 GRAPEFRUIT TWIST

Stir all the ingredients over ice, then strain into a coupe. Garnish with the grapefruit twist.

. . . .

LIGHT AND DAY

ALEX DAY, 2008

The first drink I created for Death & Co breaks a few rules (e.g., using fresh orange juice in a stirred cocktail), but it turned out delicious enough to not get me fired.—AD

2 OUNCES PLYMOUTH GIN

½ OUNCE YELLOW CHARTREUSE

¼ OUNCE MARASKA MARASCHINO LIQUEUR

¼ OUNCE ORANGE JUICE

4 DASHES HOUSE PEYCHAUD'S BITTERS (PAGE 284)

Stir all the ingredients over ice, then strain into a coupe. No garnish.

LUCINO'S DELIGHT

PHIL WARD, 2007

2 OUNCES BEEFEATER LONDON DRY GIN
¾ OUNCE CARPANO ANTICA FORMULA VERMOUTH
¼ OUNCE LUXARDO MARASCHINO LIQUEUR
¼ OUNCE AMARO LUCANO

Stir all the ingredients over ice, then strain into a coupe. No garnish.

....

MAINLAND

THOMAS WAUGH, 2009

This is a riff on the Alaska cocktail, which first appeared in The Savoy Cocktail Book. *The Alaska is a martini made with yellow Chartreuse; I subbed in Galliano, which is similar but with more pronounced vanilla and anise flavors.—TW*

2 GRAPEFRUIT TWISTS
2 OUNCES TANQUERAY NO. TEN GIN
½ OUNCE GALLIANO L'AUTENTICO
1 TEASPOON SIMPLE SYRUP (PAGE 277)
1 DASH ANGOSTURA BITTERS

Squeeze the grapefruit twists over the mixing glass, then drop them in. Add the remaining ingredients and stir over ice. Strain into a coupe. No garnish.

....

MAY FAIR

ERYN REECE, 2013

I combined traditional and modern styles of aquavit in this Vieux Carré variation: Krogstad is an unaged, American-made aquavit that's more anise-forward, while Linie is a classic Scandinavian aquavit with big caraway flavors.—ER

1 OUNCE TANQUERAY LONDON DRY GIN
½ OUNCE KROGSTAD AQUAVIT

½ OUNCE LINIE AQUAVIT
1 OUNCE HOUSE SWEET VERMOUTH (PAGE 284)
¼ OUNCE BÉNÉDICTINE
2 DASHES ANGOSTURA BITTERS
2 DASHES HOUSE PEYCHAUD'S BITTERS (PAGE 284)
GARNISH: 1 ORANGE TWIST

Stir all the ingredients over ice, then strain into a double rocks glass over 1 large ice cube. Garnish with the orange twist.

....

MEXI-GIN MARTINI

PHIL WARD, 2012

This drink started with the name. I wanted to create a martini with both tequila and mezcal, so I paired them with a softer gin and added Chartreuse and celery bitters to provide even more complexity.—PW

2 OUNCES PLYMOUTH GIN
½ OUNCE DOLIN DRY VERMOUTH
¼ OUNCE DEL MAGUEY CREMA DE MEZCAL
¼ OUNCE JALAPEÑO-INFUSED SIEMBRA AZUL
    BLANCO TEQUILA (PAGE 279)
¼ OUNCE GREEN CHARTREUSE
1 DASH BITTER TRUTH CELERY BITTERS

Stir all the ingredients over ice, then strain into a coupe. No garnish.

....

THE MONROE

SCOTT TEAGUE, 2013

A friend pointed out that there aren't any old-fashioned-style drinks made with orgeat. So I thought up this cocktail, which is very pretty but a little bit crazy, just like Marilyn.—ST

1½ OUNCES ANCHOR JUNIPERO GIN
½ TEASPOON MASSENEZ CRÈME DE PÊCHE
    PEACH LIQUEUR

¼ OUNCE ORGEAT (PAGE 278)

3 DASHES HOUSE PEYCHAUD'S BITTERS (PAGE 284)

1 DASH HOUSE ORANGE BITTERS (PAGE 284)

½ OUNCE CLUB SODA

Stir all the ingredients (except the club soda) over ice, then strain into a double rocks glass over 1 large ice cube. Add the club soda. No garnish.

....

MOON COCKTAIL

THOMAS WAUGH, 2008

2 OUNCES PLYMOUTH GIN

¾ OUNCE LUSTAU AMONTILLADO SHERRY

1 TEASPOON MASSENEZ CRÈME DE PÊCHE
    PEACH LIQUEUR

¼ OUNCE ACACIA HONEY SYRUP (PAGE 276)

1 LEMON TWIST

Stir all the ingredients (except the lemon twist) over ice, then strain into a coupe. Squeeze the lemon twist over the drink and discard. No garnish.

....

NIGHT WATCH

JESSICA GONZALEZ, 2011

A lot of the guys like to name drinks after songs or movies. I prefer works of art, like this Rembrandt painting.—JG

1½ OUNCES RANSOM OLD TOM GIN

½ OUNCE CRUZAN BLACK STRAP RUM

¾ OUNCE LUSTAU EAST INDIA SOLERA SHERRY

1 TEASPOON SIMPLE SYRUP (PAGE 277)

1 DASH ANGOSTURA BITTERS

Stir all the ingredients over ice, then strain into a coupe. No garnish.

PRESSURE DROP

THOMAS WAUGH, 2009

1½ OUNCES RANSOM OLD TOM GIN

1 OUNCE AMARO MELETTI

½ OUNCE DOLIN DRY VERMOUTH

1 TEASPOON CLEAR CREEK PEAR BRANDY

1 DASH ANGOSTURA BITTERS

Stir all the ingredients over ice, then strain into a coupe. No garnish.

. . . .

SENTIMENTAL JOURNEY

BRIAN MILLER, 2008

This cocktail was inspired by what many consider the original martini recipe, which consisted of gin, Sauvignon Blanc, and grated cinnamon.—BM

1½ OUNCES TANQUERAY NO. TEN GIN

1 OUNCE MORRO BAY CHARDONNAY

½ OUNCE CINNAMON BARK SYRUP (PAGE 276)

GARNISH: 1 LEMON TWIST

Stir all the ingredients over ice, then strain into a coupe. Garnish with the lemon twist.

. . . .

SUMMER SHACK

JOAQUÍN SIMÓ, 2009

1½ OUNCES MARTIN MILLER'S WESTBOURNE-STRENGTH GIN

¾ OUNCE LILLET BLANC

½ OUNCE SAUVIGNON BLANC

¼ OUNCE ST-GERMAIN

1 TEASPOON SIMPLE SYRUP (PAGE 277)

1 ORANGE TWIST

Stir all the ingredients (except the orange twist) over ice, then strain into a coupe. Squeeze the orange twist over the drink and discard. No garnish.

SURE SHOT

JILLIAN VOSE, 2011

1½ OUNCES HAYMAN'S OLD TOM GIN

½ OUNCE BOLS GENEVER

¾ OUNCE ANCHO CHILE–INFUSED DOLIN ROUGE VERMOUTH (PAGE 279)

1 TEASPOON GALLIANO RISTRETTO

1 TEASPOON DEMERARA SYRUP (PAGE 277)

1 DASH HOUSE ORANGE BITTERS (PAGE 284)

Stir all the ingredients over ice, then strain into a coupe. No garnish.

. . . .

WOODEN SHIP

THOMAS WAUGH, 2011

1 OUNCE TANQUERAY NO. TEN GIN

1 OUNCE BOLS GENEVER

½ OUNCE GRAND MARNIER

½ TEASPOON CANE SUGAR SYRUP (PAGE 276)

1 DASH FEE BROTHERS WHISKEY BARREL-AGED BITTERS

GARNISH: 1 LEMON TWIST

Stir all the ingredients over ice, then strain into a rocks glass. Garnish with the lemon twist.

. . . .

YEOMEN WARDER

PHIL WARD, 2008

2 OUNCES BEEFEATER LONDON DRY GIN

¾ OUNCE DOLIN DRY VERMOUTH

¼ OUNCE CYNAR

¼ OUNCE LUXARDO MARASCHINO LIQUEUR

Stir all the ingredients over ice, then strain into a coupe. No garnish.

RUM

SHAKEN

18TH CENTURY

PHIL WARD, 2008

This variation on the classic 20th Century cocktail (page 139) is my love letter to Batavia arrack.—PW

1½ OUNCES VAN OOSTEN BATAVIA ARRACK

¾ OUNCE MARIE BRIZARD WHITE CRÈME DE CACAO

¾ OUNCE CARPANO ANTICA FORMULA VERMOUTH

¾ OUNCE LIME JUICE

Shake all the ingredients with ice, then strain into a coupe. No garnish.

. . . .

BOO-YA CACHAÇA

SCOTT TEAGUE, 2013

This is my "fuck you" to cachaça, because I really don't like the stuff—it's basically an inferior version of rhum agricole.—ST

1½ OUNCES LA FAVORITE RHUM AGRICOLE BLANC

½ OUNCE LUSTAU LOS ARCOS AMONTILLADO SHERRY

¼ OUNCE CRÈME YVETTE

¾ OUNCE LIME JUICE

¾ OUNCE GINGER SYRUP (PAGE 277)

CLUB SODA

Short shake all the ingredients (except the club soda) with 3 ice cubes, then strain into a highball glass over 3 ice cubes. Top with club soda and serve with a straw. No garnish.

CARIBBEAN SHRUB

JOAQUÍN SIMÓ, 2008

This cocktail was inspired by the colonial-era family of drinks known as shrubs, in which a vinegar syrup is mixed with spirits.—JS

1 OUNCE APPLETON ESTATE V/X RUM

1 OUNCE LA FAVORITE RHUM AGRICOLE BLANC

¾ OUNCE STRAWBERRY-BALSAMIC GASTRIQUE (PAGE 285)

¼ OUNCE CANE SUGAR SYRUP (PAGE 276)

GARNISH: ½ STRAWBERRY

Short shake all the ingredients with 3 ice cubes, then strain into a highball glass filled with crushed ice. Garnish with the half strawberry and serve with a straw.

. . . .

COMPANY BUCK

PHIL WARD, 2007

2 OUNCES GOSLING'S BLACK SEAL RUM

1 OUNCE PINEAPPLE JUICE

¾ OUNCE LIME JUICE

½ OUNCE GINGER SYRUP (PAGE 277)

1 DASH ANGOSTURA BITTERS

CLUB SODA

GARNISH: 1 LIME WHEEL

Shake all the ingredients (except the club soda) with ice, then strain into a highball glass filled with ice cubes. Top with club soda. Garnish with the lime wheel and serve with a straw.

FLOR DE JEREZ

Joaquín Simó, 2009

Apricots are such a frustrating fresh fruit to work with because they're so inconsistent. You can buy a dozen of them and have two that are perfect beyond belief, three that are almost delicious, and seven others that are a mealy bunch of nothing. That's why I use a good apricot liqueur in this drink instead of fresh fruit. I was after a light-bodied cocktail that shone forth with fruit and nuts yet remained dry and refreshing.—JS

½ OUNCE APPLETON ESTATE RESERVE RUM

1½ OUNCES LUSTAU AMONTILLADO SHERRY

¼ OUNCE ROTHMAN & WINTER APRICOT LIQUEUR

¾ OUNCE LEMON JUICE

½ OUNCE CANE SUGAR SYRUP (PAGE 276)

1 DASH ANGOSTURA BITTERS

Shake all the ingredients with ice, then strain into a coupe. No garnish.

. . . .

GET LUCKY

Scott Teague, 2013

This drink comes from me not taking myself too seriously. I wanted to make something that looks like it could come from TGI Fridays but tastes like a Death & Co drink.—ST

3 BLACKBERRIES

2 OUNCES FLOR DE CAÑA EXTRA-DRY WHITE RUM

¾ OUNCE LEMON JUICE

¼ OUNCE GINGER SYRUP (PAGE 277)

¼ OUNCE ORGEAT (PAGE 278)

¼ OUNCE ACACIA HONEY SYRUP (PAGE 276)

GARNISH: HOUSE PEYCHAUD'S BITTERS (PAGE 284)

In a pilsner glass, gently muddle the blackberries. Fill the glass with crushed ice. In a shaker, whip the remaining ingredients, shaking with a few pieces of crushed ice just until incorporated. Strain into the glass. Garnish with a thin layer of bitters and serve with a straw.

Get Lucky

THE GIFT SHOP

THOMAS WAUGH, 2011

3 CUCUMBER WHEELS

2 OUNCES BANKS 5-ISLAND WHITE RUM

½ OUNCE CARDAMARO

¾ OUNCE LIME JUICE

¾ OUNCE SIMPLE SYRUP (PAGE 277)

1 DASH ANGOSTURA BITTERS

GARNISH: 3 CUCUMBER WHEELS

In a shaker, muddle the cucumber wheels. Add the remaining ingredients and shake with ice. Double strain into a double rocks glass over 1 large ice cube. Garnish with the cucumber wheels fanned on top of the drink.

....

THE GREAT PRETENDER

THOMAS WAUGH, 2011

This is basically a rum version of Brian's Gilda Cocktail (page 183), hence the name. It's also the only drink I've made that uses a full two ounces of overproof rum.—TW

CINNAMON-SUGAR RIM (PAGE 283)

2 OUNCES SMITH & CROSS RUM

½ OUNCE PINEAPPLE JUICE

½ OUNCE LIME JUICE

½ OUNCE VANILLA SYRUP (PAGE 277)

1 TEASPOON CINNAMON BARK SYRUP (PAGE 276)

Rim a coupe with cinnamon-sugar. Shake the remaining ingredients with ice, then strain into the coupe. No garnish.

....

THE GREEN MILE

PHIL WARD, 2008

I borrowed the template for this drink—liquor, Chartreuse, citrus juice, and simple syrup—from the Daisy de Santiago cocktail in Charles H. Baker's The Gentleman's

Companion. *It's a very versatile ratio that I've used for a bunch of drinks.—PW*

2 OUNCES BARBANCOURT WHITE RUM

½ OUNCE GREEN CHARTREUSE

2 DASHES VIEUX PONTARLIER ABSINTHE

¾ OUNCE LIME JUICE

½ OUNCE SIMPLE SYRUP (PAGE 277)

4 THAI BASIL LEAVES

GARNISH: 1 THAI BASIL LEAF

Shake all the ingredients with ice, then double strain into a coupe. Garnish with the basil leaf.

....

JULIUS ORANGE

BRAD FARRAN, 2012

This concept drink was inspired by, you guessed it, the Orange Julius. The curaçao really makes for a dry drink, which allowed me to add other sweet flavors without making it cloying.—BF

2 OUNCES PIERRE FERRAND DRY CURAÇAO

½ OUNCE CRUZAN SINGLE-BARREL RUM

½ OUNCE LEMON JUICE

1 TEASPOON VANILLA SYRUP (PAGE 277)

½ OUNCE HEAVY CREAM

1 DASH HOUSE ORANGE BITTERS (PAGE 284)

GARNISH: NUTMEG

Short shake all the ingredients with 3 ice cubes. Strain into a double rocks glass filled with crushed ice. Garnish with a few grates of nutmeg and serve with a straw.

....

KERALA

JOAQUÍN SIMÓ, 2008

5 CARDAMOM PODS

1 OUNCE SCARLET IBIS RUM

1 OUNCE BUFFALO TRACE BOURBON

½ OUNCE PINEAPPLE JUICE
½ OUNCE LEMON JUICE
½ OUNCE CANE SUGAR SYRUP (PAGE 276)
1 DASH ANGOSTURA BITTERS
1 DASH HOUSE PEYCHAUD'S BITTERS (PAGE 284)

In a shaker, gently muddle the cardamom pods.
Add the remaining ingredients and shake with ice.
Double strain into a coupe. No garnish.

. . . .

KOKO B. WARE

THOMAS WAUGH, 2009

*I wanted to craft a drink that tastes like coconut without
any in it, and the combination of rhum agricole, orgeat,
and cream does just that. Then I named it, fittingly, after
one of my favorite WWF wrestlers.—TW*

1½ OUNCES APPLETON ESTATE V/X RUM
¼ OUNCE LA FAVORITE RHUM AGRICOLE AMBRE
½ OUNCE LIME JUICE
½ OUNCE ORGEAT (PAGE 278)
1 TEASPOON VANILLA SYRUP (PAGE 277)
½ OUNCE HEAVY CREAM
2 DASHES ANGOSTURA BITTERS
PINCH OF FRESHLY GROUND NUTMEG
GARNISH: NUTMEG

Short shake all the ingredients with 3 ice cubes, then
strain into a coconut mug filled with crushed ice. Garnish
with a few grates of nutmeg and serve with a straw.

. . . .

PATOIS PUNCH

JOAQUÍN SIMÓ, 2009

This is fall in a glass, or a potable pumpkin pie.—JS

1 OUNCE RON DEL BARRILITO 3-STAR RUM
1 OUNCE BUSNEL VSOP CALVADOS
½ TEASPOON DONN'S SPICES #2 (PAGE 284)

½ OUNCE LEMON JUICE
½ OUNCE MAPLE SYRUP
1 TEASPOON PUMPKIN PUREE (PAGE 285)

Shake all the ingredients with ice, then strain into a
coupe. No garnish.

. . . .

PELÉE'S BLOOD

THOMAS WAUGH, 2010

*Mount Pelée is a volcano that erupted on Martinique
in 1902, resulting in the worst volcanic disaster of the
twentieth century.—TW*

1½ OUNCES RHUM JM 100-PROOF
    AGRICOLE BLANC
1½ OUNCES DONN'S SPICES #2 (PAGE 284)
2 DASHES VIEUX PONTARLIER ABSINTHE
¾ OUNCE LIME JUICE
½ OUNCE GRENADINE (PAGE 284)
1 TEASPOON CANE SUGAR SYRUP (PAGE 276)
GARNISH: 1 LIME WHEEL AND CHERRY FLAG

Shake all the ingredients with ice, then strain into a
double rocks glass filled with ice cubes. Garnish with the
lime wheel and cherry flag.

. . . .

SEA B3

PHIL WARD, 2008

*This is one of several cocktails inspired by the
worst days of our battles with our community board,
aka CB3.—PW*

2 OUNCES GOSLING'S BLACK SEAL RUM
½ OUNCE LEMON JUICE
½ OUNCE ORANGE JUICE
½ OUNCE GRENADINE (PAGE 284)

Shake all the ingredients with ice, then strain into a
coupe. No garnish.

SEERSUCKER

BRIAN MILLER, 2009

1 STRAWBERRY

2 OUNCES FLOR DE CAÑA EXTRA-DRY WHITE RUM

1 OUNCE LEMON JUICE

½ OUNCE CINNAMON BARK SYRUP (PAGE 276)

GARNISH: 1 STRAWBERRY

In a shaker, gently muddle the strawberry. Add the remaining ingredients and short shake with 3 ice cubes. Strain into a pilsner glass filled with crushed ice. Garnish with the strawberry and serve with a straw.

SLING OF APHRODITE

JOAQUÍN SIMÓ, 2009

2 OUNCES LA FAVORITE RHUM AGRICOLE AMBRE

½ OUNCE CLEAR CREEK PEAR BRANDY

1 OUNCE FUJI APPLE JUICE

¼ OUNCE LEMON JUICE

½ OUNCE CINNAMON BARK SYRUP (PAGE 276)

GARNISH: 1 APPLE FAN

Shake all the ingredients with ice, then strain into a highball glass filled with ice cubes. Garnish with the apple fan and serve with a straw.

RUM

AMITYVILLE

JILLIAN VOSE, 2013

The rum used here was released to celebrate the 150th anniversary of Bacardi and made according to the distillery's original recipe. The drink takes on a cloudy, off-green color, which I thought was kind of ghostly.—JV

1½ OUNCES BACARDI RON SUPERIOR LIMITED EDITION
¼ OUNCE BANKS 5-ISLAND WHITE RUM
½ OUNCE DOLIN BLANC VERMOUTH
1 DASH VIEUX PONTARLIER ABSINTHE
½ OUNCE GRANNY SMITH APPLE JUICE
¼ OUNCE VANILLA SYRUP (PAGE 277)
½ TEASPOON ACID PHOSPHATE
1 DASH HOUSE ORANGE BITTERS (PAGE 284)
GARNISH: 1 GRANNY SMITH APPLE SLICE

Stir all the ingredients over ice, then strain into a Nick & Nora glass. Garnish with the apple slice.

. . . .

ANGIE'S SECRET

JILLIAN VOSE, 2011

Every D&C bartender hates certain drinks others make. Joaquín hates this one, but I love it because it tastes like Christmas—more specifically, a plate of Christmas cookies in a glass.—JV

1 OUNCE BARBANCOURT WHITE RUM
1 OUNCE APPLETON ESTATE V/X RUM
1 OUNCE BECHEROVKA

1 TEASPOON CANE SUGAR SYRUP (PAGE 276)
2 DASHES BITTERMENS XOCOLATL MOLE BITTERS

Stir all the ingredients over ice, then strain into a coupe. No garnish.

. . . .

ARRACK STRAP

BRAD FARRAN, 2012

At some point, every Death & Co bartender takes on the challenge of Batavia arrack. One of the best ways to combat arrack is by balancing it with another strong flavor, in this case Black Strap rum.—BF

1 OUNCE CRUZAN BLACK STRAP RUM
1 OUNCE VAN OOSTEN BATAVIA ARRACK
1 OUNCE COCCHI VERMOUTH DI TORINO
1 TEASPOON CAMPARI
½ TEASPOON DEMERARA SYRUP (PAGE 277)
2 DASHES BITTERMENS XOCOLATL MOLE BITTERS
2 DASHES HOUSE ORANGE BITTERS (PAGE 284)
GARNISH: 1 ORANGE TWIST

Stir all the ingredients over ice, then strain into an old-fashioned glass over 1 large ice cube. Garnish with the orange twist.

BUMBOO

BRIAN MILLER, 2009

Pirates used to drink a concoction made with rum, water, sugar, and spices—usually nutmeg, sometimes cinnamon—called bumboo (or bumbo). This is my take.—BM

2 OUNCES SANTA TERESA 1796 RUM

1 TEASPOON DEMERARA SYRUP (PAGE 277)

1 TEASPOON VANILLA SYRUP (PAGE 277)

1 DASH HOUSE PEYCHAUD'S BITTERS (PAGE 284)

1 DASH ABBOTT'S BITTERS

1 DASH BITTER TRUTH JERRY THOMAS' BITTERS

GARNISH: NUTMEG

Stir all the ingredients over ice, then strain into a fizz glass. Garnish with a few grates of nutmeg.

....

COBRA VERDE

THOMAS WAUGH, 2009

This is an adaptation of the classic Diamondback cocktail. The combination of so many intense ingredients gives it, well, extra bite.—TW

1½ OUNCES NEISSON RHUM AGRICOLE BLANC

1 OUNCE CHAMOMILE-INFUSED OLD OVERHOLT RYE (PAGE 285)

½ OUNCE YELLOW CHARTREUSE

½ OUNCE GREEN CHARTREUSE

Stir all the ingredients over ice, then strain into a coupe. No garnish.

....

CORTADO

THOMAS WAUGH, 2009

This drink doesn't taste anything like a cortado—it's more like a mocha, but cortado sounds better.—TW

2 OUNCES PAMPERO ANIVERSARIO RUM

½ OUNCE LEMON HART 151 RUM

½ OUNCE COFFEE-INFUSED CARPANO ANTICA FORMULA VERMOUTH (PAGE 282)

¼ OUNCE MARIE BRIZARD WHITE CRÈME DE CACAO

½ TEASPOON DEMERARA SYRUP (PAGE 277)

1 DASH BITTERMENS XOCOLATL MOLE BITTERS

1 DASH ANGOSTURA BITTERS

GARNISH: 1 ORANGE TWIST

Stir all the ingredients over ice, then strain into a coupe. Garnish with the orange twist.

....

EAGLE-EYE CHERRY

BRAD FARRAN, 2013

2 OUNCES FLOR DE CAÑA 7-YEAR RUM

½ OUNCE CHERRY HEERING

½ OUNCE ALVEAR FESTIVAL PALE CREAM SHERRY

½ OUNCE LUSTAU EAST INDIA SOLERA SHERRY

¼ OUNCE ALCHEMIA CHOCOLATE VODKA

1 TEASPOON CARPANO ANTICA FORMULA VERMOUTH

½ TEASPOON SUZE SAVEUR D'AUTREFOIS LIQUEUR

1 DASH BITTERCUBE CHERRY BARK AND VANILLA BITTERS

1 ORANGE TWIST

GARNISH: 1 BRANDIED CHERRY

Stir all the ingredients (except the orange twist) over ice, then strain into a port glass. Squeeze the orange twist over the drink and discard. Garnish with the cherry.

....

EAST INDIA TRADING CO.

BRIAN MILLER, 2009

2 OUNCES APPLETON ESTATE RESERVE RUM

¾ OUNCE LUSTAU EAST INDIA SOLERA SHERRY

½ OUNCE RAMAZZOTTI

2 DASHES BITTERMENS XOCOLATL MOLE BITTERS

Stir all the ingredients over ice, then strain into a coupe. No garnish.

East India Trading Co.

HADLEY'S TEARS

JILLIAN VOSE, 2013

One of my favorite after-dinner drinks, this was named after Ernest Hemingway's first wife, Elizabeth Hadley Richardson.—JV

1 OUNCE APPLETON ESTATE V/X RUM

1 OUNCE BOLS GENEVER

1 TEASPOON GALLIANO RISTRETTO

½ TEASPOON ST. GEORGE ABSINTHE

¼ OUNCE CANE SUGAR SYRUP (PAGE 276)

1 DASH BITTER TRUTH AROMATIC BITTERS

GARNISH: 1 ORANGE TWIST

Stir all the ingredients over ice, then strain into a double rocks glass over 1 large ice cube. Garnish with the orange twist.

Puerto Rican Racer

HISPANIOLA

BRIAN MILLER, 2008

2 OUNCES SUMMER ROYALE TEA–INFUSED FLOR DE CAÑA WHITE RUM (PAGE 282)

¾ OUNCE LIME JUICE

½ OUNCE CANE SUGAR SYRUP (PAGE 276)

¼ OUNCE GINGER SYRUP (PAGE 277)

GARNISH: 1 LIME WHEEL

Stir all the ingredients over ice, then strain into a double rocks glass over 1 large ice cube. Garnish with the lime wheel.

....

HOWL ON THE HILL

JESSICA GONZALEZ, 2009

It's an unwritten rule that the name of any drink we create containing Fernet-Branca needs to reference San Francisco. Fernet and rum usually go great together, especially rum from Venezuela, where it's common to mix it with amaro.—JG

1½ OUNCES EL DORADO 15-YEAR RUM

½ OUNCE SANTA TERESA 1796 RUM

¾ OUNCE CARPANO ANTICA FORMULA VERMOUTH

½ OUNCE FERNET-BRANCA

¼ OUNCE YELLOW CHARTREUSE

1 DASH VIEUX PONTARLIER ABSINTHE

Stir all the ingredients over ice, then strain into a coupe. No garnish.

....

MIDNIGHT MASS

JOAQUÍN SIMÓ, 2009

2 OUNCES SCARLET IBIS RUM

¾ OUNCE CARDAMARO

¼ OUNCE BÉNÉDICTINE

1 DASH BITTER TRUTH JERRY THOMAS' BITTERS

GARNISH: 1 ORANGE TWIST

Stir all the ingredients over ice, then strain into a coupe. Garnish with the orange twist.

....

OLD IRONSIDES

BRIAN MILLER, 2009

Black strap rum is tricky: you can't use a lot or it will take over the drink. I almost always use it as a modifier.—BM

1½ OUNCES SCARLET IBIS RUM

½ OUNCE CRUZAN BLACK STRAP RUM

1 OUNCE DOLIN ROUGE VERMOUTH

1 TEASPOON LAZZARONI AMARETTO

1 DASH FEE BROTHERS WHISKEY BARREL-AGED BITTERS

Stir all the ingredients over ice, then strain into a coupe. No garnish.

....

PASSING ADEN

ALEX DAY, 2008

Batavia arrack, with its intense, funky hogo flavor, can be a challenge to work with. Here I use it in a classic punch formula with Demerara Syrup. Including a cinnamon stick when stirring the drink subtly heightens the cinnamon notes in the infused vermouth.—AD

2 OUNCES VAN OOSTEN BATAVIA ARRACK

1 OUNCE CINNAMON ORANGE TEA–INFUSED SWEET VERMOUTH (PAGE 281)

¼ OUNCE DEMERARA SYRUP (PAGE 277)

2 DASHES BITTER TRUTH AROMATIC BITTERS

1 CINNAMON STICK

GARNISH: 1 LEMON TWIST

Stir all the ingredients over ice, then strain into a coupe. Garnish with the lemon twist.

PIÑA COLADA DECONSTRUCTION

JOAQUÍN SIMÓ, 2008

This is a piña colada on a diet, the kind of cocktail I'd want poolside on a summer night while wearing a white linen suit, rather than a drink I'd have on the beach in a tank top and swim trunks.—JS

2 OUNCES PINEAPPLE-INFUSED FLOR DE CAÑA EXTRA-DRY WHITE RUM (PAGE 281)

1 TEASPOON KALANI RON DE COCO COCONUT LIQUEUR

1½ OUNCES COCONUT WATER

½ TEASPOON CANE SUGAR SYRUP (PAGE 276)

1 DASH ANGOSTURA BITTERS

Stir all the ingredients with ice, then strain into a coupe. No garnish.

....

PUERTO RICAN RACER

THOMAS WAUGH, 2009

This is one of several Death & Co variations on the Diamondback (a classic made with rye, apple brandy, and Chartreuse), each named after a different snake.—TW

2 OUNCES RON DEL BARRILITO 3-STAR RUM

½ OUNCE LAIRD'S BONDED APPLE BRANDY

SCANT ½ OUNCE YELLOW CHARTREUSE

1 TEASPOON GRENADINE (PAGE 284)

1 DASH HOUSE PEYCHAUD'S BITTERS (PAGE 284)

Stir all the ingredients over ice, then strain into a double rocks glass over 1 large ice cube. No garnish.

ROCK, PAPER, SCISSORS

THOMAS WAUGH, 2011

A lot of my drinks are inspired by dessert. Sometimes an idea comes from a new flavor pairing I discover at the hands of a great pastry chef; other times it comes from a childhood favorite. This drink is loosely based on the flavors of rocky road ice cream, minus the overwhelming sweetness.—TW

1½ OUNCES ZACAPA 23-YEAR RUM

¾ OUNCE CARPANO ANTICA FORMULA VERMOUTH

½ OUNCE OTIMA 10-YEAR TAWNY PORT

2½ TEASPOONS MARIE BRIZARD WHITE CRÈME DE CACAO

2½ TEASPOONS ALCHEMIA CHOCOLATE VODKA

1 DASH BITTERMENS XOCOLATL MOLE BITTERS

1 DASH ANGOSTURA BITTERS

Stir all the ingredients over ice, then strain into a martini glass. No garnish.

VELVET WARHOL

THOMAS WAUGH, 2008

I like to take the dominant flavor of a spirit and amplify it by infusing the booze with the same ingredient. In this case, I boosted the Gosling's banana notes by adding dried banana chips.—TW

2 OUNCES BANANA CHIP–INFUSED GOSLING'S BLACK SEAL RUM (PAGE 279)

¼ OUNCE MARIE BRIZARD WHITE CRÈME DE CACAO

2 DASHES BITTER TRUTH AROMATIC BITTERS

1 OUNCE HEAVY CREAM

Stir all the ingredients (except the cream) over ice, then strain into a coupe. Float the cream on top. No garnish.

AGAVE
SHAKEN

AKA COBBLER

ALEX DAY, 2008

Like sangria, cobblers were traditionally a means for making cheap wine better by fortifying it with a spirit and adding muddled fruit. I took the classic cobbler formula and removed most of the wine, using just a bit of sherry as a nod to the original recipe.—AD

1 TEASPOON SIMPLE SYRUP (PAGE 277)

1 TEASPOON LUXARDO MARASCHINO LIQUEUR

2 LEMON TWISTS

1 STRAWBERRY

1 WHITE SUGAR CUBE

1½ OUNCES SIEMBRA AZUL BLANCO TEQUILA

½ OUNCE JALAPEÑO–INFUSED SIEMBRA AZUL BLANCO TEQUILA (PAGE 279)

½ OUNCE LUSTAU EAST INDIA SOLERA SHERRY

GARNISH: ½ STRAWBERRY

In a shaker, muddle the simple syrup, maraschino liqueur, lemon twists, strawberry, and sugar cube. Add the tequilas and sherry and whip (shake with a few pieces of crushed ice, just until the ingredients are incorporated). Dump into a double rocks glass and top with crushed ice. Garnish with the half strawberry and serve with a straw.

. . . .

ALMOND BROTHER

JASON LITTRELL, 2011

2 OUNCES SIETE LEGUAS REPOSADO TEQUILA

¼ OUNCE AMARETTO

1 TEASPOON ROTHMAN & WINTER APRICOT LIQUEUR

¾ OUNCE LIME JUICE

¼ OUNCE ORGEAT (PAGE 278)

¼ OUNCE MAPLE SYRUP

Shake all the ingredients with ice, then strain into a coupe. No garnish.

. . . .

CAMP COUNCIL

JASON LITTRELL, 2011

1½ OUNCES SIETE LEGUAS REPOSADO TEQUILA

½ OUNCE ZIRBENZ STONE PINE LIQUEUR

½ OUNCE YELLOW CHARTREUSE

½ OUNCE PINEAPPLE JUICE

½ OUNCE LEMON JUICE

GARNISH: 1 MINT SPRIG

Shake all the ingredients with 3 ice cubes, then strain into a pilsner glass filled with crushed ice. Garnish with the mint sprig.

CHINGON

BRIAN MILLER, 2009

I created this drink as my dedication to all of our hardworking barbacks, naming it after the Mexican slang for "bad ass."—BM

2 OUNCES SIETE LEGUAS REPOSADO TEQUILA
¼ OUNCE BÉNÉDICTINE
½ OUNCE ORANGE JUICE
½ OUNCE LIME JUICE
½ OUNCE ORGEAT (PAGE 278)
GARNISH: 1 ORANGE TWIST

Shake all the ingredients with ice, then strain into a coupe. Garnish with the orange twist.

. . . .

CINDER

PHIL WARD, 2008

SMOKED SALT
¾ OUNCE PUEBLO VIEJO REPOSADO TEQUILA
¾ OUNCE JALAPEÑO-INFUSED SIEMBRA AZUL BLANCO TEQUILA (PAGE 279)
½ OUNCE DEL MAGUEY VIDA MEZCAL
¾ OUNCE LIME JUICE
¾ OUNCE SIMPLE SYRUP (PAGE 277)
2 DASHES ANGOSTURA BITTERS

Rim a coupe with smoked salt. Shake the remaining ingredients with ice, then strain into the coupe. No garnish.

. . . .

CINNAMON GIRL

BRAD FARRAN, 2013

2 ORANGE WEDGES
2 OUNCES SIETE LEGUAS REPOSADO TEQUILA
¼ OUNCE SMITH & CROSS RUM
¾ OUNCE LIME JUICE

½ OUNCE CINNAMON BARK SYRUP (PAGE 276)
¼ OUNCE CANE SUGAR SYRUP (PAGE 276)
1 DASH HOUSE ORANGE BITTERS (PAGE 284)
GARNISH: 1 ORANGE CRESCENT

In a shaker, muddle the orange wedges. Add the remaining ingredients and shake with ice. Strain into a double rocks glass filled with crushed ice. Garnish with the orange crescent and serve with a straw.

DHALGREN

PHIL WARD, 2008

2 OUNCES SIEMBRA AZUL BLANCO TEQUILA
1 OUNCE OTIMA 10-YEAR TAWNY PORT
½ OUNCE LIME JUICE
½ OUNCE GINGER SYRUP (PAGE 277)
1 DASH ANGOSTURA BITTERS
GARNISH: 1 LIME WHEEL

Shake all the ingredients with ice, then strain into a highball glass filled with ice cubes. Garnish with the lime wheel.

. . . .

DOS BESITOS

SCOTT TEAGUE, 2013

1 OUNCE EL TESORO REPOSADO TEQUILA
1 OUNCE SIETE LEGUAS BLANCO TEQUILA
¾ OUNCE PINEAPPLE JUICE
½ OUNCE LIME JUICE
¼ OUNCE AGAVE SYRUP
1 TEASPOON GRENADINE (PAGE 284)

Shake all the ingredients with ice, then strain into a coupe. No garnish.

EL COMPAÑERO

JASON LITTRELL, 2008

¾ OUNCE EL TESORO REPOSADO TEQUILA

¾ OUNCE JALAPEÑO-INFUSED SIEMBRA AZUL
   BLANCO TEQUILA (PAGE 279)

¾ OUNCE LIME JUICE

1 TEASPOON AGAVE NECTAR

1 DASH TABASCO CHIPOTLE SAUCE

PINCH OF KOSHER SALT

1 CILANTRO SPRIG

NEGRA MODELO BEER

GARNISH: 1 CILANTRO SPRIG

Shake all the ingredients (except the beer) with 3 ice cubes, then strain into a highball glass filled with ice cubes. Top with Negra Modelo. Garnish with the cilantro sprig and serve with a straw.

. . . .

ESPADIN QUEEN

THOMAS WAUGH, 2009

VIEUX PONTARLIER ABSINTHE

1½ OUNCES DEL MAGUEY VIDA MEZCAL

¼ OUNCE ST-GERMAIN

½ OUNCE GRAPEFRUIT JUICE

½ OUNCE LIME JUICE

½ OUNCE DONN'S MIX #1 (PAGE 284)

1 TEASPOON CANE SUGAR SYRUP (PAGE 276)

Rinse a coupe with absinthe and dump. Shake the remaining ingredients with ice, then strain into the coupe. No garnish.

. . . .

FLOR DE JALISCO

JOAQUÍN SIMÓ, 2009

In the 1980s, Julio Bermejo, an owner of Tommy's Mexican Restaurant in San Francisco, popularized a margarita sweetened with agave syrup. We've used his spec for some fun spin-offs, including this version made with lemon juice and orange marmalade.—JS

2 OUNCES SIEMBRA AZUL BLANCO TEQUILA

¾ OUNCE LEMON JUICE

¼ OUNCE AGAVE NECTAR

1 TEASPOON ORANGE MARMALADE

Shake all the ingredients with ice, then strain into a coupe. No garnish.

. . . .

FRESA BRAVA

PHIL WARD, 2009

1 STRAWBERRY

2 OUNCES JALAPEÑO-INFUSED SIEMBRA AZUL
   BLANCO TEQUILA (PAGE 279)

¾ OUNCE YELLOW CHARTREUSE

¾ OUNCE LEMON JUICE

½ OUNCE SIMPLE SYRUP (PAGE 277)

In a shaker, gently muddle the strawberry. Add the remaining ingredients and shake with ice, then double strain into a coupe. No garnish.

. . . .

GILDA COCKTAIL

BRIAN MILLER, 2009

The combination of pineapple, lime, and cinnamon in this cocktail became a popular trio of flavors at D&C, spawning other drinks like the Tom Bomb (page 161) and Blown Rose (page 198).—BM

2 OUNCES SIEMBRA AZUL BLANCO TEQUILA

½ OUNCE PINEAPPLE JUICE

½ OUNCE LIME JUICE

½ OUNCE CINNAMON BARK SYRUP (PAGE 276)

GARNISH: 1 LIME WHEEL

Shake all the ingredients with ice, then strain into a coupe. Garnish with the lime wheel.

GLANDULA DEL MONO

PHIL WARD, 2008

I guess it's pretty obvious that this is a tequila-based variation of the Monkey Gland (a gin-based cocktail). It also happens to be Brian Miller's favorite cocktail name.—PW

2 OUNCES SIEMBRA AZUL BLANCO TEQUILA

2 DASHES VIEUX PONTARLIER ABSINTHE

½ OUNCE LEMON JUICE

½ OUNCE ORANGE JUICE

½ OUNCE GRENADINE (PAGE 284)

Shake all the ingredients with ice, then strain into a coupe. No garnish.

. . . .

GOLDEN BEAUTIFUL

THOMAS WAUGH, 2009

2 OUNCES SIETE LEGUAS REPOSADO TEQUILA

¼ OUNCE CAMPARI

¾ OUNCE LIME JUICE

½ OUNCE VANILLA SYRUP (PAGE 277)

¼ OUNCE PASSION FRUIT SYRUP (PAGE 277)

½ OUNCE CLUB SODA

GARNISH: LIME ZEST

Short shake all the ingredients (except the club soda) with 3 ice cubes, then strain into a snifter over 1 large ice cube. Top with the club soda. Garnish with a fine grating of lime zest over the top.

. . . .

HEAD SPIN

JILLIAN VOSE, 2013

When I started working at the bar, one of my favorite drinks was Joaquín's Maggie Smith (page 213), which is a daiquiri variation made with Santa Teresa orange liqueur. I turned it into a margarita.—JV

1½ OUNCES CABEZA BLANCO TEQUILA

½ OUNCE SANTA TERESA ORANGE LIQUEUR

¾ OUNCE LIME JUICE

½ OUNCE ORANGE JUICE

¾ OUNCE KUMQUAT CORDIAL (PAGE 285)

¼ OUNCE VANILLA SYRUP (PAGE 277)

SPLASH OF CLUB SODA

GARNISH: 1 LIME WHEEL

Shake all the ingredients (except the club soda) with ice, then strain into a large coupe. Top with the club soda and garnish with the lime wheel.

. . . .

IN-SANDIARY

JOAQUÍN SIMÓ, 2009

SPICY SUGAR AND SALT RIM (PAGE 283)

2 OUNCES SIEMBRA AZUL BLANCO TEQUILA

2 OUNCES WATERMELON JUICE

½ OUNCE LIME JUICE

¼ OUNCE SIMPLE SYRUP (PAGE 277)

Rim a highball glass with spicy sugar and salt. Shake the remaining ingredients with ice, then pour into a highball glass filled with ice cubes. Serve with a straw. No garnish.

. . . .

LA VALENTINA

THOMAS WAUGH, 2009

The 1930s-era Blinker cocktail turned me on to the combination of rye, grapefruit, and raspberries. I substituted tequila for the rye and lightened it up with wheat beer.—TW

3 RASPBERRIES

1½ OUNCES DON JULIO BLANCO TEQUILA

1 OUNCE GRAPEFRUIT JUICE

¾ OUNCE LIME JUICE

¾ OUNCE SIMPLE SYRUP (PAGE 277)

PINCH OF KOSHER SALT

1½ OUNCES BLANCHE DE BRUXELLES BEER

GARNISH: 3 RASPBERRIES ON A COCKTAIL PICK

In a shaker, gently muddle the raspberries. Add the remaining ingredients (except the beer) and short shake with 3 ice cubes. Double strain into a pilsner glass filled with crushed ice, then pour in the beer. Garnish with the raspberries and serve with a straw.

. . . .

LOS AMARGOS

THOMAS WAUGH, 2009

1½ OUNCES CENTINELA REPOSADO TEQUILA

¾ OUNCE AMARO NONINO

¾ OUNCE CARDAMARO

1 TEASPOON MARASKA MARASCHINO LIQUEUR

¾ OUNCE LEMON JUICE

Shake all the ingredients with ice, then strain into a coupe. No garnish.

. . . .

NAKED AND FAMOUS

JOAQUÍN SIMÓ, 2011

This cocktail is the bastard child born out of an illicit Oaxacan love affair between the classic Last Word (page 144) and the Paper Plane, a drink Sam Ross created at the West Village bar Little Branch. Choosing an aggressively smoky, funky mezcal was key here, as there is relatively little of it in the drink and it needs to stand up against two liqueurs, neither of which lacks complexity.—JS

¾ OUNCE DEL MAGUEY CHICHICAPA MEZCAL

¾ OUNCE YELLOW CHARTREUSE

¾ OUNCE APEROL

¾ OUNCE LIME JUICE

Shake all the ingredients with ice, then strain into a coupe. No garnish.

Naked and Famous

Pinche Chivo

PINCHE CHIVO

JOAQUÍN SIMÓ, 2011

3 CUCUMBER WHEELS

2 OUNCES CABRITO BLANCO TEQUILA

¾ OUNCE SAGE-INFUSED DOLIN BLANC VERMOUTH (PAGE 281)

¾ OUNCE LIME JUICE

½ OUNCE ACACIA HONEY SYRUP (PAGE 276)

GARNISH: 1 CUCUMBER RIBBON

In a shaker, muddle the cucumber wheels. Add the remaining ingredients and shake with ice, then strain into a coupe. Garnish with the cucumber ribbon on a cocktail pick.

. . . .

SHORT RIB

PHIL WARD, 2008

When Death & Co opened, our kitchen served a dish of braised short ribs topped with jalapeño peppers and pomegranate molasses. I liked this combination, so I made it into a drink.—PW

2 OUNCES JALAPEÑO-INFUSED SIEMBRA AZUL BLANCO TEQUILA (PAGE 279)

¾ OUNCE LIME JUICE

1 OUNCE SIMPLE SYRUP (PAGE 277)

¾ TEASPOON POMEGRANATE MOLASSES

Shake all the ingredients with ice, then strain into a coupe. No garnish.

. . . .

SILVER MONK

PHIL WARD, 2007

At Death & Co, we also make a spicy version of this drink using jalapeño-infused tequila.—PW

2 CUCUMBER WHEELS

8 MINT LEAVES

PINCH OF KOSHER SALT

2 OUNCES SIEMBRA AZUL BLANCO TEQUILA

¾ OUNCE YELLOW CHARTREUSE

¾ OUNCE LIME JUICE

½ OUNCE SIMPLE SYRUP (PAGE 277)

In a shaker, muddle the cucumber wheels with the mint and salt. Add the remaining ingredients and shake with ice. Double strain into a coupe. No garnish.

. . . .

SINGLE ORIGIN

TYSON BUHLER, 2013

Chocolate, pineapple, coffee, and, of course, tequila are all famous Mexican ingredients, so it shouldn't be a surprise that they work well together in a cocktail.—TB

2 OUNCES CACAO NIB–INFUSED CABEZA BLANCO TEQUILA (PAGE 282)

1 TEASPOON GALLIANO RISTRETTO

½ OUNCE PINEAPPLE JUICE

½ OUNCE LEMON JUICE

½ OUNCE CANE SUGAR SYRUP (PAGE 276)

Shake all the ingredients with ice, then strain into a coupe. No garnish.

. . . .

SMOKED HORCHATA

JOAQUÍN SIMÓ, 2008

1 OUNCE FORTALEZA REPOSADO TEQUILA

1 OUNCE DEL MAGUEY CREMA DE MEZCAL

¼ OUNCE CINNAMON BARK SYRUP (PAGE 276)

2 OUNCES HOUSE HORCHATA (PAGE 284)

1 DASH ANGOSTURA BITTERS

GARNISH: 1 CINNAMON STICK

Shake all the ingredients with ice, then strain into a double rocks glass over 1 large ice cube. Garnish with the cinnamon stick.

SOUTHERN EXPOSURE

JOAQUÍN SIMÓ, 2009

This popular drink is my homage to the flavors of Mexico, made extra savory with red bell pepper and a pinch of salt, the latter an ingredient that doesn't see enough use in cocktails.—JS

1½ OUNCES JALAPEÑO-INFUSED SIEMBRA AZUL BLANCO TEQUILA (PAGE 279)

½ OUNCE LOS AMANTES JOVEN MEZCAL

½ OUNCE LIME JUICE

½ OUNCE CANE SUGAR SYRUP (PAGE 276)

½ OUNCE RED BELL PEPPER PUREE (PAGE 285)

PINCH OF KOSHER SALT

Shake all the ingredients with ice, then strain into a coupe. No garnish.

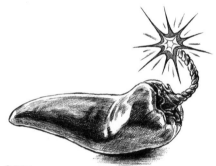

SPICY PALOMA

PHIL WARD, 2008

KOSHER SALT

2 OUNCES JALAPEÑO-INFUSED SIEMBRA AZUL BLANCO TEQUILA (PAGE 279)

1 OUNCE GRAPEFRUIT JUICE

¾ OUNCE LIME JUICE

½ OUNCE SIMPLE SYRUP (PAGE 277)

CLUB SODA

GARNISH: 1 LIME WHEEL

Rim a highball glass with kosher salt. Shake all the ingredients (except the club soda), then strain into a highball glass filled with ice cubes. Top with club soda. Garnish with the lime wheel and serve with a straw.

ST. MATILDA

PHIL WARD, 2007

½ BARTLETT PEAR, CUBED

2 OUNCES SIEMBRA AZUL BLANCO TEQUILA

¼ OUNCE MATHILDE POIRE PEAR LIQUEUR

½ OUNCE LEMON JUICE

½ OUNCE SIMPLE SYRUP (PAGE 277)

GARNISH: 1 BARTLETT PEAR SLICE

In a shaker, muddle the pear. Add the remaining ingredients and shake with ice. Double strain into a coupe. Garnish with the pear slice.

....

TOMMY AND THE RON-DELS

BRAD FARRAN, 2012

I got really excited about the flavor profile of Ron del Barrilito rum, so I worked it into a Tommy's margarita spec by including it in a split base with tequila and mezcal.—BF

¾ OUNCE EL TESORO REPOSADO TEQUILA

¼ OUNCE DEL MAGUEY CHICHICAPA MEZCAL

1 OUNCE RON DEL BARRILITO 3-STAR RUM

½ OUNCE GALLIANO L'AUTENTICO

1 DASH VIEUX PONTARLIER ABSINTHE

1 OUNCE LIME JUICE

½ OUNCE AGAVE NECTAR

1 DASH BITTERMENS 'ELEMAKULE TIKI BITTERS

GARNISH: 1 LIME WHEEL

Shake all the ingredients with ice, then strain into an old-fashioned glass over 1 large ice cube. Garnish with the lime wheel.

TY COBBLER

PHIL WARD, 2008

The combination of cherries and Cynar was an exciting revelation for me. I love the way the muddled cherries look scattered on top of the crushed ice; I refer to this as "serving it messy."—PW

3 BRANDIED CHERRIES

1 WHITE SUGAR CUBE

2 OUNCES SIETE LEGUAS BLANCO TEQUILA

½ OUNCE CYNAR

1 DASH BITTERMENS XOCOLATL MOLE BITTERS

GARNISH: 1 ORANGE WHEEL

In a shaker, muddle the cherries and sugar cube. Add the remaining ingredients and dry shake. Dump into a double rocks glass filled with crushed ice. Garnish with the orange wheel.

VILLAGE TO VILLAGE

THOMAS WAUGH, 2009

1½ OUNCES CHINACO VERDE BLANCO TEQUILA

½ TEASPOON ST. ELIZABETH ALLSPICE DRAM

1½ OUNCES FUJI APPLE JUICE

¾ OUNCE LEMON JUICE

½ OUNCE ACACIA HONEY SYRUP (PAGE 276)

½ TEASPOON GINGER SYRUP (PAGE 277)

GARNISH: 2 DASHES ANGOSTURA BITTERS AND 1 MINT SPRIG

Short shake all the ingredients with 3 ice cubes, then strain into a pilsner glass filled with crushed ice. Garnish with the bitters and the mint sprig and serve with a straw.

AGAVE

STIRRED

ALTA CALIFORNIA

ALEX DAY, 2009

2 OUNCES SIEMBRA AZUL BLANCO TEQUILA

¾ OUNCE DOLIN BLANC VERMOUTH

½ OUNCE (SCANT) YELLOW CHARTREUSE

¼ TEASPOON CINNAMON BARK SYRUP (PAGE 276)

Stir all the ingredients over ice, then strain into a coupe. No garnish.

....

AUGIE MARCH

PHIL WARD, 2008

2 OUNCES EL TESORO REPOSADO TEQUILA

¾ OUNCE CARPANO ANTICA FORMULA VERMOUTH

½ OUNCE CYNAR

GARNISH: 1 BRANDIED CHERRY

Stir all the ingredients over ice, then strain into a coupe. Garnish with the cherry.

....

BROKEN OATH

ERYN REECE, 2013

1½ OUNCES SOMBRA MEZCAL

¾ OUNCE LUSTAU AMONTILLADO SHERRY

¾ OUNCE COCCHI VERMOUTH DI TORINO

½ OUNCE GALLIANO RISTRETTO

2 DASHES BITTERMENS XOCOLATL MOLE BITTERS

Stir all the ingredients over ice, then strain into a Nick & Nora glass. No garnish.

....

CORALILLO

THOMAS WAUGH, 2011

1½ OUNCES EL TESORO AÑEJO TEQUILA

¾ OUNCE YELLOW CHARTREUSE

¾ OUNCE BUSNEL VSOP CALVADOS

¼ OUNCE CLEAR CREEK PEAR BRANDY

GARNISH: 1 FUJI APPLE SLICE

Stir all the ingredients over ice, then strain into a coupe. Garnish with the apple slice.

....

DALE COOPER

JESSICA GONZALEZ, 2011

We had a coffee pod machine at the bar that made really crappy coffee, so I would add a splash of green Chartreuse and cinnamon syrup to make it drinkable.—JG

2 OUNCES SIETE LEGUAS REPOSADO TEQUILA

½ OUNCE COFFEE-INFUSED CARPANO ANTICA FORMULA VERMOUTH (PAGE 282)

½ OUNCE GREEN CHARTREUSE

1 TEASPOON CINNAMON BARK SYRUP (PAGE 276)

1 DASH BITTERMENS XOCOLATL MOLE BITTERS

Stir all the ingredients over ice, then strain into a martini glass. No garnish.

GREEN AND RED

THOMAS WAUGH, 2012

Stirred cucumber drinks are rare; it's a lot harder to get the flavor incorporated into the drink. I got the idea for this cocktail from the Chin Up, another refreshing stirred cucumber drink, and named it after a great tequila bar in London.—TW

3 CUCUMBER WHEELS

1 OUNCE SIETE LEGUAS BLANCO TEQUILA

1 OUNCE JALAPEÑO-INFUSED SIEMBRA AZUL BLANCO TEQUILA (PAGE 279)

¾ OUNCE COCCHI AMERICANO

¾ OUNCE DOLIN DRY VERMOUTH

¼ OUNCE ALVEAR FESTIVAL PALE CREAM SHERRY

GARNISH: 1 CUCUMBER RIBBON

In a mixing glass, muddle the cucumber wheels. Add the remaining ingredients and stir over ice, then strain into a coupe. Garnish with the cucumber ribbon on a cocktail pick.

. . . .

HOT LIPS

JESSICA GONZALEZ, 2009

Joaquín's Faithful Scotsman cocktail (page 206) showed me that you can make a stirred drink with citrus juice— if you add enough fat to get the texture right.—JG

KOSHER SALT

¾ OUNCE JALAPEÑO-INFUSED SIEMBRA AZUL BLANCO TEQUILA (PAGE 279)

¾ OUNCE LOS AMANTES JOVEN MEZCAL

½ OUNCE LEMON JUICE

½ OUNCE PINEAPPLE JUICE

½ OUNCE VANILLA SYRUP (PAGE 277)

1 TEASPOON CANE SUGAR SYRUP (PAGE 276)

Rim half of a fancy fizz glass with salt and add 2 ice cubes. Stir the remaining ingredients over ice, then strain into the glass. No garnish.

IMAGINARY GRACE

JOAQUÍN SIMÓ, 2009

2 OUNCES SIETE LEGUAS REPOSADO TEQUILA

1 OUNCE MORENITA CREAM SHERRY

½ TEASPOON CLEAR CREEK PEAR BRANDY

½ TEASPOON CARPANO ANTICA FORMULA VERMOUTH

½ TEASPOON AGAVE NECTAR

1 DASH BITTERMENS XOCOLATL MOLE BITTERS

1 DASH ANGOSTURA BITTERS

Stir all the ingredients over ice, then strain into a coupe. No garnish.

. . . .

LAST TRAIN TO OAXACA

BRIAN MILLER, 2009

1½ OUNCES PUEBLO VIEJO AÑEJO TEQUILA

½ OUNCE LOS AMANTES JOVEN MEZCAL

¾ OUNCE LILLET BLANC

1 TEASPOON DONN'S SPICES #2 (PAGE 284)

GARNISH: 1 ORANGE TWIST

Stir all the ingredients over ice, then strain into a coupe. Garnish with the orange twist.

. . . .

NITTY-GRITTY

JOAQUÍN SIMÓ, 2011

In this riff on the Fitty-Fitty martini, the combination of mezcal and sherry was so drying that the cocktail needed some texture and sweetness. The smallest amount of pear liqueur and agave nectar made a huge difference.—JS

1½ OUNCES DEL MAGUEY ESPADIN ESPECIAL MEZCAL

1½ OUNCES LA CIGARRERA MANZANILLA SHERRY

½ OUNCE BÉNÉDICTINE

½ TEASPOON ROTHMAN & WINTER PEAR LIQUEUR

½ TEASPOON AGAVE NECTAR

1 DASH BAR CODE BAKED APPLE BITTERS

1 DASH BITTER TRUTH AROMATIC BITTERS

GARNISH: 1 LEMON TWIST

Stir all the ingredients over ice, then strain into a coupe. Garnish with the lemon twist.

. . . .

PERFECT CRIME

JILLIAN VOSE, 2013

Pasquet Marie-Framboise is a lovely aperitif made by soaking raspberries in cognac and freshly harvested grape juice. It lightens up this drink and bridges the smoke bomb mezcal and bitter amaro.—JV

1¾ OUNCES SOMBRA MEZCAL

½ OUNCE PASQUET MARIE-FRAMBOISE

½ OUNCE AMARO AVERNA

1 TEASPOON VANILLA SYRUP (PAGE 277)

2 DASHES HOUSE ORANGE BITTERS (PAGE 284)

GARNISH: 2 RASPBERRIES ON A COCKTAIL PICK

Stir all the ingredients over ice, then strain into a double rocks glass over 1 large ice cube. Garnish with the raspberries.

. . . .

PRIMA CHINA

JOAQUÍN SIMÓ, 2009

My wife's mother is Chinese, and one of my wife's cousins married a Mexican. So I married both cultures in this cocktail—China by way of the tea and Mexico with the tequila and bitters—and named it after my wife's Chinese cousin (prima being Spanish for "cousin").—JS

2 OUNCES SIEMBRA AZUL AÑEJO TEQUILA

¾ OUNCE EARL GREY–INFUSED DOLIN BLANC VERMOUTH (PAGE 282)

¼ OUNCE CYNAR

1 TEASPOON MARIE BRIZARD WHITE CRÈME DE CACAO

1 DASH BITTERMENS XOCOLATL MOLE BITTERS

GARNISH: 1 GRAPEFRUIT TWIST

Stir all the ingredients over ice, then strain into a coupe. Garnish with the grapefruit twist.

. . . .

REBEL REBEL

JILLIAN VOSE, 2013

This is an example of a drink that can easily go off the rails if you use too much of one ingredient. It breaks a bunch of rules, the first being that it seems like it should be a shaken drink.—JV

½ CHERRY TOMATO

1 OUNCE SIETE LEGUAS BLANCO TEQUILA

1½ OUNCES WATERMELON-INFUSED DOLIN DRY VERMOUTH (PAGE 281)

1 OUNCE COCCHI AMERICANO ROSA

½ TEASPOON FUSION VERJUS BLANC

SMALL PINCH OF KOSHER SALT

1 DASH HOUSE ORANGE BITTERS (PAGE 284)

In a mixing glass, muddle the cherry tomato. Add the remaining ingredients and stir over ice. Double strain into a Nick & Nora Glass. No garnish.

. . . .

SARAMAGO

PHIL WARD, 2008

DEL MAGUEY VIDA MEZCAL

2 OUNCES SIEMBRA AZUL BLANCO TEQUILA

¾ OUNCE DOLIN BLANC VERMOUTH

½ OUNCE ST-GERMAIN

1 DASH HOUSE ORANGE BITTERS (PAGE 284)

1 GRAPEFRUIT TWIST

Rinse a coupe with mezcal and dump. Stir the remaining ingredients (except the grapefruit twist) over ice, then strain into the coupe. Squeeze the grapefruit twist over the drink and discard. No garnish.

SHATTERED GLASSER

PHIL WARD, 2008

I love it when one of our regulars asks us to create a cocktail on the spot based on crazy criteria—and it's even better when we can pull off a decent drink on the first try. One night Avery Glasser, the man behind Bittermens bitters and one of the bar's original regulars, asked me to make him a drink that contained all of his favorite ingredients. The problem was that he likes a lot of weird shit. But I gave it a shot, splitting both the base spirit and its modifiers, and it resulted in a surprisingly balanced drink.—PW

1 OUNCE EL TESORO REPOSADO TEQUILA
½ OUNCE LOS AMANTES JOVEN MEZCAL
¾ OUNCE CARPANO ANTICA FORMULA VERMOUTH
½ OUNCE VAN OOSTEN BATAVIA ARRACK
¼ OUNCE ST. ELIZABETH ALLSPICE DRAM
¼ OUNCE BÉNÉDICTINE
2 DASHES BITTERMENS XOCOLATL MOLE BITTERS

Stir all the ingredients over ice, then strain into a coupe. No garnish.

. . . .

SPAGHETTI WESTERN

JESSICA GONZALEZ, 2011

1 OUNCE SIETE LEGUAS REPOSADO TEQUILA
½ OUNCE LOS NAHUALES MEZCAL
¾ OUNCE AMARO NONINO
1 DASH HOUSE ORANGE BITTERS (PAGE 284)
GARNISH: 1 GRAPEFRUIT TWIST

Stir all the ingredients over ice, then strain into an old-fashioned glass over 1 large ice cube. Garnish with the grapefruit twist.

SERGIO LEONE

BRIAN MILLER, 2009

This is one of the few tequila-based cocktails I've created for D&C. It's based on the spec for a Red Hook.—BM

2 OUNCES EL TESORO REPOSADO TEQUILA
¾ OUNCE CARPANO ANTICA FORMULA VERMOUTH
¼ OUNCE SOLERNO BLOOD ORANGE LIQUEUR
1 DASH BITTERMENS XOCOLATL MOLE BITTERS

Stir all the ingredients over ice, then strain into a coupe. No garnish.

SPANISH CARAVAN

BRIAN MILLER, 2008

This is a variation on the Chas, a bourbon-based drink created by Murray Stenson at Seattle's Zig Zag Café.—BM

2 OUNCES LAPSANG SOUCHONG–INFUSED SIEMBRA AZUL BLANCO TEQUILA (PAGE 282)

¼ OUNCE LAZZARONI AMARETTO

¼ OUNCE GRAND MARNIER

¼ OUNCE BÉNÉDICTINE

¼ OUNCE COINTREAU

1 DASH ANGOSTURA ORANGE BITTERS

GARNISH: 1 ORANGE TWIST

Stir all the ingredients over ice, then strain into a coupe. Garnish with the orange twist.

. . . .

TE AMO

BRAD FARRAN, 2012

Some of our cocktails use several ingredients in such tiny amounts that we premix them in a cheater bottle to speed up service. Tickle Juice—a two-to-one blend of white crème de cacao and Cynar—originated with this drink.—BF

2 OUNCES EL TESORO AÑEJO TEQUILA

¾ OUNCE COCCHI VERMOUTH DI TORINO

2 TEASPOONS MARIE BRIZARD WHITE CRÈME DE CACAO

1 TEASPOON CYNAR

1 DASH HOUSE ORANGE BITTERS (PAGE 284)

1 DASH BITTERMENS XOCOLATL MOLE BITTERS

1 DASH BITTERMENS HELLFIRE HABANERO SHRUB

GARNISH: 1 ORANGE TWIST

Stir all the ingredients over ice, then strain into a martini glass. Garnish with the orange twist.

TERRIBLE LOVE

PHIL WARD, 2013

1½ OUNCES DEL MAGUEY CHICHICAPA MEZCAL

¾ OUNCE SUZE SAVEUR D'AUTREFOIS LIQUEUR

½ OUNCE ST-GERMAIN

1 DASH HOUSE ORANGE BITTERS (PAGE 284)

GARNISH: 1 GRAPEFRUIT TWIST

Stir all the ingredients over ice, then strain into an old-fashioned glass over 1 large ice cube. Garnish with the grapefruit twist.

. . . .

VIPERA

BRIAN MILLER, 2008

I based my spiced pear-infused tequila on the pear-, apple-, and spice-infused vodka from a Dale DeGroff recipe for an apple martini.—BM

2 OUNCES SPICED PEAR–INFUSED SIEMBRA AZUL BLANCO TEQUILA (PAGE 281)

½ OUNCE LAIRD'S BONDED APPLE BRANDY

½ OUNCE YELLOW CHARTREUSE

GARNISH: 1 ANJOU PEAR SLICE

Stir all the ingredients over ice, then strain into a coupe. Garnish with the pear slice.

. . . .

YAMA BLANCA

JESSICA GONZALEZ, 2009

1½ OUNCES CENTINELA REPOSADO TEQUILA

½ OUNCE JALAPEÑO-INFUSED SIEMBRA AZUL BLANCO TEQUILA (PAGE 279)

¾ OUNCE DOLIN BLANC VERMOUTH

¼ OUNCE VELVET FALERNUM

Stir all the ingredients over ice, then strain into a coupe. No garnish.

WHISKEY

SHAKEN

19TH CENTURY

BRIAN MILLER, 2009

1½ OUNCES WOODFORD RESERVE BOURBON
¾ OUNCE LILLET ROUGE
¾ OUNCE MARIE BRIZARD WHITE CRÈME DE CACAO
¾ OUNCE LEMON JUICE

Shake all the ingredients with ice, then strain into a coupe. No garnish.

. . . .

202 STEPS

PHIL WARD, 2008

¼ TANGERINE, PEELED
2 OUNCES BAKER'S BOURBON
½ OUNCE SIMPLE SYRUP (PAGE 277)
2 DASHES HOUSE ORANGE BITTERS (PAGE 284)
GARNISH: 1 ORANGE TWIST

In a shaker, muddle the tangerine. Add the remaining ingredients and shake with ice, then double strain into a double rocks glass over 1 large ice cube. Garnish with the orange twist.

. . . .

BANKS OF ISLAY

THOMAS WAUGH, 2012

6 FRESH CURRY LEAVES
1½ OUNCES LAPHROAIG 10-YEAR SCOTCH

¾ OUNCE LIME JUICE
½ OUNCE CANE SUGAR SYRUP (PAGE 276)
1 TEASPOON GRENADINE (PAGE 284)
GARNISH: 1 FRESH CURRY LEAF

In a shaker, gently muddle the curry leaves. Add the remaining ingredients and shake with ice, then double strain into a coupe. Garnish with the curry leaf.

. . . .

BLAZING SADDLES

BRAD FARRAN, 2013

High West's oat whiskey is one of the few unaged whiskeys that I really like; it has enough of its own flavor profile to stand out in a drink, like this grapefruit- and cinnamon-flavored sour.—BF

2 OUNCES HIGH WEST SILVER OAT WHISKEY
½ OUNCE COMBIER PAMPLEMOUSSE
    ROSE LIQUEUR
¾ OUNCE LEMON JUICE
½ OUNCE CINNAMON BARK SYRUP (PAGE 276)
1 DASH BITTERMENS 'ELEMAKULE TIKI BITTERS
GARNISH: 1 GRAPEFRUIT TWIST

Shake all the ingredients with ice, then strain into a coupe. Garnish with the grapefruit twist.

BLOWN ROSE

THOMAS WAUGH, 2009

3 FUJI APPLE SLICES

2 OUNCES CHAMOMILE-INFUSED OLD OVERHOLT
 RYE (PAGE 281)

½ OUNCE PINEAPPLE JUICE

½ OUNCE LIME JUICE

½ OUNCE CINNAMON BARK SYRUP (PAGE 276)

GARNISH: 1 LIME WHEEL

In a shaker, muddle the apple slices. Add the remaining ingredients and shake with ice. Double strain into a coupe and garnish with the lime wheel.

....

BLUE RUN SLING

JOAQUÍN SIMÓ, 2009

2 OUNCES ELIJAH CRAIG 12-YEAR BOURBON

¼ OUNCE AMARO AVERNA

¾ OUNCE FUJI APPLE JUICE

½ OUNCE LEMON JUICE

¾ OUNCE VANILLA SYRUP (PAGE 277)

1 DASH HOUSE ORANGE BITTERS (PAGE 284)

GARNISH: 1 ORANGE FLAG AND FEE BROTHERS
 WHISKEY BARREL-AGED BITTERS

Shake all the ingredients with ice, then strain into a highball glass filled with ice cubes. Garnish the orange flag, topped with few drops of bitters, and serve with a straw.

....

CASTLE TO CASTLE

THOMAS WAUGH, 2009

1½ OUNCES KNAPPOGUE CASTLE 12-YEAR IRISH
 WHISKEY

1½ OUNCES FUJI APPLE JUICE

¾ OUNCE LEMON JUICE

½ OUNCE ACACIA HONEY SYRUP (PAGE 276)

GARNISH: 1 BASIL SPRIG

Short shake all the ingredients with 3 ice cubes, then strain into a pilsner glass filled with crushed ice. Garnish with the basil sprig and serve with a straw.

....

CRANE KICK

BRAD FARRAN, 2012

I wanted to devise a tiki cocktail based on Japanese whiskey. But just a little bit of Kalani completely dominated the drink, so I added a teaspoon of peaty Scotch to balance it and create extra layers of depth.—BF

2 OUNCES YAMAZAKI 12-YEAR WHISKEY

1 TEASPOON LAPHROAIG 10-YEAR SCOTCH

2 TEASPOONS KALANI RON DE COCO COCONUT
 LIQUEUR

1 OUNCE ORANGE JUICE

½ OUNCE LEMON JUICE

½ OUNCE ORGEAT (PAGE 278)

1 DASH ANGOSTURA BITTERS

Short shake all the ingredients with 3 cubes of ice, then strain into a pilsner glass filled with crushed ice. Serve with a straw. No garnish.

....

DANGEROUS LIAISONS

JOAQUÍN SIMÓ, 2012

1½ OUNCES LAVENDER-INFUSED BERNHEIM
 ORIGINAL WHEAT WHISKEY (PAGE 281)

¾ OUNCE DOLIN BLANC VERMOUTH

¾ OUNCE GRAPEFRUIT JUICE

½ OUNCE LEMON JUICE

½ OUNCE ACACIA HONEY SYRUP (PAGE 276)

GARNISH: 1 GRAPEFRUIT CRESCENT

Shake all the ingredients with ice, then strain into a highball glass filled with ice. Garnish with the grapefruit crescent on a cocktail pick and serve with a straw.

DEADPAN FIX

JESSICA GONZALEZ, 2011

Rye is harder to use in shaken drinks than bourbon; it can be a bully. But it works when combined with more aggressive flavors, like the Campari, ginger, and grapefruit here.—JG

1½ OUNCES RITTENHOUSE 100 RYE

¼ OUNCE CAMPARI

¼ OUNCE GRAND MARNIER

¾ OUNCE GRAPEFRUIT JUICE

½ OUNCE LEMON JUICE

¼ OUNCE GINGER SYRUP (PAGE 277)

GARNISH: 1 ORANGE TWIST

Shake all the ingredients with ice, then strain into a coupe. Garnish with the orange twist.

. . . .

DOC'S DRAM

JOAQUÍN SIMÓ, 2011

You don't usually see rye and gin together in a split base, but the Old Tom is malty enough and the Overholt so soft that they work fantastically together in this fall-spiced sour.—JS

1½ OUNCES OLD OVERHOLT RYE

½ OUNCE RANSOM OLD TOM GIN

½ OUNCE LUSTAU EAST INDIA SOLERA SHERRY

¾ OUNCE LEMON JUICE

½ OUNCE MAPLE SYRUP

1 TEASPOON APPLE BUTTER

1 DASH ANGOSTURA BITTERS

GARNISH: 1 APPLE FAN

Shake all the ingredients with ice, then strain into a double rocks glass over 1 large ice cube. Garnish with the apple fan.

DOUBLE FILL-UP

PHIL WARD, 2008

2 OUNCES RITTENHOUSE 100 RYE

¾ OUNCE LEMON JUICE

¾ OUNCE SIMPLE SYRUP (PAGE 277)

1 TEASPOON POMEGRANATE MOLASSES

3 MINT LEAVES

GARNISH: 1 MINT LEAF

Shake all the ingredients with ice, then double strain into a coupe. Garnish with the mint leaf.

. . . .

DR. FEELGOOD

JILLIAN VOSE, 2013

This is a good example of a drink that looks sweet on paper but actually isn't, thanks to the bone-dry apple eau-de-vie and fig-infused bourbon.—JV

2 OUNCES FIG-INFUSED ELIJAH CRAIG BOURBON (PAGE 279)

½ OUNCE CLEAR CREEK APPLE BRANDY

¼ OUNCE GRAND MARNIER

½ OUNCE LEMON JUICE

½ OUNCE GRANNY SMITH APPLE JUICE

¼ OUNCE ORGEAT (PAGE 278)

¼ OUNCE GINGER SYRUP (PAGE 277)

1 DASH ANGOSTURA BITTERS

Shake all the ingredients with ice, then strain into a large coupe. No garnish.

EYE OF THE TORINO

JILLIAN VOSE, 2013

You probably wouldn't think of using peaty Scotch in a creamy tiki drink, but its smoky flavor really stands out over all the richness.—JV

2 OUNCES BOWMORE 12-YEAR SCOTCH

½ OUNCE COCCHI VERMOUTH DI TORINO

½ OUNCE PINEAPPLE JUICE

½ OUNCE LEMON JUICE

½ OUNCE ORGEAT (PAGE 278)

1 TEASPOON VANILLA SYRUP (PAGE 277)

½ OUNCE COCO LOPEZ

¼ OUNCE HEAVY CREAM

1 DASH ANGOSTURA BITTERS

1 DASH BITTERMENS XOCOLATL MOLE BITTERS

GARNISH: 1 PINEAPPLE WEDGE AND CHERRY FLAG

Short shake all the ingredients with 3 ice cubes, then strain into a coconut mug filled with crushed ice. Garnish with the pineapple wedge and cherry flag.

. . . .

FIX ME UP

THOMAS WAUGH, 2009

1 OUNCE SAZERAC 6-YEAR RYE

1½ OUNCES LUSTAU AMONTILLADO SHERRY

½ OUNCE LEMON JUICE

½ OUNCE ORANGE JUICE

¾ OUNCE ORGEAT (PAGE 278)

2 DASHES ANGOSTURA BITTERS

¾ OUNCE CLUB SODA

Short shake all the ingredients (except the club soda) with 3 ice cubes, then strain into a snifter over 1 large ice cube. Pour in the club soda. No garnish.

GROUSE RAMPANT

ALEX DAY, 2008

This whiskey sour variation is full of fall flavors. I make an X with the bitters on top to evoke the Scottish flag.—AD

2 OUNCES FUJI APPLE–INFUSED FAMOUS GROUSE SCOTCH (PAGE 279)

¾ OUNCE LEMON JUICE

¼ OUNCE ACACIA HONEY SYRUP (PAGE 276)

¼ OUNCE CINNAMON BARK SYRUP (PAGE 276)

1 EGG WHITE

GARNISH: HOUSE PEYCHAUD'S BITTERS (PAGE 284)

Dry shake all the ingredients, then shake again with ice. Double strain into a coupe and garnish with 2 swipes of the bitters to form an X.

. . . .

HONSHU PUNCH

THOMAS WAUGH, 2009

2 OUNCES YAMAZAKI 12-YEAR WHISKEY

¾ OUNCE LEMON JUICE

½ OUNCE PINEAPPLE JUICE

½ OUNCE CANE SUGAR SYRUP (PAGE 276)

2 DASHES FEE BROTHERS WHISKEY BARREL-AGED BITTERS

2 DASHES BITTER TRUTH AROMATIC BITTERS

1 OUNCE CLUB SODA

Shake all the ingredients (except the club soda), then strain into a snifter over 1 large ice cube. Pour in the club soda. No garnish.

LITTLE ENGINE

ALEX DAY, 2009

2 OUNCES FAMOUS GROUSE SCOTCH

½ OUNCE OTIMA 10-YEAR TAWNY PORT

½ OUNCE LEMON JUICE

½ OUNCE MAPLE SYRUP

1 TEASPOON APPLE BUTTER

GARNISH: 1 APPLE FAN

Short shake all the ingredients with 3 ice cubes, then double strain into a double rocks glass filled with crushed ice. Garnish with the apple fan and serve with a straw.

....

MONONGAHELA MULE

PHIL WARD, 2007

4 RASPBERRIES

6 MINT LEAVES

2 OUNCES OLD OVERHOLT RYE

¾ OUNCE LEMON JUICE

½ OUNCE GINGER SYRUP (PAGE 277)

GARNISH: 1 MINT SPRIG

In a shaker, gently muddle the raspberries and mint. Add the remaining ingredients and shake with ice. Double strain into a highball glass filled with ice cubes. Garnish with the mint sprig and serve with a straw.

....

MRS. DOYLE

ERYN REECE, 2013

2 OUNCES REDBREAST 12-YEAR IRISH WHISKEY

¼ OUNCE KRONAN SWEDISH PUNSCH

¾ OUNCE LEMON JUICE

½ OUNCE SIMPLE SYRUP (PAGE 277)

Shake all the ingredients with ice, then strain into a coupe. No garnish.

PADDY MELT

JOAQUÍN SIMÓ, 2011

Guests who swear up and down that they hate whiskey will gulp down four of these in an evening.—JS

1½ OUNCES KNAPPOGUE CASTLE 12-YEAR IRISH WHISKEY

½ OUNCE CHAMOMILE-INFUSED OLD OVERHOLT RYE (PAGE 281)

½ OUNCE AMARO MELETTI

¾ OUNCE LEMON JUICE

½ OUNCE CANE SUGAR SYRUP (PAGE 276)

Shake all the ingredients with ice, then strain into a fancy fizz glass. No garnish.

Paddy Melt

PETE'S WORD

PHIL WARD, 2008

It doesn't make sense, but peaty Scotch and lime juice are amazing together, so I used this surprising combo in a variation on the Last Word (page 144).—PW

¾ OUNCE LAPHROAIG 10-YEAR SCOTCH

¾ OUNCE LUXARDO MARASCHINO LIQUEUR

¾ OUNCE GREEN CHARTREUSE

¾ OUNCE LIME JUICE

Shake all the ingredients with ice, then strain into a coupe. No garnish.

. . . .

SCOTCH LADY

PHIL WARD, 2008

1½ OUNCES FAMOUS GROUSE SCOTCH

½ OUNCE LAIRD'S BONDED APPLE BRANDY

¾ OUNCE LEMON JUICE

¾ OUNCE SIMPLE SYRUP (PAGE 277)

¼ OUNCE GRENADINE (PAGE 284)

1 EGG WHITE

GARNISH: 1 BRANDIED CHERRY

Dry shake all the ingredients, then shake again with ice. Double strain into a coupe and garnish with the cherry.

. . . .

STRAW DOG

THOMAS WAUGH, 2009

1 STRAWBERRY

1½ OUNCES COMPASS BOX ASYLA SCOTCH

1 OUNCE DOLIN BLANC VERMOUTH

¾ OUNCE LEMON JUICE

½ OUNCE SIMPLE SYRUP (PAGE 277)

1 DASH BITTERMENS HOPPED GRAPEFRUIT BITTERS

GARNISH: ½ STRAWBERRY

In a shaker, gently muddle the strawberry. Add the remaining ingredients and shake with ice, then strain into a coupe. Garnish with the strawberry half.

. . . .

SWEARENGEN SLING

BRIAN MILLER, 2009

2 BRANDIED CHERRIES

2 OUNCES BULLEIT BOURBON

½ OUNCE AMARO NONINO

½ OUNCE CHERRY HEERING

½ OUNCE LEMON JUICE

½ OUNCE SIMPLE SYRUP (PAGE 277)

GARNISH: 1 BRANDIED CHERRY

In a shaker, muddle the cherries. Add the remaining ingredients and shake with ice. Strain into a highball glass filled with ice cubes. Garnish with the cherry on a cocktail pick and serve with a straw.

. . . .

SWEEP THE LEG

BRAD FARRAN, 2013

2 OUNCES SUNTORY HAKASHU 12-YEAR WHISKY

¾ OUNCE ORGEAT (PAGE 278)

½ OUNCE LUSTAU AMONTILLADO SHEERY

½ OUNCE LEMON JUICE

½ OUNCE ORANGE JUICE

¼ OUNCE ACACIA HONEY SYRUP (PAGE 276)

1 TEASPOON LUXARDO AMARO ABANO

1 DASH ANGOSTURA BITTERS

1 DASH BITTERMENS XOCOLATL MOLE BITTERS

GARNISH: 1 LIME WHEEL, 1 ORANGE CRESCENT, 1 BRANDIED CHERRY, 1 MINT SPRIG

Short shake all the ingredients with 3 ice cubes, then strain into a pilsner glass filled with crushed ice. Skewer the lime wheel, orange crescent, and cherry on a cocktail pick and insert into the ice along with a mint sprig.

VAMPIRE BLUES

JESSICA GONZALEZ, 2009

1½ OUNCES OLD WELLER ANTIQUE 107 BOURBON

½ OUNCE EAST INDIA SOLERA SHERRY

½ OUNCE LEMON JUICE

½ OUNCE SIMPLE SYRUP (PAGE 277)

1 TEASPOON PUMPKIN BUTTER

2 DASHES ANGOSTURA BITTERS

GARNISH: 1 CINNAMON STICK

Shake all the ingredients with ice, then strain into a double rocks glass filled with ice cubes. Garnish with a few grates of the cinnamon stick over the top, then garnish with the cinnamon stick and serve with a straw.

. . . .

VEJK SLING

PHIL WARD, 2008

The sling is a one of the oldest cocktail templates, combining some kind of booze with lemon, sugar, and water, which could be drunk hot or cold. I named this loose interpretation after the Czech inspiration for the novel Catch-22.*—PW*

2 OUNCES COMPASS BOX ASYLA SCOTCH

1 OUNCE CHAMOMILE-INFUSED BIANCO VERMOUTH (PAGE 281)

½ OUNCE LEMON JUICE

¾ OUNCE SIMPLE SYRUP (PAGE 277)

1 DASH HOUSE ORANGE BITTERS (PAGE 284)

CLUB SODA

GARNISH: 1 LEMON TWIST

Shake all the ingredients (except the club soda) with ice, then strain into a highball glass filled with ice cubes. Top with club soda. Garnish with the lemon twist and serve with a straw.

WAREHOUSE C

JILLIAN VOSE, 2013

The combination of orgeat, Cinnamon Bark Syrup, and Ginger Syrup is a popular trifecta of sweeteners at the bar. Why use one when you can use three?—JV

1 STRAWBERRY

1½ OUNCES BUFFALO TRACE BOURBON

¾ OUNCE LEMON JUICE

¼ OUNCE LIME JUICE

¼ OUNCE ORGEAT (PAGE 278)

¼ OUNCE CINNAMON BARK SYRUP (PAGE 276)

¼ OUNCE GINGER SYRUP (PAGE 277)

1 DASH BITTER TRUTH AROMATIC BITTERS

In a shaker, gently muddle the strawberry. Add the remaining ingredients and shake with ice, then strain into a coupe. No garnish.

. . . .

WHIRLING TIGER

BRIAN MILLER, 2008

This bourbon-based cocktail is inspired by the Dark and Stormy (page 142) and named after a storm chaser group based out of Kentucky.—BM

2 OUNCES BUFFALO TRACE BOURBON

1 OUNCE FUJI APPLE JUICE

¾ OUNCE LEMON JUICE

½ OUNCE GINGER SYRUP (PAGE 277)

GARNISH: 1 FUJI APPLE SLICE

Shake all the ingredients with ice, then strain into a highball glass filled with ice cubes. Garnish with the apple slice and serve with a straw.

WHISKEY

STIRRED

B.A.F.

ERYN REECE, 2012

When we were developing this drink at a menu tasting, someone took a sip and said, "This is bitter as fuck . . . but I love it." The name stuck.—ER

1 OUNCE MACALLAN FINE OAK 10-YEAR SCOTCH

1 OUNCE LUSTAU OLOROSO SHERRY

½ OUNCE APEROL

½ OUNCE GRAN CLASSICO BITTER

1 LEMON TWIST

Stir all the ingredients (except the lemon twist) over ice, then strain into a double rocks glass. Squeeze the lemon twist over the drink and discard. No garnish.

. . . .

BELLA COHEN

JESSICA GONZALEZ, 2011

1½ OUNCES KNAPPOGUE CASTLE 12-YEAR IRISH WHISKEY

1½ OUNCES ALVEAR FESTIVAL PALE CREAM SHERRY

½ OUNCE COINTREAU

1 TEASPOON ST-GERMAIN

1 DASH HOUSE PEYCHAUD'S BITTERS (PAGE 284)

GARNISH: 1 LEMON TWIST

Stir all the ingredients over ice, then strain into a coupe. Garnish with the lemon twist.

BLACK MARKET MANHATTAN

BRIAN MILLER, 2008

I found an incredible cinnamon-orange black tea in Seattle's Pike Place Market, then brought it to the bar and started playing around with infusions. Our tea-infused sweet vermouth has proven to be a key ingredient in various stirred drinks and punches.—BM

2 OUNCES BERNHEIM WHEAT WHISKEY

1 OUNCE CINNAMON ORANGE TEA–INFUSED SWEET VERMOUTH (PAGE 281)

1 DASH ANGOSTURA BITTERS

GARNISH: 1 LEMON TWIST

Stir all the ingredients over ice, then strain into a coupe. Garnish with the lemon twist.

. . . .

BUFFALO SOLDIER

BRIAN MILLER, 2008

The pecan-infused bourbon tasted great on its own, but it needed some fat. I tried pretty much every sweetener at the bar and finally settled on Demerara Syrup.—BM

2 OUNCES PECAN–INFUSED BUFFALO TRACE BOURBON (PAGE 282)

¼ OUNCE DEMERARA SYRUP (PAGE 277)

Stir the bourbon and syrup over ice, then strain into a double rocks glass over 1 large ice cube. No garnish.

CARROLL GARDENS

JOAQUÍN SIMÓ, 2008

This is one of several D&C spin-offs on the Brooklyn cocktail (page 140), in this case named after the borough's Italian-American neighborhood.—JS

2 OUNCES RITTENHOUSE 100 RYE

½ OUNCE PUNT E MES

½ OUNCE AMARO NARDINI

1 TEASPOON LUXARDO MARASCHINO LIQUEUR

1 LEMON TWIST

Stir all the ingredients (except the lemon twist) over ice, then strain into a coupe. Squeeze the lemon twist over the drink and discard. No garnish.

....

COFFEE AND CIGARETTES

THOMAS WAUGH, 2011

I'd never seen a variation on the classic Rob Roy (page 150) made with coffee liqueur. It's such a simple idea, but it completely changes the drink.—TW

2 OUNCES CAOL ILA 12-YEAR SCOTCH

½ OUNCE GALLIANO RISTRETTO

1 TEASPOON CARPANO ANTICA FORMULA VERMOUTH

2 DASHES BITTERMENS XOCOLATL MOLE BITTERS

Stir all the ingredients over ice, then strain into a martini glass. No garnish.

....

CURE FOR PAIN

BRIAN MILLER, 2009

I created this twist on the Boulevardier (page 140) in honor of one of our longtime regulars, Anthony Sarnicola.—BM

1½ OUNCES RITTENHOUSE 100 RYE

½ OUNCE STAGG BOURBON

½ OUNCE OTIMA 10-YEAR TAWNY PORT

½ OUNCE CARPANO ANTICA FORMULA VERMOUTH

1 TEASPOON CAMPARI

1 TEASPOON MARIE BRIZARD WHITE CRÈME DE CACAO

GARNISH: 1 ORANGE TWIST

Stir all the ingredients over ice, then strain into a coupe. Garnish with the orange twist.

....

THE DANGEROUS SUMMER

JOAQUÍN SIMÓ, 2009

This stirred variation of the classic Blood and Sand (page 140) is named after a Hemingway book about bullfighters. I replaced the rich Cherry Heering with dry cherry brandy and the orange juice with blood orange liqueur.—JS

1½ OUNCES YAMAZAKI 12-YEAR WHISKEY

¾ OUNCE DOLIN ROUGE VERMOUTH

½ OUNCE SOLERNO BLOOD ORANGE LIQUEUR

½ OUNCE MASSENEZ KIRSCH VIEUX CHERRY BRANDY

1 ORANGE TWIST

Stir all the ingredients (except the orange twist) over ice, then strain into a martini glass. Flame the orange twist over the drink and discard. No garnish.

FAITHFUL SCOTSMAN

JOAQUÍN SIMÓ, 2008

The name of this single-serving, Scotch-based punch is derived from the medieval notion that cumin keeps chickens—and husbands—from straying from the coop.—JS

1½ OUNCES COMPASS BOX ASYLA SCOTCH

¼ OUNCE MASSENEZ CRÈME DE PÊCHE PEACH LIQUEUR

½ OUNCE PINEAPPLE JUICE

½ OUNCE LEMON JUICE

¼ OUNCE CUMIN SYRUP (PAGE 277)

GARNISH: 1 PINEAPPLE LEAF

Stir all the ingredients, then strain into a double rocks glass over 1 large ice cube. Garnish with the pineapple leaf.

. . . .

FOUR IN HAND

SCOTT TEAGUE, 2013

This is a no-apologies, complicated, high-proof drink— the kind Death & Co is famous for making.—ST

¾ OUNCE OLD GRAND-DAD 114 BOURBON

¾ OUNCE LAIRD'S BONDED APPLE BRANDY

¼ OUNCE SMITH & CROSS RUM

¼ OUNCE GREEN CHARTREUSE

1 TEASPOON CINNAMON BARK SYRUP (PAGE 276)

1 TEASPOON VANILLA SYRUP (PAGE 277)

GARNISH: 1 ORANGE TWIST

Stir all the ingredients over ice, then strain into a rocks glass. Garnish with the orange twist.

LA DOLCE VITA

THOMAS WAUGH, 2008

This is a variation on the Old Pal (page 148), with St-Germain in place of vermouth. It's a great example of the kind of simple drink we come up with using the stuff we find in our home bars.—TW

2 OUNCES CHAMOMILE-INFUSED OLD OVERHOLT RYE (PAGE 281)

¾ OUNCE CAMPARI

½ OUNCE ST-GERMAIN

Stir all the ingredients over ice, then strain into a double rocks glass over 1 large ice cube. No garnish.

. . . .

LA VIÑA

ALEX DAY, 2009

For this, my first foray into lower-alcohol cocktails, I used two of my pet ingredients: sherry and Amaro Nonino. It tastes similar to a Manhattan but much lighter.—AD

1 OUNCE RUSSELL'S RESERVE RYE

1 OUNCE AMARO NONINO

1 OUNCE LUSTAU EAST INDIA SOLERA SHERRY

1 DASH REGANS' ORANGE BITTERS

Stir all the ingredients over ice, then strain into a coupe. No garnish.

. . . .

MANHATTAN TRANSFER

PHIL WARD, 2008

1½ OUNCES RITTENHOUSE 100 RYE

1 OUNCE DRY VERMOUTH

1 OUNCE RAMAZZOTTI

1 DASH HOUSE ORANGE BITTERS (PAGE 284)

Stir all the ingredients over ice, then strain into a coupe. No garnish.

Manhattan Transfer

SCOTCH DRAM

PHIL WARD, 2008

2 OUNCES COMPASS BOX ASYLA SCOTCH
¾ OUNCE CARPANO ANTICA FORMULA VERMOUTH
¼ OUNCE DRAMBUIE
1 DASH HOUSE PEYCHAUD'S BITTERS (PAGE 284)

Stir all the ingredients over ice, then strain into a coupe.
No garnish.

....

SHRUFF'S END

PHIL WARD, 2008

*Bénédictine can make almost any two ingredients
love each other. Here it's the perfect bridge between
peaty Scotch and apply brandy. The result tastes like
a smoked apple.—PW*

1 OUNCE LAPHROAIG 10-YEAR SCOTCH
1 OUNCE LAIRD'S BONDED APPLE BRANDY
½ OUNCE BÉNÉDICTINE
2 DASHES HOUSE PEYCHAUD'S BITTERS (PAGE 284)

Stir all the ingredients over ice, then strain into a coupe.
No garnish.

....

ST. COLUMBUS RILL

PHIL WARD, 2008

2 OUNCES BUSHMILLS IRISH WHISKEY
¾ OUNCE DOLIN BLANC VERMOUTH
¼ OUNCE GREEN CHARTREUSE
¼ OUNCE LUXARDO MARASCHINO LIQUEUR

Stir all the ingredients over ice, then strain into a coupe.
No garnish.

SWEET AND VICIOUS

ALEX DAY, 2008

*Using muddled apples quickly infuses this variation on
the Manhattan (page 145) with their bright, yeasty flavor,
giving it a light quality.—AD*

2 FUJI APPLE SLICES
2 OUNCES OLD OVERHOLT RYE
½ OUNCE DOLIN DRY VERMOUTH
½ OUNCE AMARO NONINO
1 TEASPOON MAPLE SYRUP
GARNISH: 1 APPLE FAN

In a mixing glass, gently muddle the apple slices.
Add the remaining ingredients and stir over ice. Double
strain into a coupe and garnish with the apple fan.

....

TEA IN THE SAHARA

BRIAN MILLER, 2009

1 LEMON COIN WITH A BIT OF PITH
2 OUNCES COCONUT GREEN TEA–INFUSED FAMOUS
    GROUSE SCOTCH (PAGE 282)
1 TEASPOON STREGA
1 TEASPOON ACACIA HONEY SYRUP (PAGE 276)

Squeeze the lemon over a mixing glass and drop it in.
Add the remaining ingredients and stir with ice.
Strain into a double rocks glass. No garnish.

TREMBLING BELL

THOMAS WAUGH, 2012

1½ OUNCES CHAMOMILE-INFUSED OLD
    OVERHOLT RYE (PAGE 281)

1 OUNCE KNAPPOGUE CASTLE 12-YEAR
    IRISH WHISKEY

¾ OUNCE COCCHI AMERICANO

1 TEASPOON MASSENEZ CRÈME DE PÊCHE
    PEACH LIQUEUR

½ TEASPOON ACACIA HONEY SYRUP (PAGE 276)

1 LEMON TWIST

Stir all the ingredients (except the lemon twist) over ice, then strain into a coupe. Squeeze the lemon twist over the drink and discard. No garnish.

WICKED KISS

PHIL WARD, 2007

This variation on the classic Widow's Kiss was one of the first drinks I developed for the original Death & Co menu.—PW

1 OUNCE RITTENHOUSE 100 RYE

1 OUNCE LAIRD'S BONDED APPLE BRANDY

¼ OUNCE YELLOW CHARTREUSE

¼ OUNCE BÉNÉDICTINE

1 DASH ANGOSTURA BITTERS

Stir all the ingredients over ice, then strain into a coupe. No garnish.

BRANDY

SHAKEN

BANANA COGNAC

TYSON BUHLER, 2013

Inspired by a Dave Chappelle sketch, this concept drink uses Avuá amburana, which has awesome fruit and chocolate notes that you don't find in other cachaças.—TB

1 OUNCE PIERRE FERRAND 1840 COGNAC
½ OUNCE AVUÁ AMBURANA CACHAÇA
¾ OUNCE LEMON JUICE
½ OUNCE ORANGE JUICE
¾ OUNCE BANANA SYRUP (PAGE 276)
¼ OUNCE ORGEAT (PAGE 278)
2 DASHES ANGOSTURA BITTERS
GARNISH: 1 DRIED BANANA CHIP

Short shake all the ingredients with 3 ice cubes, then strain into a pilsner glass filled with crushed ice. Garnish with the dried banana chip and serve with a straw.

········

DON'T SIT UNDER THE APPLE TREE

BRIAN MILLER, 2008

I use only the flavorful cores and peels of apples to make the Braeburn syrup in this cocktail.—BM

2 OUNCES LAIRD'S BONDED APPLE BRANDY
½ OUNCE LEMON JUICE
1 OUNCE BRAEBURN APPLE SYRUP (PAGE 276)
1 EGG WHITE
1 DASH FEE BROTHERS WHISKEY BARREL-AGED BITTERS
GARNISH: 1 BRAEBURN APPLE SLICE

Dry shake all the ingredients, then shake again with ice. Double strain into a coupe. Garnish with the apple slice.

········

ENCHANTED ORCHARD

JOAQUÍN SIMÓ, 2011

1½ OUNCES CAMPO DE ENCANTO ACHOLADO PISCO
½ OUNCE BUSNEL VSOP CALVADOS
½ OUNCE BÉNÉDICTINE
½ OUNCE PINEAPPLE JUICE
½ OUNCE LEMON JUICE
½ OUNCE ACACIA HONEY SYRUP (PAGE 276)
GARNISH: 1 CINNAMON STICK

Shake all the ingredients with ice, then strain into a double rocks glass over 1 large ice cube. Garnish with the cinnamon stick.

········

GINGER SNAP

JOAQUÍN SIMÓ, 2009

1½ OUNCES PIERRE FERRAND AMBRE COGNAC
½ OUNCE SMITH & CROSS RUM
½ OUNCE RHUM CLÉMENT CRÉOLE SHRUBB
¾ OUNCE LEMON JUICE
¼ OUNCE CINNAMON BARK SYRUP (PAGE 276)
¼ OUNCE GINGER SYRUP (PAGE 277)

Shake all the ingredients with ice, then strain into a coupe. No garnish.

GOLDEN GATE

THOMAS WAUGH, 2009

It may seem odd to use Grand Marnier as a base spirit, but it's a blend of cognac and triple sec, and it can work if you balance its richness with something bitter, like Campari, and lots of citrus juice.—TW

¾ OUNCE GRAND MARNIER

½ OUNCE BÉNÉDICTINE

½ OUNCE CAMPARI

¾ OUNCE GRAPEFRUIT JUICE

½ OUNCE LIME JUICE

GARNISH: 1 LIME TWIST

Short shake all the ingredients with 3 ice cubes, then strain into a highball glass filled with crushed ice. Garnish with the lime twist and serve with a straw.

. . . .

HEART-SHAPED BOX

BRAD FARRAN, 2013

1 STRAWBERRY

2 OUNCES HINE H COGNAC

¾ OUNCE ST-GERMAIN

¾ OUNCE LEMON JUICE

¼ OUNCE CINNAMON BARK SYRUP (PAGE 276)

½ TEASPOON AGED BALSAMIC VINEGAR

1 DASH ANGOSTURA BITTERS

GARNISH: ½ STRAWBERRY

In a shaker, gently muddle the strawberry. Add the remaining ingredients and short shake. Strain into a double rocks glass filled with crushed ice. Garnish with the strawberry half and serve with a straw.

HOI POLLOI

JESSICA GONZALEZ, 2009

1 OUNCE HINE H COGNAC

½ OUNCE DRIED CURRANT–INFUSED WILD TURKEY RYE (PAGE 279)

½ OUNCE MARIE BRIZARD WHITE CRÈME DE CACAO

1 OUNCE PINEAPPLE JUICE

¾ OUNCE LEMON JUICE

½ OUNCE SIMPLE SYRUP (PAGE 277)

1 DASH ANGOSTURA BITTERS

GARNISH: 1 PINEAPPLE WEDGE

Short shake all the ingredients with 3 ice cubes, then strain into a pilsner glass filled with crushed ice. Garnish with the pineapple wedge and serve with a straw.

. . . .

JOKER'S WILD

THOMAS WAUGH, 2011

Pacharán is a Basque liqueur flavored with sloe berries, coffee beans, and anise.—TW

½ OUNCE LA DIABLADA PISCO

1½ OUNCES ZOCO PACHARÁN NAVARRO LIQUEUR

2 DASHES VIEUX PONTARLIER ABSINTHE

¾ OUNCE LEMON JUICE

½ OUNCE SIMPLE SYRUP (PAGE 277)

¼ OUNCE VANILLA SYRUP (PAGE 277)

CLUB SODA

Dry shake all the ingredients (except the club soda), then shake again with ice. Strain into a highball glass filled with ice cubes. Top with club soda and garnish with a spoonful of the foam left in the tin.

LITTLE BIRDY

JOAQUÍN SIMÓ, 2009

This is one that I call a "roast chicken" drink, meaning everyone likes it. I didn't name it after chicken, though, but for pisco, the Quechuan word for "bird."—JS

2 OUNCES STRAWBERRY- AND PINEAPPLE-INFUSED
    MACCHU PISCO (PAGE 281)

½ OUNCE ST-GERMAIN

¾ OUNCE GRAPEFRUIT JUICE

½ OUNCE LEMON JUICE

1 TEASPOON SIMPLE SYRUP (PAGE 277)

Shake all the ingredients with ice, then strain into a coupe. No garnish.

....

LITTLE MISS ANNABELLE

JOAQUÍN SIMÓ, 2009

I named this variation on the Sidecar (page 151) after the daughter of Alexandre Gabriel, who owns Pierre Ferrand. It has a rich mouthfeel for using such a small amount of sweetener.—JS

2 OUNCES PIERRE FERRAND AMBRE COGNAC

¼ OUNCE MATHILDE POIRE PEAR LIQUEUR

¼ OUNCE BÉNÉDICTINE

¾ OUNCE LEMON JUICE

¼ OUNCE CANE SUGAR SYRUP (PAGE 276)

1 DASH HOUSE PEYCHAUD'S BITTERS (PAGE 284)

Shake all the ingredients with ice, then strain into a coupe. No garnish.

....

MAGGIE SMITH

JOAQUÍN SIMÓ, 2009

This is a variation on Between the Sheets, a classic cocktail that's a rarity in having a split base. Here, I've replaced the cognac with pisco.—JS

1 OUNCE CAMPO DE ENCANTO ACHOLADO PISCO

1 OUNCE BANKS 5-ISLAND WHITE RUM

½ OUNCE SANTA TERESA ORANGE LIQUEUR

¾ OUNCE LIME JUICE

¼ OUNCE ORGEAT (PAGE 278)

1 TEASPOON ACACIA HONEY SYRUP (PAGE 276)

GARNISH: 1 LIME WHEEL

Shake all the ingredients with ice, then strain into a coupe. Garnish with the lime wheel.

....

MORNING BUZZ

JILLIAN VOSE, 2012

1 OUNCE HINE H COGNAC

¾ OUNCE ZACAPA 23-YEAR RUM

½ OUNCE LUSTAU AMONTILLADO SHERRY

¼ OUNCE ORGEAT (PAGE 278)

¼ OUNCE ACACIA HONEY SYRUP (PAGE 276)

¾ OUNCE HONEY NUT CHEERIO–INFUSED CREAM
    (PAGE 284)

1 EGG YOLK

Dry shake all the ingredients, then shake with ice. Double strain into a fancy fizz glass. No garnish.

....

MUCHO PICCHU

JOAQUÍN SIMÓ, 2008

1½ OUNCES MACCHU PISCO

¼ OUNCE LUXARDO MARASCHINO LIQUEUR

½ OUNCE GRAPEFRUIT JUICE

½ OUNCE SIMPLE SYRUP (PAGE 277)

DRY CHAMPAGNE

GARNISH: 1 GRAPEFRUIT TWIST

Shake all the ingredients (except the champagne) with ice, then strain into a flute. Top with champagne and garnish with the grapefruit twist.

PEACHY PACHACUTI

THOMAS WAUGH, 2011

I created the drink for a pisco cocktail competition in Peru, using Greek yogurt instead of egg whites. I named it after an Inca emperor, figuring that would increase my chances of winning. Unfortunately, I forgot to add the yogurt when I made the drink for the judges, and they hated it.—TW

3 RIPE PEACH SLICES

2 OUNCES MACCHU PISCO

½ OUNCE LIME JUICE

½ OUNCE LEMON JUICE

¾ OUNCE ACACIA HONEY SYRUP (PAGE 276)

1 TEASPOON GREEK YOGURT

In a shaker, muddle the peach slices. Add the remaining ingredients and shake with ice. Double strain into a snifter over 1 large ice cube. No garnish.

. . . .

POIRE MAN'S COBBLER

PHIL WARD, 2008

¼ RIPE BARTLETT PEAR, CUBED

2 OUNCES BUSNEL VSOP CALVADOS

¼ OUNCE BÉNÉDICTINE

2 DASHES HOUSE PEYCHAUD'S BITTERS (PAGE 284)

GARNISH: 1 BARTLETT PEAR SLICE

In a shaker, muddle the pear. Add the remaining ingredients and shake with ice. Strain into a double rocks glass filled with crushed ice. Garnish with the pear slice.

. . . .

PORT AUTHORITY

THOMAS WAUGH, 2008

4 BLACKBERRIES

2 OUNCES COGNAC

¾ OUNCE OTIMA 10-YEAR TAWNY PORT

½ OUNCE CRÈME DE CASSIS

½ OUNCE LEMON JUICE

2 DASHES BITTERMENS XOCOLATL MOLE BITTERS

GARNISH: 1 BLACKBERRY

In a shaker, gently muddle the blackberries. Add the remaining ingredients and shake with ice. Double strain into a coupe and garnish with the blackberry.

. . . .

SLOE SCOBEYVILLE SLING

PHIL WARD, 2008

2 OUNCES LAIRD'S BONDED APPLE BRANDY

1 OUNCE PLYMOUTH SLOE GIN

½ OUNCE LEMON JUICE

¾ OUNCE SIMPLE SYRUP (PAGE 277)

2 DASHES PEYCHAUD'S BITTERS

CLUB SODA

GARNISH: 1 FUJI APPLE SLICE

Short shake all the ingredients (except the club soda) with 3 ice cubes, then strain into a highball glass filled with ice cubes. Top with club soda. Garnish with the apple slice and serve with a straw.

SOLERA SIDECAR

JOAQUÍN SIMÓ, 2009

This play on the Sidecar (page 151) tastes like a dessert pastry: the sherry lends a nutty flavor, the amaro provides a biscotti note, and the cognac is fruity and floral.—JS

1½ OUNCES HINE H COGNAC

½ OUNCE EAST INDIA SOLERA SHERRY

¼ OUNCE GRAND MARNIER

¼ OUNCE LAZZARONI AMARETTO

½ OUNCE LEMON JUICE

¼ OUNCE SIMPLE SYRUP (PAGE 277)

Shake all the ingredients with ice, then strain into a coupe. No garnish.

STICK THE LANDING

BRAD FARRAN, 2012

1 OUNCE LOUIS ROYER FORCE 53 COGNAC

1 OUNCE REDBREAST 12-YEAR IRISH WHISKEY

1 TEASPOON MASSENEZ CRÈME DE PÊCHE PEACH LIQUEUR

¾ OUNCE LEMON JUICE

½ OUNCE CANE SUGAR SYRUP (PAGE 276)

2 DASHES ANGOSTURA BITTERS

Shake all the ingredients with ice, then strain into a coupe. No garnish.

Sloe Scobeyville Sling

BRANDY

STIRRED

BLACK MAGIC

THOMAS WAUGH, 2009

This drink isn't as harsh as the recipe makes it look. The minute amounts of absinthe and Fernet add a light herbaceous note to the duo of brandy and crème de menthe in the classic Stinger cocktail (page 152).—TW

VIEUX PONTARLIER ABSINTHE

1 OUNCE HINE H COGNAC

1 OUNCE ANGOSTURA 5-YEAR RUM

½ OUNCE MARIE BRIZARD WHITE CRÈME DE MENTHE

1 TEASPOON FERNET-BRANCA

1 TEASPOON SIMPLE SYRUP (PAGE 277)

Rinse a coupe with absinthe and dump. Stir the remaining ingredients over ice, then strain into the coupe. No garnish.

. . . .

BLACK MARKET BRANDY

JOAQUÍN SIMÓ, 2008

Vermouth infused with Market Spice Cinnamon-Orange Tea has become one of D&C's signature ingredients— everyone loves playing with it. This is my brandy version of Brian's Black Market Manhattan (page 204).—JS

1 OUNCE LAIRD'S BONDED APPLE BRANDY

1 OUNCE HINE H COGNAC

¾ OUNCE CINNAMON ORANGE TEA–INFUSED SWEET VERMOUTH (PAGE 281)

1 DASH HOUSE PEYCHAUD'S BITTERS (PAGE 284)

1 DASH ANGOSTURA BITTERS

GARNISH: 3 BRANDIED CHERRIES ON A COCKTAIL PICK

Stir all the ingredients over ice, then strain into a coupe. Garnish with the cherries.

. . . .

CASTLE OF CÓRDOBA

JOAQUÍN SIMÓ, 2009

¾ OUNCE BUSNEL VSOP CALVADOS

½ OUNCE PIERRE FERRAND AMBRE COGNAC

2 OUNCES ALVEAR FESTIVAL PALE CREAM SHERRY

2 DASHES HOUSE PEYCHAUD'S BITTERS (PAGE 284)

GARNISH: 1 APPLE SLICE

Stir all the ingredients over ice, then strain into a coupe. Garnish with the apple slice.

. . . .

JARNAC SHRUB

TOBY CECCHINI, 2009

2 OUNCES HINE H COGNAC

1 OUNCE CARPANO ANTICA FORMULA VERMOUTH

1 OUNCE TOBY'S SOUR CHERRY SHRUB (PAGE 285)

1 DASH HOUSE ORANGE BITTERS (PAGE 284)

GARNISH: 3 BRANDIED CHERRIES ON A COCKTAIL PICK

Stir all the ingredients over ice, then strain into a coupe. Garnish with the cherries.

LEGEND

JILLIAN VOSE, 2012

1 OUNCE PIERRE FERRAND 1840 COGNAC

½ OUNCE APPLETON ESTATE V/X RUM

¾ OUNCE LUSTAU AMONTILLADO SHERRY

½ OUNCE AMARO NONINO

¼ OUNCE DEMERARA SYRUP (PAGE 277)

1 DASH BITTER TRUTH AROMATIC BITTERS

1 DASH ANGOSTURA BITTERS

Stir all the ingredients over ice, then strain into a coupe. No garnish.

....

LES VERTS MONTS

JILLIAN VOSE, 2013

This drink showcases the many ways we use grape-based ingredients behind the bar, combining the best products from France and Spain.—JV

1 OUNCE TARIQUET VS CLASSIQUE
    BAS-ARMAGNAC

¾ OUNCE GUILLON-PAINTURAUD COGNAC GRANDE
    CHAMPAGNE VSOP

¾ OUNCE BUSNEL VSOP CALVADOS

¾ OUNCE DOLIN BLANC VERMOUTH

¼ OUNCE ALVEAR FESTIVAL PALE CREAM SHERRY

¼ OUNCE MAPLE SYRUP

1 DASH ANGOSTURA BITTERS

1 LEMON TWIST

GARNISH: 1 FUJI APPLE SLICE

Stir all the ingredients (except the lemon twist) over ice, then strain into a Nick & Nora glass. Squeeze the lemon twist over the drink and discard. Garnish with the apple slice.

Les Verts Monts

LILYWHACKER

PHIL WARD, 2008

2 OUNCES LAIRD'S BONDED APPLE BRANDY

¾ OUNCE CARPANO ANTICA FORMULA VERMOUTH

½ OUNCE COINTREAU

1 DASH BITTERMENS XOCOLATL MOLE BITTERS

Stir all the ingredients over ice, then strain into a coupe. No garnish.

. . . .

LITTLE SPARROW

BRIAN MILLER, 2008

I didn't think this drink would be as popular as it is, but when St-Germain is involved, you never know. I cut the calvados with a bit of Laird's because otherwise it would taste too sweet; Laird's is good for drying drinks out.—BM

2 OUNCES BUSNEL VSOP CALVADOS

¼ OUNCE LAIRD'S BONDED APPLE BRANDY

¾ OUNCE CARPANO ANTICA FORMULA VERMOUTH

½ OUNCE ST-GERMAIN

2 DASHES HOUSE PEYCHAUD'S BITTERS (PAGE 284)

GARNISH: 1 LEMON TWIST

Stir all the ingredients over ice, then strain into a coupe. Garnish with the lemon twist.

. . . .

MARTICA

PHIL WARD, 2007

1 OUNCE HINE H COGNAC

1 OUNCE APPLETON ESTATE V/X RUM

¾ OUNCE CARPANO ANTICA FORMULA VERMOUTH

¼ OUNCE LUXARDO MARASCHINO LIQUEUR

1 DASH ANGOSTURA BITTERS

Stir all the ingredients over ice, then strain into a coupe. No garnish.

NIGHT OWL

ALEX DAY, 2009

This Manhattan variation uses Batavia arrack as a modifier, which adds a bit of complexity without making the drink too funky.—AD

2 OUNCES PIERRE FERRAND AMBRE COGNAC

½ OUNCE PUNT E MES

½ OUNCE LUSTAU EAST INDIA SOLERA SHERRY

¼ OUNCE VAN OOSTEN BATAVIA ARRACK

Stir all the ingredients over ice, then strain into a coupe. No garnish.

SADE'S TABOO

JESSICA GONZALEZ, 2009

2 OUNCES HINE H COGNAC

¾ OUNCE COCCHI AMERICANO

¾ OUNCE DOLIN ROUGE VERMOUTH

1 DASH BITTERMENS HOPPED GRAPEFRUIT
  BITTERS

Stir all the ingredients over ice, then strain into a coupe.
No garnish.

. . . .

SIDEWINDER

PHIL WARD, 2008

2 OUNCES HINE H COGNAC

½ OUNCE LAIRD'S BONDED APPLE BRANDY

¼ OUNCE BÉNÉDICTINE

¼ OUNCE YELLOW CHARTREUSE

1 DASH VIEUX PONTARLIER ABSINTHE

1 DASH HOUSE PEYCHAUD'S BITTERS (PAGE 284)

Stir all the ingredients over ice, then strain into a coupe.
No garnish.

. . . .

SOUL CLENCH

JILLIAN VOSE, 2013

2 OUNCES WAQAR PISCO

¾ OUNCE DOLIN DRY VERMOUTH

½ OUNCE COMBIER PAMPLEMOUSSE ROSE LIQUEUR

½ OUNCE ST-GERMAIN

¼ OUNCE VELVET FALERNUM

GARNISH: 1 GRAPEFRUIT TWIST

Stir all the ingredients over ice, then strain into a double
rocks glass over 1 large ice cube. Garnish with the
grapefruit twist.

SWEET HEREAFTER

JOAQUÍN SIMÓ, 2009

*This is the opposite of a pisco sour. Instead of shaking
the drink with citrus and egg whites, which can blanket
the flavors of pisco, I showcased its fruit and floral notes
by stirring it with vermouth and Cocchi Americano, an
aperitif flavored with cinchona bark and orange.—JS*

1 GRAPEFRUIT TWIST

2 OUNCES CAMPO DE ENCANTO ACHOLADO PISCO

½ OUNCE COCCHI AMERICANO

½ OUNCE DOLIN BLANC VERMOUTH

1 TEASPOON ST-GERMAIN

1 DASH BITTERMENS HOPPED GRAPEFRUIT
  BITTERS

Squeeze the grapefruit twist over a mixing glass and
discard. Add the remaining ingredients and stir over ice,
then strain into a coupe. No garnish.

. . . .

WIDOW'S LAUREL

JOAQUÍN SIMÓ, 2009

*A riff on the Widow's Kiss cocktail, which dates back to
1895, this version is spicier and less boozy.—JS*

2 OUNCES BUSNEL VSOP CALVADOS

½ OUNCE DRAMBUIE

½ OUNCE CARPANO ANTICA FORMULA VERMOUTH

1 TEASPOON ST. ELIZABETH ALLSPICE DRAM

1 DASH ANGOSTURA BITTERS

GARNISH: 3 BRANDIED CHERRIES ON A
  COCKTAIL PICK

Stir all the ingredients over ice, then strain into a coupe.
Garnish with the cherries.

SPARKLING COCKTAILS

Champagne's primary function in a cocktail is to add acid and bubbles. If you want to taste the nuanced complexity of a fine prestige cuvée, then pour yourself a glass. The truth is, a fine champagne usually doesn't taste that great in a drink; plus, the use of actual champagne (produced in the Champagne region of France) has become prohibitively expensive for a bar. When Death & Co opened, we got a great deal on Pol Roger Champagne, but these days we use Crémant du Jura, which has a similar flavor profile at a fraction of the price. So when the recipes below call for champagne, feel free to substitute a similar sparkling wine. The best wines for sparkling cocktails are dry (which leaves room to add sweet ingredients) and crisp and have a decent amount of yeastiness.

THE BITTENBENDER

JILLIAN VOSE, 2013

This started as a punch that was quite rich. I think it works even better as a cocktail.—JV

4 RASPBERRIES

1 LEMON TWIST

1 ORANGE TWIST

2 OUNCES RUSSELL'S RESERVE 10-YEAR BOURBON

¾ OUNCE CACAO NIB–INFUSED CAMPARI (PAGE 282)

¾ OUNCE LEMON JUICE

¾ OUNCE GINGER SYRUP (PAGE 277)

1 OUNCE DRY CHAMPAGNE

GARNISH: 1 LEMON WHEEL

In a shaker, muddle the raspberries with the lemon and orange twists. Add the remaining ingredients (except the champagne) and shake with ice. Strain into a snifter over 1 large ice cube and top with the champagne. Garnish with the lemon wheel.

BITTER FRENCH

PHIL WARD, 2008

In my opinion, this French 75 (page 143) variation is the best beginner Campari drink in history.—PW

1 OUNCE PLYMOUTH GIN

¼ OUNCE CAMPARI

½ OUNCE LEMON JUICE

½ OUNCE SIMPLE SYRUP (PAGE 277)

DRY CHAMPAGNE

1 GRAPEFRUIT TWIST

Shake all the ingredients (except the champagne and grapefruit twist) with ice, then strain into a flute. Top with champagne. Squeeze the grapefruit twist over the drink and discard. No garnish.

....

BOOMIN' GRANNY

JILLIAN VOSE, 2012

1½ OUNCES HINE H COGNAC

1 OUNCE GRANNY SMITH APPLE JUICE

½ OUNCE LIME JUICE

½ OUNCE ACACIA HONEY SYRUP (PAGE 276)

DRY CHAMPAGNE

GARNISH: 1 GRANNY SMITH APPLE SLICE

Shake all the ingredients (except the champagne) with ice, then strain into a flute. Top with champagne. Garnish with the apple slice, dropped into the drink.

CALVA DORSA ROYALE

PHIL WARD, 2008

1½ OUNCES BUSNEL VSOP CALVADOS

½ OUNCE ST-GERMAIN

2 DASHES VIEUX PONTARLIER ABSINTHE

DRY CHAMPAGNE

Stir all the ingredients (except the champagne) over ice, then strain into a coupe. Top with champagne. No garnish.

The Bittenbender

CIDER HOUSE RULES

THOMAS WAUGH, 2009

¾ OUNCE FLOR DE CAÑA EXTRA-DRY WHITE RUM

¾ OUNCE APPLETON ESTATE V/X RUM

¼ OUNCE VELVET FALERNUM

½ OUNCE LIME JUICE

¼ OUNCE ACACIA HONEY SYRUP (PAGE 276)

1 DASH BITTERMENS 'ELEMAKULE TIKI BITTERS

DOC'S HARD PEAR CIDER

Stir all the ingredients (except the cider) in a mixing glass over ice, then strain into a flute. Top with cider. No garnish.

....

DARK 'N' BUBBLY

JOAQUÍN SIMÓ, 2008

1½ OUNCES GOSLING'S BLACK SEAL RUM

¼ OUNCE LIME JUICE

½ OUNCE CURRIED GINGER SYRUP (PAGE 277)

DRY CHAMPAGNE

Shake all the ingredients (except the champagne) with ice, then strain into a flute. Top with champagne. No garnish.

....

DICK AND JANE

TOBY CECCHINI, 2009

1½ OUNCES TANQUERAY NO. TEN GIN

½ OUNCE ST-GERMAIN

½ OUNCE LEMON JUICE

½ OUNCE HIBISCUS SYRUP (PAGE 277)

2 DASHES HOUSE PEYCHAUD'S BITTERS (PAGE 284)

DRY CHAMPAGNE

GARNISH: 1 LONG, SKINNY LEMON TWIST

Shake all the ingredients (except the champagne) with ice, then strain into a flute. Top with champagne. Garnish with the lemon twist.

DIRTY MARY, CRAZY LARRY

THOMAS WAUGH, 2012

2 OUNCES LAIRD'S BONDED APPLE BRANDY

FULL SAIL SESSION BLACK LAGER

Fill a pilsner glass with ice cubes and add the apple brandy. Top with Full Sail.

. . . .

DOC DANEEKA ROYALE

ALEX DAY, 2008

In my play on the French 75 (page 143), I make it more about the gin and less about citrus. Grapefruit and maple syrup work so well together.—AD

2 OUNCES PLYMOUTH GIN

½ OUNCE LEMON JUICE

½ OUNCE GRADE B MAPLE SYRUP

1 DASH BITTERMENS HOPPED GRAPEFRUIT BITTERS

DRY CHAMPAGNE

1 GRAPEFRUIT COIN

Shake all the ingredients (except the champagne and grapefruit coin) with ice, then double strain into a coupe. Top with champagne. Squeeze the grapefruit coin over the drink and discard. No garnish.

. . . .

DRAGON LILY

JOAQUÍN SIMÓ, 2008

1½ OUNCES SIEMBRA AZUL BLANCO TEQUILA

¾ OUNCE TARRAGON AND AGAVE NECTAR GASTRIQUE (PAGE 285)

1 DASH HOUSE PEYCHAUD'S BITTERS (PAGE 284)

DRY CHAMPAGNE

Stir all the ingredients (except the champagne) over ice, then strain into a flute. Top with champagne. No garnish.

DRUNKEN SKULL

BRIAN MILLER, 2009

¾ OUNCE EL DORADO 12-YEAR RUM

¾ OUNCE APPLETON ESTATE V/X RUM

2 DASHES VIEUX PONTARLIER ABSINTHE

½ OUNCE LIME JUICE

½ OUNCE GRENADINE (PAGE 284)

DRY CHAMPAGNE

Shake all the ingredients (except the champagne) with ice, then strain into a flute. Top with champagne. No garnish.

. . . .

ELDER FASHION ROYALE

PHIL WARD, 2008

1½ OUNCES PLYMOUTH GIN

½ OUNCE ST-GERMAIN

1 DASH HOUSE ORANGE BITTERS (PAGE 284)

DRY CHAMPAGNE

GARNISH: 1 GRAPEFRUIT TWIST

Stir all the ingredients (except the champagne) over ice, then strain into a flute. Top with champagne. Garnish with the grapefruit twist.

. . . .

FAIR LADY

JILLIAN VOSE, 2011

1 OUNCE SAGE-INFUSED DOLIN BLANC VERMOUTH (PAGE 281)

¾ OUNCE KROGSTAD AQUAVIT

¾ OUNCE GRAPEFRUIT JUICE

1 TEASPOON CANE SUGAR SYRUP (PAGE 276)

DRY CHAMPAGNE

Shake all the ingredients (except the champagne) with ice, then strain into a flute. Top with champagne. No garnish.

FANCY HOLLAND ROYALE

THOMAS WAUGH, 2008

This started as a genever-based martini, then Phil topped it with champagne.—TW

1½ OUNCES BOLS GENEVER

¾ OUNCE GRAND MARNIER

1 TEASPOON CANE SUGAR SYRUP (PAGE 276)

1 DASH FEE BROTHERS WHISKEY BARREL-AGED BITTERS

DRY CHAMPAGNE

Stir all the ingredients (except the champagne) over ice, then strain into a flute. Top with champagne. No garnish.

． ． ． ． ． ． ． ．

FLAQUITA

JESSICA GONZALEZ, 2011

Flaquita was my nickname back when I worked in restaurant kitchens in Florida. I was determined to make tequila and champagne like each other, and the combination of chocolate liqueur and Campari did the trick.—JG

1 OUNCE EL TESORO PLATINUM TEQUILA

½ OUNCE DOLIN BLANC VERMOUTH

¼ OUNCE MARIE BRIZARD WHITE CRÈME DE CACAO

¼ OUNCE CAMPARI

½ OUNCE LEMON JUICE

1 TEASPOON GINGER SYRUP (PAGE 277)

DRY CHAMPAGNE

Shake all the ingredients (except the champagne) with ice, then strain into a flute. Top with champagne. No garnish.

GREEN FLASH

BRIAN MILLER, 2009

1½ OUNCES RHUM JM 100-PROOF AGRICOLE BLANC

¼ OUNCE VIEUX PONTARLIER ABSINTHE

¾ OUNCE LEMON JUICE

½ OUNCE ACACIA HONEY SYRUP (PAGE 276)

DRY CHAMPAGNE

GARNISH: 1 BRANDIED CHERRY

Shake all the ingredients (except the champagne) with ice, then strain into a flute. Top with champagne. Garnish with the cherry.

． ． ． ． ． ． ． ．

IRISH SEELBACH

ALEX DAY, 2009

A variation on the Seelbach, a classic champagne drink from the Seelbach Hotel in Louisville, Kentucky.—AD

1 OUNCE CLONTARF 1014 IRISH WHISKEY

½ OUNCE COINTREAU

4 DASHES HOUSE PEYCHAUD'S BITTERS (PAGE 284)

4 DASHES ANGOSTURA BITTERS

DRY CHAMPAGNE

GARNISH: 1 ORANGE TWIST

Stir all the ingredients (except the champagne) over ice, then strain into a flute. Top with champagne. Garnish with the orange twist.

． ． ． ． ． ． ． ．

IRON CHANCELLOR

JOAQUÍN SIMÓ, 2008

2 OUNCES MACKESON STOUT

¼ OUNCE ESPRESSO-INFUSED DEMERARA SYRUP (PAGE 277)

DRY CHAMPAGNE

Combine the beer and syrup in a flute, then slowly add the champagne over the back of a teaspoon. No garnish.

JANE ROSE

JOAQUÍN SIMÓ, 2011

1 OUNCE LAIRD'S BONDED APPLE BRANDY
½ OUNCE LEMON JUICE
½ OUNCE TOBY'S LIME CORDIAL (PAGE 285)
½ OUNCE GRENADINE (PAGE 284)
DRY CHAMPAGNE

Shake all the ingredients (except the champagne) with ice, then strain into a coupe. Top with champagne. No garnish.

. . . .

JULIEN SOREL

PHIL WARD, 2008

A variation on the Last Word (page 144), with champagne (and simply the worst drink name ever).—PW

½ OUNCE COURVOISIER COGNAC
½ OUNCE GREEN CHARTREUSE
½ OUNCE LUXARDO MARASCHINO LIQUEUR
½ OUNCE LEMON JUICE
DRY CHAMPAGNE
1 LEMON TWIST

Shake all the ingredients (except the champagne and lemon twist) with ice, then strain into a flute. Top with champagne. Squeeze the lemon twist over the drink and discard. No garnish.

. . . .

LILY'S CARTEL

ERYN REECE, 2013

1 OUNCE MACCHU PISCO
¾ OUNCE APEROL
¾ OUNCE BLOOD ORANGE JUICE
¼ OUNCE LEMON JUICE
½ OUNCE SIMPLE SYRUP (PAGE 277)
DRY CHAMPAGNE

Shake all the ingredients (except the champagne) with ice, then strain into a flute. Top with champagne. No garnish.

. . . .

LIVE FREE OR DIE

JOAQUÍN SIMÓ, 2011

1½ OUNCES EAGLE RARE 10-YEAR BOURBON
½ OUNCE ROTHMAN & WINTER CHERRY LIQUEUR
½ OUNCE RUBY PORT
1 DASH VIEUX PONTARLIER ABSINTHE
DRY CHAMPAGNE
GARNISH: 1 ORANGE TWIST

Shake all the ingredients (except the champagne) with ice, then strain into a flute. Top with champagne. Garnish with the orange twist.

. . . .

MIG ROYALE

PHIL WARD, 2007

1 OUNCE PLYMOUTH GIN
¾ OUNCE COINTREAU
½ OUNCE LUXARDO MARASCHINO LIQUEUR
½ OUNCE LEMON JUICE
DRY CHAMPAGNE

Shake all the ingredients (except the champagne) with ice, then strain into a coupe. Top with champagne. No garnish.

Mig Royale

MISS BEHAVIN'

BRIAN MILLER, 2008

¾ OUNCE CLEAR CREEK PEAR BRANDY

¾ OUNCE LAIRD'S BONDED APPLE BRANDY

¾ OUNCE LEMON JUICE

1 OUNCE SIMPLE SYRUP (PAGE 277)

DRY CHAMPAGNE

GARNISH: 1 ANJOU PEAR SLICE

Stir all the ingredients (except the champagne) over ice, then strain into a flute. Top with champagne. Garnish with the Anjou pear slice.

....

MORFEO

JOAQUÍN SIMÓ, 2009

1½ OUNCES CHAMOMILE-INFUSED OLD OVERHOLT RYE (PAGE 281)

¼ OUNCE GALLIANO L'AUTENTICO

¾ OUNCE LEMON JUICE

½ OUNCE ACACIA HONEY SYRUP (PAGE 276)

DRY CHAMPAGNE

Shake all the ingredients (except the champagne) with ice, then strain into a flute. Top with champagne. No garnish.

....

NORTH BY NORTHWEST

BRIAN MILLER, 2008

When developing this cocktail, I tried to imagine something Cary Grant would drink at the Plaza Hotel. The name comes from the title of the movie in which he fittingly says, "I've got a job, a secretary, a mother, two ex-wives, and several bartenders that depend on me . . ."—BM

1½ OUNCES AVIATION GIN

¼ OUNCE ST. GEORGE ABSINTHE

¾ OUNCE LEMON JUICE

¾ OUNCE SIMPLE SYRUP (PAGE 277)

DRY CHAMPAGNE

Shake all the ingredients (except the champagne) with ice, then strain into a flute. Top with champagne. No garnish.

....

PILLOW TALK

JOAQUÍN SIMÓ, 2009

1½ OUNCES BEEFEATER 24 GIN

¼ OUNCE PLYMOUTH SLOE GIN

¼ OUNCE CRÈME YVETTE

¾ OUNCE GRAPEFRUIT JUICE

½ TEASPOON VANILLA SYRUP (PAGE 277)

SPARKLING ROSÉ

Shake all the ingredients (except the sparkling rosé) with ice, then strain into a flute. Top with sparkling rosé. No garnish.

....

RADIO DAYS

ALEX DAY, 2013

I like splitting an aperitif wine with gin to make the base for champagne drinks.—AD

1 ORANGE CRESCENT

1 DASH ANGOSTURA BITTERS

1 OUNCE TANQUERAY LONDON DRY GIN

¾ OUNCE SALERS GENTIEN APERITIF

¾ OUNCE LEMON JUICE

½ OUNCE ACACIA HONEY SYRUP (PAGE 276)

DRY CHAMPAGNE

GARNISH: 1 ORANGE CRESCENT

In a shaker, muddle the orange crescent and bitters. Add the remaining ingredients (except the champagne) and shake with ice. Strain into a large coupe and top with champagne. Garnish with the orange crescent.

RUN FOR THE ROSES

JOAQUÍN SIMÓ, 2012

½ OUNCE KNAPPOGUE CASTLE 12-YEAR
    IRISH WHISKEY

2 OUNCES ROSE-INFUSED LILLET ROSÉ (PAGE 282)

½ OUNCE MASSENEZ KIRSCH VIEUX CHERRY
    BRANDY

1 TEASPOON CANE SUGAR SYRUP (PAGE 276)

DRY CHAMPAGNE

Stir all the ingredients (except the champagne) over ice, then strain into a coupe. Top with champagne. No garnish.

. . . .

SEDA DE NARANJA

PHIL WARD, 2007

¾ OUNCE EL TESORO REPOSADO TEQUILA

¾ OUNCE GRAND MARNIER

1 DASH HOUSE ORANGE BITTERS (PAGE 284)

DRY CHAMPAGNE

Stir all the ingredients (except the champagne) over ice, then strain into a coupe. Top with champagne. No garnish.

. . . .

SOUTH SIDER

ALEX DAY, 2009

This drink is inspired by the Chicago Cocktail from the iconic New York speakeasy Milk & Honey, which is essentially a rum Manhattan. The splash of champagne acts more like a garnish, lightening up the drink a bit.—AD

2 OUNCES EL DORADO 12-YEAR RUM

1 OUNCE CARPANO ANTICA FORMULA VERMOUTH

1 DASH ANGOSTURA BITTERS

1 DASH HOUSE PEYCHAUD'S BITTERS (PAGE 284)

½ OUNCE DRY CHAMPAGNE

GARNISH: 1 ORANGE TWIST

Stir all the ingredients (except the champagne) over ice, then strain into a coupe. Top with the champagne. Garnish with the orange twist.

. . . .

SUSIE Q

JOAQUÍN SIMÓ, 2009

1½ OUNCES BUSNEL VSOP CALVADOS

½ OUNCE LEMON JUICE

¼ OUNCE CINNAMON BARK SYRUP (PAGE 276)

¼ OUNCE GINGER SYRUP (PAGE 277)

¼ OUNCE VANILLA SYRUP (PAGE 277)

1 DASH ANGOSTURA BITTERS

SPARKLING ROSÉ

Shake all the ingredients (except the sparkling rosé) with ice, then strain into a flute. Top with sparkling rosé. No garnish.

. . . .

TRAPEZE

THOMAS WAUGH, 2011

½ OUNCE ROYAL COMBIER

½ OUNCE YELLOW CHARTREUSE

½ OUNCE CAMPARI

1 DASH FEE BROTHERS WHISKEY BARREL-AGED
    BITTERS

DRY CHAMPAGNE

GARNISH: 1 ORANGE TWIST

Stir all the ingredients (except the champagne) over ice, then strain into a flute. Top with champagne. Garnish with the orange twist.

FORTIFIED WINE
COCKTAILS

Fortified wines are woefully underused as base ingredients for cocktails. We've tried to remedy this by adding a section to our menu devoted to these drinks. What's more, they're often lower in alcohol than other cocktails, which makes them a great start to a long evening of imbibing.

CAFÉ SANDINISTA

JOAQUÍN SIMÓ, 2012

This is an example of how to get a lot of flavor and texture into a drink without a ton of booze.—JS

1 OUNCE LUSTAU EAST INDIA SOLERA SHERRY

¼ OUNCE COFFEE- AND CHILE-INFUSED CAMPARI (PAGE 279)

½ OUNCE ORANGE JUICE

½ OUNCE LIME JUICE

½ OUNCE DEMERARA SYRUP (PAGE 277)

SMALL PINCH OF KOSHER SALT

GARNISH: COFFEE BEAN

Short shake with 3 ice cubes, then strain into a double rocks glass filled with crushed ice. Garnish with a few grates of coffee bean and serve with a straw.

. . . .

CYNARO DE BERGERAC

BRAD FARRAN, 2013

This is a concept drink that started with the name and the combination of Cynar and red wine from France's Bergerac region. I bridged the two unlikely partners with Black Strap rum and Demerara Syrup to create our Bergerac Mix, which has since been used in other drinks.—BF

1½ OUNCES BERGERAC MIX (PAGE 284)

1 OUNCE BOLS BARREL-AGED GENEVER

½ OUNCE HAYMAN'S OLD TOM GIN

½ OUNCE BÉNÉDICTINE

1 DASH VIEUX PONTARLIER ABSINTHE

1 DASH BITTERMENS XOCOLATL MOLE BITTERS

GARNISH: 1 ORANGE TWIST

Stir all the ingredients over ice, then strain into a Nick & Nora glass. Garnish with the orange twist.

. . . .

DERBY GIRL

JILLIAN VOSE, 2013

Juleps are typically such boozy, one-and-done affairs. I created this to be a lower-octane, aperitif-style julep.—JV

3 SMALL NECTARINE SLICES

1½ OUNCES LILLET BLANC

½ OUNCE SUZE SAVEUR D'AUTREFOIS LIQUEUR

½ OUNCE KOVAL ROSE HIP LIQUEUR

¼ OUNCE ACACIA HONEY SYRUP (PAGE 276)

GARNISH: 1 MINT BOUQUET

In a shaker, muddle the nectarine slices. Add the remaining ingredients and short shake with ice. Strain into a julep tin filled with crushed ice. Garnish with the mint bouquet in the center of the ice and serve with a straw.

FAIR FAULT

TYSON BUHLER, 2013

This cocktail is inspired by a vintage British drink called the Treacle, which is a rum old-fashioned topped with a layer of apple juice. The Black Strap rum float in my version is almost like topping the drink with pancake syrup: first you smell the rum's massive molasses aromas, then the acidic Pineau des Charentes, an aperitif made with grape must and cognac, cuts right through it.—TB

2 OUNCES PASQUET PINEAU DES CHARENTES

½ OUNCE CRUZAN SINGLE-BARREL RUM

½ OUNCE GRANNY SMITH APPLE JUICE

½ OUNCE LEMON JUICE

¼ OUNCE CANE SUGAR SYRUP (PAGE 276)

1 TEASPOON CRUZAN BLACK STRAP RUM

Shake all the ingredients (except the Black Strap rum) with ice, then strain into a port glass. Float the Black Strap rum on top. No garnish.

. . . .

HAVE AT IT

ALEX DAY, 2013

1½ OUNCES WILLIAMS & HUMBERT DRY SACK MEDIUM SHERRY

¾ OUNCE FORDS GIN

¾ OUNCE GRAPEFRUIT JUICE

½ OUNCE LEMON JUICE

¾ OUNCE SIMPLE SYRUP (PAGE 277)

1 DASH ANGOSTURA BITTERS

CLUB SODA

GARNISH: 1 ORANGE WEDGE

Short shake all the ingredients (except the club soda) with ice, then strain into a highball glass filled with ice cubes. Top with club soda. Garnish with the orange wedge and serve with a straw.

MELANCHOLY SUMMER

ERYN REECE, 2013

2 CUCUMBER WHEELS

1 OUNCE LUSTAU MANZANILLA SHERRY

1 OUNCE FORDS GIN

½ OUNCE SUZE SAVEUR D'AUTREFOIS LIQUEUR

¾ OUNCE CANTALOUPE JUICE

½ OUNCE LEMON JUICE

½ OUNCE ACACIA HONEY SYRUP (PAGE 276)

GARNISH: 1 CUCUMBER RIBBON

In a shaker, muddle the cucumber wheels. Add the remaining ingredients and shake with ice. Double strain into a Nick & Nora glass. Garnish with the cucumber ribbon on a cocktail pick.

. . . .

MIDNIGHT MOUNTAIN

BRAD FARRAN, 2013

1½ OUNCES AMARO NARDINI

1 OUNCE CARPANO ANTICA FORMULA VERMOUTH

¼ OUNCE MARIE BRIZARD WHITE CRÈME DE MENTHE

¼ OUNCE MARIE BRIZARD WHITE CRÈME DE CACAO

GARNISH: 1 ORANGE TWIST

Stir all the ingredients over ice, then strain into a double rocks glass over 1 large ice cube. Garnish with the twist.

. . . .

SCHUMAN'S ALLEY

JILLIAN VOSE, 2013

¾ OUNCE CONTRATTA VERMOUTH BIANCO

¾ OUNCE DOLIN DRY VERMOUTH

¾ OUNCE COCCHI AMERICANO

1 OUNCE FORDS GIN

½ OUNCE YELLOW CHARTREUSE

1 DASH BITTERMENS HOPPED GRAPEFRUIT BITTERS

1 DASH DALE DEGROFF'S PIMENTO BITTERS

GARNISH: 1 LEMON TWIST

Stir all the ingredients over ice, then strain into a Nick & Nora glass. To garnish, squeeze the lemon twist over the drink, then roll it up, skewer it on a cocktail pick, and drop it in the drink.

. . . .

SHOOTS AND LADDERS

ERYN REECE, 2013

1½ OUNCES BASIL-INFUSED DOLIN BLANC VERMOUTH (PAGE 281)

1½ OUNCES LUSTAU AMONTILLADO SHERRY

½ OUNCE JALAPEÑO-INFUSED SIEMBRA AZUL BLANCO TEQUILA (PAGE 279)

½ TEASPOON CANE SUGAR SYRUP (PAGE 276)

Stir all the ingredients over ice, then strain into a rocks glass. No garnish.

. . . .

STRINGER BELL

TYSON BUHLER, 2013

This was going to be a light, aperitif-style drink built around sherry and celery, but I made it spicy and vegetal with chile-infused tequila and Cynar.—TB

1½ OUNCES LUSTAU AMONTILLADO SHERRY

½ OUNCE JALAPEÑO-INFUSED SIEMBRA AZUL BLANCO TEQUILA (PAGE 279)

¼ OUNCE CYNAR

¾ OUNCE LIME JUICE

½ OUNCE CELERY JUICE

½ OUNCE CANE SUGAR SYRUP (PAGE 276)

PINCH OF KOSHER SALT

GARNISH: 1 CELERY STICK

Shake all the ingredients with ice, then strain into a double rocks glass over 1 large ice cube. Garnish with the celery stick.

PUNCH

For a punch to be authentic, the communal bowl needs to contain five elements: spirits, sugar, citrus, water, and spice. Without the spice component, it's not technically punch. (We're fully aware that we occasionally break this rule.) Spice can be added in many forms, including bitters, teas, infusions, and fresh ingredients. When Phil launched Death & Co's punch program in 2008, he borrowed a tea-infused sweet vermouth that Brian had recently created. This was another *Aha!* moment for our cocktail program. Using a method in which sugar cubes are muddled with citrus and club soda before the remaining ingredients are added and stirred over ice, we quickly developed an entire menu of punches that made Death & Co the epicenter of America's renewed interest in boozy punches. We've continued to create punches for each new menu, and in recent years some bartenders have replaced Phil's stirring method with the practice of rolling the ingredients back and forth between two pitchers. Unless noted otherwise, each punch recipe serves 4 to 6 people.

ARRACK PUNCH

PHIL WARD, 2008

16 DEMERARA SUGAR CUBES

10 OUNCES CLUB SODA

6 OUNCES APPLETON ESTATE V/X RUM

3 OUNCES VAN OOSTEN BATAVIA ARRACK

1 OUNCE LUXARDO MARASCHINO LIQUEUR

3 OUNCES LIME JUICE

5 DASHES BITTER TRUTH AROMATIC BITTERS

GARNISH: 6 LIME WHEELS

In a pitcher, muddle the sugar cubes with 4 ounces of the club soda until the sugar is fully broken up. Add the remaining ingredients (except the remaining club soda) and fill the pitcher three-quarters full with ice cubes. Stir until cold, then strain into a punch bowl over 1 large block of ice. Top with the remaining 6 ounces of club soda. Garnish with the lime wheels and serve with a ladle and punch glasses.

....

BILLINGSLEY PUNCH

ALEX DAY, 2009

I wanted to build a punch around Aperol, so I paired it with a bunch of refreshing flavors, which always works with this aperitif. The combination of gin, Aperol, and grapefruit is something we use a lot. It turned out to be quite a festive punch, so I named it after Sherman Billingsley, an ex-bootlegger who owned New York's famously festive Stork Club.—AD

12 WHITE SUGAR CUBES

8 OUNCES CLUB SODA

6 OUNCES TANQUERAY NO. TEN GIN

2 OUNCES APEROL

2 OUNCES GRAPEFRUIT JUICE

2 OUNCES LEMON JUICE

4 DASHES HOUSE PEYCHAUD'S BITTERS
(PAGE 284)

GARNISH: 6 GRAPEFRUIT CRESCENTS

In a pitcher, muddle the sugar cubes with 4 ounces of the club soda until the sugar is fully broken up. Add the remaining ingredients (except the remaining club soda) and fill the pitcher three-quarters full with ice cubes. Stir until cold, then strain into a punch bowl over 1 large block of ice. Top with the remaining 4 ounces of club soda. Garnish with the grapefruit crescents and serve with a ladle and punch glasses.

Arrack Punch

BLOODHOUND PUNCH

JASON LITTRELL, 2009

8 OUNCES ELIJAH CRAIG 12-YEAR BOURBON

4 OUNCES DONN'S SPICES #1 (PAGE 284)

3 OUNCES LEMON JUICE

4 OUNCES BLUEBERRY SYRUP (PAGE 276)

6 OUNCES CLUB SODA

GARNISH: 6 LEMON WHEELS

In a pitcher, combine all the ingredients (except the club soda). Fill the pitcher three-quarters full with ice cubes. Stir until cold, then strain into a punch bowl over 1 large block of ice. Top with the club soda. Garnish with the lemon wheels and serve with a ladle and punch glasses.

. . . .

BOOKHOUSE BOYS PUNCH

JESSICA GONZALEZ, 2011

3 OUNCES CHAMOMILE-INFUSED OLD OVERHOLT RYE (PAGE 281)

3 OUNCES OLD WELLER ANTIQUE 107 BOURBON

3 OUNCES DONN'S MIX #1 (PAGE 284)

1½ OUNCES GRAPEFRUIT JUICE

1½ OUNCES LEMON JUICE

¾ OUNCE ACACIA HONEY SYRUP (PAGE 276)

¾ OUNCE GINGER SYRUP (PAGE 277)

5 OUNCES CLUB SODA

GARNISH: 6 GRAPEFRUIT CRESCENTS

In a pitcher, combine all the ingredients (except the club soda). Fill the pitcher three-quarters full with ice cubes. Stir until cold, then strain into a punch bowl over 1 large block of ice. Top with the club soda. Garnish with the grapefruit crescents and serve with a ladle and punch glasses.

DRUNKEN PUNCH

PHIL WARD, 2008

12 DEMERARA SUGAR CUBES

7½ OUNCES CLUB SODA

6 OUNCES FUJI APPLE–INFUSED FAMOUS GROUSE
    SCOTCH (PAGE 279)

1½ OUNCES ST. ELIZABETH ALLSPICE DRAM

4½ OUNCES FUJI APPLE JUICE

3 OUNCES LEMON JUICE

6 DASHES HOUSE PEYCHAUD'S BITTERS (PAGE 284)

GARNISH: 6 APPLE SLICES

In a pitcher, muddle the sugar cubes with 3 ounces of
the club soda until the sugar is fully broken up. Add the
remaining ingredients (except the remaining club soda)
and fill the pitcher three-quarters full with ice cubes.
Stir until cold, then strain into a punch bowl over 1 large
block of ice. Top with the remaining 4½ ounces of club
soda. Garnish with the apple slices and serve with a ladle
and punch glasses.

....

EAST RIVER UNDERGROUND

PHIL WARD, 2012

*I love how La Favorite plays with jalapeño-infused
tequila, so I made up this punch on my subway ride
to one of our tastings.—PW*

18 WHITE SUGAR CUBES

8 CUCUMBER WHEELS

8 FRESH KAFFIR LIME LEAVES

PINCH OF KOSHER SALT

4 OUNCES CLUB SODA

4 OUNCES LA FAVORITE RHUM AGRICOLE BLANC

4 OUNCES JALAPEÑO-INFUSED SIEMBRA AZUL
    BLANCO TEQUILA (PAGE 279)

2 OUNCES YELLOW CHARTREUSE

4 OUNCES LIME JUICE

GARNISH: 6 CUCUMBER WHEELS AND 6 FRESH
    KAFFIR LIME LEAVES

In a pitcher, muddle the sugar cubes, cucumber wheels,
Kaffir lime leaves, and salt with the club soda until the
sugar is fully broken up. Add the remaining ingredients
and fill the pitcher three-quarters full with ice cubes. Stir
until cold, then strain into a punch bowl over 1 large block
of ice. Garnish with the cucumber wheels and Kaffir lime
leaves and serve with a ladle and punch glasses.

....

EVIL DEAD PUNCH

BRAD FARRAN, 2012

*One Halloween night I was kind of drunk and challenged
myself to use 3 ounces of St-Germain in a drink. The result
was a somewhat voluminous punch.—BF*

6 OUNCES SANTA TERESA 1796 RUM

3 OUNCES BONAL GENTIANE-QUINA

3 OUNCES ST-GERMAIN

¾ OUNCE ROTHMAN & WINTER APRICOT LIQUEUR

½ OUNCE DONN'S SPICES #2 (PAGE 284)

3 OUNCES LIME JUICE

3 OUNCES ORANGE JUICE

½ OUNCE CANE SUGAR SYRUP (PAGE 276)

½ OUNCE GINGER SYRUP (PAGE 277)

3 DASHES ANGOSTURA BITTERS

6 OUNCES CLUB SODA

GARNISH: 6 LIME AND 6 ORANGE WHEELS

In a pitcher, combine all the ingredients (except the club
soda). Fill the pitcher three-quarters full with ice cubes.
Stir until cold, then strain into a punch bowl over 1 large
block of ice. Top with the club soda. Garnish with
the lime and orange wheels and serve with a ladle and
punch glasses.

Billingsley Punch, page 232

HOIST THE COLOURS PUNCH

BRIAN MILLER, 2009

9 WHITE SUGAR CUBES

6 OUNCES CLUB SODA

4½ OUNCES APPLETON ESTATE V/X RUM

3 OUNCES GOSLING'S BLACK SEAL RUM

1½ OUNCES EL DORADO 151 RUM

4½ OUNCES DONN'S MIX #1 (PAGE 284)

3 OUNCES LEMON JUICE

1½ OUNCES PINEAPPLE JUICE

3 DASHES ANGOSTURA BITTERS

GARNISH: NUTMEG

In a pitcher, muddle the sugar cubes with 3 ounces of the club soda until the sugar is fully broken up. Add the remaining ingredients (except the remaining club soda) and fill the pitcher three-quarters full with ice cubes. Stir until cold, then strain into a punch bowl over 1 large block of ice. Top with the remaining 3 ounces of club soda. Garnish with several grates of nutmeg and serve with a ladle and punch glasses.

. . . .

JERSEY LIGHTNING

PHIL WARD, 2008

12 WHITE SUGAR CUBES

9 OUNCES CLUB SODA

6 OUNCES LAIRD'S BONDED APPLE BRANDY

3 OUNCES CINNAMON ORANGE TEA–INFUSED
    SWEET VERMOUTH (PAGE 281)

3 OUNCES LEMON JUICE

GARNISH: 6 APPLE SLICES AND 3 CINNAMON STICKS,
    SNAPPED IN HALF

In a pitcher, muddle the sugar cubes with 3 ounces of the club soda until the sugar is fully broken up. Add the remaining ingredients (except the remaining club soda) and fill the pitcher three-quarters full with ice cubes. Stir until cold, then strain into a punch bowl over 1 large block of ice. Top with the remaining 6 ounces of club soda. Garnish with the apple slices and cinnamon sticks and serve with a ladle and punch glasses.

KILL-DEVIL PUNCH

PHIL WARD, 2008

We originally made this punch extra festive by freezing raspberries in large cubes of ice. But then nobody wanted to deal with making the raspberry ice cubes, so we killed the idea.—PW

12 WHITE SUGAR CUBES

15 RASPBERRIES

3 OUNCES CLUB SODA

6 OUNCES APPLETON ESTATE V/X RUM

3 OUNCES LIME JUICE

3 OUNCES PINEAPPLE JUICE

3 OUNCES DRY CHAMPAGNE

GARNISH: 12 RASPBERRIES

In a pitcher, muddle the sugar cubes with the raspberries and club soda until the sugar is fully broken up. Add the remaining ingredients (except the champagne) and fill the pitcher three-quarters full with ice cubes. Stir until cold, then strain into a punch bowl over 1 large block of ice. Top with the champagne. Garnish with the raspberries and serve with a ladle and punch glasses.

. . . .

LA FÉE NOIR PUNCH

THOMAS WAUGH, 2009

9 WHITE SUGAR CUBES

9 BLACKBERRIES

6 OUNCES CLUB SODA

6 OUNCES HAYMAN'S OLD TOM GIN

¾ OUNCE LUXARDO MARASCHINO LIQUEUR

SCANT ¾ OUNCE ST. GEORGE ABSINTHE

3 OUNCES ORANGE JUICE

2 OUNCES LEMON JUICE

GARNISH: 6 ORANGE SLICES

In a pitcher, muddle the sugar cubes with the blackberries and 3 ounces of the club soda until the sugar is fully broken up. Add the remaining ingredients (except the remaining club soda) and fill the pitcher three-quarters full with ice cubes. Stir until cold, then strain into a punch bowl over 1 large block of ice. Top with the remaining 3 ounces of club soda. Garnish with the orange slices and serve with a ladle and punch glasses.

. . . .

LIGHTS OUT PUNCH

JOAQUÍN SIMÓ, 2009

6 OUNCES CENTINELA REPOSADO TEQUILA

3 OUNCES CINNAMON ORANGE TEA–INFUSED SWEET VERMOUTH (PAGE 281)

3 OUNCES APPLE JUICE

2 OUNCES LEMON JUICE

1 OUNCE DEMERARA SYRUP (PAGE 277)

4 DASHES ANGOSTURA BITTERS

4 DASHES FEE BROTHERS WHISKEY BARREL-AGED BITTERS

6 OUNCES CLUB SODA

GARNISH: 6 APPLE SLICES AND CINNAMON

In a pitcher, combine all the ingredients (except the club soda). Fill the pitcher three-quarters full with ice cubes. Stir until cold, then strain into a punch bowl over 1 large block of ice. Top with the club soda. Garnish with the apple slices and some cinnamon grated over the bowl and serve with a ladle and punch glasses.

. . . .

LUST FOR LIFE PUNCH

JOAQUÍN SIMÓ, 2009

9 DEMERARA SUGAR CUBES

3 LONG ORANGE TWISTS

3 OUNCES CLUB SODA

3 OUNCES LEMON JUICE

1½ OUNCES PINEAPPLE JUICE

6 OUNCES KROGSTAD AQUAVIT

3 OUNCES GRAPEFRUIT-INFUSED PUNT E MES (PAGE 281)

4½ OUNCES DRY CHAMPAGNE

GARNISH: 6 LEMON WHEELS

In a pitcher, muddle the sugar cubes with the orange twists. Add the club soda, lemon juice, and pineapple juice and stir until the sugar is dissolved. Add the aquavit and infused vermouth and fill the pitcher three-quarters full with ice cubes. Stir until cold. Pour the champagne into a punch bowl over 1 large block of ice, then strain the contents of the pitcher over the top. Garnish with the lemon wheels and serve with a ladle and punch glasses.

. . . .

MOTHER'S RUIN PUNCH

PHIL WARD, 2008

This was one of our very first punches. Traditionally punch is made with some kind of spice element, satisfied here with a tea infusion, which was a real game changer for us.—PW

8 WHITE SUGAR CUBES

2 OUNCES CLUB SODA

4 OUNCES PLYMOUTH GIN

2 OUNCES CINNAMON ORANGE TEA–INFUSED SWEET VERMOUTH (PAGE 281)

4 OUNCES GRAPEFRUIT JUICE

2 OUNCES LEMON JUICE

3 OUNCES DRY CHAMPAGNE

GARNISH: 6 GRAPEFRUIT WHEELS

In a pitcher, muddle the sugar cubes with the club soda until the sugar is fully broken up. Add the remaining ingredients (except the champagne) and fill the pitcher three-quarters full with ice cubes. Stir until cold, then strain into a punch bowl over 1 large block of ice. Top with the champagne. Garnish with the grapefruit wheels and serve with a ladle and punch glasses.

NUTS AND SHERRY PUNCH

PHIL WARD, 2008

8 WHITE SUGAR CUBES

8 OUNCES CLUB SODA

6 OUNCES LUSTAU EAST INDIA SOLERA SHERRY

3 OUNCES PECAN-INFUSED BUFFALO TRACE BOURBON (PAGE 282)

½ OUNCE ST. ELIZABETH ALLSPICE DRAM

2 OUNCES LIME JUICE

1 OUNCE PINEAPPLE JUICE

2 DASHES BITTERMENS XOCOLATL MOLE BITTERS

In a pitcher, muddle the sugar cubes with 2 ounces of the club soda until the sugar is fully broken up. Add the remaining ingredients (except the remaining club soda) and fill the pitcher three-quarters full with ice cubes. Stir until cold, then strain into a punch bowl over 1 large block of ice. Top with the remaining 6 ounces of club soda. Serve with a ladle and punch glasses. No garnish.

P-FIVE PUNCH

TYSON BUHLER, 2013

12 WHITE SUGAR CUBES

2 OUNCES ORGEAT (PAGE 278)

4 OUNCES CAMPO DE ENCANTO ACHOLADO PISCO

2 OUNCES APPLETON WHITE RUM

2 OUNCES OLD RAJ GIN

3 OUNCES GRAPEFRUIT JUICE

2 OUNCES LEMON JUICE

2 OUNCES BECHEROVKA BITTERS

GARNISH: 6 LEMON WHEELS

In a pitcher, muddle the sugar cubes with the orgeat until the sugar is fully broken up. Add the remaining ingredients and fill the pitcher three-quarters full with ice cubes. Roll the drink into another pitcher and repeat until the drink is very cold and the sugar is completely dissolved. Strain into a punch bowl over 1 large block of ice. Garnish with the lemon wheels and serve with a ladle and punch glasses.

PIC-A-DE-CROP PUNCH

JESSICA GONZALEZ, 2011

{Serves 2}

The night before our menu tastings, we're often scrambling to come up with new drinks. On a whim, I thought apricot and Batavia arrack would pair well with the banana notes in the Plantation rum, and it worked out. This is intended to be a two-person punch, but you can easily double or triple it.—JG

3 OUNCES PLANTATION BARBADOS 5-YEAR RUM

½ OUNCE EL DORADO 151 RUM

½ OUNCE VAN OOSTEN BATAVIA ARRACK

1 OUNCE ROTHMAN & WINTER APRICOT LIQUEUR

1½ OUNCES LIME JUICE

1½ OUNCES PINEAPPLE JUICE

1 OUNCE GRAPEFRUIT JUICE

1 OUNCE CANE SUGAR SYRUP (PAGE 276)

2 DASHES ANGOSTURA BITTERS

1 OUNCE CLUB SODA

GARNISH: 6 LIME WHEELS AND NUTMEG

In a pitcher, combine all the ingredients (except the club soda) and fill the pitcher three-quarters full with ice cubes. Stir until cold, then strain into a small punch bowl over ice cubes. Top with the club soda. Garnish with the lime wheels and several grates of nutmeg and serve with two straws.

....

PISCO PUNCH

PHIL WARD, 2008

A lot of our punches are complex and boozy, but we also try to include an easy-drinking punch on every menu.—PW

12 WHITE SUGAR CUBES

9 OUNCES CLUB SODA

9 OUNCES STRAWBERRY- AND PINEAPPLE-INFUSED MACCHU PISCO (PAGE 281)

1½ OUNCES LUXARDO MARASCHINO LIQUEUR

3 OUNCES LIME JUICE

GARNISH: 6 STRAWBERRY SLICES AND 6 LIME WHEELS

In a pitcher, muddle the sugar cubes with 3 ounces of the club soda until the sugar is fully broken up. Add the remaining ingredients (except the remaining club soda) and fill the pitcher three-quarters full with ice cubes. Stir until cold, then strain into a punch bowl over 1 large block of ice. Top with the remaining 6 ounces of club soda. Garnish with the strawberries and lime wheels and serve with a ladle and punch glasses.

....

PORFIRIAN PUNCH

ALEX DAY, 2009

Among sherry's many friends behind the bar is tequila. Doubling up on infusions gives this punch extra layers of complexity.—AD

9 WHITE SUGAR CUBES

9 OUNCES CLUB SODA

6 OUNCES SPICED PEAR–INFUSED SIEMBRA AZUL BLANCO TEQUILA (PAGE 281)

1½ OUNCES CINNAMON ORANGE TEA–INFUSED SWEET VERMOUTH (PAGE 281)

1½ OUNCES LA GITANA MANZANILLA SHERRY

3 OUNCES LEMON JUICE

GARNISH: 6 PEAR SLICES

In a pitcher, muddle the sugar cubes with 3 ounces of the club soda until the sugar is fully broken up. Add the remaining ingredients (except the remaining club soda) and fill the pitcher three-quarters full with ice cubes. Stir until cold, then strain into a punch bowl over 1 large block of ice. Top with the remaining 6 ounces of club soda. Garnish with the pear slices and serve with a ladle and punch glasses.

Billingsley Punch, page 232

RAZZLE-DAZZLE PUNCH

BRAD FARRAN, 2013

This punch combines two caraway-forward spirits:
Old Overholt and Kümmel.—BF

18 RASPBERRIES

1 OUNCE SUPERFINE SUGAR

6 ORANGE TWISTS

12 OUNCES OLD OVERHOLT RYE

1½ OUNCES KÜMMEL LIQUEUR

3 OUNCES LEMON JUICE

3 OUNCES GRAPEFRUIT JUICE

1½ OUNCES CANE SUGAR SYRUP (PAGE 276)

2 OUNCES DRY CHAMPAGNE

GARNISH: 12 RASPBERRIES AND 6 LEMON WHEELS

In a pitcher, muddle the raspberries with the sugar and orange twists. Add the remaining ingredients (except the champagne) and fill the pitcher with ice cubes. Stir until cold. Pour the champagne into a punch bowl, then strain the contents of the pitcher over the top. Add 1 large block of ice. Garnish with the raspberries and lemon wheels and serve with a ladle and punch glasses.

....

RUGBY PUNCH

JESSICA GONZALEZ, 2009

I so loved our green tea–infused Scotch that I created
this punch to keep it around a bit longer.—JG

9 WHITE SUGAR CUBES

3 LEMON TWISTS

2 OUNCES CLUB SODA

6 OUNCES COCONUT GREEN TEA–INFUSED FAMOUS
    GROUSE SCOTCH (PAGE 282)

1½ OUNCES AMARO NONINO

1 OUNCE GRAND MARNIER

3 OUNCES LEMON JUICE

4 OUNCES DRY CHAMPAGNE

GARNISH: 6 LEMON WHEELS

In a pitcher, muddle the sugar cubes with the lemon twists and club soda until the sugar is fully broken up. Add the remaining ingredients (except the champagne) and fill the pitcher three-quarters full with ice cubes. Stir until cold, then strain into a punch bowl over 1 large block of ice. Top with the champagne. Garnish with the lemon wheels and serve with a ladle and punch glasses.

....

VALLEY OF KINGS PUNCH

JOAQUÍN SIMÓ, 2009

6 WHITE SUGAR CUBES

4 OUNCES CLUB SODA

8 OUNCES SCARLET GLOW TEA–INFUSED MACCHU
    PISCO (PAGE 282)

3 OUNCES PINEAPPLE JUICE

2 OUNCES GRAPEFRUIT JUICE

2 OUNCES LIME JUICE

6 OUNCES DRY CHAMPAGNE

GARNISH: 6 PINEAPPLE WEDGES

In a pitcher, muddle the sugar cubes with the club soda until the sugar is fully broken up. Add the remaining ingredients (except the champagne) and fill the pitcher three-quarters full with ice cubes. Stir until cold, then strain into a punch bowl over 1 large block of ice. Top with the champagne. Garnish with the pineapple wedges and serve with a ladle and punch glasses.

JULEPS

There are two schools of thought on how to make a proper julep. One camp says you muddle the mint inside the tin, then build the drink on top of it. We usually save the mint for garnish in the form of a lavish bouquet; this method gives you a headful of minty aroma as you sip the drink through a straw. As you'll see, juleps require more patience than most cocktails. The secret to a proper julep is slowly adding crushed ice as you stir the drink to the proper dilution and temperature. In addition to being the most handsome of serving vessels, a julep tin is an excellent indicator of temperature: you should stir the drink until the tin is completely covered in a frosty patina.

APERITIVO JULEP

ALEX DAY, 2009

This is basically a big glass of vermouth, but the amaro makes it seem more complex than it is. Peach and amaro get along famously.—AD

2 OUNCES DOLIN DRY VERMOUTH

¾ OUNCE AMARO CIOCIARO

1 TEASPOON MASSENEZ CRÈME DE PÊCHE PEACH LIQUEUR

GARNISH: 1 MINT BOUQUET

Put all the ingredients in a julep tin. Fill the tin halfway with crushed ice. Stir with a teaspoon, churning the ice as you go, for about 10 seconds, holding the tin by the rim so the entire tin can eventually frost up. Add more crushed ice to fill the tin two-thirds full and stir until the tin is completely frosted. Add more ice to form a cone above the rim. Garnish with the mint bouquet in the center of the ice and serve with a straw.

CHAMOMILE JULEP

PHIL WARD, 2008

I'd tasted a chamomile-infused grappa that I loved and decided to try the same thing with Old Overholt rye. The results blew my mind. I decided to show it off in its most naked form: a julep. It has since become one of our most-used infusions.—PW

2 OUNCES CHAMOMILE-INFUSED OLD OVERHOLT RYE (PAGE 281)

¼ OUNCE SIMPLE SYRUP (PAGE 277)

GARNISH: 1 MINT BOUQUET

Put the rye and simple syrup in a julep tin. Fill the tin halfway with crushed ice. Stir with a teaspoon, churning the ice as you go, for about 10 seconds, holding the tin by the rim so the entire tin can eventually frost up. Add more crushed ice to fill the tin two-thirds full and stir until the tin is completely frosted. Add more ice to form a cone above the rim. Garnish with the mint bouquet in the center of the ice and serve with a straw.

....

DOUBLE-BARREL JULEP

JOAQUÍN SIMÓ, 2009

1½ OUNCES OLD GRAND-DAD 114 BOURBON

½ OUNCE DIPLOMÁTICO RESERVA EXCLUSIVA RUM

1 TEASPOON MASSENEZ CRÈME DE PÊCHE PEACH LIQUEUR

1 TEASPOON DEMERARA SYRUP (PAGE 277)

¼ OUNCE SMITH & CROSS RUM

4 DASHES FEE BROTHERS WHISKEY BARREL-AGED
    BITTERS

GARNISH: 1 MINT BOUQUET

Put the bourbon, Diplomático rum, peach liqueur, and syrup in a julep tin. Fill the tin halfway with crushed ice. Stir with a teaspoon, churning the ice as you go, for about 10 seconds, holding the tin by the rim so the entire tin can eventually frost up. Add more crushed ice to fill the tin two-thirds full and stir until the tin is completely frosted. Add more ice to form a cone above the rim. Float the Smith & Cross rum over the drink and top with the bitters. Garnish with the mint bouquet in the center of the ice and serve with a straw.

. . . .

JUST ANOTHER JULEP

BRIAN MILLER, 2008

The Kentucky-born humorist Irvin S. Cobb once said, "Any guy who'd put rye in a mint julep and crush the leaves would put scorpions in a baby's bed." Taking this to heart, I rub the inside of the julep tin with mint leaves, then discard them before building the drink.—BM

2 MINT SPRIGS

2 OUNCES BUFFALO TRACE BOURBON

¼ OUNCE DEMERARA SYRUP (PAGE 277)

½ OUNCE GOSLING'S BLACK SEAL RUM

GARNISH: 1 MINT BOUQUET

Rub the mint around the inside of a julep tin and discard. Fill the tin with crushed ice and add the bourbon and syrup. Swizzle briefly, then top with crushed ice. Pour the rum over the top. Garnish with the mint bouquet in the center of the ice and serve with a straw.

MAPLE JULEP

PHIL WARD, 2008

2 OUNCES OLD OVERHOLT RYE

¼ OUNCE MAPLE SYRUP

GARNISH: 1 MINT BOUQUET

Put the rye and maple syrup in a julep tin. Fill the tin halfway with crushed ice. Stir with a teaspoon, churning the ice as you go, for about 10 seconds, holding the tin by the rim so the entire tin can eventually frost up. Add more crushed ice to fill the tin two-thirds full and stir until the tin is completely frosted. Add more ice to form a cone above the rim. Garnish with the mint bouquet in the center of the ice and serve with a straw.

Maple Julep

NOT-QUITE-GEORGIA JULEP

PHIL WARD, 2008

1 OUNCE COGNAC

1 OUNCE LAIRD'S BONDED APPLE BRANDY

1 TEASPOON MASSENEZ CRÈME DE PÊCHE
 PEACH LIQUEUR

1 TEASPOON SIMPLE SYRUP (PAGE 277)

GARNISH: 1 MINT BOUQUET

Put all the ingredients in a julep tin. Fill the tin halfway with crushed ice. Stir with a teaspoon, churning the ice as you go, for about 10 seconds, holding the tin by the rim so the entire tin can eventually frost up. Add more crushed ice to fill the tin two-thirds full and stir until the tin is completely frosted. Add more ice to form a cone above the rim. Garnish with the mint bouquet in the center of the ice and serve with a straw.

. . . .

RACKETEER JULEP

JESSICA GONZALEZ, 2009

1 MINT SPRIG

2 OUNCES BOLS GENEVER

½ OUNCE SMITH & CROSS RUM

1 TEASPOON DEMERARA SYRUP (PAGE 277)

1 TEASPOON VANILLA SYRUP (PAGE 277)

1 DASH BITTER TRUTH AROMATIC BITTERS

GARNISH: 1 MINT BOUQUET

Rub the mint around the inside of a julep tin and discard. Put the remaining ingredients (except the bitters) in the tin. Fill the tin halfway with crushed ice. Stir with a teaspoon, churning the ice as you go, for about 10 seconds, holding the tin by the rim so the entire tin can eventually frost up. Add more crushed ice to fill the tin two-thirds full and stir until the tin is completely frosted. Add more ice to form a cone above the rim. Top with the bitters. Garnish with the mint bouquet in the center of the ice and serve with a straw.

SMOKED JULEP

PHIL WARD, 2008

1 OUNCE LAPHROAIG 12-YEAR SCOTCH

1 OUNCE LAIRD'S BONDED APPLE BRANDY

¼ OUNCE MAPLE SYRUP

GARNISH: 1 APPLE FAN AND 1 MINT BOUQUET

Put all the ingredients in a julep tin. Fill the tin halfway with crushed ice. Stir with a teaspoon, churning the ice as you go, for about 10 seconds, holding the tin by the rim so the entire tin can eventually frost up. Add more crushed ice to fill the tin two-thirds full and stir until the tin is completely frosted. Add more ice to form a cone above the rim. Garnish with the apple fan and mint bouquet in the center of the ice and serve with a straw.

. . . .

ZIHUATANEJO JULEP

BRIAN MILLER, 2009

Although no cinnamon is grated directly into the drink, grating the cinnamon stick before you use it to garnish the drink releases its aromas and makes it more fragrant when you stick it into the ice.—BM

1 MINT SPRIG

2 OUNCES EL TESORO REPOSADO TEQUILA

1 TEASPOON DEMERARA SYRUP (PAGE 277)

½ OUNCE DEL MAGUEY CHICHICAPA MEZCAL

GARNISH: 1 CINNAMON STICK AND 1 MINT BOUQUET

Rub the mint around the inside of a julep tin and discard. Fill the tin with crushed ice and add the tequila and syrup. Swizzle briefly, then top with crushed ice. Float the mezcal on top. Grate the side of a cinnamon stick away from the drink to release its aromas, then place the cinnamon and mint bouquet in the center of the ice and serve with a straw.

FLIPS and FIZZES

Cocktail historians might take issue with our simplified definition, but for our purposes flips contain a whole egg or yolks alone; fizzes contain a whole egg or whites alone. Either way, the almighty egg adds distinctive body and texture to any drink it touches. As always, heed the standard raw-egg warnings.

CELINE FIZZ

PHIL WARD, 2008

2 OUNCES PLYMOUTH GIN

¾ OUNCE ST-GERMAIN

¾ OUNCE LEMON JUICE

¾ OUNCE SIMPLE SYRUP (PAGE 277)

1 EGG WHITE

CLUB SODA

Dry shake all the ingredients (except the club soda), then shake again with ice. Double strain into a fizz glass and top with club soda. No garnish.

CHINESE FIZZ

PHIL WARD, 2008

A fizz variation on the Chinese cocktail from The Savoy Cocktail Book, *by Harry Craddock.—PW*

2 OUNCES APPLETON ESTATE V/X RUM

¼ OUNCE COINTREAU

¼ OUNCE LUXARDO MARASCHINO LIQUEUR

½ OUNCE LEMON JUICE

½ OUNCE SIMPLE SYRUP (PAGE 277)

¼ OUNCE GRENADINE (PAGE 284)

1 EGG WHITE

1 DASH ANGOSTURA BITTERS

GARNISH: 1 ORANGE WHEEL

Dry shake all the ingredients, then shake again with ice. Double strain into a fizz glass filled with ice cubes. Garnish with the orange wheel and serve with a straw.

. . . .

JACK SPARROW FLIP

BRIAN MILLER, 2008

2 OUNCES FLOR DE CAÑA 7-YEAR RUM

¾ OUNCE SANDEMAN RAINWATER MADEIRA

¾ OUNCE DEMERARA SYRUP (PAGE 277)

1 EGG

2 DASHES FEE BROTHERS WHISKEY BARREL-AGED BITTERS

GARNISH: CINNAMON

Dry shake all the ingredients, then add 3 ice cubes and shake again. Double strain into a fancy fizz glass. Garnish with a few grates of cinnamon.

JELLY ROLL MORTON

THOMAS WAUGH, 2009

We don't make a lot of flips at Death & Co (not everyone loves eggy cocktails, and they can make an awful mess behind the bar), but this jammy flip, named for the jazz musician, is a crowd-pleaser.—TW

1½ OUNCES HINE H COGNAC

½ OUNCE DRIED CURRANT–INFUSED WILD TURKEY RYE (PAGE 279)

¾ OUNCE SANDEMAN RUBY PORT

½ OUNCE SIMPLE SYRUP (PAGE 277)

1 EGG YOLK

½ OUNCE HEAVY CREAM

1 DASH ANGOSTURA BITTERS

Dry shake all the ingredients, then shake again with ice. Double strain into a coupe. No garnish.

....

LE GIGOT FLIP

PHIL WARD, 2008

2 OUNCES SANTA TERESA 1796 RUM

½ OUNCE CHERRY HEERING

¼ OUNCE DEMERARA SYRUP (PAGE 277)

1 EGG YOLK

½ OUNCE HEAVY CREAM

2 DASHES BITTERMENS XOCOLATL MOLE BITTERS

GARNISH: 1 BRANDIED CHERRY

Dry shake all the ingredients, then shake again with ice. Double strain into a coupe. Garnish with the cherry.

....

PEARLS BEFORE SWINE

JOAQUÍN SIMÓ, 2009

I wanted to come up with a Ramos Gin Fizz (page 150) that was less of a pain in the ass to make (you have to shake them forever). Replacing the egg with yogurt and lemon curd did the trick.—JS

2 OUNCES MARTIN MILLER'S WESTBOURNE-STRENGTH GIN

½ OUNCE LEMON JUICE

½ OUNCE ORGEAT (PAGE 278)

1 TEASPOON GREEK YOGURT

1 TEASPOON LEMON CURD

3 DROPS ROSE WATER

Shake all the ingredients (except the rose water) with ice, then double strain into a coupe. Top with the rose water. No garnish.

....

PIT STOP FLIP

ALEX DAY, 2008

By nature, flips are rich and decadent. This drink is as well, but the madeira is light and stretches out the flavors to create a more delicate flip.—AD

1½ OUNCES LAIRD'S BONDED APPLE BRANDY

½ OUNCE SANDEMAN RAINWATER MADEIRA

½ OUNCE MAPLE SYRUP

1 EGG YOLK

½ OUNCE HEAVY CREAM

GARNISH: NUTMEG AND 1 APPLE SLICE

Dry shake all the ingredients, then shake again with ice. Double strain into a coupe. Garnish with a few grates of nutmeg and rest the apple slice on the edge of the coupe.

....

RAISIN BURN

THOMAS WAUGH, 2008

2 OUNCES DRIED CURRANT–INFUSED WILD TURKEY RYE (PAGE 279)

¾ OUNCE LUSTAU EAST INDIA SOLERA SHERRY

1 WHOLE EGG

½ OUNCE HEAVY CREAM

1 DASH ANGOSTURA BITTERS

GARNISH: CINNAMON

Dry shake all the ingredients, then add 1 large ice cube and shake again. Double strain into a coupe. Garnish with a few grates of cinnamon.

....

SATURDAY MORNING FLIP

JOAQUÍN SIMÓ, 2008

1 OUNCE APPLETON ESTATE V/X RUM

1 OUNCE GOSLING'S BLACK SEAL RUM

¾ OUNCE RUBY PORT

1 TEASPOON ESPRESSO-INFUSED DEMERARA SYRUP (PAGE 277)

1 EGG YOLK

1 DASH ANGOSTURA BITTERS

Dry shake all the ingredients, then shake again with ice. Double strain into a coupe. No garnish.

....

SLEEPY HOLLOW FIZZ

BRIAN MILLER, 2008

This Halloween-inspired drink was the first of many D&C drinks named after Johnny Depp movies. Technically a "golden fizz," this rich drink is stylistically more like a flip.—BM

1½ OUNCES FLOR DE CAÑA 7-YEAR RUM

½ OUNCE EL DORADO HIGH-STRENGTH 151 RUM

½ OUNCE LEMON JUICE

½ OUNCE MAPLE SYRUP

1 EGG YOLK

2 TEASPOONS PUMPKIN PUREE (PAGE 285)

CLUB SODA

Dry shake all the ingredients (except the club soda), then shake again with ice. Strain into a fizz glass and top with club soda. No garnish.

Celine Fizz, page 245

SWIZZLES

Swizzles hail from the Caribbean, where they are traditionally mixed with the stem of the *Quararibea turbinata* tree (see page 70). We like to premix the drink by dry shaking or whipping the ingredients with a few ice pellets, which speeds the swizzling process and saves valuable time during service. But if you have the time, feel free to build the cocktail as you would a julep, swizzling the ingredients with a mixing spoon—or a *bois lélé* if you're lucky enough to own one.

6TH STREET SWIZZLE

PHIL WARD, 2008

1½ OUNCES LA FAVORITE RHUM AGRICOLE BLANC

1 OUNCE LIME JUICE

¾ OUNCE CANE SUGAR SYRUP (PAGE 276)

2 DASHES ANGOSTURA BITTERS

GARNISH: 1 MINT SPRIG AND 1 LIME WHEEL

Whip all the ingredients, shaking with a few pieces of crushed ice just until incorporated. Pour into a pilsner glass filled with crushed ice and swizzle until cold. Garnish with the mint sprig and lime wheel and serve with a straw.

. . . .

BOURBONNAIS SWIZZLE

BRIAN MILLER, 2008

2 OUNCES PECAN-INFUSED BUFFALO TRACE BOURBON (PAGE 282)

1 OUNCE MARIE BRIZARD WHITE CRÈME DE CACAO

½ OUNCE LILLET ROUGE

¾ OUNCE LEMON JUICE

Dry shake all the ingredients, then add 3 ice cubes and short shake. Strain into a pilsner glass filled with crushed ice. Serve with a straw. No garnish.

. . . .

CIRQUE SWIZZLE

JESSICA GONZALEZ, 2011

This drink's pretty pink color gives it a cotton candy–like appearance.—JG

1½ OUNCES ANCHOR JUNIPERO GIN

½ OUNCE YELLOW CHARTREUSE

1 TEASPOON CRÈME YVETTE, PLUS MORE FOR TOPPING THE DRINK

¾ OUNCE LEMON JUICE

½ OUNCE VANILLA SYRUP (PAGE 277)

¼ OUNCE SIMPLE SYRUP (PAGE 277)

Dry shake all the ingredients, then dump into a pilsner glass filled with crushed ice. Swizzle until cold, then top with a thin layer of Crème Yvette. Serve with a straw. No garnish.

COFFEY PARK SWIZZLE

ALEX DAY, 2008

This was the first of many sherry cocktails I've created. It's my tribute to the Queen's Park Swizzle (page 150), the most classic drink in the category.—AD

1 OUNCE BARBANCOURT 3-STAR RUM

1 OUNCE LUSTAU AMONTILLADO SHERRY

¼ OUNCE VELVET FALERNUM

¾ OUNCE LIME JUICE

¾ OUNCE GINGER SYRUP (PAGE 277)

3 DASHES ANGOSTURA BITTERS

GARNISH: 1 MINT SPRIG

Whip all the ingredients (except the bitters), shaking with a few pieces of crushed ice just until incorporated. Strain into a pilsner glass filled with crushed ice. Swizzle until cold. Add the bitters and swizzle them into the top of the drink. Garnish with the mint sprig and serve with a straw.

. . . .

DJ FLAMETHROWER

JOAQUÍN SIMÓ, 2012

Some of our favorite ingredient pairings are represented in this drink: grapefruit and cinnamon, tequila and chiles, and tequila and mezcal.—JS

1 OUNCE SIETE LEGUAS REPOSADO TEQUILA

½ OUNCE DEL MAGUEY VIDA MEZCAL

1 OUNCE ANCHO CHILE-INFUSED DOLIN ROUGE VERMOUTH (PAGE 279)

½ OUNCE GRAPEFRUIT JUICE

½ OUNCE LIME JUICE

¾ OUNCE CINNAMON BARK SYRUP (PAGE 276)

ANGOSTURA BITTERS

GARNISH: 1 CINNAMON STICK

Short shake all the ingredients (except the bitters) with 3 ice cubes, then strain into a pilsner glass filled with crushed ice. Add the bitters and swizzle them on top of the drink. Grate a bit of the cinnamon over the drink, then garnish with the cinnamon stick and serve with a straw.

. . . .

DOLLY DAGGER

ALEX DAY, 2009

When used judiciously, Vanilla Syrup can add a lot of elegance to a drink. Here it softens a big, funky rum, making it play nice with the sherry.—AD

1 OUNCE SMITH & CROSS RUM

1½ OUNCES WILLIAMS & HUMBERT DRY SACK MEDIUM SHERRY

¾ OUNCE LIME JUICE

½ OUNCE CANE SUGAR SYRUP (PAGE 276)

1 TEASPOON VANILLA SYRUP (PAGE 277)

GARNISH: 1 MINT SPRIG

Whip all the ingredients, shaking with a few pieces of crushed ice just until incorporated. Strain into a pilsner glass filled with crushed ice. Swizzle until cold. Garnish with the mint sprig and serve with a straw.

. . . .

DOLORES PARK SWIZZLE

THOMAS WAUGH, 2009

1 OUNCE EL TESORO AÑEJO TEQUILA

1 OUNCE LUSTAU AMONTILLADO SHERRY

¼ OUNCE VELVET FALERNUM

¾ OUNCE LIME JUICE

¾ OUNCE GINGER SYRUP (PAGE 277)

3 DASHES ANGOSTURA BITTERS

GARNISH: 1 MINT SPRIG

Dry shake all the ingredients (except the bitters), then dump into a pilsner glass filled with crushed ice. Add the bitters and swizzle them into the top of the drink. Garnish with the mint sprig and serve with a straw.

Robert Johnson Swizzle

HYDE PARK SWIZZLE

PHIL WARD, 2008

3 OR 4 MINT SPRIGS
2 OUNCES PLYMOUTH GIN
¾ OUNCE LIME JUICE
¾ OUNCE SIMPLE SYRUP (PAGE 277)
2 DASHES ANGOSTURA BITTERS
2 DASHES PEYCHAUD'S BITTERS
GARNISH: 1 MINT SPRIG

In a shaker, gently muddle the mint. Add the remaining ingredients (except the bitters) and dry shake, then dump into a pilsner glass. Fill the glass with crushed ice and swizzle until cold. Add the bitters and swizzle them into the top of the drink. Garnish with the mint sprig and serve with a straw.

....

JALISCO SWIZZLE

PHIL WARD, 2008

1½ OUNCES SIEMBRA AZUL BLANCO TEQUILA
½ OUNCE DEL MAGUEY VIDA MEZCAL
¾ OUNCE LIME JUICE
½ OUNCE CANE SUGAR SYRUP (PAGE 276)
2 DASHES ANGOSTURA BITTERS
GARNISH: 1 LIME WHEEL

Dry shake all the ingredients, then dump into a pilsner glass filled with crushed ice. Swizzle until cold. Garnish with the lime wheel and serve with a straw.

....

MYRA BRECKINRIDGE

PHIL WARD, 2008

Anthony Sarnicola, a regular at the bar, named this drink and described it as "a sex change for Laphroaig."—PW

2 OUNCES LAPHROAIG 10-YEAR SCOTCH
2 DASHES VIEUX PONTARLIER ABSINTHE

¾ OUNCE LIME JUICE

½ OUNCE CANE SUGAR SYRUP (PAGE 276)

GARNISH: 1 MINT SPRIG

Dry shake all the ingredients, then dump into a pilsner glass filled with crushed ice. Swizzle until cold. Garnish with the mint sprig and serve with a straw.

....

PARK LIFE SWIZZLE

THOMAS WAUGH, 2009

1 OUNCE RANSOM OLD TOM GIN

1 OUNCE LUSTAU AMONTILLADO SHERRY

½ OUNCE VELVET FALERNUM

¾ OUNCE LIME JUICE

½ OUNCE GINGER SYRUP (PAGE 277)

6 DASHES ANGOSTURA BITTERS

GARNISH: 1 MINT SPRIG

Dry shake all the ingredients (except the bitters), then dump into a pilsner glass filled with crushed ice. Top with the bitters. Garnish with the mint sprig, and serve with a straw.

....

ROBERT JOHNSON SWIZZLE

BRIAN MILLER, 2009

Swizzling the bitters on top of the swizzle, instead of with the other ingredients, gives you a blast of aromatics as you sip the drink.—BM

2 OUNCES EVAN WILLIAMS SINGLE-BARREL BOURBON

¾ OUNCE OTIMA 10-YEAR TAWNY PORT

½ OUNCE LEMON JUICE

¾ OUNCE VANILLA SYRUP (PAGE 277)

2 DASHES FEE BROTHERS WHISKEY BARREL-AGED BITTERS

3 DASHES HOUSE PEYCHAUD'S BITTERS (PAGE 284)

GARNISH: 1 MINT SPRIG

Dry shake all the ingredients (except the bitters), then dump into a pilsner glass filled with crushed ice. Swizzle until cold. Add the bitters and swizzle them into the top of the drink. Garnish with the mint sprig and serve with a straw.

....

SANGRIA SWIZZLE

THOMAS WAUGH, 2009

Build this swizzle slowly; the wine needs time to marry with the currant-infused rye.—TW

1½ OUNCES DRIED CURRANT–INFUSED WILD TURKEY RYE (PAGE 279)

1 OUNCE RED RIOJA WINE

¾ OUNCE COINTREAU

½ OUNCE LIME JUICE

1 TEASPOON SIMPLE SYRUP (PAGE 277)

1 DASH BITTERMENS XOCOLATL MOLE BITTERS

GARNISH: 1 ORANGE WHEEL

Combine all the ingredients in a pilsner glass and swizzle while adding crushed ice little by little. Garnish with the orange wheel and serve with a straw.

....

SNAKE HIPS SWIZZLE

JOAQUÍN SIMÓ, 2009

1½ OUNCES HINE H COGNAC

¼ OUNCE GRAND MARNIER

½ OUNCE MORENITA CREAM SHERRY

½ OUNCE LEMON JUICE

½ OUNCE MAPLE SYRUP

1 TEASPOON CINNAMON BARK SYRUP (PAGE 276)

2 DASHES ANGOSTURA BITTERS

Dry shake all the ingredients (except the bitters), then dump into a pilsner glass filled with crushed ice. Swizzle the drink until cold. Add the bitters and swizzle them into the top of the drink. Serve with a straw. No garnish.

MULTIPLE CHOICE

In 2008 we put the Mr. Potato Head method (see page 118) into practice on our cocktail menu by devoting a section to drinks that could be made by swapping a variety of base spirits. Inevitably we had a favorite spirit for each recipe, so we phased out the Multiple Choice section of our menu, but it did accurately demonstrate the Mr. Potato Head method in that the same formula works equally well (or nearly as well) if you just swap out one base spirit for another.

BLACK MARKET SLING

PHIL WARD, 2008

2 OUNCES PLYMOUTH GIN, SCARLET IBIS RUM, BERNHEIM WHEAT WHISKEY, RITTENHOUSE 100 RYE, LAIRD'S BONDED APPLE BRANDY, OR HINE H COGNAC

1 OUNCE CINNAMON ORANGE TEA–INFUSED SWEET VERMOUTH (PAGE 281)

½ OUNCE LEMON JUICE

¾ OUNCE SIMPLE SYRUP (PAGE 277)

1 DASH ANGOSTURA BITTERS

CLUB SODA

GARNISH: 3 BRANDIED CHERRIES ON A COCKTAIL PICK

Shake all the ingredients (except the club soda) with ice, then strain into a highball glass filled with ice cubes. Top with club soda. Garnish with the cherries and serve with a straw.

COIN TOSS

PHIL WARD, 2008

This was our original multiple-choice cocktail. It employs a template I've used to create a bunch of drinks: 2 ounces of booze, ¾ ounce of vermouth, and ½ ounce of something interesting—here split between Chartreuse and Bénédictine.—PW

2 OUNCES RITTENHOUSE 100 RYE, LAIRD'S BONDED APPLE BRANDY, SANTA TERESA 1796 RUM, HINE H COGNAC, OR FAMOUS GROUSE SCOTCH

¾ OUNCE CARPANO ANTICA FORMULA VERMOUTH

¼ OUNCE YELLOW CHARTREUSE

¼ OUNCE BÉNÉDICTINE

2 DASHES HOUSE PEYCHAUD'S BITTERS (PAGE 284)

Stir all the ingredients over ice, then strain into a coupe. No garnish.

....

ELECTRIC KOOL-AID ACID TEST

PHIL WARD, 2008

This is a classic Mr. Potato Head spec. With gin it becomes a Ramble (page 160); with rum it's a Seersucker (page 174); and with apple brandy it's a Sloe Scobeyville Sling (page 214).—PW

1 OUNCE PLYMOUTH GIN, SCARLET IBIS RUM, LAIRD'S BONDED APPLE BRANDY, OR SIEMBRA AZUL BLANCO TEQUILA

1 OUNCE SLOE GIN

1 OUNCE LEMON JUICE

¾ OUNCE SIMPLE SYRUP (PAGE 277)

3 BLACKBERRIES

½ OUNCE LUXARDO MARASCHINO LIQUEUR

Short shake all the ingredients (except the blackberries and maraschino liqueur) with 3 ice cubes, then strain into a pilsner glass filled with crushed ice. Empty the ice from the shaker and add the blackberries and the maraschino liqueur. Gently muddle the blackberries, then pour over the drink. Serve with a straw.

....

LITTLE KINGDOM

PHIL WARD, 2008

2 OUNCES EL TESORO REPOSADO TEQUILA, BEEFEATER LONDON DRY GIN, COMPASS BOX ASYLA SCOTCH, RITTENHOUSE 100 RYE, OR HINE H COGNAC

¾ OUNCE CARPANO ANTICA FORMULA VERMOUTH

½ OUNCE CYNAR

GARNISH: 1 BRANDIED CHERRY

Stir all the ingredients over ice, then strain into a coupe. Garnish with the cherry.

....

ST-GERMAIN REDUX

PHIL WARD, 2008

1 OUNCE BEEFEATER LONDON DRY GIN, APPLETON ESTATE V/X RUM, SIEMBRA AZUL BLANCO TEQUILA, COMPASS BOX ASYLA SCOTCH, CALVADOS, OR HINE H COGNAC

1 OUNCE DRY CHAMPAGNE

1 OUNCE ST-GERMAIN

1 OUNCE CLUB SODA

GARNISH: 1 LEMON TWIST

Combine all the ingredients in a wine glass filled with ice cubes and stir until cold. Garnish with the lemon twist.

AQUAVIT

Aquavit was never a key player in classic cocktails, so it's often overlooked as a base spirit. We've tried to remedy this by occasionally giving the ingredient its own section on our menus.

GREAT NORTHERN

JESSICA GONZALEZ, 2011

2 OUNCES LINIE AQUAVIT

¾ OUNCE LILLET BLANC

½ OUNCE COINTREAU

¾ OUNCE LEMON JUICE

½ OUNCE ACACIA HONEY SYRUP (PAGE 276)

GARNISH: 2 ORANGE CRESCENTS

Short shake all the ingredients with 3 ice cubes, then strain into a double rocks glass filled with crushed ice. Garnish with the orange crescents.

. . . .

ONE, ONE, ONE

THOMAS WAUGH, 2009

This is a play on the Fitty-Fitty, an equal-parts martini popularized by Audrey Saunders at the Pegu Club, with the addition of aquavit.—TW

1 OUNCE KROGSTAD AQUAVIT

1 OUNCE BEEFEATER LONDON DRY GIN

1 OUNCE DOLIN BLANC VERMOUTH

1 DASH REGANS' ORANGE BITTERS

Stir all the ingredients over ice, then strain into a coupe. No garnish.

OVER AND OUT

ERYN REECE, 2013

1 OUNCE KROGSTAD AQUAVIT

1 OUNCE OCHO 2012 PLATA TEQUILA

¾ OUNCE LIME JUICE

¾ OUNCE WATERMELON JUICE

½ OUNCE CANE SUGAR SYRUP (PAGE 276)

1 DASH BITTER TRUTH CELERY BITTERS

1 DASH HOUSE ORANGE BITTERS (PAGE 284)

Shake all the ingredients with ice, then strain into a large coupe. No garnish.

. . . .

SLAP 'N' PICKLE

BRIAN MILLER, 2009

3 CUCUMBER WHEELS

2 OUNCES KROGSTAD AQUAVIT

¾ OUNCE LIME JUICE

¾ OUNCE SIMPLE SYRUP (PAGE 277)

1 TEASPOON GRENADINE (PAGE 284)

2 DASHES BITTER TRUTH CELERY BITTERS

GARNISH: 1 CUCUMBER SPEAR

In a shaker, muddle the cucumber wheels. Add the remaining ingredients and shake with ice, then double strain into a double rocks glass over 1 large ice cube. Garnish with the cucumber spear.

SAZERAC VARIATIONS

The Sazerac, New Orleans's most famous contribution to the cocktail canon, is elegant in its simplicity. We, of course, have complicated and fussed with the original recipe to no end, resulting in many iterations that are true to the classic in only the loosest sense of the word. (For our classic version, see page 151.)

ALEMBIC

PHIL WARD, 2008

VIEUX PONTARLIER ABSINTHE
2 OUNCES ANCHOR GENEVIEVE GIN
¼ OUNCE DEMERARA SYRUP (PAGE 277)
3 DASHES HOUSE PEYCHAUD'S BITTERS (PAGE 284)
GARNISH: 1 LEMON TWIST

Rinse a rocks glass with absinthe and dump. Stir the remaining ingredients over ice, then strain into the glass over 1 large ice cube. Garnish with the lemon twist.

. . . .

BAY CITY ROLLER

BRIAN MILLER, 2008

2 OUNCES COMPASS BOX ASYLA SCOTCH
¼ OUNCE AMARO AVERNA
1 TEASPOON SIMPLE SYRUP (PAGE 277)
GARNISH: 1 ORANGE TWIST

Stir all the ingredients over ice, then strain into a double rocks glass. Garnish with the orange twist.

COOPER UNION

PHIL WARD, 2008

LAPHROAIG 10-YEAR SCOTCH
2 OUNCES REDBREAST 12-YEAR IRISH WHISKEY
½ OUNCE ST-GERMAIN
1 DASH HOUSE ORANGE BITTERS (PAGE 284)
1 LEMON TWIST

Rinse a double rocks glass with Laphroaig and dump. Stir the remaining ingredients (except the lemon twist) over ice, then strain into the glass. Squeeze the lemon twist over the drink and discard. No garnish.

. . . .

CREOLE SAZ

JOAQUÍN SIMÓ, 2011

This drink contains all things French: French absinthe, French cognac, French-colony rum, and bitters that originated in Haiti, a former French colony.—JS

VIEUX PONTARLIER ABSINTHE
1½ OUNCES BARBANCOURT 3-STAR RUM
½ OUNCE PIERRE FERRAND 1840 COGNAC
1 TEASPOON CANE SUGAR SYRUP (PAGE 276)
3 DASHES HOUSE PEYCHAUD'S BITTERS (PAGE 284)
1 LEMON TWIST

Rinse a rocks glass with absinthe and dump. Stir the remaining ingredients (except the lemon twist) over ice, then strain into the glass. Squeeze the lemon twist over the drink and discard. No garnish.

DEVIL INSIDE

THOMAS WAUGH, 2011

LAPHROAIG 10-YEAR SCOTCH

1½ OUNCES RITTENHOUSE 100 RYE

½ OUNCE BRUICHLADDICH PORT CHARLOTTE 7-YEAR SCOTCH

2 DASHES VIEUX PONTARLIER ABSINTHE

1 TEASPOON DEMERARA SYRUP (PAGE 277)

2 DASHES HOUSE PEYCHAUD'S BITTERS (PAGE 284)

1 LEMON TWIST

Rinse a rocks glass with Laphroaig and dump. Stir the remaining ingredients (except the lemon twist) with ice, then strain into a rocks glass. Squeeze the lemon twist over the drink and discard. No garnish.

....

ENEMY LINES

JILLIAN VOSE, 2011

Splitting aquavit and tequila is weird, but it works. You end up with a rich drink without using a lot of sugar.—JV

1½ OUNCES LINIE AQUAVIT

¾ OUNCE EL TESORO REPOSADO TEQUILA

1 TEASPOON CANE SUGAR SYRUP (PAGE 276)

4 DASHES HOUSE PEYCHAUD'S BITTERS (PAGE 284)

1 DASH BITTER TRUTH AROMATIC BITTERS

1 LEMON TWIST

Stir all the ingredients (except the lemon twist) over ice, then strain into a rocks glass. Squeeze the lemon twist over the drink and discard. No garnish.

GUNS AND ROSÉ

SCOTT TEAGUE, 2013

I like combining a high-proof spirit with something soft and delicate. Here it's a fiery overproof whiskey and an aperitif made with rosé.—ST

1½ OUNCES OLD GRAND-DAD 114 BOURBON

1 OUNCE LILLET ROSÉ

1 TEASPOON CANE SUGAR SYRUP (PAGE 276)

2 DASHES HOUSE PEYCHAUD'S BITTERS (PAGE 284)

1 GRAPEFRUIT TWIST

Stir all the ingredients (except the grapefruit twist) over ice, then strain into a rocks glass. Squeeze the grapefruit twist over the drink and discard. No garnish.

....

HALLYDAY

THOMAS WAUGH, 2011

Named after Johnny Hallyday, the French pop singer, this Sazerac variation uses a quartet of French ingredients.—TW

VIEUX PONTARLIER ABSINTHE

1½ OUNCES HINE H COGNAC

½ OUNCE DOLIN DRY VERMOUTH

½ OUNCE ROYAL COMBIER LIQUEUR

1 TEASPOON CLEAR CREEK PEAR BRANDY

1 DASH ANGOSTURA BITTERS

GARNISH: 1 LEMON TWIST

Rinse a rocks glass with absinthe and dump. Stir the remaining ingredients over ice, then strain into the glass. Garnish with the lemon twist.

LATIN QUARTER

JOAQUÍN SIMÓ, 2008

It's hard to predict which D&C drinks will be replicated elsewhere. This Sazerac variation has ended up on the menus of cocktail bars all over world.—JS

VIEUX PONTARLIER ABSINTHE

2 OUNCES ZACAPA 23-YEAR RUM

1 TEASPOON CANE SUGAR SYRUP (PAGE 276)

3 DASHES HOUSE PEYCHAUD'S BITTERS (PAGE 284)

1 DASH ANGOSTURA BITTERS

1 DASH BITTERMENS XOCOLATL MOLE BITTERS

1 LEMON TWIST

Rinse a double rocks glass with absinthe and dump. Stir the remaining ingredients (except the lemon twist) over ice, then strain into the glass. Squeeze the lemon twist over the drink and discard. No garnish.

SAZ WHO?

BRIAN MILLER, 2009

1½ OUNCES CRUZAN SINGLE-BARREL RUM

½ OUNCE CLEAR CREEK PEAR BRANDY

2 DASHES VIEUX PONTARLIER ABSINTHE

1 TEASPOON DEMERARA SYRUP (PAGE 277)

4 DASHES HOUSE PEYCHAUD'S BITTERS (PAGE 284)

1 DASH ANGOSTURA BITTERS

1 LEMON TWIST

Stir all the ingredients (except the lemon twist) over ice, then strain into a double rocks glass. Squeeze the lemon twist over the drink and discard. No garnish.

Latin Quarter

Negroni VARIATIONS

Our favorite cocktail writer, Kingsley Amis, said of the Negroni, "This is a really fine invention. It has the power, rare with drinks and indeed with anything else, of cheering you up." We couldn't agree more. Plus, the simple recipe of equal parts gin, sweet vermouth, and Campari is a great launchpad for endless modification. (For our classic version, see page 147.)

BALTASAR AND BLIMUNDA

PHIL WARD, 2008

2 OUNCES BEEFEATER LONDON DRY GIN
½ OUNCE PUNT E MES
½ OUNCE CAMPARI
½ OUNCE OTIMA 10-YEAR TAWNY PORT
GARNISH: 1 ORANGE COIN

Stir all the ingredients over ice, then strain into a coupe. To garnish, flame the orange coin over the drink, then drop it in.

. . . .

FAIL-SAFE

SCOTT TEAGUE, 2013

Some drinks are just happy accidents. One night I saw several bottles sitting next to each other behind the bar, and I thought, Why not? I started playing around with them in Negroni proportions, and it worked.—ST

¾ OUNCE PERRY'S TOT NAVY-STRENGTH GIN
¾ OUNCE PLYMOUTH SLOE GIN
½ OUNCE APEROL

½ OUNCE PIERRE FERRAND DRY CURAÇAO
2 DASHES ANGOSTURA BITTERS

Stir all the ingredients over ice, then strain into a double rocks glass over 1 large ice cube. No garnish.

. . . .

HOUSE OF PAYNE

PHIL WARD, 2012

Raspberries and Campari have a great affinity for each other, so I combined them, along with sloe gin, in this Negroni variation.—PW

3 RASPBERRIES
1½ OUNCES BEEFEATER LONDON DRY GIN
1 OUNCE PLYMOUTH SLOE GIN
1 OUNCE CAMPARI
GARNISH: 1 RASPBERRY

In a mixing glass, gently muddle the raspberries. Add the remaining ingredients and stir over ice. Double strain into a double rocks glass over 1 large ice cube. Garnish with the raspberry.

KINGSTON NEGRONI

JOAQUÍN SIMÓ, 2009

I created this Negroni variation immediately after I first tasted Smith & Cross rum. Only Carpano Antica has the balls to stand up to its intensity.—JS

1 OUNCE SMITH & CROSS RUM

1 OUNCE CARPANO ANTICA FORMULA VERMOUTH

1 OUNCE CAMPARI

GARNISH: 1 ORANGE TWIST

Stir all the ingredients over ice, then strain into a double rocks glass. Garnish with the orange twist.

. . . .

MAÑANITA

JOAQUÍN SIMÓ, 2011

In Oaxaca, it's customary to drink a small copita *of* mezcal, *called a* mañanita, *before your morning coffee. This is probably the spiciest drink we've ever served.—JS*

1 OUNCE SOMBRA MEZCAL

1 OUNCE COFFEE- AND CHILE-INFUSED CAMPARI (PAGE 279)

1 OUNCE HOUSE SWEET VERMOUTH (PAGE 284)

GARNISH: 1 ORANGE TWIST

Stir all the ingredients over ice, then strain into a double rocks glass over 1 large ice cube. Garnish with the orange twist.

. . . .

RANGE LIFE

PHIL WARD, 2008

2 OUNCES EL TESORO REPOSADO TEQUILA

½ OUNCE CAMPARI

½ OUNCE GRAND MARNIER

½ OUNCE PUNT E MES

Stir all the ingredients over ice, then strain into a coupe. No garnish.

UNO, DOS, TRES

JOAQUÍN SIMÓ, 2009

1½ OUNCES SIEMBRA AZUL REPOSADO TEQUILA

¾ OUNCE GRAPEFRUIT-INFUSED PUNT E MES (PAGE 281)

½ OUNCE CAMPARI

¼ OUNCE CYNAR

1 DASH BITTERMENS XOCOLATL MOLE BITTERS

GARNISH: 1 ORANGE TWIST

Stir all the ingredients over ice, then strain into a coupe. To garnish, flame the orange twist over the drink, then drop it in.

. . . .

THE VANDERBILT

SCOTT TEAGUE, 2013

1½ OUNCES LAIRD'S BONDED APPLE BRANDY

1 OUNCE GRAN CLASSICO BITTER

¾ OUNCE MATHILDE POIRE PEAR LIQUEUR

Stir all the ingredients over ice, then strain into a double rocks glass over 1 large ice cube. No garnish.

. . . .

WHITE NEGRONI

ALEX DAY, 2009

1½ OUNCES FORD'S GIN

¾ OUNCE DOLIN BLANC VERMOUTH

¾ OUNCE SUZE SAVEUR D'AUTREFOIS LIQUEUR

GARNISH: 1 LEMON TWIST

Stir all the ingredients over ice, then strain into a double rocks glass over 1 large ice cube. Garnish with the lemon twist.

DAIQUIRI VARIATIONS

If there is a secret handshake at Death & Co, it's the daiquiri. Just as you can learn everything about a cook's kitchen skills by watching him or her make an omelet, you can see into the soul of a bartender by ordering a daiquiri. If bartenders can execute it properly, achieving a harmonious balance of sweet, sour, and boozy—and a drink that's cold as hell but not overly diluted—they can make anything.

The daiquiri is also our preshift drink of choice, so much so that if you stop by Death & Co at the very beginning of a shift, you might be witness to GDT, or Gangster Daiquiri Time. What started as a grudge match between Thomas and Brad to shake the best daiquiri turned into a nightly ritual in which a designated bartender creates a round of daiquiris (or variations thereof) for the staff. Many of the following specs were born out of this sacred custom. (For our classic version, see page 141.)

ANGUS STORY DAIQUIRI

PHIL WARD, 2012

The venerable British bartender Angus Winchester came in one night and asked me to make him a three-rum daiquiri. This is the result.—PW

¾ OUNCE APPLETON ESTATE V/X RUM

¾ OUNCE RON DEL BARRILITO 3-STAR RUM

½ OUNCE LA FAVORITE RHUM AGRICOLE BLANC

¾ OUNCE LIME JUICE

½ OUNCE CANE SUGAR SYRUP (PAGE 276)

GARNISH: 1 LIME WEDGE

Shake all the ingredients with ice, then strain into a coupe. Garnish with the lime wedge.

ARRACKUIRI

PHIL WARD, 2008

When we first got Batavia arrack, nobody wanted to mess with it. I was determined to use it as a base spirit, though, so I mixed it with a spoonful of pomegranate molasses, which works micacles.—PW

2 OUNCES VAN OOSTEN BATAVIA ARRACK

¾ OUNCE LIME JUICE

¾ OUNCE SIMPLE SYRUP (PAGE 277)

1 TEASPOON POMEGRANATE MOLASSES

6 TO 8 MINT LEAVES

GARNISH: 1 MINT LEAF

Short shake all the ingredients, then double strain into a coupe. Garnish with the mint leaf.

....

AUTUMN DAIQUIRI

JOAQUÍN SIMÓ, 2008

I wanted to make a daiquiri with fall flavors and tried rum after rum until I landed on Mount Gay, which adds a crazy apple flavor to the drink.—JS

2 OUNCES MOUNT GAY ECLIPSE RUM

½ OUNCE LIME JUICE

½ OUNCE PINEAPPLE JUICE

¼ OUNCE DEMERARA SYRUP (PAGE 277)

¼ OUNCE CINNAMON BARK SYRUP (PAGE 276)

1 DASH ANGOSTURA BITTERS

Shake all the ingredients with ice, then strain into a coupe. No garnish.

BENJAMIN BARKER DAIQUIRI

BRIAN MILLER, 2008

The addition of Campari and absinthe makes this a real bartender's daiquiri. The drink takes on a reddish hue, which inspired me to name it after one of Sweeney Todd's aliases.—BM

2 OUNCES GOSLING'S BLACK SEAL RUM

½ OUNCE CAMPARI

2 DASHES VIEUX PONTARLIER ABSINTHE

¾ OUNCE LIME JUICE

½ OUNCE DEMERARA SYRUP (PAGE 277)

GARNISH: 1 LIME WEDGE

Shake all the ingredients with ice, then strain into a coupe. Garnish with the lime wedge.

. . . .

BOUKMAN DAIQUIRI

ALEX DAY, 2008

Boukman Dutty was a slave who helped launch the Haitian Revolution. Using rum over cognac is my nod to the French getting out of the colony.—AD

1½ OUNCES BARBANCOURT WHITE RUM

½ OUNCE HINE H COGNAC

¾ OUNCE LIME JUICE

½ OUNCE CINNAMON BARK SYRUP (PAGE 276)

Shake all the ingredients with ice, then strain into a coupe. No garnish.

. . . .

DAI, DAI MY DARLING

JILLIAN VOSE, 2012

I challenged myself to make a stirred Hemingway daiquiri. Acid phosphate, which gives acidity without adding any citrus flavor, did the trick. Instead, the citrus flavors come from the grapefruit-flavored liqueur.—JV

¾ OUNCE FLOR DE CAÑA EXTRA-DRY WHITE RUM

¾ OUNCE EL DORADO 3-YEAR RUM

½ OUNCE BANKS 5-ISLAND WHITE RUM

½ OUNCE DOLIN BLANC VERMOUTH

½ OUNCE COMBIER PAMPLEMOUSSE ROSE LIQUEUR

½ TEASPOON KIRSCH

½ TEASPOON LUXARDO MARASCHINO LIQUEUR

½ TEASPOON ACID PHOSPHATE

GARNISH: 1 LIME WEDGE

Stir all the ingredients over ice, then strain into a coupe. Garnish with the lime wedge.

. . . .

D.W.B.

PHIL WARD, 2008

This cocktail's name is short for "Daiquiri With Benefits." La Favorite makes one hell of a daiquiri, and it gets even better with the funk of Batavia arrack.—PW

2 OUNCES LA FAVORITE RHUM AGRICOLE BLANC

½ OUNCE VAN OOSTEN BATAVIA ARRACK

¾ OUNCE LIME JUICE

½ OUNCE CANE SUGAR SYRUP (PAGE 276)

GARNISH: 1 LIME WEDGE

Shake all the ingredients with ice, then strain into a coupe. Garnish with the lime wedge.

. . . .

GRANNY'S DAIQUIRI

PHIL WARD, 2008

2 OUNCES GRANNY SMITH APPLE–INFUSED RHUM BARBANCOURT (PAGE 279)

¾ OUNCE LIME JUICE

¾ OUNCE SIMPLE SYRUP (PAGE 277)

GARNISH: 1 LIME WEDGE

Shake all the ingredients with ice, then strain into a coupe. Garnish with the lime wedge.

JAVANESE DAIQUIRI

TYSON BUHLER, 2013

This started as a spin on our house gimlet, but then it took a sharp left turn. It's a confusing drink. Arrack is a funky, weird ingredient that a lot of people don't like. And when you see "curry" listed in the ingredients, you think it's going to taste like Indian food. Despite having so many weird ingredients, this ended up being a surprisingly approachable cocktail.—TB

1 OUNCE VAN OOSTEN BATAVIA ARRACK

1 OUNCE SCARLET IBIS RUM

1 OUNCE TOBY'S LIME CORDIAL (PAGE 285)

3 FRESH CURRY LEAVES

GARNISH: 1 LIME WEDGE

Shake all the ingredients with ice, then strain into a double rocks glass over cracked ice. Garnish with the lime wedge.

JOVENCOURT DAIQUIRI

PHIL WARD, 2007

This cocktail was my first epiphany about using mezcal in a mixed drink. Doing so is common now, but nobody was mixing with it back then.—PW

2 OUNCES BARBANCOURT WHITE RUM

¼ OUNCE DEL MAGUEY VIDA MEZCAL

¾ OUNCE LIME JUICE

¾ OUNCE SIMPLE SYRUP (PAGE 277)

Shake all the ingredients with ice, then strain into a coupe. No garnish.

....

LA BOMBA DAIQUIRI

JOAQUÍN SIMÓ, 2008

Here's a great example of a fruity drink that's not at all sweet. Its name is a play on the French word for pomegranate: grenade.—JS

5 RASPBERRIES

2 OUNCES BARBANCOURT WHITE RUM

¾ OUNCE LIME JUICE

½ OUNCE SIMPLE SYRUP (PAGE 277)

1 TEASPOON POMEGRANATE MOLASSES

GARNISH: 1 LIME WHEEL AND RASPBERRY FLAG

In a shaker, gently muddle the raspberries. Add the remaining ingredients and shake with ice. Double strain into a coupe. Garnish with the lime wheel and raspberry flag.

....

LINBABA DAIQUIRI

JOAQUÍN SIMÓ, 2011

The Indian subcontinent has inspired many of my drinks, including this Indian-spiced daiquiri variation named after the lead character in one of my favorite books.—JS

1½ OUNCES SCARLET IBIS RUM

½ OUNCE APPLETON ESTATE V/X RUM

¾ OUNCE LIME JUICE

¼ OUNCE CINNAMON BARK SYRUP (PAGE 276)

¼ OUNCE ORGEAT (PAGE 278)

¼ OUNCE GINGER SYRUP (PAGE 277)

2 FRESH CURRY LEAVES

1 DASH ANGOSTURA BITTERS

Shake all the ingredients with ice, then strain into a coupe. No garnish.

. . . .

MERIDIAN DAIQUIRI

JOAQUÍN SIMÓ, 2011

5 CARDAMOM PODS

1½ OUNCES LINIE AQUAVIT

½ OUNCE SCARLET IBIS RUM

¾ OUNCE PINEAPPLE JUICE

½ OUNCE LIME JUICE

½ OUNCE GINGER SYRUP (PAGE 277)

GARNISH: 1 LIME WHEEL

In a shaker, gently muddle the cardamom pods. Add the remaining ingredients and shake with ice. Strain into a double rocks glass over 1 large ice cube. Garnish with the lime wheel.

. . . .

MOSQUITO COAST

PHIL WARD, 2008

2 OUNCES SCARLET IBIS RUM

¼ OUNCE ST. ELIZABETH ALLSPICE DRAM

¾ OUNCE LIME JUICE

¾ OUNCE SIMPLE SYRUP (PAGE 277)

GARNISH: 1 LIME WEDGE

Shake all the ingredients with ice, then strain into a coupe. Garnish with the lime wedge.

SUNSET AT GOWANUS

ALEX DAY, 2008

In this decadent daiquiri variation, the bright fruity character of Santa Teresa rum becomes even more pronounced thanks to the apple brandy and maple syrup.—AD

2 OUNCES SANTA TERESA 1796 RUM

¼ OUNCE LAIRD'S BONDED APPLE BRANDY

¼ OUNCE YELLOW CHARTREUSE

¾ OUNCE LIME JUICE

½ OUNCE GRADE B MAPLE SYRUP

Shake all the ingredients with ice, then strain into a coupe. No garnish.

. . . .

TAKE TWO

TYSON BUHLER, 2013

Dark, full-bodied wine is the base of our Bergerac Mix, which Brad created for his Cynaro de Bergerac cocktail (page 229)—and which I wanted to use again in a daiquiri-style drink (hence the name). Red wine is so complex to begin with that it's fun to use in cocktails; the trick is to complement its flavor profile with other ingredients.—TB

1 OUNCE RON DEL BARRILITO 3-STAR RUM

1 OUNCE BERGERAC MIX (PAGE 284)

1 DASH VIEUX PONTARLIER ABSINTHE

¾ OUNCE LIME JUICE

½ OUNCE CANE SUGAR SYRUP (PAGE 276)

GARNISH: 1 LIME WEDGE

Shake all the ingredients with ice, then strain into a coupe. Garnish with the lime wedge.

DEATH & CO FAMILY DAIQUIRI ALBUM

The simpler the drink, the more it's open to interpretation. To illustrate this point, we asked Death & Co alums for their favorite specs for the classic daiquiri. When creating your own personal daiquiri, choose your rum first, then adjust the amount of lime and sweetener to balance it to your liking. Denser sweeteners like cane syrup will give you more of a buffer against overdilution than simple syrup. Also, use a cobbler shaker: it allows for quick chilling of the drink and lets just the right amount of tiny ice chips fall into the drink as you pour it into the glass.

JILLIAN'S DAIQUIRI

JILLIAN VOSE

¾ OUNCE FLOR DE CAÑA EXTRA-DRY WHITE RUM

¾ OUNCE EL DORADO 3-YEAR RUM

½ OUNCE BANKS 5-ISLAND WHITE RUM

1 OUNCE LIME JUICE

½ OUNCE CANE SUGAR SYRUP (PAGE 276)

GARNISH: 1 LIME WEDGE

Shake all the ingredients with ice, then strain into a coupe. Garnish with the lime wedge.

ERYN'S DAIQUIRI

ERYN REECE

1½ OUNCES FLOR DE CAÑA EXTRA-DRY WHITE RUM

½ OUNCE LA FAVORITE RHUM AGRICOLE BLANC

1 OUNCE LIME JUICE

½ OUNCE CANE SUGAR SYRUP (PAGE 276)

GARNISH: 1 LIME WEDGE

Shake all ingredients with ice, then strain into a coupe. Garnish with the lime wedge.

RAVI'S DAIQUIRI

RAVI DEROSSI

2 OUNCES FLOR DE CAÑA EXTRA-DRY WHITE RUM

¾ OUNCE LIME JUICE

½ OUNCE RICH SIMPLE SYRUP (2 PARTS SUGAR TO 1 PART WATER)

GARNISH: 1 LIME WEDGE

Shake all ingredients with ice, then double strain into a coupe. Garnish with the lime wedge.

DAVE'S DAIQUIRI

DAVE KAPLAN

2 OUNCES MATUSALEM GRAN
   RESERVA 15-YEAR RUM

1 OUNCE LIME JUICE

¾ OUNCE SIMPLE SYRUP (PAGE 277)

GARNISH: 1 LIME WEDGE

Shake all the ingredients with ice,
then strain into a coupe. Garnish
with the lime wedge.

ALEX'S DAIQUIRI

ALEX DAY

2 OUNCES FLOR DE CAÑA EXTRA-DRY
   WHITE RUM

1 OUNCE LIME JUICE

¾ OUNCE SIMPLE SYRUP (PAGE 277)

GARNISH: 1 LIME WEDGE

Shake all the ingredients with ice,
then strain into a coupe. Garnish
with the lime wedge.

THOMAS'S DAIQUIRI

THOMAS WAUGH

2 OUNCES CAÑA BRAVA RUM

1 OUNCE LIME JUICE

½ OUNCE CANE SUGAR SYRUP
   (PAGE 276)

GARNISH: 1 LIME WEDGE

Shake all the ingredients with ice,
then strain into a coupe. Garnish
with the lime wedge.

BRIAN'S DAIQUIRI

BRIAN MILLER

2 OUNCES FLOR DE CAÑA EXTRA-DRY
   WHITE RUM

¾ OUNCE LIME JUICE

½ OUNCE SIMPLE SYRUP (PAGE 277)

GARNISH: 1 LIME WEDGE

Shake all the ingredients with ice,
then strain into a coupe. Garnish
with the lime wedge.

PHIL'S DAIQUIRI

PHIL WARD

2 OUNCES BARBANCOURT WHITE RUM

¾ OUNCE LIME JUICE

½ OUNCE CANE SUGAR SYRUP
   (PAGE 276)

GARNISH: 1 LIME WEDGE

Shake all the ingredients with ice,
then strain into a coupe. Garnish
with the lime wedge.

JOAQUÍN'S DAIQUIRI

JOAQUÍN SIMÓ

1 OUNCE APPLETON ESTATE V/X RUM

1 OUNCE SCARLET IBIS RUM

1 OUNCE LIME JUICE

½ OUNCE DEMERARA SYRUP
   (PAGE 277)

Shake all the ingredients with
ice, then strain into a coupe.
No garnish.

Classic Manhattan, page 145

Manhattan
VARIATIONS

"I'll have a Manhattan" falls upon our ears more than any other off-the-menu drink order. Whiskey tempered and sweetened by vermouth and reinforced with bitters is one of the most riff-friendly cocktail templates. Long before modern bartenders began splicing and dicing classic recipes, the Manhattan was father to many spin-offs. Some of them, like the Rob Roy (page 150), are classics in their own right. (For our classic version, see page 145.)

THE BLACK PRINCE
PHIL WARD, 2008

2 OUNCES ZACAPA 23-YEAR RUM

¾ OUNCE PUNT E MES

½ OUNCE AMARO AVERNA

1 DASH HOUSE ORANGE BITTERS (PAGE 284)

Stir all the ingredients over ice, then strain into a coupe. No garnish.

. . . .

DAISY BUCHANAN
JOAQUÍN SIMÓ, 2009

This is my summertime Manhattan, a floral, herbaceous drink that's complex but not overbearing.—JS

2 OUNCES CHAMOMILE-INFUSED OLD OVERHOLT RYE (PAGE 281)

¾ OUNCE DOLIN DRY VERMOUTH

½ OUNCE APEROL

¼ OUNCE YELLOW CHARTREUSE

Stir all the ingredients over ice, then strain into a coupe. No garnish.

DRUNKEN DODO
BRIAN MILLER, 2008

2 OUNCES SCARLET IBIS RUM

¾ OUNCE CARPANO ANTICA FORMULA VERMOUTH

¼ OUNCE ST. ELIZABETH ALLSPICE DRAM

2 DASHES ANGOSTURA BITTERS

GARNISH: 1 ORANGE TWIST

Stir all the ingredients over ice, then strain into a coupe. Garnish with the orange twist.

. . . .

INGÉNUE
BRIAN MILLER, 2009

The name came to me first, then the drink followed: a cognac-based Manhattan variation with a nod to tiki.—BM

2 OUNCES PIERRE FERRAND AMBRE COGNAC

1 OUNCE DOLIN ROUGE VERMOUTH

1 TEASPOON CINNAMON BARK SYRUP (PAGE 276)

Stir all the ingredients over ice, then strain into a coupe. No garnish.

JIVE TURKEY

JESSICA GONZALEZ, 2009

1 OUNCE WILD TURKEY RYE 101

¾ OUNCE BUFFALO TRACE BOURBON

¾ OUNCE AMARO CIOCIARO

¾ OUNCE DOLIN DRY VERMOUTH

¼ OUNCE ST-GERMAIN

1 DASH ANGOSTURA BITTERS

Stir all the ingredients over ice, then strain into a coupe. No garnish.

. . . .

MI AMARO

JOAQUÍN SIMÓ, 2009

This is probably the best stirred tequila drink I've come up with, and it's quite simple: just a Manhattan variation made with some incredible ingredients.—JS

2 OUNCES EL TESORO REPOSADO TEQUILA

½ OUNCE AMARO CIOCIARO

½ OUNCE CARPANO ANTICA FORMULA VERMOUTH

¼ OUNCE ST-GERMAIN

GARNISH: 1 GRAPEFRUIT TWIST

Stir all the ingredients over ice, then strain into a coupe. Garnish with the grapefruit twist.

. . . .

NAVIGATOR

TYSON BUHLER, 2013

Once I figured out that dried apricots, rather than fresh, made the best infusion, I built the drink around that, using madeira for most of the richness and sweetness, augmented by a bit of syrup.—TB

1½ OUNCES APRICOT-INFUSED FAMOUS GROUSE SCOTCH (PAGE 279)

¾ OUNCE BLANDY'S 5-YEAR MALMSEY MADEIRA

½ TEASPOON DEMERARA SYRUP (PAGE 277)

½ TEASPOON VANILLA SYRUP (PAGE 277)

1 DASH HOUSE PEYCHAUD'S BITTERS (PAGE 284)

Stir all the ingredients over ice, then strain into a coupe. No garnish.

. . . .

ORKNEY CHAPEL

JASON LITTRELL, 2009

Just a little bit of sherry can completely transform a drink. Here it hides in the background but makes all the difference.—JL

2 OUNCES HIGHLAND PARK 12-YEAR SCOTCH

½ OUNCE DOLIN DRY VERMOUTH

¼ OUNCE LUSTAU AMONTILLADO SHERRY

¼ OUNCE GRAND MARNIER

¼ OUNCE CANE SUGAR SYRUP (PAGE 276)

GARNISH: 1 ORANGE TWIST

Stir all the ingredients over ice, then strain into a martini glass. Garnish with the orange twist.

PISCO INFERNO

BRAD FARRAN, 2012

2 OUNCES CAMPO DE ENCANTO ACHOLADO PISCO

½ OUNCE ANCHO CHILE–INFUSED DOLIN ROUGE
 VERMOUTH (PAGE 279)

2¼ TEASPOONS CHERRY HEERING

2¼ TEASPOONS MASSENEZ KIRSCH VIEUX CHERRY
 BRANDY

2 DASHES FEE BROTHERS WHISKEY BARREL-AGED
 BITTERS

1 DASH HOUSE ORANGE BITTERS (PAGE 284)

GARNISH: 1 ORANGE TWIST

Stir all the ingredients over ice, then strain into a martini
glass. Garnish with the orange twist.

. . . .

RED ANT

THOMAS WAUGH, 2011

1½ OUNCES RITTENHOUSE 100 RYE

1 TEASPOON DEL MAGUEY CHICHICAPA MEZCAL

½ OUNCE MASSENEZ KIRSCH VIEUX CHERRY
 BRANDY

½ OUNCE CHERRY HEERING

½ TEASPOON CINNAMON BARK SYRUP (PAGE 276)

2 DASHES BITTERMENS XOCOLATL MOLE BITTERS

GARNISH: 3 BRANDIED CHERRIES ON A COCKTAIL
 PICK

Stir all the ingredients over ice, then strain into a martini
glass. Garnish with the cherries.

. . . .

SFORZANDO

ERYN REECE, 2012

1 OUNCE RITTENHOUSE 100 RYE

¾ OUNCE DEL MAGUEY CHICHICAPA MEZCAL

½ OUNCE BÉNÉDICTINE

½ OUNCE DOLIN DRY VERMOUTH

2 DASHES BITTERMENS XOCOLATL MOLE BITTERS

GARNISH: 1 ORANGE TWIST

Stir all the ingredients over ice, then strain into a coupe.
Garnish with the orange twist.

. . . .

ST. JAMES INFIRMARY

JOAQUÍN SIMÓ, 2011

1½ OUNCES PLANTATION BARBADOS 5-YEAR RUM

½ OUNCE ST. JAMES ROYAL AMBRE RHUM AGRICOLE

½ OUNCE COCCHI VERMOUTH DI TORINO

½ OUNCE MORENITA CREAM SHERRY

1 TEASPOON SIMPLE SYRUP (PAGE 277)

2 DASHES BITTERMENS 'ELEMAKULE TIKI BITTERS

1 DASH BITTER TRUTH JERRY THOMAS' BITTERS

GARNISH: 1 ORANGE TWIST

Stir all the ingredients over ice, then strain into a coupe.
Garnish with the orange twist.

. . . .

STOLEN HUFFY

JILLIAN VOSE, 2013

*About a quarter of our guests ask us to make them
something spicy. Our first reaction is always to reach
for a bottle of jalapeño-infused tequila, but I wanted to
try something else to expand our spicy offerings. As it
turns out, red Thai chiles work quite nicely with a boldly
flavored rye.—JV*

1½ OUNCES RED THAI CHILE–INFUSED
 RITTENHOUSE RYE (PAGE 279)

1 TEASPOON DEL MAGUEY CHICHICAPA MEZCAL

¾ OUNCE HOUSE SWEET VERMOUTH (PAGE 284)

½ OUNCE PIERRE FERRAND DRY CURAÇAO

1 TEASPOON CANE SUGAR SYRUP (PAGE 276)

1 DASH ANGOSTURA BITTERS

Stir all the ingredients over ice, then strain into a Nick &
Nora glass. No garnish.

Old-Fashioned
Variations

 Spirit, sugar, water, bitters: the old-fashioned is the protococktail, with a charmingly vague recipe that has inspired some of our favorite and most-popular drinks. (For our classic version, see page 147.)

CONFERENCE

BRIAN MILLER, 2008

One of our servers asked me to make her something stirred and boozy. So I threw four of my favorite spirits into an old-fashioned template, splitting the base four ways. All these brown spirits needed something to tie them together. Avery Glasser (of the bitters company Bittermens) happened to be sitting at the bar, and he suggested trying his mole bitters. It was like lacing up a shoe.—BM

½ OUNCE RITTENHOUSE 100 RYE

½ OUNCE BUFFALO TRACE BOURBON

½ OUNCE CALVADOS

½ OUNCE HINE H COGNAC

1 TEASPOON DEMERARA SYRUP (PAGE 277)

2 DASHES ANGOSTURA BITTERS

1 DASH BITTERMENS XOCOLATL MOLE BITTERS

GARNISH: 1 LEMON TWIST AND 1 ORANGE TWIST

Stir all the ingredients over ice, then strain into a double rocks glass over 1 large ice cube. Garnish with the lemon and orange twists.

DEATH FROM ABOVE

THOMAS WAUGH, 2011

1 OUNCE LEMON HART 151 RUM

¾ OUNCE SCARLET IBIS RUM

¼ OUNCE CRUZAN BLACK STRAP RUM

1 TEASPOON LUSTAU EAST INDIA SOLERA SHERRY

1 TEASPOON CANE SUGAR SYRUP (PAGE 276)

1 DASH ANGOSTURA BITTERS

2 DASHES HOUSE ORANGE BITTERS (PAGE 284)

GARNISH: 1 LEMON TWIST AND 1 ORANGE TWIST

Stir all the ingredients over ice, then strain into a double rocks glass over 1 large ice cube. Garnish with the lemon and orange twists.

....

ELDER FASHION

PHIL WARD, 2007

2 OUNCES PLYMOUTH GIN

½ OUNCE ST-GERMAIN

2 DASHES HOUSE ORANGE BITTERS (PAGE 284)

GARNISH: 1 GRAPEFRUIT TWIST

Stir all the ingredients over ice, then strain into a double rocks glass over 1 large ice cube. Garnish with the grapefruit twist.

Elder Fashion

HEADSTONE

JILLIAN VOSE, 2013

I wanted to make the most expensive old-fashioned variation possible, so I started with an elegant and floral Japanese whiskey and added two orange liqueurs.—JV

2 OUNCES SUNTORY HAKUSHU 12-YEAR WHISKEY
½ OUNCE MANDARINE NAPOLÉON LIQUEUR
¼ OUNCE RHUM CLÉMENT CRÉOLE SHRUBB
¼ OUNCE CANE SUGAR SYRUP (PAGE 276)
2 DASHES HOUSE ORANGE BITTERS (PAGE 284)
1 DASH ANGOSTURA BITTERS

Stir all the ingredients over ice, then strain into a double rocks glass over 1 large ice cube. No garnish.

········

JEKYLL AND HYDE

THOMAS WAUGH, 2009

1½ OUNCES EAGLE RARE 10-YEAR BOURBON
½ OUNCE LAIRD'S BONDED APPLE BRANDY
½ TEASPOON CINNAMON BARK SYRUP (PAGE 276)
1 TEASPOON DEMERARA SYRUP (PAGE 277)
2 DASHES BITTER TRUTH AROMATIC BITTERS
2 DASHES ANGOSTURA BITTERS
GARNISH: 1 LEMON TWIST AND 1 ORANGE TWIST

Stir all the ingredients over ice, then strain into a double rocks glass over 1 large ice cube. Garnish with the lemon and orange twists.

········

LA CONFERENCIA

PHIL WARD, 2008

I was so impressed (and jealous) when Brian created his Conference cocktail (page 270) that I had to rip it off. My version replaces the whiskey with tequila, naturally.—PW

½ OUNCE EL TESORO REPOSADO TEQUILA

½ OUNCE DEL MAGUEY VIDA MEZCAL

½ OUNCE LA FAVORITE RHUM AGRICOLE BLANC

½ OUNCE SANTA TERESA RUM

¼ OUNCE CANE SUGAR SYRUP (PAGE 276)

1 DASH ANGOSTURA BITTERS

1 DASH BITTERMENS XOCOLATL MOLE BITTERS

GARNISH: 1 ORANGE TWIST

Stir all the ingredients over ice, then strain into a double rocks glass. Garnish with the orange twist.

. . . .

NORTH GARDEN

JASON LITTRELL, 2009

A guest once asked me to make a cocktail that tasted like "the great American novel." So I combined apple brandy from our country's oldest distillery with a classic bourbon.—JL

1½ OUNCES LAIRD'S BONDED APPLE BRANDY

¾ OUNCE BUFFALO TRACE BOURBON

¼ OUNCE LAPHROAIG 10-YEAR SCOTCH

1 TEASPOON DEMERARA SYRUP (PAGE 277)

1 DASH ANGOSTURA BITTERS

Stir all the ingredients over ice, then strain into a coupe. No garnish.

. . . .

OAXACA OLD-FASHIONED

PHIL WARD, 2008

1½ OUNCES EL TESORO REPOSADO TEQUILA

½ OUNCE DEL MAGUEY SAN LUIS DEL RIO MEZCAL

1 TEASPOON AGAVE NECTAR

2 DASHES ANGOSTURA BITTERS

GARNISH: 1 ORANGE TWIST

Stir all the ingredients over ice, then strain into a double rocks glass over 1 large ice cube. To garnish, flame the orange twist over the drink, then drop it in.

. . . .

TEA TIME AT GUILLERMO'S

JILLIAN VOSE, 2013

My friend Guillermo Sauza makes Fortaleza tequila in an old distillery left over from his family's sale of their famous brand. I created this rich, decadent drink in his honor, complementing his tequila with Siembra Azul reposado infused with caramel- and bergamot-flavored Queen of Earl tea.—JV

1 OUNCE FORTALEZA REPOSADO TEQUILA

1 OUNCE SCARLET IBIS RUM

½ OUNCE QUEEN OF EARL TEA–INFUSED SIEMBRA AZUL REPOSADO TEQUILA (PAGE 282)

½ OUNCE DRAMBUIE

1 TEASPOON MAPLE SYRUP

1 DASH HOUSE ORANGE BITTERS (PAGE 284)

1 DASH FEE BROTHERS WHISKEY BARREL-AGED BITTERS

Stir all the ingredients over ice, then strain into an old-fashioned glass over 1 large ice cube. No garnish.

. . . .

TIKI-TIKI TOM-TOM

THOMAS WAUGH, 2012

1½ OUNCES EL DORADO 15-YEAR RUM

½ OUNCE SCARLET IBIS RUM

½ OUNCE DRAMBUIE

1 TEASPOON STREGA

½ TEASPOON ACACIA HONEY SYRUP (PAGE 276)

Stir all the ingredients over ice, then strain into a double rocks glass over 1 large ice cube. No garnish.

APPENDICES

Sweeteners, Infusions
& Other Concoctions

SWEETENERS

In many of our cocktails, we use syrups infused with other ingredients to introduce additional flavors, heated to extract the third-party flavor. These recipes can be scaled up as necessary. Here are a few pointers on making your own syrups at home:

• When making syrup, apply heat only when necessary to dissolve the sugar or extract flavor from additional ingredients (such as in Cinnamon Bark Syrup, see below). Heating sugar changes its flavor and texture, and it's difficult to keep it consistent from one batch to another.

• Superfine sugar makes the task of dissolving a little easier, but granulated sugar will work just fine; the process will just require more time and patience. Be aware that 1 cup of superfine sugar will yield a sweeter syrup than 1 cup of granulated, so either measure by weight or make DIY superfine sugar by whizzing the correct quantity of granulated sugar in a blender or food processor. It's important to always measure the sugar and water separately. If you measure them together, the sugar will already be dissolving, so the final syrup may not have the right proportions of sweetness or density.

• Store syrups in a refrigerator until you're ready to use them. It's generally best to allow cooked syrups to cool to room temperature before transferring to a storage container and refrigerating. Most infused syrups will keep for 1 or 2 weeks before they start losing flavor, though the higher the sugar content, the longer the syrup will keep. To ensure good results, taste stored syrups before each use.

ACACIA HONEY SYRUP

In a bottle or other container with a tight lid, combine 2 cups of acacia honey with 1 cup of warm water. Shake vigorously until the honey is dissolved.

BANANA SYRUP

In a saucepan, combine 1 sliced banana, 2 cups of cane sugar, and 2 cups of water. Bring to a simmer, then remove from the heat, cover, and let cool to room temperature. Refrigerate overnight, then strain through a cheesecloth-lined sieve.

BLUEBERRY SYRUP

In a saucepan, combine 5 cups of blueberries, 1 cup of sugar, and 1 cup of water. Crush the berries with a potato masher. Bring to a boil, then lower the heat and simmer, stirring occasionally, for 15 minutes. Strain through a cheesecloth-lined sieve, pressing the berries to extract as much liquid as possible. Return the strained mixture to the pan and simmer for 10 minutes. Stir in 2 tablespoons of apple cider vinegar and simmer for 2 minutes.

BRAEBURN APPLE SYRUP

In a saucepan, combine 2 cups of water and 2 cups of sugar and bring to a simmer. Stir in the peels and cores from 5 Braeburn apples and simmer, stirring occasionally, for 30 minutes. Let cool to room temperature, then strain through a fine-mesh sieve.

CANE SUGAR SYRUP

In a saucepan, combine 2 cups of organic cane sugar (often labeled "evaporated cane juice"; note that this is different from turbinado sugar) with 1 cup of water. Cook over medium heat, stirring constantly and without bringing to a boil, until the sugar is dissolved.

CINNAMON BARK SYRUP

In a saucepan, muddle 1 ounce of cassia cinnamon sticks until it's broken up into shards. Add 2 cups of water and

2 cups of superfine sugar. Bring to a boil, stirring occasionally. Lower the heat, cover, and simmer gently for 4 minutes. Remove from the heat and let stand overnight. Strain through a cheesecloth-lined sieve.

CUMIN SYRUP

In a dry skillet, toast 6 tablespoons of cumin seeds over medium-low heat until fragrant. In a saucepan, combine 2 cups of sugar and 2 cups of water and bring to a boil, stirring constantly until the sugar is dissolved. Remove from the heat and stir in the cumin seeds. Cover and let stand for 6 hours. Strain through a cheesecloth-lined sieve.

CURRIED GINGER SYRUP

In a saucepan, toast 2 tablespoons of Tellicherry black peppercorns, 2 tablespoons of grains of paradise, and 2 tablespoons of coriander seeds over medium heat until fragrant, about 2 to 3 minutes. Add 1½ cups of demerara sugar, ½ cup of superfine sugar, and 2 cups of hot water. Bring to a boil, stirring constantly, then lower the heat and simmer for 2 minutes. Remove from the heat and add 4 muddled sprigs of fresh curry leaves to the pot. Cover and let stand for 1 hour. Strain through a cheesecloth-lined sieve, pressing firmly on the solids to extract as much flavor as possible.

DEMERARA SYRUP

In a saucepan, combine 2 cups of demerara sugar and 1 cup of water. Cook over medium heat, stirring constantly and without bringing to a boil, until the sugar is dissolved.

ESPRESSO-INFUSED DEMERARA SYRUP

Coarsely grind 4 ounces of espresso-roast coffee beans and transfer to a container. Add 2 cups of room-temperature water and stir well. Cover and let stand for 12 to 16 hours. Strain through a fine-mesh strainer, then stir in Demerara Syrup (see above) to taste.

GINGER SYRUP

Make ½ cup fresh ginger juice, either by using a juice extractor or by finely grating fresh ginger, wrapping it in a clean towel, and squeezing out the juice; you'll need about 24 ounces of ginger root to make this much juice. Put the juice in a blender, add 1 cup of superfine sugar, and blend until the sugar is dissolved.

HIBISCUS SYRUP

In a saucepan, bring 2 cups of water to a boil. Remove from the heat and stir in 3½ ounces of dried hibiscus flowers. Cover and let stand for 20 minutes. Strain through a cheesecloth-lined sieve, then return to the saucepan. Stir in 2 cups of superfine sugar and cook over low heat, stirring constantly and without bringing to a boil, until the sugar is dissolved.

ORGEAT

See page 278.

PASSION FRUIT SYRUP

Combine 1 cup of passion fruit puree and ½ cup of Simple Syrup (see below) in a blender and process until the sugar is dissolved.

SCARLET GLOW SYRUP

In a saucepan, bring 2 cups of water to a boil. Remove from the heat and stir in 4 heaping teaspoons of Scarlet Glow herbal tea (available at inpursuitoftea.com). Cover and let stand for 6 hours. Strain through a cheesecloth-lined sieve. Add 2 cups of superfine sugar and shake or stir until the sugar is dissolved.

SIMPLE SYRUP

Combine equal parts (preferably by weight, but you can also use measuring cups) of superfine sugar and warm water in a container. Shake or stir until the sugar is dissolved.

VANILLA SYRUP

Split 1 Tahitian vanilla bean in half lengthwise and put it in a saucepan. Add 2 cups of water and 2 cups of superfine sugar. Bring to a boil, stirring occasionally. Lower the heat, cover, and simmer gently for 4 minutes. Remove from the heat and let stand overnight. Strain through a cheesecloth-lined sieve.

ORGEAT

Orgeat is an almond-based syrup that has been part of cocktail culture since the mid-nineteenth century. It's a key ingredient in the vintage Japanese Cocktail (brandy, orgeat, and Angostura bitters) and especially the mai tai and its tiki brethren. Made primarily from water and almonds, along with other ingredients such as orange flower water and cognac, it has a unique flavor that's more than the sum of its ingredients and something altogether individual. It's milky and nutty but not cloying. It deepens the flavors of other ingredients and bridges magically between refreshing and savory, creating an ethereal mouthfeel that makes ingredients meld in unexpected ways, and at Death & Co, we use it in many styles of cocktails.

ORGEAT

12 OUNCES TOASTED ALMOND MILK (SEE BELOW)

16 OUNCES SUPERFINE SUGAR

2½ TEASPOONS PIERRE FERRAND AMBRE COGNAC

2½ TEASPOONS LAZZARONI AMARETTO

¼ TEASPOON ROSE WATER

In a saucepan, combine the almond milk and sugar. Cook over medium-low heat, stirring occasionally and without bringing to a boil, until the sugar is dissolved. Remove from the heat and stir in the cognac, amaretto, and rose water. Store in the refrigerator for up to one month.

. . . .

TOASTED ALMOND MILK

1 CUP BLANCHED SLICED ALMONDS

2 CUPS PLUS 2 TABLESPOONS WARM WATER

In a large, dry saucepan, toast the almonds over medium-low heat, stirring constantly, until golden brown. Transfer to a blender and add the water. Pulse until the almonds are finely chopped, then blend for 2 minutes. Strain through a cheesecloth-lined sieve.

INFUSIONS

When making your own infusions, here are a few pointers:

- **Solvent:** Infusions get a bad rap because of cheap vodka and artificially flavored candy. But when you start with top-shelf booze, you can give an already-delicious product an added layer of complexity. High proof spirits make for a speedier infusion process, sometimes only a matter of minutes, while vermouth and other lower-proof booze may take up to a week to accomplish the task.

- **Flavorings:** We love infusing with fancy, one-of-a-kind tea blends and ingredients typically found in sweet liqueurs, such as coffee, coconut, and pineapple. Fruit and any other fresh produce should be unblemished and washed before use. Surface area is important: we use loose tea and finely chopped produce to allow more contact with the solvent. This speeds the process and results in a more flavorful infusion.

- **Vessel:** Choose a nonreactive plastic or glass container with a tight lid, and be sure you can fit a spoon into it for stirring. Restaurant-grade Cambro containers are excellent, as are wide-mouthed jars. It's absolutely essential that the vessel be very clean, as alcohol will suck up the flavor of chicken soup or whatever was last in the container, even dish soap. Be sure to save the original booze bottle for storing the infusion when it's complete.

- **Temperature:** Most single-ingredient infusions can be made at room temperature in a cool, dark place. If using a variety of ingredients that will infuse at different rates, such as fresh fruit along with spices, refrigerate the infusion to give the flavors more time to meld.

- **Time:** The duration required to make a flavorful infusion can vary dramatically based on many factors: the intensity or ripeness of the ingredients, the size of the vessel, and, most importantly, your own preference. When making infusions, taste them frequently. Fresh, ripe ingredients, such as berries and tropical fruits, will infuse rather quickly, and it's important to strain them out before the fruit deteriorates too much—but not before it's given all of its flavor to the spirit. Anything involving tannins (say tea or herbs) is even less forgiving; there's a fine line between the perfect level of Earl Grey flavor in vermouth and an overly tannic mess. Dry, hard ingredients, such as pecans, require a bit more time—sometimes more than a week—to impart their flavor.

- **Storage:** Although infusions may be shelf stable in a cool, dark place, we recommend refrigerating them to help keep their flavors fresh longer. As a bonus, your infusions will be prechilled when you make cocktails.

··· Chile Infusions ···

ANCHO CHILE–INFUSED DOLIN ROUGE VERMOUTH

Stem and coarsely chop 3 dried ancho chiles. Transfer to a container, add one 750-ml bottle of Dolin rouge vermouth, and stir well. Let stand at room temperature for 1 hour and 45 minutes, stirring occasionally. Strain through a fine-mesh sieve.

COFFEE- AND CHILE-INFUSED CAMPARI

In a container, combine 22 grams each of crumbled red puya chile, crumbled morita chile, and crumbled mulato chile. Add 8 heaping teaspoons of whole coffee beans and one 1-liter bottle of Campari and stir well. Let stand at room temperature for 5 hours, stirring occasionally. Strain through a fine-mesh sieve.

JALAPEÑO-INFUSED SIEMBRA AZUL BLANCO TEQUILA

In a container, combine the ribs and seeds from 4 jalapeño chiles and the chopped flesh of ½ jalapeño with one 750-ml bottle of Siembra Azul blanco tequila and stir well. Let stand at room temperature for 20 minutes, tasting frequently so you can stop the infusion when the heat level is to your liking. Strain through a fine-mesh sieve.

RED THAI CHILE–INFUSED RITTENHOUSE RYE

In a container, combine 10 crumbled dried red Thai chiles and one 750-ml bottle of Rittenhouse 100 rye and stir well. Let stand at room temperature for 15 minutes, tasting frequently so you can stop the infusion when the heat level is to your liking. Strain through a fine-mesh sieve.

··· Fruit Infusions ···

APRICOT-INFUSED FAMOUS GROUSE SCOTCH

Coarsely chop 10 whole dried apricots. Transfer to a container, add one 1-liter bottle of Famous Grouse Scotch, and stir well. Let stand at room temperature for 24 hours, stirring occasionally. Strain through a fine-mesh sieve.

BANANA CHIP–INFUSED GOSLING'S BLACK SEAL RUM

In a container, combine 3 cups of banana chips and one 1-liter bottle of Gosling's Black Seal rum and stir well. Let stand at room temperature for 24 hours, stirring occasionally. Strain through a cheesecloth-lined sieve, return to the container, and refrigerate overnight. Strain through a cheesecloth-lined fine-mesh sieve.

DRIED CURRANT–INFUSED WILD TURKEY RYE

In a container, combine 3 cups of dried currants and one 750-ml bottle of Wild Turkey rye and stir well. Let stand at room temperature for 48 hours, stirring daily. Strain through a cheesecloth-lined sieve.

FIG-INFUSED ELIJAH CRAIG BOURBON

In a container, muddle 4 fresh figs. Add one 750-ml bottle of Elijah Craig 12-year bourbon and stir well. Let stand for 1 hour, stirring occasionally. Strain through a cheesecloth-lined sieve.

FUJI APPLE–INFUSED FAMOUS GROUSE SCOTCH

In a container, combine 3 coarsely chopped Fuji apples (cores, peels, and all) and one 750-ml bottle of Famous Grouse Scotch and stir well. Let stand at room temperature for 1 week, stirring daily. Strain through a cheesecloth-lined sieve.

GRANNY SMITH APPLE–INFUSED RHUM BARBANCOURT

In a container, combine 4 coarsely chopped Granny Smith apples (cores, peels, and all) and one 750-ml bottle of Barbancourt white rum and stir well. Let stand at room temperature for 1 week, stirring daily. Strain through a cheesecloth-lined sieve.

GRAPEFRUIT-INFUSED PUNT E MES

In a container, combine the zest of 2 Ruby Red grapefruits and one 750-ml bottle of Punt e Mes and stir well. Cover and refrigerate for 24 hours. Strain through a fine-mesh sieve.

PINEAPPLE-INFUSED FLOR DE CAÑA EXTRA-DRY WHITE RUM

In a container, combine 3 cups of cubed pineapple and one 750-ml bottle of Flor de Caña extra-dry white rum and stir well. Cover and refrigerate for 5 days, stirring daily. Strain through a cheesecloth-lined sieve.

SPICED PEAR–INFUSED SIEMBRA AZUL BLANCO TEQUILA

In a container, combine 3 coarsely chopped red Anjou pears, 1 coarsely chopped Granny Smith apple (core, peel, and all), 2 cloves, 1 cinnamon stick, and one 750-ml bottle of Siembra Azul blanco tequila and stir well. Cover and let stand at room temperature for 1 week, stirring daily. Strain through a cheesecloth-lined sieve.

STRAWBERRY- AND PINEAPPLE-INFUSED MACCHU PISCO

In a container, combine 4 cups of cubed pineapple, 4 cups of halved strawberries, and one 750-ml bottle of Macchu pisco and stir well. Cover and refrigerate for 5 days, stirring daily. Strain through a cheesecloth-lined sieve.

WATERMELON-INFUSED DOLIN DRY VERMOUTH

In a blender, combine ten 1-inch cubes of watermelon and one 750-ml bottle of Dolin dry vermouth. Pulse until smooth, then let stand at room temperature for 1 hour. Strain through a cheesecloth-lined sieve.

··· *Herb Infusions* ···

BASIL-INFUSED DOLIN BLANC VERMOUTH

In a container, combine 25 fresh basil leaves and one 750-ml bottle of Dolin blanc vermouth and stir well. Cover and let stand at room temperature for 24 hours, stirring occasionally. Strain through a fine-mesh sieve.

LAVENDER-INFUSED BERNHEIM ORIGINAL WHEAT WHISKEY

In a container, combine 1 tablespoon of dried lavender and one 750-ml bottle of Bernheim wheat whiskey and stir well. Let stand at room temperature for 30 minutes. Strain through a cheesecloth-lined sieve.

PENNYROYAL-INFUSED HAYMAN'S OLD TOM GIN

In a container, combine 2 teaspoons of dried pennyroyal and one 750-ml bottle of Hayman's Old Tom gin and stir well. Let stand for 5 minutes. Strain through a fine-mesh sieve.

SAGE-INFUSED DOLIN BLANC VERMOUTH

In a container, combine ½ ounce of dried whole-leaf sage and one 750-ml bottle of Dolin blanc vermouth and stir well. Let stand at room temperature for 1 hour and 15 minutes, stirring occasionally. Strain through a fine-mesh sieve.

··· *Tea Infusions* ···

CHAMOMILE-INFUSED BIANCO VERMOUTH

In a container, combine 3 heaping tablespoons of loose chamomile tea and one 750-ml bottle of Martini bianco vermouth and stir well. Let stand at room temperature for 1 hour and 45 minutes, stirring occasionally. Strain through a cheesecloth-lined sieve.

CHAMOMILE-INFUSED OLD OVERHOLT RYE

In a container, combine a heaping ¼ cup of loose chamomile tea and one 1-liter bottle of Old Overholt rye and stir well. Let stand at room temperature for 1 hour and 45 minutes, stirring occasionally. Strain through a cheesecloth-lined sieve.

CINNAMON ORANGE TEA–INFUSED SWEET VERMOUTH

In a container, combine 3 heaping tablespoons of loose Market Spice cinnamon-orange tea (marketspice.com) and one 750-ml bottle of Martini sweet vermouth and stir well. Let stand at room temperature for 1 hour and 30 minutes, stirring occasionally. Strain through a cheesecloth-lined sieve.

COCONUT GREEN TEA–INFUSED FAMOUS GROUSE SCOTCH

In a container, combine 6 heaping teaspoons of loose T Salon Green Tea with Coconut (available at tsalon.com) and one 750-ml bottle of Famous Grouse Scotch and stir well. Let stand at room temperature for 30 minutes, stirring occasionally. Strain through a cheesecloth-lined sieve.

EARL GREY–INFUSED DOLIN BLANC VERMOUTH

In a container, combine a heaping ¼ cup of loose Early Grey tea and one 750-ml bottle of Dolin blanc vermouth and stir well. Let stand at room temperature for 45 minutes, stirring occasionally. Strain through a cheesecloth-lined sieve.

LAPSANG SOUCHONG–INFUSED SIEMBRA AZUL BLANCO TEQUILA

In a container, combine 3 heaping tablespoons of loose Lapsang Souchong tea and one 750-ml bottle of Siembra Azul blanco tequila and stir well. Let stand at room temperature for 5 hours, stirring occasionally. Strain through a cheesecloth-lined sieve.

QUEEN OF EARL TEA–INFUSED SIEMBRA AZUL REPOSADO TEQUILA

In a container, combine 1 teaspoon of loose T Salon Queen of Earl tea (available at tsalon.com) and one 750-ml bottle of Siembra Azul reposado tequila and stir well. Let stand at room temperature for 10 minutes. Strain through a cheesecloth-lined sieve.

SCARLET GLOW TEA–INFUSED MACCHU PISCO

In a container, combine a heaping ¼ cup of loose Scarlet Glow herbal tea (available at inpursuitoftea.com) and one 750-ml bottle of Macchu pisco and stir well. Let stand at room temperature for 1 hour and 30 minutes, stirring occasionally. Strain through a cheesecloth-lined sieve.

SUMMER ROYALE TEA–INFUSED FLOR DE CAÑA WHITE RUM

In a container, combine 3 heaping tablespoons of loose T Salon Summer Royale tea (available at tsalon.com) and one 750-ml bottle of Flor de Caña extra-dry white rum and stir well. Let stand at room temperature for 1 hour, stirring occasionally. Strain through a cheesecloth-lined sieve.

··· *Other Infusions* ···

CACAO NIB–INFUSED CABEZA BLANCO TEQUILA

In a container, combine 3 tablespoons of cacao nibs and one 1-liter bottle of Cabeza blanco tequila and stir well. Let stand at room temperature for 1 hour, stirring occasionally. Strain through a cheesecloth-lined sieve.

CACAO NIB–INFUSED CAMPARI

In a container, combine 3 tablespoons of cacao nibs and one 750-ml bottle of Campari and stir well. Let stand at room temperature for 1 hour, stirring occasionally. Strain through a cheesecloth-lined sieve.

COFFEE-INFUSED CARPANO ANTICA FORMULA VERMOUTH

In a container, combine 3 tablespoons of whole coffee beans and one 1-liter bottle of Carpano Antica Formula vermouth and stir well. Cover and let stand at room temperature for 24 hours, stirring occasionally. Strain through a cheesecloth-lined sieve.

PECAN-INFUSED BUFFALO TRACE BOURBON

Soak 2 cups of pecan halves in cold water for 20 minutes. Preheat the oven to 300°F. Drain the pecans well, then spread them on a rimmed baking sheet. Season with salt, pepper, and cayenne pepper and bake for 20 minutes, stirring occasionally and being careful not to burn the pecans. Let cool to room temperature. In a container, combine the pecans and one 750-ml bottle of Buffalo Trace bourbon and stir well. Let stand at room temperature for 1 week, stirring daily. Strain through a cheesecloth-lined sieve.

ROSE-INFUSED LILLET ROSÉ

In a container, combine 4 heaping tablespoons of dried rosebuds and one 750-ml bottle of Lillet rosé and stir well. Let stand at room temperature for 1 hour and 30 minutes, stirring occasionally. Strain through a fine-mesh sieve.

SUGAR SNAP PEA–INFUSED PLYMOUTH GIN

In a container, combine 2 cups of coarsely chopped sugar snap peas and one 750-ml bottle of Plymouth gin and stir well. Let stand at room temperature for 1 hour, stirring occasionally. Strain through a cheesecloth-lined sieve.

SZECHUAN PEPPERCORN–INFUSED PLYMOUTH GIN

In a container, combine 1 ounce of Szechuan peppercorns and one 1-liter bottle of Plymouth gin and stir well. Let stand at room temperature for 35 minutes, stirring occasionally. Strain through a fine-mesh sieve.

RIMS

We don't use rims very frequently at Death & Co—and when we do, we roll the exterior and often rim only half of the glass, allowing the guest to choose how much to include in each sip. We also keep our rims modest and clean, covering about a ½ inch of the rim of the glass in a straight swath.

CINNAMON AND SUGAR

Mix equal parts finely ground cinnamon and superfine sugar.

SPICY SUGAR AND SALT

Mix equal parts kosher salt, granulated sugar, and ground ancho chiles.

TOASTED FENNEL SALT

Lightly toast 1 tablespoon of fennel seeds in a small dry skillet. Let cool, then finely grind in a spice grinder. Measure the ground fennel, then add an equivalent amount of kosher salt and mix well.

BATCHES

Some Death & Co cocktails call for minute amounts of ingredients—teaspoons of this and ¼ ounce of that—sometimes for several ingredients in one drink. To speed things up (and make for more accurate measuring), we premix some of these batches and put them in cheater bottles. The batches have a way of taking on lives of their own, inspiring future drinks and earning a permanent place atop the bar. However, for home use, you could always make these mixes to order—in other words, instead of making a large batch of House Sweet Vermouth, you could just add equal parts of Dolin rouge vermouth and Punt e Mes to whatever drink you're mixing.

BERGERAC MIX

6 OUNCES BERGERAC RED WINE

1½ OUNCES CRUZAN BLACK STRAP RUM

1½ OUNCES CYNAR

½ OUNCE DEMERARA SYRUP (PAGE 277)

DONN'S MIX #1

2 PARTS GRAPEFRUIT JUICE (PREFERABLY FROM RUBY RED GRAPEFRUITS)

1 PART CINNAMON BARK SYRUP (PAGE 276)

DONN'S SPICES #2

1 PART VANILLA SYRUP (PAGE 277)

1 PART ST. ELIZABETH ALLSPICE DRAM

HOUSE ORANGE BITTERS

1 PART FEE BROTHERS WEST INDIAN ORANGE BITTERS

1 PART REGANS' ORANGE BITTERS

1 PART ANGOSTURA ORANGE BITTERS

HOUSE PEYCHAUD'S BITTERS

2 PARTS PEYCHAUD'S BITTERS

1 PART BITTER TRUTH CREOLE BITTERS

HOUSE SWEET VERMOUTH

1 PART DOLIN ROUGE VERMOUTH

1 PART PUNT E MES

PENDENNIS MIX

2 OUNCES SIMPLE SYRUP (PAGE 277)

1 OUNCE MARIE BRIZARD APRICOT LIQUEUR

2 TEASPOONS MARIE BRIZARD CRÈME DE PECHE PEACH LIQUEUR

ZOMBIE MIX

8 OUNCES VELVET FALERNUM

1 OUNCE PLUS 4 TEASPOONS GRENADINE (SEE BELOW)

2 TEASPOONS VIEUX PONTARLIER ABSINTHE

MISCELLANY

Gastriques, cordials, purees, and so on: these "other" ingredients aren't everyday staples, but they're irreplaceable ingredients in some of our most unique cocktails.

GRENADINE

In a saucepan, combine 4 cups of organic unfiltered, unsweetened pomegranate juice and 3 cups of organic cane sugar (often labeled "evaporated cane juice"; note that this is different from turbinado sugar). Cook over medium heat, stirring constantly and without bringing to a boil, until the sugar is dissolved. Remove from the heat and let cool to room temperature. Transfer to a container and stir in 6 ounces of pomegranate molasses. Squeeze 8 half-dollar-size orange twists over the surface, discarding the twists, and stir well. Store in the refrigerator for up to 2 weeks.

HONEY NUT CHEERIO–INFUSED CREAM

In a bowl, combine 2 cups of heavy cream and 2 cups of Honey Nut Cheerios and stir gently. Cover and refrigerate for 1 hour, then strain through a cheesecloth-lined fine-mesh sieve, pressing gently on the Cheerios. Store in the refrigerator for up to 2 days.

HOUSE HORCHATA

In a dry, heavy skillet, lightly toast 1 cup of almond flour and 1 cup of shredded unsweetened coconut. In a bowl, combine 2 cups of rice milk, 1 cup of almond milk, 1 cup of coconut water, ¼ cup of light brown sugar, 2 tablespoons of Cinnamon Bark Syrup (page 276), and the toasted almond flour and unsweetened coconut and stir well. Working in batches, transfer to a blender and process on high speed for about 45 seconds. Strain through a fine-mesh sieve, pressing on the solids to extract as much liquid as possible. Store in the refrigerator for up to 3 days.

KUMQUAT CORDIAL

In a blender or food processor, combine 1 cup of granulated sugar, ½ cup of thinly sliced kumquats, ¼ cup of water, 2 tablespoons of lime juice, and 1½ tablespoons of lemon juice. Pulse until the kumquats are finely chopped. Transfer to a container, cover, and refrigerate for 24 hours. Strain through a fine-mesh sieve. Store in the refrigerator for up to 1 week.

PUMPKIN PUREE

In a bowl, combine one 15-ounce can of pure pumpkin puree, 15 ounces of Simple Syrup (page 277), 1 teaspoon of ground cinnamon, ½ teaspoon of ground ginger, and ¼ teaspoon of ground cloves. Blend with an immersion blender or whisk vigorously until combined. Store in the refrigerator for up to 1 week.

RED BELL PEPPER PUREE

In a blender, combine 1 coarsely chopped red bell pepper and a splash of water. Blend until smooth, then strain through a fine-mesh sieve. Store in the refrigerator for up to 3 days.

STRAWBERRY-BALSAMIC GASTRIQUE

In a medium saucepan, combine 1⅓ cups of superfine sugar and 1⅓ cups of water. Cook over low heat, stirring constantly and without bringing to a boil, until the sugar is dissolved. Add 2 cups of hulled and halved strawberries and simmer, stirring occasionally, for 30 minutes. Stir in 1 cup of balsamic vinegar, raise the heat, and bring to a boil. Lower the heat and simmer, stirring occasionally, until thickened, about 30 minutes. Let cool, then strain through a cheesecloth-lined fine-mesh sieve. Store in the refrigerator for up to 3 weeks.

TARRAGON AND AGAVE NECTAR GASTRIQUE

In a saucepan over medium heat, bring 12 ounces of agave nectar to a boil, stirring frequently. Slowly add 4 ounces of champagne vinegar while stirring constantly. Boil for 5 minutes, stirring occasionally. Remove from the heat and stir in ¼ cup of gently muddled tarragon leaves. Let cool, then strain through a cheesecloth-lined fine-mesh sieve, pressing firmly on the tarragon to extract as much flavor as possible. Store in the refrigerator for up to 3 weeks.

TOBY'S LIME CORDIAL

Strip the zest from 12 limes, reserving the zest, then juice the limes. Weigh the lime juice and measure an equal amount of sugar (by weight). In a nonreactive container, combine the lime juice and sugar and stir until the sugar is dissolved. Stir in the lime zest and taste; the mixture should be slightly more tart than sweet and fairly viscous. Adjust the flavor and texture as needed with more lime juice or sugar. Cover and let stand at room temperature for 24 hours, stirring occasionally. Strain through a fine-mesh sieve. Store in the refrigerator for up to 1 month.

TOBY'S SOUR CHERRY SHRUB

Rinse 2 quarts of sour cherries and trim away any rot. Put the unpitted cherries in a large nonreactive pot and mash for several minutes with your hands or a wooden spoon to break the cherries down a bit. Pour in enough apple-cider vinegar (preferably Bragg's) or other vinegar to cover the cherries. Cover and let stand at room temperature for 1 week, stirring daily. Don't be alarmed by the smell or the sludge on top. After 1 week, stir in ½ cup of raw sugar and boil gently for 1 hour, stirring occasionally. (The smell will be a bit offensive, so open the doors and windows.) Cool slightly, then strain through a cheesecloth-lined fine-mesh sieve. Make a test shrub: Cool 3 to 4 tablespoons of the cherry mixture. (Cover the pot to keep its contents warm.) Fill a 20-ounce glass with ice. Add water or club soda to almost the rim, then stir in the chilled cherry mixture. Taste and adjust as needed. If it's too tart, add another ½ cup or so of sugar, little by little, while it's still hot, stirring after each addition, until the sugar is dissolved. Once the taste is to your liking, cool completely. Store in the refrigerator, where it will keep indefinitely.

THE DEATH & CO BOOKSHELF

We're excited to share shelf space with other works that promote the craft of making fine cocktails—and the joyous act of drinking them. If you're reading this, you should also own as many of the following titles as possible.

Amis, Kingsley. *Everyday Drinking: The Distilled Kingsley Amis.* Bloomsbury, 2010.

Baker, Charles H., Jr. *Jigger, Beaker and Glass: Drinking Around the World.* Derrydale Press, 2001.

Boothby, William T. *Cocktail Boothby's American Bartender.* Anchor Distilling, 2009.

Cecchini, Toby. *Cosmopolitan: A Bartender's Life.* Broadway Books, 2003.

Chartier, Francois. *Taste Buds and Molecules: The Art and Science of Food, Wine, and Flavor.* Houghton Mifflin Harcourt, 2012.

Craddock, Harry. *The Savoy Cocktail Book.* Pavilion, 2007.

Curtis, Wayne. *And a Bottle of Rum: A History of the New World in Ten Cocktails.* Crown, 2006.

DeGroff, Dale. *Craft of the Cocktail: Everything You Need to Know to Be a Master Bartender, with 500 Recipes.* Clarkson Potter, 2002.

_____. *The Essential Cocktail: The Art of Mixing Perfect Drinks.* Clarkson Potter, 2008.

Embury, David A. *The Fine Art of Mixing Drinks.* Mud Puddle Books, 2008.

Ensslin, Hugo. *Recipes for Mixed Drinks.* Mud Puddle Books, 2009.

Grimes, William. *Straight Up or On the Rocks: A Cultural History of American Drink.* Simon & Schuster, 1993.

Haigh, Ted. *Vintage Spirits and Forgotten Cocktails: From the Alamagoozlum to the Zombie, 100 Rediscovered Recipes and the Stories Behind Them.* Quarry Books, 2009.

Jackson, Michael. *Whiskey: The Definitive World Guide.* Dorling Kindersley, 2005.

Lendler, Ian. *Alcoholica Esoterica: A Collection of Useful and Useless Information as It Relates to the History and Consumption of All Manner of Booze.* Penguin Books, 2005.

Lord, Tony. *The World Guide to Spirits, Aperitifs and Cocktails.* Sovereign Books, 1979.

McGee, Harold. *On Food and Cooking: The Science and Lore of the Kitchen.* Scribner, 2004.

Meehan, Jim. *The PDT Cocktail Book: The Complete Bartender's Guide from the Celebrated Speakeasy.* Sterling Epicure, 2011.

Myhrvold, Nathan, Chris Young, and Maxime Bilet. *Modernist Cuisine: The Art and Science of Cooking.* Cooking Lab, 2011.

O'Neil, Darcy. *Fix the Pumps.* Art of Drink, 2010.

Pacult, F. Paul. *Kindred Spirits 2.* Spirit Journal, 2008.

Page, Karen, and Andrew Dornenburg. *The Flavor Bible: The Essential Guide to Culinary Creativity, Based on the Wisdom of America's Most Imaginative Chefs.* Little, Brown, 2008.

_____. *What to Drink with What You Eat: The Definitive Guide to Pairing Food with Wine, Beer, Spirits, Coffee, Tea—Even Water—Based on Expert Advice from America's Best Sommeliers.* Bulfinch, 2006.

Parsons, Brad Thomas. *Bitters: A Spirited History of a Classic Cure-All, with Cocktails, Recipes, and Formulas.* Ten Speed Press, 2011.

Regan, Gary. *The Bartender's Gin Compendium.* Xlibris, 2009.

_____. *The Joy of Mixology: The Consummate Guide to the Bartender's Craft.* Clarkson Potter, 2003.

Schwartz, Rob, and Jeff Hollinger. *The Art of the Bar: Cocktails Inspired by the Classics.* Chronicle Books, 2006.

Stewart, Amy. *The Drunken Botanist: The Plants That Create the World's Great Drinks.* Algonquin Books, 2013.

Thomas, Jerry. *The Bartender's Guide: How to Mix Drinks.* Dick & Fitzgerald, 1862.

Uyeda, Kazuo. *Cocktail Techniques.* Mud Puddle Books, 2010.

Wondrich, David. *Imbibe!* Perigree, 2007.

_____. *Punch: The Delights (and Dangers) of the Flowing Bowl.* Perigee, 2010.

RESOURCES

We couldn't make drinks without the following resources for ingredients, tools, glassware, and more.

ART OF DRINK (artofdrink.com)
For acid phosphate and lactart.

ASTOR WINES & SPIRITS (astorwines.com)
For a vast selection of spirits.

BAR PRODUCTS (barproducts.com)
For all the bar equipment and tools under the sun.

BEVERAGE ALCOHOL RESOURCE
(beveragealcoholresource.com)
For aspiring bartenders and liquor professionals.

CHEF SHOP (chefshop.com)
For Napa Fusion verjus, honey, maraschino cherries, and other pantry staples.

COCKTAIL KINGDOM (cocktailkingdom.com)
For all matter of barware, as well as bitters, syrups, and cocktail books, including facsimiles of some vintage classics.

DRINK UP NY (drinkupny.com)
For hard-to-find spirits and other boozy ingredients.

DUAL SPECIALTIES (dualspecialty.com)
For spices, nuts, and bitters.

IN PURSUIT OF TEA (inpursuitoftea.com)
For rare and exotic teas.

INSTAWARES (instawares.com)
For an extensive assortment of bar tools, glassware, and kitchen supplies.

LIBBEY (libbey.com)
For durable glassware.

MARKET SPICE (marketspice.com)
For one-of-a-kind tea blends.

MONTEREY BAY SPICE COMPANY
(herbco.com)
For bulk herbs, spices, and teas.

STEELITE (steelite.com)
For coupes and Nick & Nora glasses.

TERRA SPICE COMPANY
(terraspice.com)
For an extensive selection of spices, sugars, and dried fruit and chiles.

T SALON (tsalon.com)
For loose-leaf teas and tisanes.

Acknowledgments

DAVE KAPLAN

This book would not exist without a near-endless number of individuals: My agent, Jonah Straus, started me on the path and was an ever-present guide through the process. He first led me to my partner in crime and fellow distraction enthusiast, Nick Fauchald. Nick did what few others could, patiently wrangling a ragtag crew of Death & Co alums, as well as chasing me down from coast to coast throughout the process. Tim Tomkinson and Katherine Tomkinson have been entrusted with the appearance of our menus and much more since we opened; they turned our proposal into an art object and, as expected, continued to outdo themselves with their work on the book.

With proposal in hand we met with Aaron Wehner at Ten Speed Press. He listened patiently as I waxed poetic about what this book could be and ultimately shared that vision, and a few cocktails, as we sat at table 7 at Death & Co. A week later, I'd just landed in Jackson Hole and was still on the plane when I received a call from Jonah saying that we were going to be part of the Ten Speed family. I had been holding my breath waiting to hear the news.

Emily Timberlake proved to be the ever-sweet voice on the Ten Speed end of the phone through times of both stress and accomplishment. William Hereford brought just the right amount of light to the darkness of Death & Co with his beautiful photos. To my partners, Ravi DeRossi and our ever nonsilent silent partner Craig Manzino, thank you for seven years now of epic highs, and for enduring the occasional lows.

To Paul Pacult, Dale DeGroff, David Wondrich, Steve Olson, Doug Frost, Simon Ford, Allen Katz, Julie Reiner, Audrey Saunders, Sasha Petraske, Lenell Smothers, and many others, thank you for inspiring, teaching, leading, or helping to hold up the bar during those first years.

Death & Co was and continues to be defined by our staff. The early days spent with our first head bartender, Phil Ward, as we decided what this thing would become were some of my favorite moments. Phil, you're an odd duck and brilliant as hell; thank you for taking a chance. The head bartender torch was then handed over to Brian Miller and his love for all things tiki and Johnny Depp. Thomas Waugh then grabbed the reins and brought a little bit of San Francisco to NYC. Jillian Vose is our current head bartender, and the position has never looked as effortless. Thank you all for putting in absurd hours and an incredible amount of energy and creativity, and for all the leadership and love you have given this place.

Thanks also to the rest of the D&C staff: Joaquín Simó gave five years to D&C, was everyone's favorite bartender, and will forever be the nicest guy to work behind the stick. Jessica Gonzalez came on as a waitress, moved up to bartender, and stayed with us for five years before moving on to be head bartender at the Nomad. To Toby Cecchini, the oldest, grumpiest, and wittiest bartender we've ever met; I hope that by the time this book is on the shelf, you finally finished the foreword—now let's go get a haircut. And a big thank-you to everyone else who has put time and energy into the bar: Anne Claire, Cabell Tomlinson, Damon Dyer, Kelvin Joyner, Sean Newell, James Flak, Placido, Alexandra Lacey, Jacquelyn Leon, Mary Berhane, Jason Littrell, Michelle Bernardi, Zach Lombardo, Edgar Crutchfield, Shannon Tebay, Wally Suarez, Katie Emmerson, Isabella Huber, Eliad Mendez, Angel Colon, Bobby Weinberger (thank you for passing the bar exam and becoming my daily counsel), Samuel Vega, Stephen Fletcher, Chris Darsch, Serena Chow, David Powell, Constance Sousek, Miguel Rivera, Eryn Reece (the fastest there is), Christina Gerasimovich, Stephanie Joyce-Solis, Devyn Sisson, John Evans, Eva McGarry, Arnie Marcella (long live purple), Tim Elledge, Brad Faran, Stephanie Borris, Felipe Colina, Peter

Mullin, Tyson Buhler (you're fired), Andrea Jaramillo, Scott Teague (insert modeling joke here), Jordan Gomez, Jane Danger, Joshua D'Oyley, Jourdan Gomez, Shae Minnillo, Edmund Marvelli, Jack Burns, Erin A. Reitz, Anthony Byron, Justice McFadden, Brittney Chadbourne, Zachery Ellis, Paul DiStefano, Oscar Valle, Drew Bushong, Valerie Zolkina, and Michael Russel. To anyone who has worked a day here that I missed, I'm sorry for the lapse in memory. I blame the booze.

Frankie Rodriguez, thank you for keeping the lights on, the leaks at bay, and the Death & Co family together. You're the best manager and friend anyone could hope for.

The acceptance speech continues: A special thank-you to my family, who have always been my support and inspiration. To my mom, Barb Kaplan, I don't know many parents who would support a son's art school education and then his leap into bars at twenty-four years old—in Manhattan, no less. The same is true for my father, Robert Kaplan, who doesn't drink cocktails and upon the opening of D&C asked what sort of a bar it was ("A pick-up bar?"). My grandpa Morry Kaplan, who has always been my hero, used to ask me how my saloon was doing until one day, before he passed, when he got to visit. I asked him what he thought of my saloon, and with his beautiful smile, he replied, "This is no saloon; this is quite the enterprise." To my sister Sarah, thank you for being my best friend and always one year ahead of me.

To Alex Day, thank you for being a brilliant bartender and an even better businessman, for sitting down in front of Joaquín on your first visit to Death & Co and drinking that French 75 that led you down this cocktail path, and for taking the risk and partnering up with me. Your drive and passion for our business keeps me going, and your friendship keeps me sane. Let's build more things.

Most importantly, thank you to all of the Death & Co customers, both regulars who visit us weekly (or more often) and who we've come to think of as family, and also the first-timers with whom we get to share our love of cocktails. Death & Co—both the bar and the book—exists only because of you.

Finally, a thank-you to our insane, loving, welcoming, brilliant, often-drunken industry. I can't imagine another job or a better place to call home.

ALEX DAY

To thank everyone responsible for making Death & Co an amazing bar—and for making this book a possibility—might result in a census of the global bar industry. For the honor of having Death & Co be a place that our industry loves to visit, I will be forever grateful. Thank you to every single bartender, chef, spirits maker, brand ambassador, and liquor-industry hooligan for making Death & Co your first stop in NYC and your home away from home, and for teaching us something new every single night.

Above all else, thank you to my partner in all these boozy shenanigans, Dave Kaplan. He gave me a gig at his exciting new bar when I was in no way qualified to be there, and has since become the counterbalance to my professional neurosis. The day I became a co-owner of Death & Co will forever be one of the greatest of my life. Thank you for including me in this book and allowing me to smudge some pages up here and there.

Dave has probably thanked the same people I thank here, but I love them, too, so there. The D&C crew changed my life, both professionally and personally, and I will forever be grateful for the chance to work with such passionate people. That first cocktail Joaquín Simó made me opened my eyes to great drinks, and experiencing it became the most important moment in my professional life. It sent me down the path to putting words on this page. That first terrifyingly shaky trial shift (I forgot the agave nectar in a Oaxaca Old-Fashioned!) with Phil Ward, who turned into a mentor—a man of few words, certainly, but always with insight and wisdom—taught me the value of not accepting mediocrity. Brian Miller, dodging your formidable shake and blistering wit, and being inspired by your obsessive commitment to your work, has been invaluable to every page in this book. Jessica Gonzalez kept pretending she wasn't a badass bartender, but then she stepped behind the stick and made us all look like newbies. Thomas Waugh, thank you for moving to New York, changing our perspective on cocktails, and bringing an unbridled creativity to the table. Jillian Vose, your leadership in the next era of Death & Co has been invaluable, your dedication unmatched, and your cocktails jaw-dropping; we'd be lost without you. Brad Farran, a lot of your ideas seemed so ridiculous at first, but goddamn do your drinks taste good; thank you for livening up the bar every night and making our guests excited to be on our bar stools. Eryn Reece, by the time this book is out, I'm sure your maniacal professionalism will have taken you great places; I just hope you don't forget us little people, okay? Tyson Buhler, I couldn't be more grateful for your time at Death & Co; as with Eryn, your assured greatness will take you far—you'll probably be a senator or something by the time this book is in print. Way to make us all look like dumb-asses, Ty! Al Sotack, I couldn't be more honored that you joined the team; since we first worked together in Philly, you've developed into one of the most creative bartenders I've ever met. Lane Ford, we didn't get any time behind the stick together, but having the opportunity to drink in front of you many times was nothing less than inspirational; I always left with a new idea. Cabel Tomlinson and Katie Stipe, thank you for being the loveliest women on the planet (aside from my mother). You are both better bartenders than everyone—anywhere.

It all comes back to my first coveted Sunday night shift at D&C and the coworkers who held my hand through it. Maria Diamond, wherever you are in Ireland, thank you for dealing with me dropping stuff and running amuck. Sam Kershaw, I'll always be thankful for the marmalade you put in every cocktail. You'd be surprised how much that impacted the rest of my career. Damon Dyer, your genial demeanor and ever-present smile, not to mention your perfectly timed dirty jokes, will continue to be the envy of every smart-ass who has worked at this bar. Well done, sir.

In any job, you can get numb with the day-to-day monotony of things and tend to lose sight of the magic that surrounds you. I can confidently say that on my nights off, when I'd stop by the bar for a drink and sit in front of everyone listed above while they made me cocktails, my excitement about bartending was quickly reignited. A greater group of professionals has never been assembled.

Frankie Rodriguez, our longtime general manager and all-around nicest guy in the room, deserves more thanks than most. Although we fancy bartenders hog the limelight while you shy away, Death & Co surely wouldn't exist without you, Frankie. We're all so grateful for your leadership and for directing the service culture at Death & Co.

D&C's tireless group of door hosts, servers, and other staff deserve more praise than I can possibly put into words here. Shannon, Connie, Andrea, Valerie, Anne-Claire, Fletch, Bobby . . . so many! Anyone I forgot, forgive me, please. This is all very overwhelming.

To our partners Ravi DeRossi and Craig Manzino, thank you for being so supportive of all the crazy decisions made in support of the lofty Death & Co ambition. Your business sense and guidance are immeasurably helpful and appreciated.

Death & Co has always been a beacon for great restaurant pros, who mostly fill our bar stools after closing down their restaurants and kitchens for the night. Phillip Kirschen-Clark, I miss getting to make you drinks and being challenged in the most productive and exciting ways by your enthusiasm and intelligence, but I take solace that you're there to properly vet new bartenders. Amador and Alina Acosta, I love you both so much; by simply being present in a room, you make everyone feel better. Nadine Proctor, I've never experienced a boring conversation with you and can't imagine that anyone else has, either; you make our bar a more interesting place. Arnie Marcella, first a regular patron of D&C and now a good friend, thank you for stepping in and leading our kitchen—a task far below your pedigree and skill, but you've never once scoffed at it. All our Plymouth gin has your name on it.

I first met Nick Fauchald years ago, while I was making mediocre drinks in teacups, and he somehow became convinced that I'd be useful in putting together a book. Thank you, Nick, for your unbelievable patience in what could only be described as a full-time job herding drunk kittens as you gathered the material in this book from me and my ilk. I couldn't be more honored to have my name on the cover of this book, and to have it next to yours implies that I know what I'm doing! As always, thank you for allowing me to cop your style.

Thank you Aaron, Emily, and everyone at Ten Speed for believing in this book and making it happen. Did we do okay?

Last, but definitely not least, a bar is nothing without the people who come and enjoy it. Press accolades and awards mean absolutely nothing without the folks who walk down East Sixth Street every night, newbies and regulars alike—many of whom have become like family. As a bartender, I hope to have been your counselor at some point, and many of you have been mine as well. Thank you, of course, for coming to our little bar, but more than anything, thank you for your friendship.

NICK FAUCHALD

My first experience at Death & Co happened to fall on their first official day of business. I'd lived nearby for years and had heard whispers of a new, ambitious cocktail bar opening up in the neighborhood. I opened the ominous-looking door on a chilly January evening and found a stool near the end of the bar. From my perch I recognized Phil Ward, who had served me on many illuminating occasions at the Pegu Club, which at that time offered one of the most progressive cocktail programs in New York. Phil's presence alone gave this fledgling bar an instant aura of serious cred. I'd just begun my own self-education in cocktails and asked Phil to make me his favorite drink on the inaugural menu. (Little did I know then that bartenders hate this request.) He made me an Oaxaca Old-Fashioned, and my first sip of that electrifying drink told me that Death & Co was going to be a big player in the new cocktail craze.

As I started writing more about cocktails, Death & Co became my most reliable fountain of knowledge. Any time I needed to know what was happening next in drink trends, I paid a visit to Sixth Street to see what those innovative bartenders were up to—and figure out what other bars across the country would be serving next. Over the years, Death & Co introduced me to many firsts: my first punch service, my first swizzle, my first proper tiki drink, my first tastes of countless spirits, bitters, and other exotic ingredients, and so on. I never planned on writing a cocktail book, but at some point a few years ago, I decided that if I did, I would want it to be about this bar that has taught me so much.

So it was with great kismet that Dave and his agent, Jonah Straus, approached me about writing this book. We quickly realized that we shared a vision for a different kind of cocktail book—one that could teach both professionals and home bartenders the hows and whys of making great drinks. Jonah, thank you for putting us all together and for selling our stubborn proposal to Ten Speed Press. Aaron Wehner, thank you for believing in us enough to add this book to Ten Speed's ever-impressive legacy.

To my agent, advocate, and sounding board, David Larabell, you were right: this book was a beast. Is it too late to renegotiate?

Dave Kaplan, thank you for dragging me from coast to coast (and points in between) as we cobbled this thing together. Without your innate knack for hospitality and refusal to let Goliath win, 433 East Sixth Street would be some shitty Indian restaurant today. Your contagious enthusiasm for your bar, its staff, and this project has never wavered and keeps us all striving to reinvent the wheel. Let's do it again sometime.

Alex Day, before you took me under your tiny wing, everything I knew about cocktails I'd learned from watching *Cocktail*. Thank you for unteaching me my Tom Cruise ways and showing me the path to enlightenment, beginning with a pair of chopsticks and an empty water glass in that Chinese restaurant on St. Mark's Place. Your many contributions to the book turned the impossible into the enjoyable. *Arigato, sensei*.

To all of the past and present Death & Co bartenders and staff, thank you for sharing your hard-earned knowledge, for answering my dumb questions, and for keeping my liver lively. Jillian Vose and Frankie Rodriguez, you get an extra round of thanks for all of the organizing, wrangling, double-checking, correcting, and moral support. Please get some sleep.

To Death & Co's always affable and accommodating doormen (and women), thank you for letting me inside (usually).

Will Hereford, I'm honored to have worked with you on your first big-boy book. You literally gave the shirt off your back to this project and made the bar and its drinks come alive on the page. Along with Tim and Kate Tomkinson, you've created the handsomest cocktail book on the shelf.

Don Lee, I wish I had one-tenth of your cocktail brain (and one-fifth of your magnificent mane). Thanks for all of the invaluable input on equipment, science, and all the rest, and thanks for letting me hang out in Cocktail Kingdom's library. I promise I didn't steal anything.

Toby Cecchini, thanks for adding your wit and writerly touch to this tome. In case anyone doesn't already know, Toby invented the cosmopolitan; ask him to make you one next time you see him.

Jasmine Star, your impressive cocktail knowledge, copy editing skills and tireless sleuthing did way more than polish our prose.

Finally, a thank-you to Emily Timberlake. You're the most patient and proficient editor I've ever worked with. I'm grateful to you for organizing a mess of ideas, and for asking the right questions and answering the tough ones. The next round's on me.

INDEX

Copyright © 2014 by David Kaplan
Photographs copyright © 2014 by William Hereford
Foreword copyright © 2014 by Toby Cecchini
All rights reserved.

Published in the United States by Ten Speed Press, an imprint of the Crown Publishing Group, a division of Random House LLC, a Penguin Random House Company, New York.
www.crownpublishing.com
www.tenspeed.com

Ten Speed Press and the Ten Speed Press colophon are registered trademarks of Random House LLC.

Library of Congress Cataloging-in-Publication Data

Kaplan, David (Bartender)
Death & Co: Modern Classic Cocktails / David Kaplan, Nick Fauchald, Alex Day;
photographs by William Hereford; illustrations by Tim Tomkinson.
      pages cm
Includes bibliographical references and index.
1. Cocktails. 2. Death & Co. (Bar: New York, N.Y.) I. Fauchald, Nick. II. Day, Alex. III. Title.
TX951.K1654 2014
641.87'4—dc23

                    2014004245

Hardcover ISBN: 978-1-60774-525-9
eBook ISBN: 978-1-60774-526-6

Printed in China

Design by Katherine Tomkinson
Illustrations by Tim Tomkinson

10 9 8 7 6 5 4 3

First Edition

MEASUREMENT CONVERSION CHARTS

COCKTAIL VOLUMES

U.S.	METRIC
¼ oz	7.5 ml
½ oz	15 ml
¾ oz	22.5 ml
1 oz	30 ml
1¼ oz	37.5 ml
1½ oz	45 ml
1¾ oz	52.5 ml
2 oz	60 ml

COOKING VOLUMES

U.S.	METRIC
1 tablespoon	15 ml
2 tablespoons	30 ml
¼ cup	60 ml
⅓ cup	90 ml
½ cup	120 ml
⅔ cup	150 ml
¾ cup	180 ml
1 cup	240 ml
1¼ cups	300 ml
2 cups (1 pint)	480 ml
2½ cups	600 ml
1 quart	1 L

WEIGHT

U.S./IMPERIAL	METRIC
½ oz	15 g
1 oz	30 g
2 oz	60 g
¼ lb	115 g
⅓ lb	150 g
½ lb	225 g
¾ lb	350 g
1 lb	450 g

LENGTH

INCH	METRIC
¼ inch	6 mm
½ inch	1.25 cm
¾ inch	2 cm
1 inch	2.5 cm
6 inches (½ foot)	15 cm
12 inches (1 foot)	30 cm

TEMPERATURE

FAHRENHEIT	CELSIUS
250°F	120°C
275°F	135°C
300°F	150°C
325°F	160°C
350°F	175°C
375°F	190°C
400°F	200°C
425°F	220°C
450°F	230°C
475°F	245°C
500°F	260°C

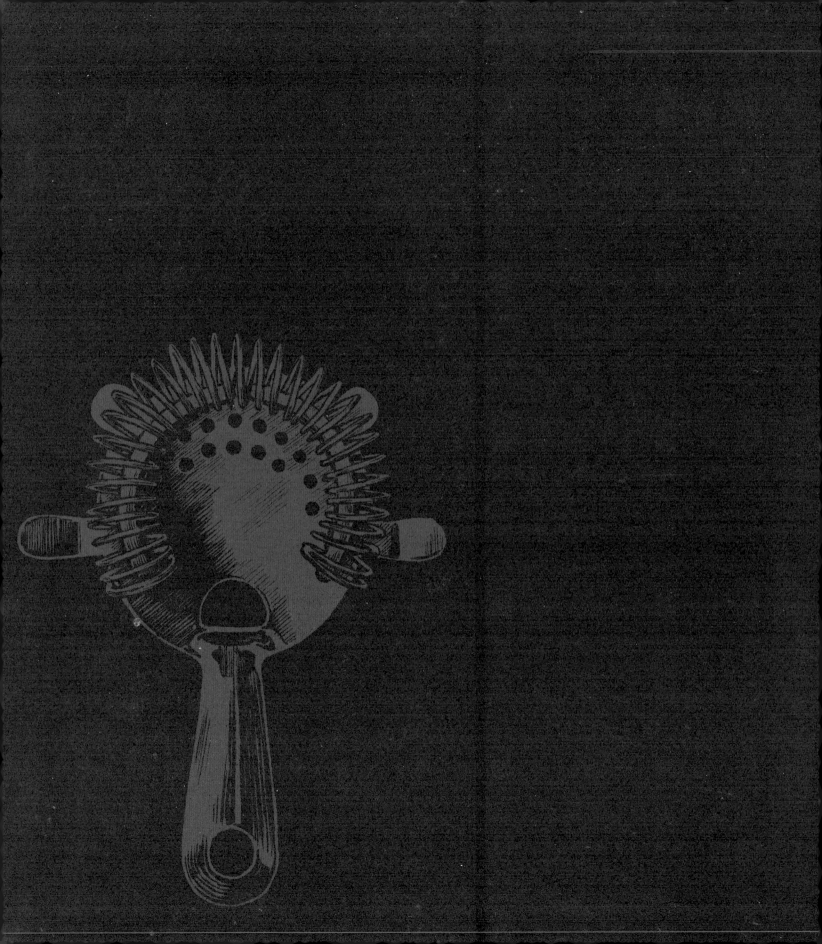